At the Margins of Orthodoxy

AT THE MARGINS OF ORTHODOXY

*Mission, Governance,
and Confessional Politics
in Russia's Volga-Kama
Region, 1827–1905*

P AUL W. W ERTH

Cornell University Press

ITHACA AND LONDON

First published 2002 by Cornell University Press

Printed in the United States of America

Library of Congress Cataloging-in-Publication Data

Werth, Paul W. (Paul William), 1986–
    At the margins of orthodoxy : mission, governance, and confessional politics in Russia's Volga-Kama region, 1827–1905 / Paul W. Werth.
        p. cm.
    Includes bibliographical references and index.
    ISBN 0-8014-3840-3 (cloth : alk. paper)
    1. Russkaia pravoslavanaia tserkov—Missions—Russia (Federation)—Volga River Region—History—19th century. 2. Russkaia pravoslavnaia tserkov—Missions—Russia (Federation)—Kama River Region—History—19th century. 3. Russkaia pravoslavnaia tserkov—Missions—Russia (Federation)—Volga River Region—History—20th century. 4. Russkaia pravoslavnaia tserkov—Missions—Russia (Federation)—Kama River Region—History—20th century.   I. Title.
    BV3033.V65 W47 2001
    281.9'474—dc21

                                            2001002510

For Liza and Danila

Contents

Maps

Acknowledgments

Many people and institutions have provided essential guidance, help, and support for the completion of this book. My largest debt is undoubtedly to my wife, Elizaveta, for her loving support and indispensable aid with numerous translations from Russian, and my little son, Daniil Pavlovich, who distracted me with his silly antics. I wish also to thank my mentors at Knox College for supporting my work and for pointing me in the direction of graduate school. At the University of Michigan William Rosenberg, Jane Burbank, Valerie Kivelson, Müge Göçek, and Ronald Suny (now at the University of Chicago) contributed immensely to this project. Adeeb Khalid (as a semi-anonymous reader for Cornell University Press), Allen Frank, Nicholas Breyfogle, Charles Steinwedel, and a second reader for Cornell all took on the arduous task of reading full versions of the manuscript in earlier incarnations. Other colleagues read portions of the manuscript: David Althoen, Swapna Bannerjee, Thomas Barrett, Andrew Bell, Gregory Brown, Heather Coleman, Marianne Kamp, Andreas Kappeler, Sviatoslav Kaspe, Nadia Kizenko, Lawrence Klein, Nathaniel Knight, Hugo Lane, Edward Lazzerini, Seppo Lallukka, Colin Loader, Virginia Martin, Lynda Park, Yuri Slezkine, Willard Sunderland, Rein Taagepera, Gregory Vitarbo, William Wagner, Theodore Weeks, Elise Kimerling Wirtschafter, and Andrei Znamenski. The photographs were printed expertly by Ingrid Spaffend. John G. Ackerman and his staff at Cornell University Press have made significant contributions to this book as well. I gratefully acknowledge the contributions of all.

Numerous scholars, archivists, and librarians in Russia likewise offered indispensable guidance over the course of several visits to that country. In Kazan I thank in particular M. A. Usmanov, Diliara Usmanova, D. M. Iskhakov, the late Äbrar Kärimullin, Jämil Zäinullin, F. S. Safiullina, Azat Akhunov, and the staffs of the National Archive of the Republic of Tatarstan

(NART) and the N. I. Lobachevskii Library of Kazan University. In St. Petersburg I thank the entire staff of Russian State Historical Archive (RGIA), and in particular Ol'ga Krstich, Larisa Sinitsyna, Nadezhda Korneva, Serafima Varekhova, Irina Mulina, David Raskin, and Vladimir Lapin. In Kirov the staffs of the State Archive of the Kirov Region (GAKO) and of the Regional Division of the A. I. Herzen Regional Library, in particular Lena Novikova, helped to make my "exile" in Viatka enjoyable and tremendously productive. The staff of the Central State Historical Archive of the Bashkir Republic (TsGIARB) did much to accommodate me during a short term of work there in 1999, while Danil' Azamatov and Iurii Afanas'ev made my stay in Ufa stimulating and enjoyable. N. S. Popov, V. E. Vladykin, and Aleksei Zagrebin served as gracious hosts and knowledgeable interlocutors during my brief stays in Ioshkar-Ola (Mari El) and Izhevsk (Udmurt Republic).

A number of institutions provided generous funding for the research and writing of this study: the International Research and Exchanges Board (IREX), with funds provided by the National Endowment for the Humanities, the U.S. Information Agency, and the U.S. Department of State, which administers the Russian, Eurasian, and East European Research Program (Title VIII); the American Council of Teachers of Russian (ACTR); the Social Science Research Council (SSRC); the Kennan Institute for Advanced Russian Studies; the Rackham School of Graduate Studies at the University of Michigan; the Advanced Study Center of the International Institute, University of Michigan; Mellon Fellowship in the Humanities; and the University of Nevada at Las Vegas.

Parts of this book were presented and discussed at a conference on regionalism in Russia in Omsk (July 1999); at the Shelby Cullom Davis Center for Historical Studies at Princeton University (February 2000); at the Congress of the Canadian Association of Slavists, University of Alberta (May 2000); and at the VI ICCEES World Congress in Tampere, Finland (July 2000). A portion of chapters 6 and 9 appeared in *Russian Review* 59, 4 (2000): 493–511, and another portion of chapter 9 was published in *Ab Imperio* 2 (2000): 105–34. I gratefully acknowledge permission to use this material here in revised form.

Finally, it is a source simultaneously of great pleasure and immense sorrow to acknowledge the contribution of Jenifer Stenfors, who carefully read a draft of the entire manuscript and enthusiastically supported my work even as she courageously struggled against an aggressive case of cancer. To my intense anguish, Jen did not live to see this book in published form, but her spirit undoubtedly inheres within it.

Note on Terminology

For the non-Russians in this book, I use current ethnic designations (which are closer to their respective self-designations), rather than prerevolutionary Russian terminology. Thus, while retaining the original designations in citations, I refer to Maris rather than Cheremis, Udmurts rather than Votiaks, and Kräshens for at least part of the baptized-Tatar population. I leave a number of Russian terms untranslated in certain contexts, either out of convenience or in order to impart a sense of the original even in paraphrase. Thus *novokreshchenye* (lit. "the newly baptized") refers to non-Russians baptized in the eighteenth century and after. *Inorodtsy* (lit. "those of other origin") was a blanket term for non-Russians in the Volga-Kama region that gained broad currency in the mid-nineteenth century, while *obrusenie* ("Russification") was used, beginning principally in the 1860s, to refer to the cultural assimilation of non-Russians.

I have used "Mohammedanism" where Russian sources write *magometanstvo* or *mukhammedanstvo*, while I use "Islam" and "Muslim" in my own voice or where sources offer *musul´manstvo*. I use the term "animism" when referring to practices and rituals that were neither Christian nor Muslim, although I use the more tendentious "pagan" when official status was at issue. The term "apostasy" (in Russian usually *otpadenie* or *otstupnichestvo*) refers to the open rejection of Orthodox status. As regards territorial and administrative demarcations, I translate *guberniia* as "province," both *uezd* and *okrug* as "district," *volost´* as "canton," and *eparkhiia* as "diocese." By 1832 provinces and dioceses coincided territorially, and the two terms are therefore often used interchangeably.

I have used the Library of Congress system for transliteration, while usually eliminating the soft sign (´) in the final position, except in source citations and bracketed passages indicating the original Russian. All dates are given according to the prerevolutionary calendar.

Abbreviations

Archives and Sources

GAKO	Gosudarstvennyi Arkhiv Kirovskoi Oblasti (State Archive of the Kirov Region), Kirov
GARME	Gosudarstvennyi Arkhiv Respubliki Marii El (State Archive of the Republic Marii El), Ioshkar-Ola
IKE	*Izvestiia po Kazanskoi eparkhii*
IOAIE	*Izvestiia Obshchestva Arkheologii, Istorii i Etnografii pri Imperatorskom Kazanskom universitete*
NART	Natsional'nyi Arkhiv Respubliki Tatarstan (National Archive of the Republic of Tatarstan), Kazan
NRF MarNII	Nauchno-Rukopisnyi Fond Mariiskogo Nauchno-Issledovatel'skogo Instituta (Manuscript Division of the Mari Research Institute), Ioshkar-Ola
PSZ	*Polnoe Sobranie Zakonov Rossiiskoi Imperii* (Complete Collection of the Laws of the Russian Empire), 3 series
RGIA	Rossiiskii Gosudarstvennyi Istoricheskii Arkhiv (Russian State Historical Archive), St. Petersburg
SZ	*Svod Zakonov Rossiiskoi Imperii* (Law Digest of the Russian Empire)
TsGIARB	Tsentral'nyi Gosudarstvennyi Istoricheskii Arkhiv Respubliki Bashkortostan (Central State Historical Archive of the Republic of Bashkortostan), Ufa
VEV	*Viatskie eparkhial'nye vedomosti*

Government Institutions

DDDII	Departament Dukhovnykh Del Inostrannykh Ispovedanii (Department for Religious Affairs of Foreign Faiths)
MGI	Ministerstvo Gosudarstvennykh Imushchestv (Ministry of State Domains)
MNP	Ministerstvo Narodnogo Prosveshcheniia (Ministry of Education)
MVD	Ministerstvo Vnutrennikh Del (Ministry of Internal Affairs)

Archival Citations

f.	*fond* (collection)
op.	*opis'* (inventory)
d.	*delo* (file)
ch.	*chast'* (part)
l. (ll.)	*list, listy* (leaf, leaves)
ob.	*oborot* (verso)

At the Margins of Orthodoxy

European Russia, with the provinces of the Volga-Kama region (prior to 1850)

Introduction

In early 1827 baptized Tatars from a series of villages in the Volga-Kama region submitted petitions to Emperor Nicholas I requesting that they be allowed to confess Islam. Claiming that their ancestors had been forcibly converted to Orthodoxy, they denied having any comprehension of the Christian faith and therefore sought admittance to the Muslim community. Shortly thereafter, officials in neighboring districts uncovered two large "idolatrous" gatherings involving representatives of a Finnic minority, Maris, also indigenous to the region. Without the prior knowledge or approval of local authorities, both baptized and unbaptized Maris from several provinces had convened to perform a collective native prayer with a ritual sacrifice of livestock. According to Orthodox canons and the laws of the Russian empire, Orthodox Christians were permitted neither to convert to other faiths nor to practice them in any way. The state accordingly rejected the baptized Tatars' petitions, and ecclesiastical authorities initiated investigations into both incidents.

Although Orthodox Christianity had long served as perhaps the central defining element of the "Russian" people,[1] in fact not all Orthodox Christians in the Russian empire were Russians or even Slavs. By the early nineteenth century the empire had expanded to include a number of other peoples—most notably Georgians and the Rumanian-speaking population of Bessarabia—who had confessed Orthodoxy long before their incorporation into imperial Russia. Moreover, both the Muscovite and the imperial Russian state had overseen the conversion of still other peoples to Orthodoxy, such as Karelians, Komi, and some native Siberians. But the largest group of

---

[1] In the view of imperial officialdom and most educated observers, "Little Russians" (Ukrainians), "White Russians" (Belorussians), and "Great Russians" (Russians) represented three branches of a single people.

such converts were the Finnic and Turkic peoples settled to the east of Moscow, around the confluence of the Volga and Kama rivers. Indeed, these converts represented the largest segment of the Eurasian population to have been baptized into Orthodoxy since the East Slavs' own conversion in the tenth century. As such, they represented a crucial test case concerning the potential for Orthodoxy to serve as an instrument of imperial integration beyond the East Slavic heartland.

From this perspective, the events of the late 1820s represented a significant setback. By making painfully clear the weak presence of Orthodoxy among non-Russians of the Volga-Kama region, these disquieting examples of "apostasy" and "delusion" underscored the need for converts' further "reinforcement" in Orthodoxy. In response to a directive of the Emperor, the Most Holy Governing Synod in St. Petersburg in 1828 began to consider measures "for the spread and consolidation" of the Orthodox faith "in those parts of the state where there live people who have not yet come to know Christianity, or where, after their conversion, they have not been sufficiently reinforced and instructed in it."[2] By 1830 missions had been established in several provinces of the Volga-Kama region.

The object of this book is to account for the origins, evolution, and consequences of this missionary effort from its inception in the late 1820s to the government's reform of religious policy in 1905. Throughout this period, issues of conversion, religious deviance, and official confessional status were the source of frequent interaction, some of it contentious, between state officials, Orthodox clerics, and non-Russian inhabitants. Although these interactions encompassed a range of different questions, there were essentially two principal axes of contention. One concerned the specific religious confession to which particular individuals, households, and communities were to be officially ascribed. Not only did many baptized Tatars continue to reject their formal Orthodox status, but in some cases recently converted animists complained to central authorities that they had been illegally coerced into accepting baptism. At issue in these disputes was the degree to which the government would respect the assertions of its subjects in the matter of religious affiliation or, alternatively, whether state officials would arrogate for themselves the prerogative of ascribing confessional status as they saw fit.

A second axis of contention concerned the *meanings* of specific religious affiliations, above all of Orthodoxy itself. What did it *mean* to be an Orthodox Christian? Were there particularistic standards and expectations for non-Russian converts to Orthodoxy? What, in fact, *were* non-Russians converting to? How did non-Russian expectations and aspirations affect prevailing conceptions of religious affiliation? In some cases, non-Russians apparently came to accept the notion that they somehow "belonged" to

2 RGIA, f. 797, op. 3, d. 12652, l. 1.

Orthodoxy but asserted that this did not obviate their need to venerate indigenous spirits. Missionaries and priests, unable to reconcile such a view with Christianity's exclusivist claims, sought to eliminate the dependence of non-Russian parishioners on native spirits, in some cases by physically destroying sites and objects of non-Russian veneration. By the second half of the nineteenth century, some non-Russians were willing to embrace Orthodoxy more consciously and even enthusiastically, but even then they had their own ideas about what Orthodoxy meant for their communities and about the possibilities for autonomy and indigenous cultural development within the Orthodox fold. Church officials themselves often disagreed about the kinds of compromises that were appropriate for deepening the attachments of otherwise marginal Christians to Orthodoxy. And just as "Russification" (*obrusenie*) came to be identified more explicitly as a goal of state policy toward non-Russians in the 1860s, Orthodox and secular officials alike became less certain about the exact relationship between Orthodoxy and Russianness. In short, the act of baptizing non-Christians and ensuring converts' religious conformity raised a series of important questions about Orthodoxy itself.

Central to my analysis are the ways in which the imperial state sought to use confessional affiliation and religious institutions as tools in the governance of its ethnically and religiously diverse empire. Under Catherine II (1762–96) and especially Alexander I (1801–25), the government constructed a system of administration that subordinated "foreign faiths" to state supervision, even as it endowed their hierarchies with substantial spiritual authority within their respective communities. In this book, however, I concentrate principally on how the Orthodox church and the tsarist government attempted to instigate religious change among the Finnic and Turkic peoples of the Volga-Kama region, either by promoting the baptism of Muslims and animists or by fostering stronger attachments to Orthodoxy among those who already had been formally converted. These efforts took a variety of forms, from itinerant missionary excursions, the translation of religious texts into native languages, and the establishment of missionary schools, to the imposition of restrictions on competing religions (particularly Islam), the extirpation of indigenous sacred sites, and the use of coercion to effectuate baptism. Although the outright persecution of religious deviance fluctuated over the course of the century, attempts to impose religious discipline—that is, to secure compliance with the norms of Orthodox practice and unequivocal recognition of the church's spiritual authority—remained central throughout.

Equally important to this book are the ways in which local communities responded to these initiatives and shaped their own cultural identities in a process of interaction with representatives of the state. Deeply attached to indigenous forms of community and religious practice, non-Russians subverted missionary overtures in a variety of ways. They absconded from their villages and homes when missionaries appeared. They challenged missionaries' authority to preach and convert. They exploited contradictions in the empire's laws and policies by, for example, invoking provisions of religious tolerance to justify their religious "deviance" and "apostasy." And they sent petitions and even emissaries to St. Petersburg to contest what they saw as local abuses and to request formal transfer from Orthodoxy. Yet eventually some of these non-Russians also accepted significant elements of the Orthodox message, recognized the possibilities for "enlightenment" offered by Orthodox institutions, and began the process of forging indigenous Orthodoxies. Even in such cases, however, the proper balance between the indigenous and the Orthodox was rarely beyond dispute, and could therefore be established—and then only provisionally—as a synthesis of official dictate and popular aspiration.

Indeed, this book treats confessional politics as a matter of negotiation and interaction, whereby non-Russians' articulations and behavior shaped state perspectives and policies, just as state structures, practices, and categories influenced non-Russians' aspirations and forms of protest. This is not to say that the power of the state and that of non-Russians were somehow equal (this was certainly not the case), but simply that state officials formed their perspectives and policies on the basis of interactions with the population they ruled and could never entirely control policies once they were implemented. Indeed, much of our story can be understood as a process whereby the state, confronted with the complex consequences of its own practices and principles, struggled with itself, its own local representatives, and its non-Russian subjects to establish a desirable religious order.[3]

Tsars and emperors had long made toleration of cultural difference an important aspect of their attempt to rule a remarkably diverse polity. Nevertheless, in particular instances the state energetically promoted religious conversion in order to foster greater unity of its domains and to subordinate non-Russians more effectively to its authority. Although the secular government was concerned above all with issues of state building, administrative modernization, and social order, religious institutions were in fact crucial to all these imperatives. Particularly in Russia's undergoverned countryside these institutions represented indispensable tools for promoting education and literacy, keeping vital statistics on the rural population, and inculcating respect for authority and compliance with state directives. To be sure, the state's relative success in enlisting—and even *creating*—Islamic institutions

[3] In highlighting the limited ability of the state and missionaries to effectuate religious change and the interactive character of the confessional politics in this book, I draw on the insights of John and Jean Comaroff, *Of Revelation and Revolution*, vol. 1: *Christianity, Colonialism, and Consciousness in South Africa* (Chicago, 1991), and vol. 2: *The Dialectics of Modernity on a South African Frontier* (Chicago, 1997); Vicente L. Rafael, *Contracting Colonialism: Translation and Christian Conversion in Tagalog Society under Early Spanish Rule* (Durham, 1993); and Gauri Viswanathan, *Outside the Fold: Conversion, Modernity, and Belief* (Princeton, 1998).

and clergy to perform these functions among Muslims implied that Orthodoxy was not absolutely necessary for good governance. Nevertheless, most state officials continued to nourish a preference for Orthodoxy, not only because it was the official state religion and therefore implied a higher degree of loyalty to sovereign and state, but also because Christianity was presumed to be intrinsically related to enlightenment, civic-mindedness (*grazhdanstvennost'*), and similar values that the autocracy sought to promote among its subjects. From this perspective, Orthodoxy offered the soundest moral foundation for the development and improvement of the empire's population. Thus, while upholding a basic level of tolerance for recognized religious groups, the tsarist regime sought nonetheless to encourage conversion to Orthodoxy, if not always through active missionary work, then at least by offering would-be converts significant material incentives, such as tax breaks and exemptions from military service.

By the early nineteenth century, several bursts of aggressive missionary activity in the Volga-Kama region had produced a substantial number of baptized non-Russians, who were referred to as *novokreshchenye* (the newly converted). Indeed, most of the region's animists and perhaps 10 percent of its Muslims had been formally brought into the Orthodox fold. But many of these conversions turned out eventually to be serious liabilities for church and state, which both felt compelled to combat "apostasy" and to discipline "those who have gone astray" (*zabludivshiesia*). Converted animists continued to perform rituals prescribed by indigenous tradition, while baptized Tatars sought to fulfill basic Islamic obligations and intermittently petitioned for official recognition as Muslims. Nor did the remaining Muslims and animists show much desire for baptism, despite the proffered incentives. As the century progressed, the tenacious attachment of local communities to native confessions and cultural practices became a source of growing discomfort, frustration, and even anxiety for state officials, many of whom became convinced of the need for a more thoroughly integrated and unified state. While cultural diversity and particularism were acceptable to state authorities in the distant periphery of the empire, they were more difficult to countenance in the state's interior provinces.

In examining contestation over religious affiliation and practice in the Volga-Kama region, this book brings together a series of themes central to Russian, and to European, history in the nineteenth century. Perhaps most obvious are the tensions between the fact of confessional diversity, on one hand, and state aspirations to maintain and promote social and political unity, on the other. In this regard, imperial Russian authorities were confronted with an extreme version of a problem that faced many European states. In Britain, France, the Ottoman Empire, Austria, Prussia and other German states, government authorities established hierarchies of religious confession on the basis of which they delineated the boundaries between various religious groups and differentiated the rights and privileges of Catholics, Calvinists, Lutherans, Uniates, Orthodox Christians, dissenters, and Jews. They sought also to define the relationship of different confessions to state authority, to delineate realms of autonomy for each religious association, and in some cases to promote and enforce religious orthodoxy. At the same time, both the clergy and the laity of unofficial and minority confessions sought to improve their status, in some cases by negotiating new privileges for their religions and in some cases through conversion.[4] The Russian case was distinct in this regard primarily because of the tremendous religious diversity of the tsars' realm, which included, aside from Orthodoxy itself, the major Christian denominations, a wide range of sectarian beliefs, and numerous non-Christian confessions, from Islam, Judaism, and Buddhism to various local forms of shamanism and animism. Thus missionary activity was part of a larger process whereby the state sought to manage confessional diversity.

This diversity in turn suggests a second crucial theme: empire. The Russian state had been construed explicitly as an empire and the sovereign as emperor ever since Peter the Great laid claim to these distinctions in 1721, and the state's substantial territorial acquisitions since that time—Finland, Lithuania, Poland, west-central Ukraine, New Russia, Crimea, Transcaucasia, the Kazakh steppe, and (by the 1860s) Central Asia—could only serve to reinforce this designation. Within the context of Russia as empire, the Volga-Kama region acquires special significance, both as Russia's first major non-Russian and non-Christian territorial acquisition, dating from the conquest of the Kazan Khanate in 1552,[5] and as a region whose location *between* the state's Slavic core and its distant, alien borderlands casts into particularly sharp relief the tensions between imperial and national identity in Russian history.[6]

---

[4] Rainer Liedtke and Stephan Wendehorst, eds., *The Emancipation of Catholics, Jews and Protestants: Minorities and the Nation State in Nineteenth-Century Europe* (Manchester, U.K., 1999); Christopher Clark, "The Limits of the Confessional State: Conversions to Judaism in Prussia, 1814–1843," *Past and Present* 147 (1995): 159–79; Benjamin Braude, ed., *Christians and Jews in the Ottoman Empire: The Functioning of a Plural Society*, 2 vols. (New York, 1982); Selim Deringil, *The Well-Protected Domains: Ideology and the Legitimation of Power in the Ottoman Empire, 1876–1909* (London, 1998); idem, "There is No Compulsion in Religion': On Conversion and Apostasy in the Late Ottoman Empire, 1839–1856," *Comparative Studies in Society and History* 42, 3 (2000): 547–75; Keith Hitchins, *Orthodoxy and Nationality: Andreiu Saguna and the Rumanians of Transylvania, 1846–1873* (Cambridge, Mass., 1977); Paul Brödy, *Joseph Eötvös and the Modernization of Hungary, 1840–1870* (Boulder, 1985); and John-Paul Himka, *Religion and Nationality in Western Ukraine: The Greek Catholic Church and the Ruthenian National Movement in Galicia, 1867–1900* (Montreal, 1999).

[5] Andreas Kappeler has suggestively labeled the peoples of the Volga "Russia's first nationalities." See his *Rußlands erste Nationalitäten: Das Zarenreich und die Völker der Mittleren Wolga vom 16. bis 19. Jahrhundert* (Cologne, 1982) and his "Die Moskauer 'Nationalitäten Politik' unter Ivan IV," *Russian History* 14 (1987): 263–83.

[6] A number of scholars have highlighted this tension, including Nathaniel Knight, "Constructing the Science of Nationality: Ethnography in Mid-Nineteenth Century Russia" (Ph.D. diss., Columbia University, 1994); idem, "Science, Empire, and Nationality: Ethnography in the

I argue here that the period from the late 1820s to the reform era of the 1860s initiated a transition—never completed under the old regime—from an imperial model featuring tolerance of ethnic and religious diversity and emphasizing dynastic loyalty above all else, to one of a unitary national state, which aspired to a higher degree of integration of its diverse popula-tion.[7] Because imperial rulers could not hope to assimilate the state's more distant and alien periphery—indeed, the state's relentless expansion ren-dered this task all but impossible—this shift also involved the transforma-tion of Russia into a different *kind* of empire, one more akin to overseas em-pires featuring the domination of largely non-European colonies by a modern European metropole. Thus, I contend, Russia in the nineteenth cen-tury represented something *between*, on one hand, an essentially premod-ern, composite state made up of different peoples and regions ruled by a hereditary non-national dynasty, and, on the other, a multinational state characterized by the subordination of diverse, culturally distinct, and at least implicitly "inferior" peoples to a core, dominant nation.[8] Once again, the Volga-Kama region offers unique insights into these issues, since it was one of the key territories of the premodern Russian empire and yet re-mained sufficiently alien in cultural terms to be subordinated, at least par-tially, to the logic of more modern forms of colonial rule.

At the same time, however, this study should be understood in terms of the history of Orthodoxy itself. Undoubtedly, the non-Russian parishes of the Volga-Kama region were situated at the margins of the Orthodox world, as this book shows. But in some respects the non-Russian Orthodox experi-ence can be understood as a variation on a predominantly Slavic theme. If baptized animists were often denigrated by observers for their darkness, ig-norance, and "pagan" proclivities, then the same was true of the Russian peasantry as well. Among both Russians and non-Russians, popular or

---

Russian Geographical Society, 1845–1855," in *Imperial Russia: New Histories for the Empire*, ed. Jane Burbank and David L. Ransel (Bloomington, 1998), pp. 108–41; Geoffrey Hosking, *Russia: People and Empire, 1552–1917* (Cambridge, Mass., 1997); Mark Bassin, *Imperial Vi-sions: Nationalist Imagination and Geographical Expansion in the Russian Far East* (Cam-bridge, 1999); and David G. Rowley, "'Redeemer Empire': Russian Millenarianism," *American Historical Review* 104, 5 (1999): 1582–1602.

[7] In this regard I concur with Andreas Kappeler, *Russland als Vielvölkerreich: Entstehung, Geschichte, Zerfall* (Munich, 1992); Charles Robert Steinwedel, "Invisible Threads of Empire: State, Religion, and Ethnicity in Tsarist Bashkiria, 1773–1917" (Ph.D. diss., Columbia Uni-versity, 1999); John W. Slocum, "The Boundaries of National Identity: Religion, Language, and Nationality Politics in Late Imperial Russia" (Ph.D. diss., University of Chicago, 1993); and Svi-atoslav Kaspe, "Imperskaia politicheskaia kul'tura i modernizatsiia v Rossii: Peremeny vtoroi poloviny XIX veka" (paper presented at the conference "Empire and Region: The Russian Case, 1700–1917," Omsk, 1999).

[8] Terry Martin usefully raises such a contrast in a recent review of Daniel R. Brower and Edward J. Lazzerini, eds., *Russia's Orient: Imperial Borderlands and Peoples, 1700–1917* (Bloomington, 1997) in *The Journal of Modern History* 71, 2 (1999): 508–11.

"lived" Orthodoxy was characterized by deviation from officially prescribed Orthodoxy.[9] Indeed, if Gregory Freeze is correct that Russian Orthodoxy should be regarded as "Russian Heterodoxy," consisting of "an aggregate of local Orthodoxies, each with its own cults, rituals, and customs,"[10] then non-Russian Orthodoxies certainly merit inclusion in the study of Orthodox experience in Russia. Furthermore, Russian peasants' aspirations for more meaningful participation in their own religious affairs and the remarkable growth of monasticism in the nineteenth century had their equivalents among non-Russian Orthodox Christians. Even baptized-Tatar "apostates" had rough counterparts in the various Russian sectarians, who rejected important elements of official Orthodoxy and spurned association with its church, and in the Uniates, many of whom resisted their incorporation into Orthodoxy after the elimination of their church in 1839. In some respects, these Slavic dissenters represented an even greater threat to state authority than did non-Russian renegades, in part because of the strange practices that some of them adopted—most notably ritual castration in the case of Skoptsy—but more importantly because their rejection of official Orthodoxy constituted a repudiation of the confessional unity of the Russian people that the state deemed one of its cornerstones.[11] Given the unevenness of the religious landscape within Russian Orthodoxy, how *does* the experience of baptized non-Russians fit into a broader history of Orthodoxy?

Because the Orthodox church was so closely associated with the tsarist state, and because the distinction between secular and religious authority remained ambiguous, the problems of "apostasy" and dissent were inextricably linked to broader issues of law and authority. Gregory Freeze has argued that the church enjoyed a significant degree of operational autonomy from the secular state and that although its array of powers had been narrowed as a result of Peter I's ecclesiastical reform, they had also been "absolutized" within a more clearly delineated "spiritual domain."[12] Undoubtedly there is

---

[9] Christopher Chulos, "Myths of the Pious or Pagan Peasant in Post-Emancipation Central Russia (Voronezh Province)," *Russian History* 22, 2 (1995): 181–216; Gregory L. Freeze, "The Rechristianization of Russia: The Church and Popular Religion, 1750–1850," *Studia Slavica Finlandensia* 7 (1990): 101–36; and Nadieszda Kizenko, *A Prodigal Saint: John of Kronstadt and the Russian People* (University Park, Pa., 2000).

[10] Gregory L. Freeze, "Institutionalizing Piety: The Church and Popular Religion, 1750–1850," in Burbank and Ransel, eds., *Imperial Russia*, p. 215.

[11] Chulos, "Myths of the Pious or Pagan Peasant," 202–7; Nicholas Breyfogle, "Heretics and Colonizers: Religious Dissent and Russian Colonization of Transcaucasia, 1830–1890" (Ph.D. diss., University of Pennsylvania, 1998), esp. pp. 31–35; and Laura Engelstein, *Castration and the Heavenly Kingdom: A Russian Folktale* (Ithaca, 1999). This threat to confessional unity would grow as other non-Orthodox forms of Christianity became available to Russians toward the end of the nineteenth century. On this issue, see Heather Jean Coleman, "The Most Dangerous Sect: Baptists in Tsarist and Soviet Russia, 1905–1929" (Ph.D. diss., University of Illinois, 1998).

[12] Freeze, "Institutionalizing Piety," p. 214. On this theme see also his article, "Handmaiden of the State? The Church in Imperial Russia Reconsidered," *Journal of Ecclesiastical History* 1 (1985): 82–102.

much truth to these assertions, but church and state remained intimately connected, with the Emperor at the head of both and the former largely dependent on the latter. The imperial state continued to foster the church's moral preeminence and privileged status and provided substantial support for Orthodox religious principles. Standards of religious practice and the boundaries of existing religious communities were regulated and maintained by secular tsarist law, as well as by extralegal administrative provisions, to the benefit of Orthodoxy. Indeed, the state sometimes equated religious offenses with crimes against the state and prescribed secular penalties for religious transgressions.[13] At the same time, secular ministries could block the church's introduction of missionary activity for either financial or political reasons. Thus much of the confessional politics addressed in this book centers on the authority of local officials, and in particular ecclesiastical ones, to promote baptism and to enforce religious discipline. In light of the growing commitment of an important segment of imperial officialdom to "legality" (*zakonnost´*) in the administration of the state, the law afforded at least some protection to imperial subjects by, for example, prohibiting the use of force and coercion in the promotion of baptism and by upholding a certain level of religious tolerance for recognized confessional groups.[14] Although their spirit and letter were at times violated on the local level, these laws tempered local officials' arbitrariness and gave subjects a basis for contesting violations of the order that these laws were designed to uphold. What, then, were the effects of tsarist law as it was applied by officials and at times appropriated and challenged by individuals and communities on the local level?

Finally, this book represents an exercise in peasant studies, to the extent that virtually all the non-Russians of the region were rural inhabitants and members of the peasant estate.[15] Some belonged to one of the many particularistic social groups that continued to exist prior to the Great Reforms of the 1860s (*lashmany*, Bashkirs, Teptiars, etc.), while others were serfs either of individual landowners or of the imperial family itself. But the vast majority were state peasants, or "free rural inhabitants," a segment of rural

[13] Laura Engelstein, *The Keys to Happiness: Sex and the Search for Modernity in Fin-de-Siècle Russia* (Ithaca, 1992), pp. 28–29.

[14] The best and most comprehensive analyses of the law and religious toleration remain those of prerevolutionary Russian scholars, such as M. A. Reisner, *Gosudarstvo i veruiushchaia lichnost´* (St. Petersburg, 1905); K. K. Arsen´ev, *Svoboda sovesti i veroterpimost´* (St. Petersburg, 1905); S. V. Poznyshev, *Religioznye prestupleniia s tochki zreniia religioznoi svobody* (Moscow, 1906); and V. N. Shiriaev, *Religioznye prestupleniia: Istoriko-dogmaticheskie ocherki* (Iaroslavl, 1909). But see also Peter Waldron, "Religious Toleration in Late Imperial Russia," in *Civil Rights in Imperial Russia*, ed. Olga Crisp and Linda Edmondson (Oxford, U.K., 1989), pp. 103–19.

[15] Tatars were the only non-Russian ethnic group in the region with any substantial presence in towns. In 1857 about 2% of the Tatar population was urban, rising to almost 5% by 1897. See D. M. Iskhakov, *Istoricheskaia demografiia tatarskogo naroda: XVIII–nachalo XX vv.* (Kazan, 1993), pp. 73–78; and RGIA, f. 821, op. 8, d. 1096.

Russia that continues to be virtually ignored in what is otherwise a robust literature on the empire's peasantry.[16] More generally, the efforts of non-Russians to reject state-imposed religious identities and to subvert the enforcement of religious discipline offer an excellent series of case studies of peasant resistance. Often the appearance of rumors among Muslims and animists that the state was preparing their wholesale conversion to Orthodoxy induced officials to abandon or postpone new policies and plans for fear of generating unrest. And in some instances—especially during the mass "apostasy" of baptized Tatars in the late 1860s—non-Russians defied authorities quite openly. But because the state remained capable of marshaling substantial physical force when necessary, and because non-Russians appear to have accepted many elements of the tsarist order, indigenous protest most often took decidedly deferential forms, above all petitions and similar forms of supplication. To what extent did non-Russians participate in a broadly-based "culture of peasant resistance"?[17] In what ways did they differ from the Russian peasantry, whom officialdom at times regarded as a "domestic other" that itself required discipline and enlightenment?[18] How prominent was resistance in the broad set of interactions involving clergy, local officials, and non-Russians?

This book is organized along both thematic and chronological lines. Chapter 1 considers how best to understand the place of the Volga-Kama region in the larger Russian empire and describes both the mass conversions of non-Russians in the eighteenth century and the basic contours of animism and Islam in the region in the early to mid-nineteenth century. The next three chapters focus on the period of Nicholas I (1825–55). Chapter 2 analyzes the apostasy and large animist prayer noted above and shows how these events led to the establishment of Orthodox missions in several provinces by the mid-1830s. Chapter 3 considers the basic structure of these missions and the issue of baptism—that is, the ways in which church and state sought to bring the remaining non-Christians, but principally pagans, into the Orthodox fold. Chapter 4 describes the missions' efforts to "reinforce" novokreshchenye in Orthodoxy and considers the many problems that the missions faced in their day-to-day activity.

---

[16] The central work on state peasants remains N. M. Druzhinin, *Gosudarstvennye krest'iane i reforma P. D. Kiseleva*, 2 vols. (Moscow, 1946 and 1958), although see also G. Bolotenko, "Administration of the State Peasants in Russia Before the Reforms of 1838" (Ph.D. diss., University of Toronto, 1979).

[17] I take the phrase "culture of peasant resistance" from Lynne Viola, *Peasant Rebels under Stalin: Collectivization and the Culture of Peasant Resistance* (New York, 1996).

[18] I take the term "domestic other" from Stephen P. Frank, "Confronting the Domestic Other: Rural Popular Culture and Its Enemies in Fin-de-Siècle Russia," in *Cultures in Flux: Lower-Class Values, Practices, and Resistance in Late Imperial Russia*, ed. Stephen P. Frank and Mark D. Steinberg (Princeton, 1994), pp. 74–107. For a fuller discussion, see also idem, *Crime, Cultural Conflict, and Justice in Rural Russia, 1856–1914* (Berkeley, 1999).

The next several chapters collectively chart a series of important shifts in Russia across the middle portion of the nineteenth century. Chapter 5 analyzes a crucial reorientation in the character of the imperial polity and argues that in the Great Reform era officials began to abandon the premodern model of a non-national composite state and took several important steps toward the construction of a unified national state. This shift also produced new imperial ideologies and a more thoroughly developed sense of a "civilizing mission" in the eastern part of the empire. Chapter 6 considers the mass apostasy of baptized Tatars in the late 1860s, which helped to reinforce the shifts described in chapter 5. Chapter 7 analyzes the appearance of new official (and above all missionary) perceptions of Islam. Over the course of the nineteenth century Muslims came to be regarded as intractable "fanatics," bitterly hostile to the spread of "Russian civilization." Chapter 8 explores an important missionary success (though one still beset by significant ambiguities): the religious movement of highland Maris in Kazan province that led to the establishment of the region's first explicitly non-Russian monastery. Finally, chapter 9 considers the reform of missionary practice associated with N. I. Il′minskii and its impact on religious life in the region. The chapter ends with a consideration of the ways in which the intractable problem of apostasy contributed to a fundamental (if limited) religious reform in 1905.

The non-Russians addressed in this study are Maris and Udmurts (both linguistically Finnic) and Tatars and Chuvash (both Turkic), although I also offer some observations concerning Mordvins, Bashkirs, and Teptiars. The most detailed source material at my disposal concerns Tatars and Maris, and therefore my account concerns these groups somewhat more than the others. In geographical terms, I construe the Volga-Kama region as including Kazan, Simbirsk, Viatka, and northwestern Orenburg provinces (based on pre-1850 boundaries)—in short, the area where the selected non-Russian peoples were concentrated.[19] Most of this region was incorporated into the Russian state after the conquest of the Khanate of Kazan in 1552, although the region to the east of the Kama river remained only tenuously attached to Russia until at least the eighteenth century.[20]

Although some non-Russians were baptized into Orthodoxy in the decades immediately after the conquest, it was in the eighteenth century that the largest

---

[19] In 1850 Samara province was established along the left bank of the Volga river from parts of Simbirsk and Orenburg province, and in 1865 Ufa province was carved out of northwestern Orenburg province.

[20] On the conquest and administration prior to the nineteenth century, see Kappeler, *Ruß-lands erste Nationalitäten*; Nikolai Firsov, *Inorodcheskoe naselenie prezhnego Kazanskogo tsarstva v novoi Rossii do 1762 goda i kolonizatsiia zakamskikh zemel′ v eto vremia* (Kazan, 1869); Alton S. Donnelly, *The Russian Conquest of Bashkiria, 1552–1740: A Case Study in Imperialism* (New Haven, 1968); and S. Kh. Alishev, *Istoricheskie sud′by narodov Srednego Povolzh′ia, XVI—nachalo XIX v.* (Moscow, 1990).

numbers of the region's indigenous population became formally Orthodox.[21] Already toward the end of the seventeenth century, Tsar Fedor promoted the baptism of Mordvins by offering them a six-year tax break and threatening them with enserfment if they did not convert.[22] Peter the Great (reigned 1682–1725) was even more energetic in promoting conversion, although it was principally under his successors, in the 1740s–50s, that the majority of animists and a segment of the Tatar population were baptized. Because of their larger significance for our story, the nature and consequences of these conversions are considered in greater detail in chapter 1. Here I wish to sketch out briefly the development of religious policy from the time of the mass baptisms to the start of Nicholas I's reign in 1825, for it was principally in these years that the empire's major institutions for coping with confessional diversity were established.

The reign of Catherine II witnessed a "compromise" in the governance of Russia's diverse subject population, involving a combination of religious tolerance and at least temporary accommodation of ethnic and cultural differences.[23] In line with her Enlightenment rationalism, Catherine's government ended aggressive Orthodox proselytism in the Volga-Kama region in 1764, eliminated the interference of Orthodox clergy in the construction of mosques in 1773, and in 1788 created an institutional structure and religious hierarchy for Muslims based on both Ottoman and Orthodox models.[24] Although her tolerant policies did not apply equally to all—Uniates in particular faced persecution by the 1790s—her reign nonetheless established a set of progressive principles that continued to influence imperial rule until the end of the tsarist regime.[25] The reign of Paul I (1796–1801) was for the

---

[21] For accounts of these early conversions, see A. Mozharovskii, *Izlozhenie khoda missionerskogo dela po prosveshcheniiu kazanskikh inorodtsev s 1552 po 1867 goda* (Moscow, 1880), pp. 1–28; I. K. Zagidullin, "Khristianizatsiia tatar Srednego Povolzh'ia vo vtoroi polovine XVI–XVII vv.," *Uchenye zapiski Tatarskogo Gosudarstvennogo Gumanitarnogo Instituta* 1 (1997): 111–65; Chantal Lemercier-Quelquejay, "Les Missions Orthodoxes en pays Musulmans de Moyenne- et Basse-Volga, 1552–1865," *Cahiers du monde russe et soviétique* 8, 3 (1967): 369–403; and Michael Khodarkovsky, "'Not by Word Alone': Missionary Policies and Religious Conversion in Early Modern Russia," *Comparative Studies in Society and History* 38, 2 (1996): 267–93. The number of early converts is not clear from existing sources.

[22] On the decree of 1681 and its consequences, see A. Mozharovskii, "Po istorii prosveshcheniia nizhegorodskoi mordvy," *Nizhegorodskie eparkhial'nye vedomosti* 16 (1890): 664–65. See also James Cracraft, *The Church Reform of Peter the Great* (New York, 1971), pp. 62–79.

[23] The notion of a "Catherinian compromise" is developed by Brower and Lazzerini in *Russia's Orient*, pp. 312–13.

[24] Steinwedel, "Invisible Threads of Empire," pp. 47–76; Robert D. Crews, "Allies in God's Command: Muslim Communities and the State in Imperial Russia" (Ph. D. diss., Princeton University, 1999), pp. 61–79; D. D. Azamatov, *Orenburgskoe Magometanskoe Dukhovnoe Sobranie v kontse XVIII–XIX vv.* (Ufa, 1999), pp. 20–39; and Alan W. Fisher, "Enlightened Despotism and Islam under Catherine II," *Slavic Review* 27 (1968): 542–53.

[25] For a general overview of Catherine's religious policy, see Isabel de Madariaga, *Russia in the Age of Catherine the Great* (New Haven, 1981), pp. 503–18. On Uniates specifically, see James T. Flynn, "Iraklii Lisovskii, Metropolitan of the Uniate Church (1806–09) and Reform in the Russian Empire," *Slavonic and East European Review* 77, 1 (1999): 102–4; and

most part too brief to have a major impact on religious policy, although his government eased the pressure on Uniates, established a governing board for the Roman Catholic Church, and created a special arm of the Orthodox church known as "unified faith" (*edinoverie*), designed to draw dissident Old Believers back into the official fold with certain concessions on ritual.[26]

Alexander I continued and extended the main trends of his grandmother's "compromise," at least until the last years of his life. Initially embracing her Enlightenment rationalism and then turning toward an essentially Protestant mysticism in about 1812, he made tolerance a cornerstone of his religious policy and indeed sought to transcend distinctions between different Christian confessions in the name of Christian unity. Alexander held that his subjects should continue to adhere to the confessions into which they were born, and he therefore disapproved of conversion (especially among Christian faiths), censured interfaith polemics, and gave special protection to several Protestant sects in his realm. Still, though he and his fellow mystics believed that even non-Christian faiths offered at least partial versions of the truths fully revealed in the New Testament, Alexander was convinced of Christianity's superiority over other religions and was therefore eager to spread the Gospel throughout his realm. Combining this aspiration with a strong sense of Christian universalism, he granted several foreign (mostly Protestant) groups the right to proselytize in more distant parts of the empire, even as the state refrained from any concerted effort to promote Orthodox missionary activity.[27] But for the most part, spreading the Gospel meant literally that—the distribution of holy scripture in many of the empire's languages, unaccompanied by active proselytism. This was one of the principal functions of the Russian Bible Society (established in 1812), through which Alexander hoped to unite representatives of various Christians denominations (and even a few non-Christians!) under the auspices of his "utopian ecumenism."[28] For a period, then, the state in effect put

---

M. I. Koialovich, *Istoriia vozsoedineniia zapadnorusskikh uniatov starykh vremen* (St. Petersburg, 1873), pp. 352–400.

[26] Flynn, "Iraklii Lisovskii," 104–5; Roy Robson, *Old Believers in Modern Russia* (DeKalb, 1995), pp. 17, 29–30; *Sobranie postanovlenii po chasti raskola* (St. Petersburg, 1875), pp. 7–16.

[27] A. Vasil'ev, "Veroterpimost' v zakonodatel'stve i zhizni v tsarstvovanie imperatora Aleksandra I (1801–1825)," *Nabliudatel'* 6–8 (1896): 35–56, 257–96, 98–113. On foreign missionaries in Russia, see M. V. Jones, "The Sad and Curious Story of Karass, 1802–1835," *Oxford Slavonic Papers* 8 (1975): 53–81; D. S. M. Williams, "The 'Mongolian Mission' of the London Missionary Society: An Episode in the History of Religion in the Russian Empire," *Slavonic and East European Review* 56 (1978): 329–45; and C. R. Bawden, *Shamans, Lamas, and Evangelicals: The English Missionaries in Siberia* (London, 1985).

[28] Georges Florovsky, *Ecumenism II: A Historical Approach, Collected Works of Georges Florovsky* (Vaduz, 1989), 14: 110–12; E. A. Vishlenkova, *Religioznaia politika: Ofitsial'nyi kurs i "obshchee mnenie" Rossii Aleksandrovskoi epokhi* (Kazan, 1997), pp. 97–134; and Alexander Martin, *Romantics, Reformers, and Reactionaries: Russian Conservative Thought and Politics in the Reign of Alexander I* (DeKalb, 1997), pp. 185–96.

Orthodoxy and other Christian confessions on almost equal footing, while also respecting non-Christian faiths and even decriminalizing adherence to certain forms of Russian sectarianism.

More significant in the long term, Alexander's government took major steps in the further institutionalization of non-Orthodox faiths with the creation in 1810 of the Main Administration of the Religious Affairs of Foreign Faiths, which in 1817 became part of A. N. Golitsyn's "Dual Ministry" (the Ministry of Religious Affairs and Enlightenment). Focusing its work principally on Christian confessions that had recently come under Russian rule, the Main Administration set about collecting statistical data, studying canon law, and composing historical surveys of the relations of those churches to secular authority. Although this new administration undoubtedly created the possibility—indeed, perhaps the necessity—of deeper state intervention into non-Orthodox religious affairs, it also signified official recognition of the confessions in question. In effect, Alexander's government aspired to stand above confessional distinctions, promoting harmony among them in the interests of a higher religious sensibility and a unified religious policy.[29]

Not surprisingly, many Orthodox clerics and their allies were deeply offended by the essentially Protestant orientation of the Bible Society and the equalization of Orthodoxy and other faiths implicit in the unified spiritual administration. Their aspirations to reverse the prevailing policy earned broader support in ruling circles in the aftermath of student unrest in German universities in 1819 and the mutiny of the Semenovskii regiment in Russia that year, which seemed to confirm the proposition that enlightenment pursued in the mystical Protestant spirit characteristic of the Bible Society would lead eventually to irreligion and rebellion. The obvious solution was to re-enshrine Orthodoxy as the indisputably predominant faith of the empire. Initially securing the expulsion of Jesuits from Russia in 1820 and the elimination of freemasonry in 1822, conservatives subsequently attacked Golitsyn's Dual Ministry–Bible Society complex and succeeded in dismantling both of its components in 1824.

Notably, however, the reaction was directed primarily against various forms of "freethinking," and Golitsyn's successor as head of the Main Administration, A. S. Shishkov, upheld the idea of tolerating and even protecting recognized non-Orthodox faiths. He believed that one of the state's principal goals should be to combat "sects and heresy" among *all* the empire's officially acknowledged faiths.[30] In essence, then, the principle that emerged

---

[29] On the creation of this administration and its implications, see the informed discussions in Crews, "Allies in God's Command," pp. 22–26; and Vishlenkova, *Religioznaia politika*, pp. 52–96, 135–83. Much of Transcaucasia was incorporated into the empire in the first decade of the nineteenth century, as was the Grand Duchy of Finland in 1809. Though a portion of Poland was taken in 1772, the lion's share was annexed only in 1793–95, followed by the inclusion of the Congress Kingdom in 1815.

[30] Vasil'ev, "Veroterpimost'," 101–5; and Vishlenkova, *Religioznaia politika*, p. 177.

by the mid-1820s and was to serve as a foundation for religious policy in the reign of Nicholas I was the idea of state protection and patronage of orthodoxy in *both* senses of the term—that is, of Russian Orthodoxy as the "supreme and predominant" confession of the Russian imperial state, *and* of the doctrinal uniformity and clerical authority of all tolerated faiths. If Alexander's regime by the 1820s abandoned its previously tolerant policy toward Russian sectarians and began to focus on their segregation and / or conversion back to official Orthodoxy, then it also aided the Lutheran clergy in combating Protestant sectarians and Islamic religious elites in dealing with Sufis, itinerant teachers, and other religious figures lacking official sanction.[31] Admittedly, official attitudes toward Catholicism worsened considerably after the Polish insurrection of 1830–31, thus contributing to an atmosphere conducive to the wholesale "reunification" of Uniates with Orthodoxy in 1839.[32] But the administrative agency for non-Orthodox faiths, now titled the Department for the Religious Affairs of Foreign Faiths, was retained after the elimination of the Dual Ministry. Non-Orthodox faiths thus continued to enjoy explicit institutional recognition.

Still, the predominance of the Orthodox church was unequivocally reaffirmed in the last years of Alexander's reign and received full ideological elaboration under Nicholas I. Indeed, in its search for new forms of legitimation, Nicholas's government sought to enlist the Orthodox church as a symbolic guardian of Russia's national past and as one of the principal factors differentiating Russia from the West. According to Sergei Uvarov, the minister of education and the principal ideologue of the Nikolaevan period, one of the central benefits of Orthodoxy was that it provided a cultural, ethical, and political source of unity. Although he had no profound views about Orthodoxy as such, Uvarov did believe that in this regard it was superior to the Protestantism that had so recently been in vogue. As he wrote, Protestant churches "do not contain a Protestant dogma, but the central Protestant principle: '*that each judges by his own conscience the tenets of his own belief,*' and this places the churches in a state of eternal ferment. Vainly would one search for an anchor in the midst of this unending agitation."[33]

[31] Breyfogle, "Heretics and Colonizers," pp. 42–62; Vasil'ev, "Veroterpimost'," 107–9; and Crews, "Allies in God's Command," pp. 28–30, 501–51.

[32] On the "reunification," see Julian Pelesz, *Geschichte der Union der Ruthenischen Kirche mit Rom von aeltesten Zeiten bis auf die Gegenwart* (Würzburg, 1881), 2: 803–31; Adrien Boudou, *Le Saint-Siège et la Russie: Leurs Relations Diplomatiques au XIXe Siècle*, vol. 1: *1814–1847* (Paris, 1922), pp. 153–69, 213–40; Wasyl Lencyk, *The Eastern Catholic Church and Czar Nicholas I* (Rome, 1966); and Theodore Weeks, "Between Rome and Tsar'grad: The Uniate Church in Imperial Russia," in *Of Religion and Empire: Missions, Conversion, and Tolerance in Tsarist Russia*, ed. Robert Geraci and Michael Khodarkovsky (Ithaca, 2001), pp. 70–91. After 1839 the Uniate church continued to exist within the Russian empire only in the Kholm region of the Kingdom of Poland, and this church was itself eliminated in 1875.

[33] Cited in Cynthia H. Whittaker, *The Origins of Modern Russian Education: An Intellectual Biography of Count Sergei Uvarov, 1786–1855* (DeKalb, 1984), p. 96 (emphasis in the original).

In this context, as the foreign missionaries were forced to terminate their activities and in some cases to leave Russia, new Orthodox missions were established in several parts of the empire.[34] Indeed, the Holy Synod was presumably quite aware of the prevailing atmosphere when it argued for the establishment of missionary activity in the Volga-Kama region by emphasizing "the well-known influence of religious unity on civil unanimity" (*izvestnoe vliianie edinoveriia na edinodushie grazhdanskoe*).[35]

The history of Russia as an imperial entity has usually been construed in terms of an opposition between a center and a periphery. Particularly when viewed from St. Petersburg, or perhaps from Central Asia or Poland, this opposition illuminates important dimensions of imperial Russian governance. But there were also lands that did not fall clearly into one category or the other. These regions straddled the central Russian provinces and the outer, predominantly non-Russian territories and therefore incorporated elements of both. This book rests on the proposition that the tensions and contradictions of Russia's imperial development were most clearly registered in this zone, which included the Volga-Kama region. Yet I propose also that because Russia was a contiguous empire, these tensions were present, to one degree or another, throughout the vast expanse of Eurasia that was claimed by the House of Romanov.

[34] RGIA, f. 796, op. 116, d. 560, ll. 1–3; f. 797, op. 10, d. 26614, ll. 1–4. Orthodox missions appeared in Alaska and Arkhangel'sk province (1824), the Altai (1830), Buriatia (1833), and various locations in the north (1832, 1844, 1845), as well as in the Volga-Kama region in 1830. See Andrei A. Znamenski, *Shamanism and Christianity: Native Encounters with Russian Orthodox Missions in Siberia and Alaska, 1820–1917* (Westport, Conn., 1999); and Joseph Glazik, *Die Russische-Orthodoxe Heidenmission seit Peter dem Grossen* (Munster, 1954).

[35] RGIA, f. 797, op. 3, d. 12652, l. 1.

I Historical and Cultural Contexts

Already by the mid-sixteenth century the Muscovite state had brought a number of non-Russian peoples, principally Finnic tribes, under its rule. But most historians agree that with the conquest of the Khanate of Kazan in 1552, Muscovy began a new project of empire building. As Geoffrey Hosking has written of this event, Moscow "had embarked on a course of conquest and expansion which was to last for more than three centuries and create the largest and most diverse territorial empire the world has ever seen."[1] From this perspective the Volga-Kama region represented Russia's first imperial acquisition, and its indigenous inhabitants became, to adopt Andreas Kappeler's formulation, "Russia's first nationalities."[2] But aside from regarding its incorporation as the first chapter in a longer narrative of Russian imperial expansion, how should we situate the Volga-Kama region within the larger Russian empire? How did the status of its peoples compare to that of others in the empire? In what sense was this region an object of imperial rule?

After providing a basic historical and ethnographic sketch, I conclude that the region represented a transitional zone between the core Slavic lands of old Muscovy and the state's more recently acquired non-Russian borderlands. As a result, the status of the region remained ambiguous. The mass conversion of Volga-Kama peoples in the mid-eighteenth century may be seen as a continuation of the process whereby the Muscovite grand princes and tsars had "gathered" and integrated the Rus´ lands in the medieval period.[3] Yet by the late eighteenth century the government had become more accepting of the region's diversity—an approach characteristic of the state's

---

[1] Geoffrey Hosking, *Russia: People and Empire, 1552–1917* (Cambridge, Mass., 1997), p. 3.
[2] Andreas Kappeler, *Rußlands erste Nationalitäten: Das Zarenreich und die Völker der Mittleren Wolga vom 16. bis 19. Jahrhundert* (Cologne, 1982).
[3] The conversion to Orthodoxy of the predominantly Slavic, but also Finnic, tribes had been central to the extension of political control of both Kievan Rus´ and later Muscovy.

practice in more recently acquired territories. In part, of course, these fluctuations corresponded to changes of rulers and the overall imperatives facing the imperial government at different times. Fundamentally, however, the Volga-Kama region was sufficiently "close" to the center in geographical and cultural terms to be considered part of a more limited Russia, yet sufficiently distant and alien to be subjected to a broader imperial logic.

Settlement and Population

After the Muscovite conquest in 1552, Russian colonization of the region began with the construction of several strategically located towns and fortresses, followed by Russian peasant settlement around major waterways and towns. Non-Russians were accordingly pushed into the interior, while many fled Russian encroachments by migrating across the Kama river into the more sparsely populated Bashkir lands. By the end of the eighteenth century, the lands to the northwest of the Kama river were largely settled, and Russian colonization of the trans-Kama lands began to accelerate.[4] By the mid-nineteenth century, Russians constituted an outright majority in Simbirsk and Viatka provinces and a substantial minority in Kazan province and the northwestern districts of Orenburg province.[5] Non-Russians nonetheless continued to be concentrated in particular districts and locales.

Virtually all the region's non-Russians spoke either Turkic or Finnic languages. Tatars, a Turkic people, represented the largest and most prominent non-Russian group of the region. Consisting of a variety of different sub-ethnicities and usually referring to themselves as Muslims, they lived more or less throughout eastern Russia, in small pockets or in more concentrated masses. Tatars supplemented agriculture with beekeeping, animal husbandry, and domestic crafts (principally sewing and weaving), which served as a basis for their trading within the Russian empire and even beyond its borders.[6] Tatars also had a substantial merchant class and a highly educated segment, the *ulema*. Bashkirs, for the most part nomads or seminomads in

---

[4] On Russian colonization of the Volga-Kama region see G. Peretiatkovich, *Povolzh'e v XVII i nachale XVIII veka: Ocherki iz istorii kolonizatsii kraia* (Odessa, 1882); and N. V. Firsov, *Inorodcheskoe naselenie prezhnego Kazanskogo tsarstva v novoi Rossii do 1762 goda i kolonizatsiia zakamskikh zemel'v eto vremia* (Kazan, 1869). On the non-Russian migrations across the Kama, see U. Kh. Rakhmatullin, *Naselenie Bashkirii v XVII–XVIII vv.: Voprosy formirovaniia nebashkirskogo naseleniia* (Moscow, 1988), pp. 80–90.

[5] Data from the tenth revision (1857) indicate that Russians represented approximately the following percentages in each of the region's provinces: Kazan—42%, Viatka—81%; Orenburg—53%, and Simbirsk—72%.

[6] M. Laptev, *Materialy dlia geografii i statistiki Rossii, sobrannye ofitserami General'nogo shtaba: Kazanskaia guberniia* (St. Petersburg, 1861), pp. 195–97, 219; D. M. Iskhakov, *Etnograficheskie gruppy tatar Volgo-ural'skogo regiona* (Kazan, 1993); R. K. Urazmanova, ed., *Etnokul'turnoe raionirovanie tatar Srednego Povolzh'ia* (Kazan, 1991); N. I. Vorob'ev and G. M. Khisamutdinov, eds., *Tatary Srednego Povolzh'ia i Priural'ia* (Moscow, 1967), pp. 38–56; N. A. Khalikov, *Zemledelie tatar Srednego Povolzh'ia i Priural'ia, XIX–nachala XX v.* (Moscow, 1981); and idem, *Khoziaistvo tatar Povolzh'ia i Urala* (Kazan, 1995).

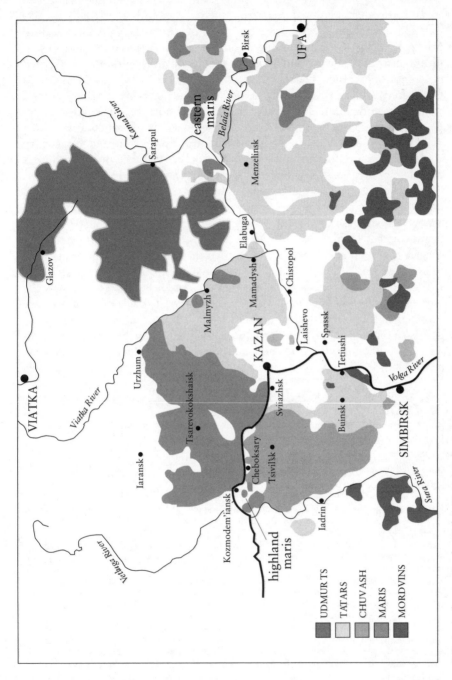

Ethnic settlement in the Volga-Kama region

Orenburg province, were also Muslims. Until 1863 they enjoyed a special social status that exempted them from the poll tax and regular military service and gave them special property rights over their land.[7] Chuvash lived primarily to the southwest of the Volga and constituted large majorities in several districts of Kazan and Simbirsk provinces, although some also settled in Orenburg province. For the most part animists before their conversion to Orthodoxy, Chuvash apparently sought to avoid contact with Russians and sometimes settled in deep forests, far from neighbors and big roads.[8]

Among the Finnic peoples, Mordvins were usually identified as the most assimilated to Russians. Already in 1826 the Kazan Spiritual Consistory contended, no doubt with some exaggeration, that "the Mordvin people is completely Russified [*obrusen*], and everyone down to the last person speaks Russian very well."[9] Similarly, highland Maris, settled on the right bank of the Volga, were almost always contrasted favorably with their counterparts across that river on the meadow side, because they exhibited a stronger attachment to Christianity and had become agriculturalists. Some accounts suggest that highland Maris even regarded their meadow counterparts with a certain scorn.[10] Meadow Maris constituted a majority in the isolated and sparsely populated forests along much of the border between Kazan and Viatka provinces, where trades based on forest products were crucial to their subsistence.[11] Eastern Mari communities, made up of eighteenth-century migrants to Orenburg and Perm provinces, for the most part escaped baptism and were therefore able to practice animism with relatively little interference. Many did, however, appropriate customs and practices from their

---

[7] V. M. Cheremshanskii, *Opisanie Orenburgskoi gubernii v khoziaistvenno-statisticheskom, etnograficheskom i promyshlennom otnosheniiakh* (Ufa, 1859), pp. 130–68; and Charles Robert Steinwedel, "Invisible Threads of Empire: State, Religion, and Ethnicity in Tsarist Bashkiria, 1773–1917" (Ph.D. diss., Columbia University, 1999), pp. 76–83.

[8] A. I. Lipinskii, *Materialy dlia geografii i statistiki Rossii, sobrannye ofitserami General'nogo shtaba: Simbirskaia guberniia* (St. Petersburg, 1868), 1:322; V. Lebedev, "Simbirskie chuvashi," *Zhurnal MVD* 30 (1850): 306, 318–20; and Vasilii Sboev, *Issledovaniia ob inorodtsakh Kazanskoi eparkhii* (Kazan, 1856), pp. 41–49.

[9] N. V. Nikol'skii, *Sbornik istoricheskikh materialov o narodnostiakh Povolzh'ia* (Kazan, 1920), pp. 273–74. For similar assessments, see Laptev, *Materialy*, pp. 255–56; Karl Fuks, "Poezdka iz Kazani k mordve Kazanskoi gubernii v 1839 godu," *Zhurnal MVD* 34, 12 (1839): 102–10; and RGIA, f. 797, op. 3, d. 12654, l. 10.

[10] The highland Maris were so named because the terrain on the right bank of the Volga was considerably more rugged than the terrain on the left bank. "Gornye cheremisy v Kazanskoi gubernii," *Zhurnal MVD* 41, 2 (1853): 223; and L. Iznoskov, "Gorno-cheremiskie prikhody Kozmodem'ianskogo uezda," *Trudy Kazanskogo gubernskogo statisticheskogo komiteta*, no. 2 (1869): 20–27. The dialects of the two groups differed considerably. See K. I. Kozlova, *Ocherki etnicheskoi istorii mariiskogo naroda* (Moscow, 1978), p. 214; and M. Veske, "Issledovaniia o narechiiakh cheremiskogo iazyka," *IOAIE* 7 (1888): 1–50.

[11] Laptev, *Materialy*, pp. 46–49, 289–331; D. E. Kazantsev, *Formirovanie dialektov mariiskogo iazyka* (Ioshkar-Ola, 1985), pp. 134–39; G. N. Aiplatov and A. G. Ivanov, eds., *Istoriia Mariiskogo kraia v dokumentakh i materialakh*, no. 1 (Ioshkar-Ola, 1992): 346–48, 352–53, 516–26; and Ivan N. Smirnov, *Cheremisy: Istoriko-etnograficheskii ocherk* (Kazan, 1889), p. 84. On the Mari economy in the eighteenth century, see A. G. Ivanov, *Ocherki po istorii Mariiskogo kraia XVIII veka* (Ioshkar-Ola, 1995), pp. 107–98.

Highland and meadow Maris in the 1870s. From S. K. Kuznetsov, "Ocherki iz byta cheremis," *Drevniaia i Novaia Rossiia* 8 (1877), facing p. 349.

Muslim neighbors, and some adopted the Tatar language and eventually sought to convert to Islam.[12] Udmurts occupied primarily the southeastern districts of Viatka province, though they could be found in neighboring provinces as well. Although they remained a predominantly peasant population, a number was ascribed to the two large iron factories in Izhevsk and Votkinsk in the early nineteenth century.[13]

Inhabited by several different ethno-confessional groups, the Volga-Kama region was in fact characteristic of several areas in the Russian empire. In the Baltic and western provinces, New Russia in the south, and in the North Caucasus and Transcaucasia, several—often many—peoples of diverse background and traditions converged in a single area. Indeed, many non-Russian

[12] On the eastern Maris, see Cheremshanskii, *Opisanie*, pp. 179–93; G. A. Sepeev, *Vostochnye mariitsy: Istoriko-etnograficheskoe issledovanie material'noi kul'tury, seredina XIX–nachalo XX vv.* (Ioshkar-Ola, 1975); and N. I. Isanbaev, "Mezhetnicheskie sviazi vostochnykh mariitsev," *Etnogenez i etnicheskaia istoriia mariitsev* (Ioshkar-Ola, 1988), pp. 87–98.
[13] V. Bekhterev, "Votiaki: Ikh istoriia i sovremennoe sostoianie," *Vestnik Evropy* 8 (1880): 620–54; P. N. Luppov, *Volneniia votiakov Viatskoi gubernii po povodu prikrepleniia ikh k gornym zavodam v 1807 i 1808 g.* (Viatka, 1909); and V. V. Pimenov, ed., *Udmurty: Istoriko-etnograficheskie ocherki* (Izhevsk, 1993).

subjects faced the problem of having to relate not just to Russians and representatives of state authority, but to other non-Russians, with whom their relations were not always entirely peaceful. Likewise, state officials, in governing many portions of the empire, had to manage several populations at once, which sometimes involved the self-appointed task of rescuing one non-Russian group from the "pernicious influence" of another.[14] This problem was to grow over the course of the nineteenth century.

The Eighteenth-Century Baptisms and Their Legacy

Undoubtedly, one of the most dramatic events in the history of the Volga-Kama region was the mass induction of over four hundred thousand non-Christians into Orthodoxy in the mid-eighteenth century. Building on Peter the Great's efforts earlier in the century, the state launched an aggressive missionary campaign in the 1740s that created a large class of newly baptized non-Russians, or *novokreshchenye*. Centered in the city of Sviiazhsk, an institution known as the Office for the Affairs of New Converts (*Kontora novokreshchenykh del*) was the principal agent of conversion before it was finally closed by Catherine II in 1764.[15] In the 1740s it was not uncommon for clerics to report the baptism of tens of thousands of non-Russians over a short period or the conversion of all residents of a given locale "to the very last child without exception."[16]

Non-Russians were in some cases attracted to Christianity by various benefits that the government offered in return for baptism: freedom from the military draft, a three-year tax break instituted by Peter the Great, and even direct payment in money and goods. Although sometimes skeptical about relying on cash to promote baptism—in some cases new converts returned for baptism several times in order to maximize their receipts!—most clerics

---

[14] Recent works that seriously address the complexities of these multiethnic situations include: Theodore R. Weeks, *Nation and State in Late Imperial Russia: Nationalism and Russification on the Western Frontier, 1863–1914* (DeKalb, 1996); Paul Robert Magosci, *A History of Ukraine* (Toronto, 1996); Willard Sunderland, "Making the Empire: Colonists and Colonization in Russia, 1800–1850s" (Ph.D. diss., Indiana University, 1997); Nicholas Breyfogle, "Heretics and Colonizers: Religious Dissent and Russian Colonization of Transcaucasia, 1830–1890" (Ph.D. diss., University of Pennsylvania, 1998); Adeeb Khalid, *The Politics of Muslim Cultural Reform: Jadidism in Central Asia* (Berkeley, 1998); and Thomas M. Barrett, *At the Edge of Empire: The Terek Cossacks and the North Caucasus Frontier, 1700–1860* (Boulder, 1999).

[15] E. A. Malov, *O Novokreshchenskoi kontore* (Kazan, 1878); S. L. Ursynovich, "Novokreshchenskaia Kontora: K voprosu o roli pravoslavnogo missionerstva v kolonizatsionnoi i natsional'noi politike samoderzhaviia," *Ateist* 54 (1930): 22–50; and Michael Khodarkovsky, "'Not by Word Alone': Missionary Policies and Religious Conversion in Early Modern Russia," *Comparative Studies in Society and History* 38, 2 (1996): 267–97.

[16] This report documented the baptism of 18,090 Mordvins. *Opisanie dokumentov i del, khraniashchikhsia v arkhive Sviateishogo Sinoda* (St. Petersburg, 1906), 16:62.

were forced to admit that without such incentives, "proselytism itself has almost no force and effect whatsoever." Once the association between baptism and cash awards had been established, moreover, "it is impossible for proselytizers to show up in non-Christian dwellings without any [money], for some of them, when they run out of money (which has been demanded from them by some of the newly baptized), have scarcely been able to save themselves and have been protected by accompanying soldiers."[17]

Material encouragement was supplemented with a liberal dose of coercion, especially when converts became too insistent on getting their money. Records suggest that violence was frequently central to these "conversions," and that sometimes missionaries became the objects of angry retribution. In one notable instance, the missionary Dmitrii Sechenov was attacked by a group of Mordvins, one-thousand-strong, after he destroyed a Mordvin ancestral graveyard, and barely escaped with his life.[18] To judge by Chuvash legends, baptism sometimes involved merely driving people into a river or lake and giving each of them a cross and a Russian name. To escape this missionary juggernaut, some non-Russians fled into the dense forests and lived there for extended periods, while others migrated permanently across the Kama river into Bashkiria, where the state's authority was much weaker.[19] Still, in one way or another, most of the region's animists—Chuvash, Maris, Mordvins, and Udmurts—and at least some Muslims were baptized.

Following baptism, novokreshchenye faced a host of threats both from Russian officials, who exploited their new status for personal gain, and from those non-Russians who remained unbaptized. The latter conflict became especially aggravated when the government decreed that the taxes from which converts had been freed should be imposed on the unconverted members of the same communities. Thus, as one observer related, "Difference of faith creates tremendous disagreement among them, so that baptized and unbaptized cannot tolerate one another and do all kinds of nasty things to one another."[20] While missionary sources typically made the new converts out to be the victims of these "injuries" (*obidy*), Muslim and pagan testimony before the Legislative Commission in the 1760s described how new converts took advantage of protection from local officials, and "not having

[17] Ibid., 23:481.
[18] A. Mozharovskii, "Teriushevskoe deistvie 1743 g.," *Nizhegorodskie gubernskie vedomosti* 1, 2, 4 (1892); and Paul W. Werth, "Armed Defiance and Biblical Appropriation: Assimilation and the Transformation of Mordvin Resistance, 1740–1810," *Nationalities Papers* 27, 2 (1999): 248–59. Thirty-five Mordvins were less fortunate and perished in subsequent confrontation with the authorities.
[19] V. D. Dimitriev, *Chuvashskie istoricheskie predaniia: Ocherki istorii chuvashskogo naroda s drevnikh vremen do serediny XIX veka* (Cheboksary, 1993), pp. 284–86; and Rakhmatullin, *Naselenie Bashkirii*, pp. 80–90.
[20] Cited in N. V. Nikol'skii, *Khristianstvo sredi chuvash Srednego Povolzh'ia v XVI–XVIII vekakh* (Kazan, 1912), p. 164.

to answer to anyone . . . [they] give themselves over to great impudence and mischief."[21] Whoever was oppressing whom in actuality, sources report that new converts continued to experience various "injuries" at the hands of both Russians and non-Christians. Plans for their resettlement to separate no-vokreshchenye villages ran up against the fact that converts were usually too poor and almost never eager to resettle, "injuries" notwithstanding.[22]

The government soon became convinced that in addition to the promotion of Christianity, successful missionary activity also required the weakening of Islamic influence in the region. The result was a wholesale destruction of hundreds of mosques, accompanied by extensive prohibitions on the construction of new ones.[23] These measures exacerbated conflicts between new converts and non-Christians, since mosques were destroyed precisely in those locales where they presented the greatest danger of "seduction" for new converts.[24] The state's assaults on Islamic institutions soon provoked Muslim resistance, which took its most violent and coherent form in the Batyrsha uprising of 1755.[25] From this point forward, Russian authorities promoted a more cooperative relationship with Muslims and eschewed further attempts to convert them on a large scale. Muslim expressions of apprehension for their mosques and religious status, as articulated by their delegates to the Legislative Commission, heightened the government's deference toward Islamic religious practice and contributed to Catherine's edict granting Muslims religious tolerance in 1773.[26] The Pugachev uprising (1773–75), in which many Muslims and even baptized non-Russians participated, accelerated the policy of integrating Islamic elites into the Russian imperial system, culminating in the establishment in 1788 of the Orenburg Muslim Spiritual Assembly.[27]

After the closing of the Kontora in 1764, missionary activity continued for the next few decades in a much softer form. Several "proselytizers"

---

[21] Cited in S. F. Tashkin, *Inorodtsy Privolzhsko-Priural'skogo kraia i Sibiri po materialam Ekaterininskoi zakonodatel'noi komissii* (Kazan, 1922), pp. 168–69.

[22] Malov, *O Novokreshchenskoi kontore*, pp. 83–87. In 1756 a directive established that only if new converts made up less than 10% of the population of a given settlement should they be resettled. Otherwise, non-Christians should be resettled.

[23] A decree of 1744 reports that of 536 mosques, 418 were destroyed. See E. A. Malov, "O tatarskikh mechetiakh v Rossii," *Pravoslavnyi sobesednik* 3 (1867): 295–300.

[24] Nikol'skii, *Khristianstvo*, pp. 101–3.

[25] Malov, *O Novokreshchenskoi kontore*, p. 176. For a Soviet account that sees the uprising in class terms, see S. Bikbulatov, "Bashkirskie vosstaniia i tatary," *Vestnik Nauchnogo Obshchestva Tatarovedeniia* 9–10 (1930): 61–87. For a hagiographic account that sees Batyrsha as the leader of a "national liberation movement of the Tatar people," see F. G. Islaev, *Pravoslavnye missionery v Povolzh'e* (Kazan, 1999), pp. 68–76.

[26] PSZ I, vol. 19, no. 13996 (1773).

[27] On the Assembly, see Steinwedel, "Invisible Threads of Empire," pp. 47–76; and D. D. Azamatov, *Orenburgskoe Magometanskoe Dukhovnoe Sobranie v kontse XVIII–XIX vv.* (Ufa, 1999). On the participation of non-Russians in the Pugachev uprising, see S. Kh. Alishev, *Tatary Srednego Povolzh'ia v Pugachevskom vosstanii* (Kazan, 1973); A. G. Ivanov, ed., *Krest'ianskaia voina pod predvoditel'stvom E. I. Pugacheva v Mariiskom krae* (Ioshkar-Ola, 1989); and V. A. Nestorov, ed., *Krest'ianskaia voina pod predvoditel'stvom Emel'iana Pugacheva v Chuvashii* (Cheboksary, 1972).

(*propovedniki*) were assigned to each diocese and were dispatched to trouble spots—for example, where new converts refused to attend church or continued to perform animist rituals. But as one proselytizer reported, though new converts tended to listen to him and even tried to present themselves as good Christians, they usually returned to animism after he had left. Nor did proselytizers receive much help from local secular authorities, and their presence generated conflict with the local clergy, which viewed them as an unwelcome intrusion. Such open rifts within the Orthodox clergy could hardly have made a positive impression on non-Russians, and on the whole proselytizers enjoyed little success.[28] They were ordered to cease their activities in 1789 when threats of unrest began to appear once again in the trans-Kama region, and after the few non-Russian schools that had been established in conjunction with the Kontora were closed in 1800, not even a semblance of missionary activity remained.[29]

Like all Orthodox Christians in Russia, novokreshchenye were ascribed to Orthodox parishes and became responsible for supporting their clergy economically. In Russia generally, the inadequacy of the local clergy's material support constituted an intractable problem for the church. Lacking state salaries, clergy were forced to subsist on voluntary contributions from parishioners, given in exchange for the performance of important religious rites (above all, baptism, marriage, and burial), and sometimes on a fixed collection in kind (*ruga*). While the state provided a special supplement to the poorest parishes beginning in 1829, this measure did not solve the fundamental problem in local parishes: the clergy's economic dependence on parishioners complicated the proper execution of their religious duties.[30] Not surprisingly, this problem was especially great among new converts, who were in particular need of "worthy church servitors." The fact that most non-Russian parishioners could not understand Russian and had a poor grasp of Orthodoxy's religious requirements "serve[d] the rural clergy as a plentiful source for the satisfaction of their interests."[31] While authorities issued directives designed to protect non-Russian parishioners from clerical abuses, local priests found ways to bully or trick the latter into fulfilling unlawful *ruga* demands, indeed to such an extent that clergy in non-Russian

---

[28] Nikol'skii, *Khristianstvo*, pp. 160–67; and M. Dobrovol'skii, "Nekotorye cherty religioznoi zhizni novokreshchen-inorodtsev Nizhegorodskoi eparkhii vo vtoroi polovine XVIII stoletiia," *Nizhegorodskie eparkhial'nye vedomosti* 1 (1892): 11–18.

[29] RGIA, f. 796, op. 70, d. 47; and A. Mozharovskii, *Izlozhenie khoda missionerskogo dela po prosveshcheniiu kazanskikh inorodtsev s 1552 po 1867 goda* (Moscow, 1880), pp. 107–8. On the schools, see K. V. Kharlampovich, "Kazanskie novokreshchenskie shkoly v XVIII veke," *Pravoslavnyi blagovestnik* 5 (1905): 203–7, 6 (1905): 243–48, 7 (1905): 300–305, 8 (1905): 355–58, 9 (1905): 19–22.

[30] Gregory L. Freeze, *The Parish Clergy in Nineteenth-Century Russia: Crisis, Reform, Counter-Reform* (Princeton, 1983), pp. 51–101. Although Freeze remarks that *ruga* (fixed support) was quite rare, it appears to have been fairly standard in non-Russian parishes.

[31] RGIA, f. 383, op. 3, d. 2332, l. 70b.

parishes viewed the first half of the nineteenth century as a "golden age."[32] This problematic relationship between clergy and parishioners not only produced various "misunderstandings" and "incidents" but also dissuaded remaining pagans and Muslims from converting to Christianity.

While several officials and later publicists drew attention to the plight of non-Russian parishes, their superiors in St. Petersburg typically viewed parish economics as a more general problem and did not take account of the region's specificities.[33] Though the Synod attempted to alleviate some of the burden by providing subsidies to several new Mari parishes established in 1838,[34] its more general solution was to promote the formation of parishes with a number of parishioners sufficient to ensure the clergy's adequate support, above all by eliminating undersized parishes and reducing the size of clerical staffs.[35] Less secure financially and covering relatively large geographical areas, non-Russian parishes were particularly vulnerable to the cold rationality of this policy. Thus in 1869 Kazan Archbishop Antonii (Amfiteatrov) identified the reckless introduction of new registries of clerical positions to his diocese in 1846 without regard for the prevailing local circumstances as a principal reason for persistent apostasy among baptized Tatars. The standards imposed by the registries "might be convenient where parishioners are all Russian and the settlements are not scattered. But Kazan diocese is not like that."[36] Non-Russians required more clergy, smaller parishes, and subsidies from the Synod. While in some cases the limited salaries accompanying the introduction of the registries alleviated tensions,[37] they were usually not sufficient to eliminate the problem altogether. Established and maintained by government directive and in most cases not yet enjoying full legitimacy in the eyes of their parishioners, non-Russian parishes could not hope to attain the independent and organic state to which many church reformers aspired by the 1860s, and in most cases still required financial support from the government.[38]

Thus the eighteenth-century baptisms created a large number of non-Russian Christians whose conversion was so superficial that they continued

[32] S. Nurminskii, "Inorodcheskie prikhody," *Pravoslavnoe obozrenie* 12 (1863): 254–55; NRF MarNII op. 1, d. 43, l. 36; P. N. Luppov, ed., *Materialy dlia istorii khristianstva u votiakov v pervoi polovine XIX veka* (Viatka, 1911), p. 257; and L. A. Taimasov, *Khristianizatsiia chuvashskogo naroda v pervoi polovine XIX veke* (Cheboksary, 1992), pp. 37–42.

[33] RGIA, f. 383, op. 3, d. 2332, ll. 23–230b.

[34] RGIA, f. 796, op. 124, d. 1795.

[35] Freeze, *Parish Clergy*, esp. pp. 92–98.

[36] RGIA, f. 796, op. 150, d. 816, ll. 5–18 (citation from l. 6). Antonii requested a ten thousand-ruble subsidy for these parishes, but the Synod was unsympathetic to his requests and told him to make do with the resources on hand (ll. 1–4).

[37] See Nurminskii, "Inorodcheskie prikhody," 261; and Sboev, *Issledovaniia*, p. 5.

[38] This was the view, for example, of Nurminskii in "Inorodcheskie prikhody." On discussions in the 1860s concerning the need for independent and organic Orthodox parishes, see A. Papkov, *Tserkovno-obshchestvennye voprosy v epokhu tsaria-osvoboditelia, 1855–1870* (St. Petersburg, 1902).

to practice animism and Islam, even if only surreptitiously, well into the nineteenth century. We will encounter some new baptisms in chapter 3, but the nineteenth-century mission was concerned principally with "reinforcing" these already-baptized non-Russians in Christianity. Aside from creating large numbers of novokreshchenye, the Kontora's actions also served to link Christian affiliation inextricably with imperial authority, so that missionaries' later attempts to conduct activity with a more genuine emphasis on spirituality floundered on non-Russians' refusal to agree to baptism unless it had been specifically decreed by the Emperor or the "higher authorities." Having once endured such a missionary assault, the remaining non-Christians (above all Muslims) were also now inclined to see any significant government initiative—for example, the promotion of the potato among state peasants in the 1840s or the introduction of new fire regulations for mosques—as the thin wedge of yet another coercive missionary campaign. Indeed, the fear and long-term suspicion generated by the Kontora among non-Russians was perhaps its most lasting legacy.

Even so, at least until the Soviet period there was never such an assault on indigenous religious institutions and practices, and the state was particularly circumspect in its dealings with Muslims. In accordance with the "Catherinian compromise," Russian law and administration in the nineteenth century combined tolerance for recognized religious groups with a privileged status for Orthodoxy. Because only the Orthodox church, as the embodiment of the "supreme and predominant" religion of the imperial state, enjoyed the right to proselytize, non-Orthodox believers were prohibited from promoting their faiths. Similarly, apostasy from Orthodoxy, even to another Christian faith, was strictly forbidden, thus rendering Orthodox status both hereditary and unalterable.[39] At the same time, adherents to recognized religions—even paganism—had the right to practice their religions without undue interference. In short, the law offered basic religious toleration (*veroterpimost´*) to recognized religious groups, but not freedom of conscience (*svoboda sovesti*) to the individual.

Animism and Islam

In religious terms, the Volga-Kama region stood at the intersection of three worlds: the Orthodox, the Islamic, and the animist. Especially in certain communities, these different worlds overlapped and intersected, although Orthodoxy was by far the most recent addition and remained, for the most part,

[39] *SZ* (1832), vol. 1, part 1, articles 44–45; vol. 14, articles 40–41, 73; *PSZ* II, vol. 16, no. 14409 (1842), article 25. Each Orthodox husband / father was required to ensure that his wife and children did not accept another faith. *SZ* (1832), vol. 14, article 41; and Ardalion Popov, *Sud i nakazaniia za prestupleniia protiv very i nravstvennosti po russkomu pravu* (Kazan, 1904), p. 317.

only superficially integrated into indigenous life at the beginning of the nineteenth century. Islam, by contrast, appeared in the region by the early tenth century and was central to the identity of many Turkic communities throughout the Volga and Ural region, western Siberia, and the steppe. A deeper understanding of the confessional politics considered in this book requires at least a brief consideration of animist and Islamic beliefs, practices, and institutions, as they appeared roughly in the first half of the nineteenth century.

Animists throughout the Russian empire differed from most other confessional groups in that they had no officially recognized hierarchy or religious institutions, presumably because they lacked the scripture and other accoutrements by which officials defined religion. But if animists had no "clergy" with formal ordination or religious hierarchy, they did have religious specialists, known in Mari as *karty* (elders), who had acquired wisdom and experience about particular prayers and rituals and were elected by their communities to deal with specific religious occasions.[40] Similarly, so-called *muzhany* were consulted to prescribe remedies for particular misfortunes, such as offerings to one or another spirit. While Russian authorities often regarded *muzhany* as self-interested tricksters who profited materially from their spurious expertise,[41] neither *karty* nor *muzhany* differed outwardly from other peasants, and thus could not be easily identified. Udmurts and Chuvash had similar specialists.[42]

Animists seem to have had a conception of a supreme god (Mari: *Kugu Iomo*, Udmurt: *Inmar*, Chuvash: *Tora*), but this being was functionally less significant than the wide range of spirits that had jurisdiction over various aspects of human life.[43] Prayers were accordingly directed to a particular spirit depending on the situation, and the concerns behind these religious rites appear to have been very concrete, often involving health, success in agriculture and raising livestock and bees, help in paying state taxes, and so on.[44] But while many animist rituals were geared toward satisfying super-

---

[40] V. P. Vishnevskii, "O religii nekreshchennykh cheremis Kazanskoi gubernii," *Etnograficheskii sbornik*, no. 4 (1858): 209–14; and F. Alonzov, "O religioznykh verovaniiakh nekreshchenykh cheremis Birskogo uezda," *Pamiatnaia kniga Orenburgskoi gubernii na 1865* (Ufa, 1865), p. 8.

[41] GAKO, f. 237, op. 131, d. 1283, l. 20b.; and RGIA, f. 808, op. 1, d. 134, l. 43.

[42] P. M. Bogaevskii, "Ocherki religioznykh predstavlenii votiakov," *Etnograficheskoe obozrenie* 1 (1890): 123–24; and V. E. Vladykin, "Religioznye verovaniia," in *Udmurty*, pp. 234–37.

[43] Vladykin, "Religioznye verovaniia," p. 232; Sboev, *Issledovaniia*, pp. 100–108; and S. Nurminskii, "Ocherk religioznykh verovanii cheremis," *Pravoslavnyi sobesednik* 3 (1862): 284–85. By the nineteenth century indigenous concepts seem already to have been inflected by Christianity. See A. Filimonov, "O religii kreshchenykh cheremis i votiakov Viatskoi gubernii," *Viatskie gubernskie vedomosti* 12–14 (1868). For a listing of various spirits, see "Imena bogov cheremiskikh," *Zavolzhskii muravei* 16 (1833): 924–25; RGIA, f. 808, op. 1, d. 134, l. 410b.; and Thomas A. Sebeok and Frances J. Ingemann, *Studies in Cheremis: The Supernatural* (New York, 1956).

[44] "Sobranie molitv, chitaemykh cheremisami kreshchenymi i nekreshchenymi pri zhertvoprinoshenii Keremeti," *Zavolzhskii muravei* 10 (1833): 584–87.

natural entities to receive some benefit or to alleviate some misfortune, it is misleading to view these religious practices as strictly "utilitarian," as some observers did.[45] Rather, it seems more accurate to suggest that the well-being of family and community was itself invested with sacred significance.[46]

Among the most significant spiritual entities locally were *keremets*, which required sacrifices—including livestock, fowl, agricultural products (bread, honey, and beer), and even money—performed in sacred groves located near each village. While sometimes these rituals involved many participants from distant villages, there were also smaller keremets, representing ancestors, which were venerated through private offerings, usually involving a single household or family. Though some observers labeled keremets "evil spirits," a more sensitive reading suggests that their diabolical character was introduced by missionaries seeking to demonize indigenous practices, and that some Maris—particularly in the east, where the influence of Christianity was weak—viewed keremets as beneficial protectors who were nonetheless capable of visiting disaster when not venerated properly.[47] The keremet cult was widespread in the Volga-Kama region—even among some Muslims—and constituted a main distinguishing feature of local religious life.[48]

As was true for many faiths in the empire, religious practice for animists was not a matter of individual discretion but instead served as the basis for defining and sustaining community. At least until mid-century or so, definitions of community that might appear ethnic or linguistic are better understood in religious terms. Maris thus referred to their own beliefs as "Mari faith" (*marla vera*) and viewed the abandonment of native practices in favor of Orthodox ones as an act of "becoming Russian." They accordingly called

[45] P. Znamenskii, "Gornye cheremisy Kazanskogo kraia (iz nabliudenii ochevidtsa)," *Vestnik Evropy* 4 (1867): 47. See also F. Zemlianitskii, "Neskol'ko slov po povodu iazycheskikh sueverii cheremis Tsarevokokshaiskogo uezda," *IKE* 8 (1871): 244–45.

[46] Devin DeWeese has identified this outlook as being characteristic of the Inner Asian religious environment more broadly. See his *Islamization and Native Religion in the Golden Horde: Baba Tükles and the Conversion to Islam in Historical and Epic Tradition* (University Park, Penn., 1994), p. 30.

[47] V. M. Vasil'ev, *Materialy dlia izucheniia verovanii i obriadov naroda Marii* (Krasnokokshaisk, 1927), pp. 21–28. Demonization of native beliefs was characteristic of missionary efforts elsewhere as well. See, for example, Birgit Meyer, "Modernity and Enchantment: The Image of the Devil in Popular African Christianity," in *Conversion to Modernities: The Globalization of Christianity*, ed. Peter van der Veer (London, 1996), pp. 199–230; and Kenneth Mills, *Idolatry and Its Enemies: Colonial Andean Religion and Extirpation, 1640–1750* (Princeton, 1997), pp. 211–42.

[48] Keremets seem to have had their origins in the Turkic conversion to Islam—the term is itself etymologically of Arabic origin—and their veneration may have been a local adaptation of the Islamic Central Asian cult of saints' tombs. For more on keremets, see Sboev, *Issledovaniia*, pp. 110–20; N. Zolotnitskii, "Nevidimyi mir po shamanskim vozzreniiam cheremis," *Uchenye zapiski Imperatorskogo Kazanskogo universiteta* 4 (1877): 735–59; Il'ia Sofiiskii, "O keremetiakh kreshchennykh tatar Kazanskogo kraia," *IKE* 24 (1877): 674; V. K. Magnitskii, *Materialy k ob"iasneniiu staroi chuvashskoi very* (Kazan, 1881), pp. 1–11; R. G. Akhmet'ianov, *Obshchaia leksika dukhovnoi kul'tury narodov Srednego Povolzh'ia* (Moscow, 1981), pp. 31–33; and Allen J. Frank, "The Traditional Religion of the Volga-Turkic peoples" (M.A. thesis, Indiana University, 1990), pp. 68–76.

the practicing Christians in their midst "Russian-believers" (*ruskovery*). Widespread among the peoples of the region was the proposition that God had given each people its own faith, and that each faith was equally pleasing to God.[49] Animists therefore did not view Christianity as a false religion, but they nonetheless considered it impossible to abandon their own practices and to confess Orthodoxy exclusively, as the church required. Indeed, animists considered that their well-being and even their lives depended on performance of native rituals. As one missionary reported in 1829, Maris claimed, "If all Cheremis are brought into the Russian faith, then all will inevitably perish."[50] Thus, whereas the Orthodox church focused on baptism as the defining moment in conversion and viewed converts' subsequent performance of "pagan rituals" as a temporary "going astray" (*zabluzhdenie*), for animists conversion occurred when a person abandoned native practices and thereby rejected the community. Thus many novokreshchenye were viewed by ecclesiastical authorities as Orthodox Christians (if rather shaky ones) but saw themselves as *chii Marii* (that is, "pure Maris" or animists), even though they might conform with Orthodox prescriptions to avoid trouble with the authorities.

At the same time, however, animists' religious worldview was not sternly exclusivist, and they were therefore reasonably open to new practices that they considered to be effective. Observers thus reported a fair degree of syncretism, by which Christian elements were incorporated into indigenous pantheons. To Orthodox observers, baptized animists appeared to occupy an ambiguous religious space between Christianity and their native traditions. The priest Andrei Al'binskii wrote in 1820 about his Mari parishioners, "Almost all those who have heard the Gospel feel and believe its truth, and it is only the entrenched habit of their faith, and even more the fear of the calamities that the *muzhany* say they will suffer from keremets on account of their defiance, that prevents them from abandoning their delusions."[51] Another priest related in 1828 that most baptized Maris "because of close habitation, blind attachment to their inborn prejudices, and crude superstition, adhere to the church of Christ with one hand, and with the other, just as much or even more, they adhere to the very same rules of paganism as do the unbaptized."[52] While Orthodox clergy described this syncretism as a kind of religious schizophrenia, it is not clear that baptized animists were themselves plagued by a sense of cognitive dissonance.

The geographic scope of animist practices varied considerably. Some rituals were clearly very localized. Individual households often had their own sa-

---

[49] Usually they spoke of seventy-seven peoples and religions. Vishnevskii, "O religii," 209; and N. I. Zolotnitskii, *Kornevoi chuvashsko-russkii slovar'* (Kazan, 1875), pp. 181–85.

[50] RGIA, f. 797, op. 3, d. 12654, ll. 124–124ob.

[51] RGIA, f. 808, op. 1, d. 134, ll. 43–44.

[52] GAKO, f. 237, op. 131, d. 1283, ll. 73–73ob.

cred groves, and some important holidays, such as the Mari *Aga-Pairam*, were celebrated separately in each village.[53] However, other holidays and sacred sites could have a much broader geographic scope. A single sacred grove might be known as far away as neighboring provinces and could serve as a center of animist activity for the whole region. Sometimes Maris even shared shrines with nearby Muslims, who associated the sites with Sufis or Islamic saints.[54] A large cliff in Urzhum district, known as *Kuruk kuguza* ("hill grandfather"), was considered by Maris to be the resting place of a Mari hero and was famous as far away as Perm province. Maris conducted collective offerings to this spirit every few years in special groves, each serving about ten villages.[55] On occasion, ritual gatherings could involve thousands of participants, including representatives from distant provinces who had been called to the location by special messengers.[56] Arguably, the introduction of Orthodoxy, with religiosity focused on the parish church, may in fact have served to *localize* religious practice to a greater degree, by breaking apart these larger networks and in some cases even destroying the objects of veneration that united animists across a broad geographic space.[57]

Novokreshchenye Tatars were settled primarily along the right bank of the Volga and in most cases had not been baptized as whole villages. Rather, a handful of families or individuals in each village had either succumbed to the Kontora's assault or had accepted baptism subsequently to avoid military service or to receive tax breaks or pardons for certain crimes.[58] As a result, relatively small numbers of baptized Tatars resided in villages that were otherwise entirely Muslim. Novokreshchenye therefore differed from their

---

[53] *Istoriia Mariiskogo kraia*, p. 480.

[54] Allen J. Frank, "The Veneration of Muslim Saints among the Maris of Russia," *Eurasian Studies Yearbook* 70 (1998): 79–84.

[55] S. K. Kuznetsov, "Poezdka k drevnei cheremiskoi sviatyne, izvestnoi so vremen Oleariia," *Etnograficheskoe obozrenie* 1 (1905): 129; and A. F. Rossolovskii, "Statisticheskoe opisanie Tsarevokokshaiskogo uezda v 1837 g.," *Kazanskie gubernskie vedomosti* 49 (1853).

[56] See, for example, A. G. Ivanov, "Vsemariiskoe iazycheskoe molenie 1827 goda i deistviia vlastei," *Mariiskii arkheograficheskii vestnik* 8 (1998): 48–74; and N. S. Popov, "Na mariiskom iazycheskom molenii," *Etnograficheskoe obozrenie* 3 (1996): 130–45.

[57] Scholars of religion in Africa have similarly challenged the notion that "traditional" religions are necessarily "microscopic" in their orientations (in contrast to major "world religions"). See in particular the work of Terence Ranger, "The Local and the Global in Southern African Religious History," in *Conversion to Christianity: Historical and Anthropological Perspectives on a Great Transformation*, ed. Robert W. Hefner (Berkeley, 1993), pp. 65–98; and idem, "Power, Religion, and Community: The Matobo Case," in *Subaltern Studies VII: Writings on South Asian History and Society*, ed. Partha Chatterjee and Gyanendra Pandey (Delhi, 1992), pp. 221–46.

[58] See Aleksei Maslovskii, "O kreshchenykh tatarakh Saranskogo uezda," *Penzenskie eparkhial'nye vedomosti* 11 (1871): 335–37; and N. I. Il'minskii, ed., *Opyty perelozheniia khristianskikh verouchitel'nykh knig na tatarskii i drugie inorodcheskie iazyki v nachale tekushchego stoletiia* (Kazan, 1885), pp. 36–70. Islaev shows that in the most intense years of the Kontora's activities (1744–52), only somewhat more than eight thousand Tatars were baptized, compared to over four hundred thousand baptisms for the region as a whole (*Pravoslavnye missionery*, p. 78).

Muslim neighbors only in terms of their formal religious affiliation. It is hardly surprising that apostasy—the open renunciation of Orthodox status—appeared among this group first and foremost.

Matters were more complex as regards "old-convert" (*starokreshchenye*) Tatars (known in Tatar as *Kräshens*), who were settled primarily to the east of the Volga, especially around the intersection of Kazan, Viatka, and Orenburg / Ufa provinces. Most Kräshens had been baptized before the eighteenth century and tended to live separately from Muslims.[59] In effect, they were situated at the very intersection of Christian, Islamic, and animist worlds and incorporated elements of each into their cosmology. Nonetheless, until the 1860s or so, they were generally considered good Christians by religious authorities—principally because of the church's focus on the mechanical execution of "Christian obligations"—and were therefore not the object of specific missionary attention. Although their religious identity seems to have varied from parish to parish, most Kräshens apparently viewed themselves as distinct from Muslims. Some scholars suggest that

Table 1
Number and Distribution of Baptized Tatars (circa 1862)

Province	Starokreshchenye	Novokreshchenye	"Apostates"
Kazan	27,901	12,693	3,517
Nizhnii/Novgorod	0	1,160	0
Samara	681	34	182
Simbirsk	348	2,251	64
Ufa	12,002	0	0
Viatka	7,463	1,382	0
Total	48,395	17,520	3,763

Sources: D. M. Iskhakov, *Istoricheskaia demografiia tatarskogo naroda: XVIII–nachalo XX vv.* (Kazan, 1993), pp. 93–98; E. A. Malov, "Statisticheskie svedeniia o kreshchenykh tatarakh Kazanskoi i nekotorykh drugikh eparkhii v volzhskom basseine," *Uchenye zapiski Kazanskogo universiteta*, no. 3–4 (1866): 311–20, 321–87. All figures refer to both sexes. I have not included the small numbers from Penza, Tambov, Perm, and (post-1865) Orenburg dioceses. Figures for Ufa province are based on Menzelinsk, Belebei, and Birsk districts and include "Bashkirs," although this term should be understood in a social sense *(bashkirtsy iz tatarskogo plemeni)*. The "apostate" category refers to those who were considered such by local clergy.

[59] The most complete account of the origins of this group is Il'dus Zagidullin, "Khristianizatsiia tatar Srednego Povolzh'ia vo vtoroi polovine XVI–XVII vv." *Uchenye zapiski Tatarskogo Gosudarstvennogo Gumanitarnogo Instituta* 1 (1997): 111–65. Missionary literature usually explained the distinction between old converts and new converts as being defined by the beginning of the Kontora's activities in the 1730s. More recently, Kappeler has demonstrated the distinction was based on whether baptisms had occurred before or after the introduction of the poll tax (*Rußlands erste Nationalitäten*, p. 357).

prior to their baptism Kräshens had not been well integrated into the Muslim world and that at least some had Finnic and Chuvash roots.[60] Russian authorities referred to them as "baptized Tatars," but for Kräshens themselves the term "Tatar" could only refer to Muslims.[61] Distinct from both Muslim Tatars and the adjacent Finnic peoples, these converts were in effect compelled to adopt a label that would differentiate them in some way. The label "Kräshen," based on the Russian term "baptized" (*kreshchennyi*), served this function reasonably well.

Though detailed information about Kräshens from before the 1860s is lacking, it would seem that they tended to view "Christian obligations" principally as a burdensome state imposition, and Islamic practices occupied an important part of their religious life. Kräshens invoked Mohammed and Allah in their prayers, maintained that Mohammed was God's prophet (or at least a saint), and could recite a multitude of legends about his activities and goodness. Most Kräshens frequented saints' tombs and other Muslim holy sites, where they interacted with Muslims. They were often skeptical of missionaries' attempts to disprove their beliefs, "because they did not want to be disappointed about their high conception of Mohammed." Many observers agreed that Kräshens "have left one shore but have not yet adhered to the other—they have left Islam but do not know Christianity."[62]

Even though the tendency among some missionaries was to plot Kräshens on an axis extending from Christianity to Islam, for many Kräshens themselves animism occupied the most important place in their religious world. When the first generation of educated Kräshens began to write about the beliefs of their fellow villagers, rather than fretting about Islamic influences, they tended to focus on various forest and water spirits, keremets, ancestor spirits, and the offerings and "superstitions" that punctuated Kräshen village life.[63]

---

[60] The Kräshen population to the northeast of Kazan, in particular, appears to have had Mari and Udmurt roots. See I. G. Mukhametshin, *Tatary-kriasheny: Istoriko-etnograficheskoe issledovanie material'noi kul'tury, seredina XIX–nachalo XX vv.* (Moscow, 1977), pp. 13, 21–22; and F. S. Baiazitova, *Govory tatar-kriashen v sravnitel'nom osveshchenii* (Moscow, 1986), pp. 17–18.

[61] E. A. Malov, *Missionerstvo sredi mukhammedan i kreshchenykh tatar* (Kazan, 1892), p. 276.

[62] Mikhail Mashanov, *Religiozno-nravstvennoe sostoianie kreshchenykh tatar Kazanskoi gubernii Mamadyshskogo uezda* (Kazan, 1875), pp. 15, 25. See also Agnès Kefeli-Clay, "L'Islam populaire chez les Tatars Chrétiens Orthodoxes au XIXe siècle," *Cahiers du monde russe* 37 (1996): 418.

[63] See Sofiiskii, "O keremetiakh"; idem, *Zagovory i zaklinaniia kreshchenykh tatar Kazanskogo kraia* (Kazan, 1878); Semen Maksimov, "Ostatki drevnikh narodno-tatarskikh (iazycheskikh) verovanii u nyneshnikh kreshchenykh tatar Kazanskoi gubernii," *IKE* 19–20 (1876): 565–82, 607–18; Mikhail Apakov, "Rasskazy kreshchenykh tatar dereven Ibelei i Alekseevskogo vyselka Iamashskogo prikhoda, Chistopol'skogo uezda, o proiskhozhdenii keremetei," *IKE* 11 (1876): 322–37; and V. Timofeev, "Moe vospitanie," in *Kazanskaia tsentral'naia kreshcheno-tatarskaia shkola: Materialy dlia istorii khristianskogo prosveshcheniia kreshchenykh tatar*, ed. N. I. Il'minskii (Kazan, 1887), pp. 9–28.

Those Kräshens who clung tenaciously to animist beliefs were called "clean, pure, or true Kräshen" (*chista, taza, chei Kräshen*).[64] In other words, as counterintuitive as it might seem semantically, the "purest" Kräshen was an animist one.

The religious constitution of each village and individual varied, depending on a variety of factors, such as their distance from the parish church, the abilities of the local priest, their relative proximity to Muslim villages, and economic and social ties with Muslims. Kräshens even developed a specialized vocabulary to describe these various dispositions. While an animist Kräshen was "pure," a Kräshen with Islamic inclinations was termed *tatarsymak* (one becoming Tatar or Muslim), while those with more Christian inclinations were called *uryssymak* (one becoming Russian or Christian).[65] Moreover, a Kräshen inclined toward Christianity was sometimes called a "black Kräshen" (*kara kräshen*), and one who began to exhibit signs of Christian belief was said to have "begun to blacken" (*karala bashlagan*). One with Muslim inclinations, on the other hand, was called "white Kräshen" (*ak kräshen*), evidently because of the ablutions connected with Islamic prayer.[66] Much of this vocabulary was shared by other non-Russians, which underscores that many religious conceptions were common across different confessional and linguistic groups.

Thus Kräshen religious beliefs, as one Kräshen himself wrote, "constitute a mixture of ancient pagan beliefs, Mohammedanism, and Christianity."[67] It is not clear to what extent Kräshens, in taking ideas and practices from different religious sources, actually synthesized them into a theologically consistent system, or whether those ideas merely coexisted as a kind of cultural mosaic.[68] In any event, their tenacious pre-Islamic commitments created favorable conditions for Christian missionary work, since experience had shown that converting Muslims was more difficult than converting animists. The Kräshen missionary Vasilii Timofeev recounted that though he had initially been "very indignant about the pagan rites of my fellow villagers," he later realized "that Kräshens' tenacious fortitude and keeping of pagan superstitions had brought great benefit. It nourished and supported religious feeling in the population and protected our old folks from the influence of outsiders. . . . If pagan superstitious rites had not been main-

---

[64] Sofiiskii, "O Keremetiakh," p. 687; and Iapei Babai [E. A. Malov], "O kreshchenykh tatarakh: Iz missionerskogo dnevnika," *IKE* 18–20 (1891): 563.

[65] Sofiiskii, "O Keremetiakh," p. 687.

[66] Ibid., p. 687.

[67] Maksimov, "Ostatki," p. 565.

[68] For more on the distinction between religious synthesis and cultural mosaic (and on syncretism generally), see J. D. Y. Peel, "Syncretism and Religious Change," *Comparative Studies in Society and History* 10 (1968): 121–41; and Charles Stewart and Rosalind Shaw, eds., *Syncretism / Anti-Syncretism: The Politics of Religious Synthesis* (London, 1994).

tained, then now, in all likelihood, the name of baptized Tatars would not have remained."[69] Still, the diverse sources of their religious outlook suggest that Kräshens' sense of religious affiliation could easily change.

If Kräshens' religious identity remained somewhat indeterminate, Muslims were by all indications firmly attached to Islam, and their conversion to Orthodoxy in the nineteenth century was quite rare. The strength of their community was in part a product of Islam's extensive institutional presence in the region. By most accounts, almost every Tatar village had a mosque with a school (*mäktäp*), in which both boys and girls received a basic education.[70] As Table 2 shows, mosques far outnumbered churches, even though they served a numerically smaller population. As a result, the literacy rate among Tatars was remarkably high, which made manuscript and printed texts accessible to Muslims on a wide scale. The introduction of Arabic-script printing presses in Kazan at the beginning of the nineteenth century made such texts more available, although many appear to have been widespread in manuscript form even before their mass publication. While Soviet scholarship highlights the secular literature produced by these presses, a significant portion of it was in fact religious.[71]

Table 2
Number of Churches, Chapels, and Mosques in the Volga-Kama Region (1860s)

Province	Orthodox churches	Orthodox chapels	Mosques	No. of souls (both sexes) per church	mosque
Kazan	450	155	677	2,302	601
Orenburg	284	126	1,687	2,942	540
Simbirsk	527	?	139	2,028	645
Viatka	577	339	139	3,901	289

Sources: M. Laptev, *Materialy dlia geografii i statistiki Rossii, sobrannye ofitserami General'nogo shtaba: Kazanskaia guberniia* (St. Petersburg, 1861), pp. 462–63; A. I. Lipinskii, *Materialy dlia geografii i statistiki Rossii, sobrannye ofitserami General'nogo shtaba: Simbirskaia guberniia* (St. Petersburg, 1868), 1:251, 2:350, 393; *Pamiatnaia knizhka Viatskoi gubernii na 1870* (Viatka, 1870), pp. 10–11, 62–63; *Pamiatnaia knizhka Orenburgskoi gubernii na 1865 god* (Ufa, 1865), appendices. Data for Simbirsk province concern number of parishes. Orenburg province includes districts that became Ufa province in 1865.

[69] Cited in Baiazitova, *Govory tatar-kriashen*, pp. 9–10. For a survey of Kräshen ritual practices (as well as an analysis of their linguistic particularities), see idem, *Keräshennär: Tel üzenchälekläre häm iola ijaty* (Kazan, 1997).
[70] NART, f. 10, op. 1, d. 1655, ll. 16–17. See also R. U. Amirkhanov, "Nekotorye osobennosti razvitiia narodnogo obrazovaniia u tatar v dooktiabr'skii period," in *Narodnoe proveshchenie u tatar v dooktiabr'skii period*, ed. Amirkhanov (Kazan, 1992), pp. 22–60.
[71] On Tatar publishing, see also E. A. Malov, *Pravoslavnaia protivomusul'manskaia missiia v Kazanskom krae v sviazi s istoriei musul'manstva v pervoi polovine XIX veka* (Kazan, 1868), pp. 1–25. The presses in Kazan and, later, other cities eventually supplied books to internal Russian markets and even for export. See Vorob'ev and Khisamutdinov, eds., *Tatary Srednego Povolzh'ia i Priural'ia*, p. 384.

Table 3
Number of Muslims, Islamic Clergy, and Mosques in Eastern European Russia (circa 1860)

Province	No. of Muslims	No. of Islamic clergy	No. of mosques/parishes
Kazan	418,504	1,558	677
Nizhnii/Novgorod	31,950	86	38
Orenburg	858,695	3,488	1,850
Penza	46,171	136	94
Perm	71,965	316	148
Samara	152,908	1,104	27
Saratov	59,897	180	132
Simbirsk	85,412	787	134
Tambov	11,647	43	21
Viatka	84,626	373	125

Sources: RGIA, f. 821, op. 8, d. 1096: "Vedomost´ o chisle magometan, mechetei, shkol pri onykh (medrias), i magometanskogo dukhovenstva, po guberniiam"; RGIA, Khranilishche pechatnykh zapisok, folder 3206; *Pamiatnaia knizhka Orenburgskoi gubernii.* The term "Islamic clergy" presumably refers to mullahs who had been officially recognized by the Muslim Spiritual Assembly and provincial authorities.

Aside from officially recognized Muslim institutions and clerics, there were also numerous unofficial mullahs and itinerant Sufis, who spread Islamic knowledge not just among Muslims but also among baptized Tatars and other non-Russians of the region. Their efforts were made easier by the fact that, despite some regional variation, Tatar was essentially the lingua franca in the region among non-Russians.[72]

The state's gradual recognition of the authority of the *ulema* within Muslim communities and its creation of the Muslim Spiritual Assembly served to legitimize Islam in the empire and helped to reinforce and promote new notions of Islamic regional identity encompassing the entire region from the Volga to western Siberia. These notions focused on the conversion to Islam of the region's first Turkic settlers, known as Bulghars, sometime before the tenth century. Gradually supplementing diverse local, tribal, and estate identities, this regional identity served to integrate the region's Muslims by reconciling various communal histories and, one may propose, thereby creating a strong incentive for those baptized communities conscious of a genealogical connection to the Bulghars to seek reinclusion in this emerging regional community. More than this, shrine catalogues and regional histories could also *create* such a historical memory even among those local communities that actually lacked such a genealogical connection.[73] All of these factors—

[72] Robert D. Crews, "Allies in God's Command: Muslim Communities and the State in Imperial Russia" (Ph.D. diss., Princeton University, 1999), pp. 47, 135–36.

[73] The elaboration of this "Bulghar" regional identity is the subject of Allen J. Frank, *Islamic Historiography and "Bulghar" Identity Among the Tatars and Bashkirs of Russia* (Leiden, 1998).

Muslims exiting a mosque in the village of Kazaklary, Laishevo district, Kazan province, ca. 1904. RGIA, f. 835, op. 4, d. 72, photograph #11.

an extensive network of mosques and schools, large numbers of published and manuscript texts, the existence of the Muslim Spiritual Assembly, and new notions of regional Islamic identity—not only made Muslims more resistant than animists to the idea of conversion to Christianity but even encouraged the conversion to Islam of other non-Russians in the region.

The Volga-Kama Region and the Problem of Empire

In a recent collection of essays entitled *Russia's Orient*, Daniel Brower and Edward Lazzerini remark that in the eighteenth and nineteenth centuries, "the relations between eastern and southern regions and the state were those of colonial lands and empire." The peoples there were dominated by an imperial center and were considered backward by contemporary Western standards. "Their status resembled that of the peoples in the overseas colonies of the French and British empires." In short, they conclude, "St. Petersburg ruled its own Russian Orient."[74] As general statements, these assertions contain much truth, and, given the conquest of the Volga-Kama region by an alien regime, colonization by Russian peasants, and a violent campaign of conversion, they would certainly seem to be valid as concerns the Finnic and Turkic peoples there. I would nonetheless stress that these propositions are accurate to different degrees depending on the time and territory in question. In chapter 5, we shall consider the appearance of more explicitly colonial discourses and practices in the mid- to late nineteenth century. Here, I wish to emphasize that in preceding years the idea of "colonial rule" in the Volga-Kama needs to be substantially qualified.

We must resist, first of all, the proposition that the state was manifestly Russian and therefore oppressed non-Russian subjects along ethnic, national, or linguistic lines. Indeed, Andreas Kappeler has emphasized the persistence of the "prenational" character of the Russian empire, whereby dynastic loyalty and social hierarchy (rule through elites) remained the most salient factors keeping the tsars' diverse territories under one rule well into the nineteenth century. Russian ethnic consciousness and the Orthodox faith were undoubtedly crucial for the integration of the more limited Russian core, Kappeler believes, but the larger empire was far too diverse to be held together by an ethnically or confessionally exclusive ideology.[75] Likewise, Richard Wortman demonstrates that tsarist rulers, rather than seeking to embody the Russian nation, long strove to dramatize their foreignness in order to affirm the permanence and inevitability of their separation from the population that they ruled. True, a "national subtheme" also ran through Russian political imagery, "but, until the late nineteenth century, only as an antithesis that was repeatedly submerged by a dominant foreign motif."[76] National motifs did begin to make their appearance under Nicholas I, but really only in the late nineteenth century—and even then with qualification—can we begin to speak of the rule of Russians, as a people, over non-Russians.

This is not to say that ethnicity was irrelevant. Russians maintained attitudes toward indigenous peoples, even the baptized, that were often con-

---

[74] Daniel R. Brower and Edward J. Lazzerini, eds., *Russia's Orient: Imperial Borderlands and Peoples, 1700–1917* (Bloomington, 1997), p. xv. This volume includes several essays on the Volga-Kama region.

[75] Andreas Kappeler, *Russland als Vielvölkerreich: Entstehung, Geschichte, Zerfall* (Munich, 1992), pp. 13, 134–38.

[76] Richard S. Wortman, *Scenarios of Power: Myth and Ceremony in Russian Monarchy*, vol. 1: *From Peter the Great to the Death of Nicholas I* (Princeton, 1995), pp. 5–6. Wortman documents the incarnation of a more explicitly national (Russian) Tsar in this work's second volume, *From Alexander II to the Abdication of Nicholas II* (Princeton, 2000).

temptuous, and they even used non-Russian ethnic designations as insults and profanity. One Mordvin related in 1828, for example, that nearby Russians "will never agree to give their daughters in marriage to a Mordvin, for that very name is repulsive to them."[77] Embedded in these Russian attitudes may well have been the consciousness of a ruling people. Yet many Tatars maintained similarly condescending attitudes toward nomadic Muslims and were willing to participate in the government's project of "civilizing" the steppe peoples by bringing them Islamic culture. There is no intrinsic reason to suppose that these Tatars identified with the empire less than Russians did, and in fact Allen Frank suggests that there was a "convergence" between their ideas and those of state officials, at least as regards the "uncultured" peoples of Inner Asia.[78]

If we consider formal social status, it is difficult to see the Russian people as being privileged over the rest. In many cases, the state offered newly incorporated non-Russian elites privileges and status equal or comparable to those of the Russian nobility (and therefore far superior to those of most Russians) in exchange for their service and support. True, Peter I compelled some native elites, such as Tatar *morzalar* and Mari *tarkhany*, to accept Orthodoxy in order to retain their privileged social status.[79] But serfdom, the lowest possible social status in Russia, was predominant above all in the state's central provinces, where the population was almost exclusively Russian. Some non-Russians in the Volga-Kama region were also enserfed, but the majority became state peasants, whose designation as "free rural inhabitants" underscores their considerable autonomy.[80] Other non-Russian groups were even more privileged. Bashkirs—a term that designated a social status more than an ethnic group—enjoyed special property rights and exemption from the poll tax. Teptiars, a multiethnic service estate closely related to Bashkirs, paid a reduced poll tax. Both these groups and *lashmany*, mostly Tatar peasants of the Admiralty, had special service obligations that exempted them from regular military conscription.[81] As a general rule, those

[77] Nikol'skii, *Sbornik*, p. 274.

[78] Allen Frank, "Volga Tatars and the 'Islamization' of Muslim Nomads: A Reverse Angle on Russia's 'Civilizing Mission' " (paper delivered at Humboldt University, Berlin, 1996).

[79] Kappeler, *Rußlands erste Nationalitäten*, p. 442; Steinwedel, "Invisible Threads of Empire," pp. 43–47; Ivanov, *Ocherki*, pp. 21–24; Ramil' Khairutdinov, "Tatarskaia feodal'naia znat' i rossiiskoe dvorianstvo: Problemy integratsii na rubezhe XVIII–XIX vv.," in Stefan Diuduan'on [Stéphane Dudoignon], Damir Iskhakov, and Rafik Mukhametshin, eds., *Islam v tatarskom mire: Istoriia i sovremennost'* (Kazan, 1997), pp. 83–101.

[80] Most of the region's non-Russians were transferred from status as tribute payers (*iasachnye liudi*) to state peasants as part of Peter the Great's tax and administrative reforms. See E. V. Anisimov, *Podatnaia reforma Petra I: Vvedenie podushnoi podati v Rossii, 1719–1728 gg.* (Leningrad, 1982), esp. pp. 179–89.

[81] A portion of those enjoying Bashkir and Teptiar social status were not Bashkir ethnically but rather Tatar, Mishar, and even Udmurt and Mari. See Steinwedel, "Invisible Threads of Empire," pp. 76–83; D. M. Iskhakov, "Teptiari: Opyt etnostatisticheskogo izucheniia," *Sovetskaia etnografiia* 4 (1979): 29–42; and M. I. Rodnov, "Chislennost' tiurkskogo krest'ianstva

further from the state's center were more likely to enjoy privileges and autonomy, and this is of course precisely where non-Russians were more likely to be located.[82]

As regards administrative institutions, too, the Volga-Kama region was only barely distinguishable from purely Russian provinces. The Prikaz (ministry) of the Kazan Court, considered by one historian to have been a kind of "colonial office" for the region, ceased functioning around 1720.[83] Nor did Catherine II's provincial reform of 1775 impose any unique institutions on the Volga. On the contrary, in the case of Bashkiria, this reform actually integrated this territory more thoroughly into Russia by extending to it the same system of territorial demarcation employed in the central provinces.[84] On the whole, Catherine's reform appears to have been quite indifferent to ethnic and even confessional distinctions, so that provincial borders cut directly across areas of compact non-Russian settlement.[85] And if the presence of a governor-general signified that a territory was a colonial borderland (at least after a reform in 1837), then the absence of such a post in the Volga-Kama region, with the exception of Orenburg province, reveals that the state no longer viewed most of the region in these terms.[86]

To be sure, because Orthodoxy was the state's "supreme and predominant" religion, discrimination against non-Russian peoples could occur along confessional lines. The Orthodox church retained a monopoly on the right to proselytize, and the toleration of non-Orthodox faiths was always limited. Yet even here the picture is complex. If Peter I decimated the region's native elites in the early eighteenth century, then in 1784 Catherine II offered former native princes the opportunity to regain noble status, and a small Tatar nobility thus reappeared toward the end of the eighteenth century,

---

Ufimskoi gubernii v nachale XX v.," *Etnograficheskoe obozrenie* 6 (1996): 121–31. *Lashmany*, who were Mordvins, Chuvash, and above all Tatars, were created as a social group in 1718 by Peter I for the purposes of supplying timber for ship construction.

[82] Kappeler likewise stresses that Russians were not privileged in the empire, adding that they were also less developed than at least some of the empire's other ethnic groups in economic, sociopolitical, and educational terms. Kappeler suggests that this circumstance was one of the reasons why the empire's diversity remained so persistent (*Russland als Vielvölkerreich*, pp. 136–37). On the privileges of non-Russians relative to Russians, see also Boris Mironov, *Sotsial'naia istoriia Rossii (XVIII–nachalo XX v.)* (St. Petersburg, 1999), 1:31–34.

[83] Michael Rywkin, "The Prikaz of the Kazan Court: First Russian Colonial Office," *Canadian Slavonic Papers* 18 (1976): 293–300.

[84] Steinwedel, "Invisible Threads of Empire," pp. 40–43.

[85] On these reforms, which seem to have been motivated above all by the interests of the ruling noble class, see Isabel de Madariaga, *Russia in the Age of Catherine the Great* (New Haven, 1981), pp. 277–91; and John P. LeDonne, *Ruling Russia: Politics and Administration in the Age of Absolutism, 1762–1796* (Princeton, 1984).

[86] On the reform, see Daniel T. Orlovsky, *The Limits of Reform: The Ministry of Internal Affairs in Imperial Russia, 1802–1881* (Cambridge, Mass., 1981), pp. 30–32; and Erik Amburger, *Geschichte der Behördenorganisation Russlands von Peter dem Grossen bis 1917* (Leiden, 1966), 374–75. At least until 1879, when governor-generalships began to appear

above all in Orenburg (later Ufa) province.[87] It is true that the state was slow to grant the privileges enjoyed by the Orthodox clergy to Muslim clerics, who were never recognized as a distinct social estate. Still, in 1850 the State Council exempted from conscription and corporal punishment mullahs and imams at least as long as they performed their clerical duties.[88] Finally, if the state limited the construction of mosques by stipulating a minimum of two hundred male tax-paying souls for every such house of worship, it also took measures to prevent the proliferation of "excess" Orthodox parishes to guarantee a basic level of economic support for the clergy.[89] In short, many of the measures applied to non-Christians appear somewhat less discriminatory when viewed in a comparative and historical context.

Although an ideology of civilizing mission akin to those in western Europe did appear in Russia by the mid-nineteenth century, the Volga-Kama region was not its principal referent. Catherine II could write to Voltaire with delight about being in "Asia" when she visited Kazan in 1767.[90] But on the whole the Volga-Kama region generated far less romantic fascination with the exotic or sense of imperial mission than has been documented for the Amur region, the Caucasus, Central Asia, or even Siberia.[91] Conquered long before, largely integrated in administrative and socio-legal terms, and having a substantial Russian population, the Volga-Kama region by the nineteenth century simply could not be construed as alien to the same extent as the empire's outlying regions.

Here, indeed, is the source of difficulty in identifying the place of the Volga-Kama region in the larger Russian empire. On one hand, the non-Russians there were simply several of the many peoples who by the early nineteenth century had been incorporated into a state that was construed explicitly as an empire, and whose leaders therefore accepted the fact of ethnic and confessional diversity as a source of their legitimation.[92] On the other

---

within Russia as a way of combating the revolutionary movement, all such posts were indeed on the empire's periphery (with the exception of the two capitals).

[87] Steinwedel, "Invisible Threads of Empire," pp. 43–47; and Khairutdinov, "Tatarskaia feodal′naia znat′," 87–90.

[88] Robert Crews sees this act as the result of a petition campaign by Muslim clerics in 1841 for the legal recognition of corporate privileges, while Steinwedel stresses the initiative of Minister of State Domains P. D. Kiselev. See Crews, "Allies in God's Command," pp. 131–53; and Steinwedel, "Invisible Threads of Empire," pp. 61–63, 73–76.

[89] *PSZ* I, vol. 14, no. 10597 (1756); Freeze, *Parish Clergy*, pp. 91–97; idem, *The Russian Levites: Parish Clergy in the Eighteenth Century* (Cambridge, Mass., 1977), pp. 107–20.

[90] "What difference in climate, in people, in customs, and even in ideas themselves! Here I am in Asia; I wanted to see it with my own eyes." Cited in Kappeler, *Rußlands erste Nationalitäten*, pp. 358–59.

[91] See Galya Diment and Yuri Slezkine, eds., *Between Heaven and Hell: The Myth of Siberia in Russian Culture* (New York, 1993); Susan Layton, *Russian Literature and Empire: Conquest of the Caucasus from Pushkin to Tolstoi* (Cambridge, 1994); Adeeb Khalid, *The Politics of Muslim Cultural Reform: Jadidism in Central Asia* (Berkeley, 1998); and Mark Bassin, *Imperial Visions: Nationalist Imagination and Geographical Expansion in the Russian Far East* (Cambridge, 1999).

[92] On the issue of empire as legitimation, see Wortman, *Scenarios of Power*, 1:6, 135–39.

hand, the Volga-Kama peoples were not simply imperial subjects like those in more distant regions. They were among the first to have been incorporated into Muscovy, and they inhabited a region that was no longer a borderland in the strict sense of the term. On the contrary, this region was immediately adjacent to the core of the old Muscovite state, which *had*—in contrast to the larger empire—been consolidated on the basis of Orthodoxy and a protonational Russian identity. Moreover, East Slavs had historically assimilated several Finnic peoples,[93] and the situation among Mordvins by the early nineteenth century seemed to suggest that such assimilation would continue among the next tier of non-Russian peoples. In other words, the Volga-Kama region was situated precisely at the place where the core lands of Muscovy shaded into the more distant and alien lands of the imperial periphery. Because there was no distinct boundary between the two, it was not clear whether the logic of the former or the latter would prevail. Particularly in the years of Catherine and her immediate successors, the situation seemed to favor the latter.[94] But by the second quarter of the nineteenth century, that situation was beginning to change.

Such, then, was the situation in the Volga-Kama region when Nicholas I became Emperor in 1825. The majority of animists to the west of the Kama had been baptized, if only superficially, while significant communities of animists continued to exist in the east, especially in the northwestern districts of Orenburg province. The numbers of baptized Tatars were considerably lower, and these communities stood in close proximity to the many Muslims in the region. The state made no effort to recognize or create a pagan "clergy," presumably because there were relatively few remaining animists, and it was assumed that sooner or later these would convert to Orthodoxy. Muslims, in contrast, appeared unlikely to convert anytime soon, and a sense of pragmatism induced the state to establish the Spiritual Assembly and gradually to acknowledge and create a Muslim clergy similar, if still legally inferior, to its Orthodox counterpart. With the exception of Bashkirs and Teptiars and a few other comparatively small and locally specific status groups, such as *lashmany*, the non-Russian inhabitants of the region had been integrated into Russia's general system of social classification, and they

---

[93] For example, the Meria, Muroma, Vod', and Chud', as well as many Veps and Izhora, were assimilated in the medieval and early modern period.

[94] The problem of ascertaining where empire "begins" geographically was not restricted to Russia. Recent scholarship on European colonialism has revealed that distinctions between metropole and colony were far more problematic than they might appear on the surface. In Britain, moreover, there was the problem of "internal colonialism," and in France official attitudes toward regional rural populations have been characterized as "imperial." On these issues, see Ann Laura Stoler and Frederick Cooper, eds., *Tensions of Empire: Colonial Cultures in a Bourgeois World* (Berkeley, 1997); Michael Hechter, *Internal Colonialism: The Celtic Fringe in British National Development, 1536–1966* (London, 1975); and Eugen Weber, *Peasants into Frenchmen: The Modernization of Rural France, 1870–1914* (Stanford, 1976).

were subject to the same secular laws and bureaucratic instances as their Russian counterparts. In the region as a whole, Russians constituted a majority of the population, even if non-Russians continued to predominate in certain specific districts or locales. But if the distinction between Russians and non-Russians no longer took legal or political forms, profound cultural and religious differences remained.

2　*Orthodoxy Challenged*

Nicholas became Emperor shortly after the closing of the Dual Ministry and the reinstatement of Orthodoxy as the indisputably predominant faith of the empire. The atmosphere created in the last years of Alexander's life set the agenda for the early years of Nicholas's reign, at least with regard to religious policy. The new Emperor continued to raise the status of Orthodoxy while subordinating the church more thoroughly to the secular state. Nicholas's government simultaneously extended the institutionalization of non-Orthodox faiths, although the status of such faiths was decidedly subordinate to that of Orthodoxy.[1] Because the elite rebellion known as the Decembrist revolt occurred within the first days of his reign, Nicholas regarded manifestations of dissent with particular apprehension.

It was precisely in the first few years of Nicholas's reign, however, that the position of Orthodoxy was dramatically challenged by two remarkable occurrences: first, an attempt by several thousand baptized Tatars in Kazan and Simbirsk provinces to gain permission for their reversion to Islam; and second, a large unauthorized gathering of baptized and unbaptized Maris in Viatka province for the performance of an animist prayer. In each case novokreshchenye had reason to hope that they might receive permission to practice their native religions openly. While their aspirations were clearly at odds with church and civil law, fissures in imperial policy and practice offered a basis for contesting the state's intransigence using deferential forms of protest. Although local authorities sought to project a certain vision with which they expected non-Russians to comply, they were not able to prevent non-Russians from appropriating elements of that vision to construct an

---

[1] After the Polish insurrection of 1830–31, the Department of Religious Affairs of Foreign Faiths (DDDII) was transferred from the Ministry of Education to the Ministry of Internal Affairs.

alternative in line with their own desires. Even so, both state and church were able, eventually, to make clear that the official Orthodox status of novokreshchenye was not negotiable, and the Maris and Tatars in question were compelled to accept this status and to redirect confessional politics in the region, at least for the time being, into different arenas.

Sources of Apostasy

In the absence of formal institutions of representation in Russia, petitioning had long played a significant role in Russian political life.[2] Though petitions cannot be construed as a legal "right" of tsarist subjects, they did provide an important channel for upward communication of interests and offered at least the possibility of redress. In broad terms, petitioning can be considered one form of what Michael Adas calls "avoidance protest," whereby dissatisfied groups "seek to attenuate their hardships and express their discontent" in ways that "minimize challenges to or clashes with those whom they view as their oppressors."[3]

It was by filing petitions that novokreshchenye Tatars initiated the encounters we consider here. By the spring and summer of 1827 several thousand Tatars from different districts west of the Volga had filed twenty-one petitions to the Emperor, in which they requested permission to practice Islam openly.[4] Nicholas quickly ordered that an experienced clergyman be sent to the petitioners, along with copies of the New Testament in Tatar. What followed was a drawn-out contest in which missionaries slowly encouraged and coerced the petitioners into abandoning their requests. Gradually whittling away at the number of resisters, by mid-1830 religious authorities were able to report that "almost all the baptized Tatars of the named districts who have deviated into Mohammedanism, having recognized their delusion, have converted once again to the Orthodox Greco-Russian Church and fulfill its sacraments."[5]

The aspirations of baptized Tatars for recognition as Muslims must be understood in terms of the awkward religious space they occupied in their

---

[2] In 1810 Alexander I established a special Commission of Petitions, which adjudicated complaints, while regulations on petitioning were codified in a single statute in 1835. See *PSZ* I, vol. 26, no. 19856 (1801); ibid., vol. 31, no. 24064 (1810), §§ 80, 88–117; *PSZ* II, vol. 10, no. 7771 (1835); and *SZ* (1832), vol. 1: *Uchrezhdeniia*, §§ 96–117.

[3] Michael Adas, "From Avoidance to Confrontation: Peasant Protest in Precolonial and Colonial Southeast Asia," *Comparative Studies in Society and History* 33 (1981): 217.

[4] The Synod later reported that in 1826–27 there were 3,274 petitioners in 97 different villages in Buinsk district (Simbirsk province) and Tetiushi, Tsivil'sk, Sviiazhsk, and Cheboksary districts (Kazan province). At this time (prior to 1832), all of Simbirsk province came under the religious jurisdiction of Kazan diocese.

[5] RGIA, f. 797, op. 3, d. 12644, l. 1200b. Seven Tatars continued to resist, and several of them were transferred to Orthodox monasteries to receive admonition. At least one was finally exiled to Siberia (RGIA, f. 796, op. 108, d. 595, ll. 49–51). Fairly lengthy narratives of this episode, along with considerable citation from primary sources, are in E. A. Malov, *Pravoslav-*

villages. On one hand, Muslims exerted considerable pressure on no-vokreshchenye to retain ties to Islam. An investigation in Nizhnii Novgorod province undertaken in response to an earlier instance of apostasy in 1802 revealed that "Tatar mullahs, who come to them [novokreshchenye] more than three times a day, encourage them to reject the Christian faith and tell them, 'even if you outwardly maintain the Christian faith, in your heart keep the Mohammedan faith.'" These mullahs and other Muslims also reproached them for having abandoned their "natural" (*prirodnaia*) faith, referred to them as "dogs," and became "angry at them if they [saw] Holy icons in their homes."[6] On the other hand, Christianity remained largely inaccessible to novokreshchenye. Because the church service was performed in Slavonic, it had virtually no meaning for baptized Tatars, as one group explained: "When we go to church, we are only bored, seeing the Russian Christians praying in their own way with zeal and knowing how to pray, and we perceive ourselves as knowing and understanding nothing." Converts also remained poorly integrated into the Christian community, marrying only among themselves and never Russians. As novokreshchenye themselves declared, "we have left Mohammedanism, but do not adhere to Christianity."[7]

But what circumstances impelled novokreshchenye to begin filing petitions at this particular moment? Part of the answer has to do with the broader political culture of the empire. Throughout the nineteenth century, baptized Tatars' petitions usually coincided with imperial coronations (1802, 1826–27, 1856, 1882–83, and 1896), which were usually accompanied by manifestations of tsarist grace toward the empire's subjects. In short, baptized Tatars understood that this was the best time to petition. But the petitions of 1826–27 were also rooted in more local circumstances. In 1807 a Tatar woman had protested her inclusion in the latest revision (census) as a Christian. Acknowledging that a mistake had been made, the Senate issued an order that made it sound as if a *baptized person* had been permitted to return to Islam—an impression deepened by the continued reference to the woman as "baptized" by judicial authorities in Simbirsk province. An investigation into the matter concluded that with its careless wording, the Simbirsk criminal court "gave the unenlightened Tatars a basis for a false

---

naia protivomusul´manskaia missiia v Kazanskom krae v sviazi s istoriei musul´manstva v pervoi polovine XIX veka (Kazan, 1868); and A. Mozharovskii, *Izlozhenie khoda missionerskogo dela po prosveshcheniiu kazanskikh inorodtsev s 1552 po 1867 goda* (Moscow, 1880), pp. 115–50; and V. Zeletnitskii, "Ocherki missionerskoi deiatel´nosti nekotorykh kazanskikh arkhipastyrei," *Pravoslavnyi blagovestnik* 1 (1901): 8–18, 5 (1901): 196–201, 6 (1901): 253–63, 7 (1901): 301–7.

[6] N. I. Il´minskii, ed., *Opyty perelozheniia khristianskikh verouchitel´nykh knig na tatarskii i drugie inorodcheskie iazyki v nachale tekushchego stoletiia* (Kazan, 1885), pp. 23–24. (This work is essentially the publication of RGIA, f. 796, op. 84, d. 4.) In several cited passages in this chapter, I have added quotation marks within citations to clarify when the cited text was actually providing direct speech.

[7] Ibid., p. 25.

opinion and desire to change religion, which is contrary to law."[8] This otherwise innocuous chancellery blunder was invested with greater subversive potential when a local secretary leaked copies of the correspondence to local novokreshchenye. Once the rumors spread that returning to Islam was as easy as filing a petition, the secretary found himself writing petitions and presumably receiving compensation for his services.[9]

Apart from this case, forty-four male souls from villages in Chistopol district (Kazan province) filed a petition in November 1826 to the Kazan Provincial Board, in which they claimed that they, too, had been falsely entered into the seventh revision with "Russian names" (i.e., as Christians) and that now their fellow villagers would not allow them to practice Islam properly. Because the Ecclesiastical Consistory was unable to produce any documentation proving the petitioners' Christian status (a fire in 1815 had destroyed most of the Consistory's files), the Provincial Board upheld their claim and ordered the clergy not to interfere with their practice of Islam.[10]

Thus in two separate cases Tatars were able to gain (re)recognition as Muslims by arguing that they had mistakenly been registered as Christians. It should be emphasized that in these cases petitioners claimed that a *mistake* had been made, that they had never been baptized and were thus *wrongfully* considered Christian. Where proof of baptism was lacking—and fire and negligence had in some cases left a very poor documentary record— there was indeed a remote chance that the bureaucracy might recognize a request. When petitioners *acknowledged* that they had been baptized, and therefore based their requests on their desire to confess Islam or their inability to understand the Orthodox service, they received no satisfaction. In short, the state privileged legal ascription of religious status over subjective articulations of belief.

If a local secretary was originally responsible for "leaking" the misworded bureaucratic correspondence, then it was two baptized Tatars—Larion and Vasilii Ivanov—who spread the word into the countryside. Visiting various villages and encouraging novokreshchenye to contribute funds for a petition, the Ivanovs procured a copy of the correspondence noted above and showed it to fellow novokreshchenye as proof that their petitions had been

---

[8] RGIA, f. 796, op. 109, d. 1189, l. 2.

[9] Ibid., ll. 1–2; RGIA, f. 796, op. 125, d. 1518, ll. 81–82; Malov, *Pravoslavnaia protivomusul'manskaia missiia*, pp. 134–38; and Mozharovskii, *Izlozhenie*, p. 124. Though the secretary was recognized as being guilty of having given out copies of the correspondence and of having written the petitions, the Senate recognized that he had done so because of the mistake of the Simbirsk judicial authorities and thus found him innocent of having willfully spread false rumors. But since he had aided the baptized Tatars in their "dreams about the faith," he was strictly forbidden from writing any more petitions and papers aside from his own personal business. (RGIA, f. 796, op. 109, d. 1189, ll. 3–4.) Not long after these events, in 1835, a law was instituted to punish those who, "for personal profit," incited others to file petitions. See *PSZ* II, vol. 10, no. 8170 (1835).

[10] Mozharovskii, *Izlozhenie*, pp. 127–29.

successful.[11] By visiting a large number of villages and producing official-looking documentation, the Ivanovs were able to invest the rumors they spread with considerable plausibility, thereby making it extremely difficult for clergy and officials to disprove them subsequently. Thus there was ample foundation for novokreshchenye, eager to terminate their estrangement from the Islamic community, to believe that a return to Islam was now possible.

In their petitions, novokreshchenye made a number of different arguments to justify their request. Some declared that their ancestors had been force-fully baptized and that they themselves had been raised as Muslims. Others reported that the circumstances behind their baptism were unclear or they had heard that their fathers converted in order to escape recruitment. A few denied that they were baptized and argued that they had come to be regarded as such either by mistake or through the deliberate machinations of the local clergy.[12] In all cases, petitioners explained that they did not at all understand Christianity, while they practiced Islam and had been married in accordance with its sacraments.

The petitioners also attempted to align their aspirations with the will of the Sovereign, stressing that their desire to practice Islam in no way compromised their loyalty to the Tsar. One petition declared directly that "faith, whichever it might be, does not change our subjecthood" (*poddanstvo*). An envoy for one group of petitioners declared, "The Mohammedan law requires [us] to fulfill unfailingly all obligations, and my clients must and should serve Your Imperial Majesty the All-Russian Autocrat to the final drop of blood." Another group of petitioners highlighted their "devotion to our All-merciful Sovereigns," while others appealed to "the loving father of true subjects."[13] Thus novokreshchenye offered an explicitly dynastic image of subjecthood, one that defined their belonging to the Russian empire not in terms of the faith they confessed but in terms of their devotion to the Sovereign.

Petitioners also claimed that they were willing to abide by the Tsar's decision on their petitions and that they would not contradict the Sovereign's will if their request were rejected. But they also refused to desist until the Sovereign had made that will indisputably clear.[14] The contest, then, revolved around the nature of the Tsar's decision—and indeed whether he had actually made one. While missionaries informed the petitioners that their requests had been rejected, baptized-Tatar envoys in St. Petersburg continued

---

[11] Ibid., pp. 122–26.

[12] RGIA, f. 797, op. 3, d. 12644, ll. 50–51; and RGIA, f. 797, op. 3, d. 12643, l. 2.

[13] RGIA, f. 797, op. 3, d. 12630, l. 4; RGIA, f. 797, op. 3, d. 12644, ll. 20b.–30b.; and RGIA, f. 796, op. 108, d. 595, ll. 90b.–10, 1300b. Similar petitions are located throughout the files listed here. The "envoy" (*poverennyi*) referred to above was a member of a community authorized to petition on its behalf.

[14] RGIA, f. 796, op. 108, d. 595, ll. 1150b., 1240b.

to assure them that the decision was still pending. Many petitioners, when presented with their rejected petitions, did agree to abandon their "pernicious enterprise," but those who held out longer invoked the belief that they would eventually be vindicated by the Tsar's decision.

The Limits of Admonition

The church's first concern was to ascertain that the petitioners were indeed baptized, whatever they themselves claimed. This proved more difficult than one might imagine, however, since religious records turned out to be chaotic and incomplete, both in Kazan and at the parish level. Clergy in one village lacked documentation and could report that "they have only heard, in part based on the accounts of elderly novokreshchenye parishioners, that they were baptized not long before 1750." Another parish reported that it had no documentation, but that "it is generally heard that they accepted baptism in order to avoid public punishment."[15] One claimant stated that he had been raised by baptized relatives when his own parents died and had actually never been baptized.[16] Thus petitioners provided only vague explanations for how they had come to be baptized, if they admitted that they were baptized at all.

Despite these difficulties, Archbishop Iona (Pavlinskii) of Kazan marshaled several circumstances that he believed proved the petitioners' Christian status: priests visited the petitioners in their villages, gave their infants names, and recorded them in parish registries, while nearby Muslim Tatars "consider them to be in Christian law and therefore do not permit them into the mosque." The petitioners were also listed in the parish registers, as well as in the seventh revision "with Russian names." Finally, the petitioners were married to baptized Tatar women (although in some cases they denied either the Christian status of their wives or the fact of the marriage itself).[17] In short, regardless of the petitioners' own claims about their religious practice and disposition, there was enough evidence to classify them as Christians. Sensing the general mood of the baptized-Tatar population, Iona added in another report that the petitioners must be left in Christianity "in order not to give others a reason for deviation as well."[18]

---

[15] Ibid., ll. 49–51. The law provided that lesser crimes might be forgiven through baptism, and sentences could be lightened in the case of more serious ones. RGIA, f. 1405, op. 63, d. 4952, ll. 1–20b.

[16] RGIA, f. 796, op. 108, d. 594, ll. 3–18. Despite these circumstances, Archbishop Iona concluded that such stories were "nothing other than their general desire to become Muslims," and that the petitioners were lying (l. 6).

[17] RGIA, f. 797, op. 3, d. 12644, ll. 35–370b.

[18] RGIA, f. 796, op. 108, d. 595, l. 530b.

Three archpriests were dispatched to the affected villages "to restrain [novokreshchenye] in the Christian faith and to explain to them the vanity of Mohammedan false teaching": Ioann Svetovidov to Tetiushi and Sviiazhsk districts, Andrian Gal'binskii to Tsivil'sk district, and Andrei Milonov to Buinsk, Simbirsk, and Stavropol districts.[19] Each accompanied by a civil official, these three figures made several trips to the affected villages in 1827–29 to admonish baptized Tatars and to evaluate the competence and performance of local clergy. The missionaries were eventually able to reach almost all baptized Tatar settlements in the districts along the right bank of the Volga (Sviiazhsk, Tetiushi, Tsivil'sk, Buinsk, and Simbirsk).

Immediately, the language problem arose, since "in Kazan diocese there is almost no one from among the church servitors who knows the Tatar language well."[20] The Kazan Ecclesiastical Consistory thus chose as missionaries persons who did not know Tatar but who, "based on good morality and knowledge of the dogmas of the Christian faith," could nonetheless admonish the affected Tatars by relying on translators and Tatars' own knowledge of Russian.[21] Despite Archbishop Iona's questionable claim that "all Tatars, and especially novokreshchenye, know Russian," the activities of the missionaries were limited by the language barrier to a significant degree.[22]

In accounting for novokreshchenye's weak attachment to Christianity, the missionaries identified two major problems. First, novokreshchenye usually lived as small minorities in villages with Muslims, "before whom the baptized are even ashamed of their Christian faith."[23] Local clergy related that Muslims "not only persecute and frighten the baptized in all kinds of ways for their fulfillment of Christian obligations" but also "scornfully jeer at the priests." They added that baptized Tatars even requested them to perform all rites as secretly as possible, "so that none of the unbaptized will see this."[24] The second problem involved the parish clergy itself, whom baptized Tatars in several cases accused of making excessive demands in return for the performance of rites. The visiting archpriest began an investigation into one priest, who allegedly took forty rubles (an enormous sum) for performing marriages, and the Consistory discovered from its own records that this same priest had earlier been disciplined for bad behavior. Local Chuvash parishioners were asked to confirm the accusations, and several of them testified that the priest had taken between ten and forty-five rubles for the per-

---

[19] Cited in Mozharovskii, *Izlozhenie*, p. 120.

[20] RGIA f. 796, op. 108, d. 595, l. 66ob. This was based on an 1824 diocesan survey. Tatar had begun to be taught in the religious educational institutions of Kazan diocese in 1800, but this teaching gained firm financial foundations only in 1820 (RGIA, f. 802, op. 1, d. 2749). See also I. Pokrovskii, "K stoletiiu kafedry tatarskogo iazyka v dukhovno-uchebnykh zavedeniiakh g. Kazani (1800–1900)," *Pravoslavnyi sobesednik* 2 (1900): 576–609.

[21] RGIA, f. 796, op. 108, d. 595, ll. 66ob.–67.

[22] Mozharovskii, *Izlozhenie*, p. 137.

[23] RGIA, f. 796, op. 108, d. 595, l. 329ob.

[24] Ibid., l. 52.

formance of various rites.[25] Investigations revealed similar problems with other priests, who were poorly educated and had previously been disciplined for failure to fulfill their duties and for drunkenness. Several officials even concluded that the poor behavior of the local clergy was the principal reason for the petitions.

The authorities took these accusations seriously. The Emperor himself wrote, "The actions of the priests, who through their rites have caused the apostasy from the church, in my eyes, are so important that they demand the sternest investigation."[26] After subsequent inquiries, five priests were removed from their parishes "for bad conduct with baptized Tatar parishioners" and had their clerical certificates revoked.[27] Other priests were left under suspicion, in part because the evidence against them was inconclusive, and in part, it would seem, because there was no one qualified to replace them.[28] In several cases, priests died before authorities were able to initiate proceedings against them, which conveniently eliminated the need for further investigation. All remaining priests were required to sign statements promising to satisfy themselves with only those payments that Tatar parishioners offered voluntarily.[29] The church thus made a genuine effort to identify and transfer the bad apples among the rural clergy and to regularize the dealings of those who remained with their parishioners.

The success of the archpriests varied greatly from locale to locale. Svetovidov and Gal'binskii in Kazan province met with comparatively little resistance in the fall of 1827. As Svetovidov explained, he admonished parishioners to return to the "womb of Christ's church," and novokreshchenye "all expressed the desire to remain steadfastly in the Christian law, announcing that their attempt to tear themselves away from Christ's church occurred exclusively because of unfounded rumors and the instigation of a small number of their fellows, who are more attached to Mohammedanism than the rest." Simultaneously, Gal'binskii reported that the baptized Tatars he visited agreed "to confess the Orthodox Christian faith as before." They explained "with open hearts" that "they were drawn into these mistakes exclusively because they live in the same villages as Mohammedans, but henceforward they promised not to pay attention to all the seductive encouragements of the Mohammedans living with them."[30] In short, large numbers of baptized Tatars saw that there was little hope of receiving satisfaction of their petitions and ascribed their temporary "delusion" to factors largely beyond their control.

---

[25] Ibid., ll. 145–51.

[26] RGIA, f. 797, op. 3, d. 12644, l. 66.

[27] RGIA, f. 796, op. 108, d. 595, l. 113. Yet one of the more remarkable aspects of the removal of such priests was that many of them were simply transferred to Russian parishes!

[28] RGIA, f. 797, op. 3, d. 12644, l. 590b.

[29] RGIA, f. 796, op. 108, d. 595, l. 59.

[30] Cited in Mozharovskii, *Izlozhenie*, p. 131.

Both Svetovidov and Gal'binskii did encounter resistance, however. In particular, Vasilii Ivanov (whom we met above as one of the instigators of the petition campaign) continued to encourage others to seek return to Islam by referring to an envoy in St. Petersburg who was petitioning the Emperor on their behalf. Others refused to acknowledge that their petitions had actually been rejected, arguing that the rejections "came from the higher Kazan authorities, and not from the Sovereign Emperor himself." But it was Milonov who ran into the greatest difficulties in Simbirsk province, where baptized Tatars showed hardly any signs of Christian inclinations:

> The holy icons have been taken out of their houses, they themselves were without crosses and belts, [they had] skull caps on their heads, as with unbaptized Tatars, their fellow residents; they considered it a kind of profanity to make the sign of the cross in the Christian way and to read Christian prayers, and thus did not want to do this; they have ceased baptizing their children, they have begun to live with their fiancées out of wedlock; in a word, in them there were no traces of Christianity.

Yet remarkably, more than six hundred of these parishioners, "with the help of God," agreed to return to Christianity and ascribed their aspirations for Islam to the extortion of local clergy.[31] Thus by 1828 only a few villages continued to resist, arguing above all that the rejection of their petitions was not genuine.

The Kazan governor therefore ordered that Tatars be shown the original petitions in order to eliminate their "ignorant prejudice" and "to protect [others] from similar mistakes." This strategy met with success in some cases, especially when the Ivanovs, who had since been apprehended and were now under prosecution, were brought back to vouch that the rejected petition presented by the authorities was indeed the original.[32] In other cases, it was the missionary's persistence that paid off. In the village of Ul'iankovo (Sviiazhsk district), Svetovidov reported the following, after villagers had refused to accept the rejection of their petition:

> Seeing their stubbornness and bitterness, we continued admonishing them well into the night, read to them from a catechism an explanation of the dogmas, sacraments, and commandments of the Lord, and moreover asked a mullah who happened to be there to read a few chapters from the New Testament in the Tatar language [!]. Then the baptized, seeing on one hand the example of gentleness and mercy accorded to their fellows who did not remain stubborn during their edification in the Christian religion and, on the other, feeling the ruinous consequences of insubordination to the holy church and the will of the higher government, and having heeded [our] persuasion

---

[31] Cited ibid., pp. 131–33.

[32] Cited ibid., pp. 136, 138. The Ivanovs, faced with severe punishment for their activities, evidently decided to minimize the fallout by cooperating with the authorities. Eventually, however, they were given thirty lashes and were subsequently subjected to strict supervision.

and admonitions, finally repented of their bitterness, readily declared their desire to remain in the wombs of the Christian faith and henceforward not to make any kind of attempt to tear themselves away from it.

For good measure, novokreshchenye added a complaint about the excessive solicitations of their clergy, which "in large part enticed them to agree to the invitation of the envoys to file a petition about conversion to Mohammedanism."[33] Probably Svetovidov's description was not far off the mark. By this time the authorities had made it clear that the petitioners would not be left alone until they acquiesced. It is also true that none of those baptized Tatars who agreed to abandon their petitions suffered any kind of punishment. In the end, for many of these baptized Tatars it was easier simply to tell the missionary what he wanted to hear so that he would go away. But Svetovidov himself recognized the disingenuousness of this repentance, noting that while baptized Tatars would now begin to fulfill the rites of the Christian faith, *"in their heart and soul they will be Muslims."*[34] Missionaries had thus done little to change the religious convictions of the baptized Tatars and had only been able to convince them of the futility of seeking a change in formal religious status.

But at least one group of baptized Tatars, even after acknowledging "that they believe the ukaz [rejection] of the Sovereign Emperor," made a more heartfelt plea to be allowed to remain in Islam. They related that their interactions were almost exclusively with Muslims, and thus they had no way of knowing Russian.[35] They had only occasional contact with their parish priest, and work made it "impossible" for them to attend church. Moreover, Christianity "allegedly causes them various illnesses and even death for their children, as well as crop failure and loss of livestock; and thus they do not wish to hear edification [about Christianity], and even if they were to be sent to Siberia, there, too, they do not wish to hear either about the church or about the Christian faith."[36] Thus novokreshchenye clearly associated religious practice with health and agricultural prosperity, in accord with prevailing inner Asian religious conceptions that constituted religious life not so much as the "worship" of some deity than as the preservation of the health and continuity of the family and community.[37] Agricultural difficulties were a clear sign that there was something fundamentally wrong with a family's or a community's religious practice. Already alienated from Christianity by other circumstances, it is not surprising that baptized Tatars should have ascribed their difficulties to that religion.

[33] Cited ibid., p. 137.
[34] Cited ibid., p. 141 (emphasis added).
[35] Svetovidov, however, claimed that the baptized Tatars in the village actually spoke Russian well.
[36] Cited ibid., p. 140.
[37] See Devin DeWeese, *Islamization and Native Religion in the Golden Horde: Baba Tükles and Conversion to Islam in Historical and Epic Tradition* (University Park, Penn., 1994), p. 37.

More important still, the practice of Islam was a matter of social conformity and should be understood in terms of the communal nature of religious life. Baptized Tatars were outsiders within their own villages, and on numerous occasions they underscored that being a Christian was simply too difficult in light of this circumstance. We unfortunately have little information on what the "ridicule and reproaches" of neighboring Muslim Tatars actually consisted of, but it seems reasonably clear that the conflict along this axis was significant. Baptized Tatars would become "true Christians," Svetovidov concluded, "only when their cohabitation with Muslims ceases and when they are settled separately and in small numbers in old-Russian settlements."[38] Subsequently the tenacious villagers "all declared unanimously that they do not wish to have even the very best priests, because living among unbaptized [Tatars], they do not want to abandon Mohammedanism." Not only was Svetovidov unable to convince them to abandon their aspirations, but even baptized Tatars who had not originally been listed on the petition asked that they be included among those "wishing to deviate into Mohammedanism."[39]

While the authorities were willing to take seriously the various factors preventing Christianization—especially the alleged excesses of the local clergy—the petitioners gradually lost the sympathy of the religious authorities, who became more and more convinced that they were disingenuous and that instigation by a small number of envoys, who had traveled to St. Petersburg and were now encouraging their fellows from there to stand firm, was the ultimate source of the trouble. Changes in administrative personnel were also decisive. The replacement of Iona as archbishop of Kazan by Filaret (Amfiteatrov) in 1828 was accompanied by a hardening toward the petitioners, as was the replacement of Archpriest Milonov by Vasilii Utekhin as missionary after the former's death in 1830. Utekhin reported that the "strong influence" of Tatar envoys was rendering all his efforts "futile," and that baptized Tatars had become considerably more "embittered." The main reason for continuing "stubbornness" among many of the petitioners, he argued, was the slow prosecution of the principal envoy, Semen Egorov (in Tatar, Abdezekov), who even from prison continued to assure his comrades "that their affair is going in accordance with their wishes and that sooner or later it will be decided in their favor." Utekhin faulted the "lenient measures of admonition" that until then had given baptized Tatars "the false impression that there are no other laws and other means, beside the desire [of the authorities], to force them to accept the Christian law that they have renounced." To counter the notion that the government would leave them alone if they resisted long enough, Utekhin urged the use of resettlement

---

[38] Cited in Mozharovskii, *Izlozhenie*, pp. 143–44. Resettlement indeed became one way that Russian authorities attempted to counteract apostasy by the late 1830s and 1840s (see chapter 6).

[39] Cited ibid., pp. 140–41.

"which will serve as a most felt punishment for the desecration of the Christian faith" and would reconcile the others to the "offended religion."[40] By 1834 Filaret, in the process of establishing a policy of resettlement, reported that "the deviation of novokreshchenye into Mohammedanism occurs not due to some kind of corruption by the [Orthodox] clergy but due to the encouragements of the unbaptized."[41] In short, religious authorities had now begun to take a harder line on "deviates," construing their apostasy as an affront to Orthodox sensibilities.

Discernible in the account presented here are various strategic layers of baptized-Tatar resistance. The first line of defense was to cling to the idea that the Emperor had not really rejected their petition. As this notion became less tenable, and especially as the church's determination to secure renunciation of their petitions became evident, baptized Tatars referred to corrupt clergy, their poor knowledge of Russian, and the instigation of others who encouraged them to join the enterprise. For those who continued to resist, their accounts turned to the difficulties of practicing Christianity while living among Muslims and the threats that Christianity posed for their economic well-being. But even the vast majority of these holdouts finally gave in, as Svetovidov reported after his trip to the same parishes in the fall of 1828. Only in Tetiushi district did it take any more work to get the last baptized Tatars to resign: "Although they at first remained somewhat stubborn, later, with the help of God, during repeated admonitions, having been softened up, they all expressed their agreement to remain in the Christian religion."[42]

As the missionaries themselves recognized, the petitioners' abandonment of their petitions did not actually signal their acceptance of Christianity. At stake first and foremost was the authority of the church and the state and their ability to force baptized Tatars to accept Orthodox religious status, thereby upholding the law. Not open to negotiation, that status constituted a boundary that baptized Tatars contested in 1827 but over which neither state nor church was willing to compromise. Nonetheless, it was clear to both the Emperor and to ecclesiastical authorities that more work was required among this population to ensure that such deviation did not occur in the future. The mission in Kazan diocese was thus a result of this apostasy.

Pagan Dreams and Ritual Prayers

Compared to baptized Tatars, baptized animists less frequently sought official reinstatement of their pagan status. Instead they simply continued to practice animism together with their unbaptized counterparts. Even so, the

[40] RGIA, f. 796, op. 108, d. 595, ll. 329–330ob.
[41] RGIA, f. 797, op. 3, d. 12644, l. 1890b.
[42] Cited in Mozharovskii, *Izlozhenie*, p. 142.

discovery by local authorities of two large animist gatherings in 1827–28 constituted a challenge to established authority and an affront to Orthodoxy no less subversive than the explicit requests of baptized Tatars.

In 1827 about four thousand baptized and unbaptized Maris from Kazan, Viatka, and Kostroma provinces gathered in Tsarevokokshaisk district "to make some kind of offering against the Christian religion," and when the police chief confronted the gathering, Maris "surrounded me and the others who were with me and began to beat [us] brutally."[43] In the ensuing investigation, Maris explained that four years earlier, in response to a period of agricultural crisis, all the residents had promised that when they received a harvest they would "make a prayer to God who lives in the sky in accordance with the ancient ritual of their ancestors." After "many admonitions," the participants "finally acknowledged that they had done such an idolatrous ritual on account of their ignorance, and having learned from the religious superintendent that such an idolatrous prayer is offensive to the Orthodox church, [they] promise to abandon it and to obey the advice of their church pastors."[44] Religious authorities by this time realized that Maris as well as Tatars maintained only tenuous ties to Christianity.

Just few months later, a similar gathering was discovered in neighboring Urzhum district of Viatka province, involving Mari participants from Viatka, Kazan, and Ufa provinces. Together with parish priest Andrei Darovskii and a group of Russian peasants, the police chief set out for the gathering and found more than three thousand Maris gathered in about one hundred small groups around fires and pots, with livestock and fowl for sacrifice "in a frightful quantity." Having identified most participants as baptized Maris, the police chief and priest attempted to break up the gathering, but neither their admonitions nor threats of legal retribution could persuade the Maris to abandon their enterprise. The gatherers claimed to be praying to God "for the health of the Sovereign, for the military, so that God would bring an end to the war [with the Ottoman Empire]; they request to be spared from recruitment, and finally they pray for the preservation of their domestic livestock and fowl, for the harvest and for the well-being of their wives and children." When the ritual ended, the Maris dispersed so quickly that the police chief was able to collect only some of their names.[45]

An investigation begun shortly thereafter traced the gathering to the dreams of three different baptized Maris that were interpreted as a call to public prayer. The dream of one Mari, Ivan Tokmetev, was recorded as follows:

---

[43] GARME, f. 165, op. 1, d. 199; NART, f. 1, op. 1, d. 112, ll. 1–2; and RGIA, f. 797, op. 3, d. 12647, l. 2. This gathering has been analyzed at considerable length in A. G. Ivanov, "Vsemariiskoe iazycheskoe molenie 1827 i deistviia vlastei," *Mariiskii arkheograficheskii vestnik* 8 (1998): 48–74.

[44] RGIA, f. 796, op. 108, d. 1850, l. 470b.

[45] RGIA, f. 797, op. 3, d. 12654, ll. 1–30b.; and GAKO, f. 237, op. 131, d. 1283, ll. 1–30b.

He had a dream that, because of crop failure and loss of livestock, he and a multitude of Cheremis were praying to god before a mountain somewhere, and having performed the prayer he and the people went up on the mountain, where they saw a wonderful light already shining in the ripened grain and beneath the mountain was a meadow in which there was a multitude of livestock.[46]

The dream of another Mari had a similar message: the dreamer "was in the fields with a multitude of Cheremis, where suddenly there appeared a kind of notable person who approached them and advised them to pray to the old god—*tiumen tiumeser iumo* . . . promising them in return an abundance of grain and livestock."[47] Given that 1827–28 had indeed been a season of deep agricultural crisis in the region, word soon spread about the dreams, and Maris from many settlements gathered together in one village, interpreted the dreams as punishment for their failure to perform prayers and sacrifices in accord with the commandments of their parents, and, influenced above all by unbaptized Maris, gave a solemn vow to conduct a prayer and sacrifice by Mari ritual. In addition, convinced by the unbaptized to ensure "that the prayer be populous" (*mnogoliudnoe*), they sent out nine emissaries to inform others in more distant settlements and even neighboring provinces of the proposed gathering. When everyone had arrived they elected elders to conduct the prayer, and the three "dreamers" (*snovidtsy*) oversaw the offering itself.[48] The participants conducted the prayer in the forest, at a place where a new spring had recently appeared, which was itself interpreted as a divine sign.[49] In short, a number of seemingly supernatural occurrences converged to produce and confirm the impression that a collective prayer was necessary.

On the local level, there was some disagreement over what to make of these events. While the local priest Darovskii labeled it "a willful gathering, contrary to civil directives and even more to the rules of the Christian religion," the civil investigator charged with the case emphasized the orderly

---

[46] GAKO, f. 237, op. 131, d. 1283, l. 1150b. A slightly different version of the dream, apparently reported to the civil authorities, is reproduced in A. Andrievskii, "Dela o sovershenii iazycheskikh obriadov i zhertvoprinoshenii kreshchenymi inorodtsami Viatskoi gubernii," in *Stoletie Viatskoi gubernii, 1780–1880: Sbornik materialov k istorii Viatskogo kraia* (Viatka, 1881), 2: 537. Tokmetev was a novokreshchenyi Mari from Kuprian-Sola, whose name "in Russian" was Fedot Alekseev.

[47] GAKO, f. 237, op. 131, d. 1283, ll. 119–1190b.; Andrievskii, "Dela o sovershenii," p. 538. Participants stressed that the prayer was directed not to keremet, Chinbulat, or other spirits, but precisely to *tiumen tiumeser iumo*, to whom the very first people had prayed after the creation of the world (and to whom Maris had allegedly never before directed prayers).

[48] The Russian term *snovidtsy* is used throughout, even by those who doubted that the Maris had actually seen such visions. I have decided to retain the term in its approximate translation as a shorthand for these three Maris, who were to figure prominently in the rest of the affair.

[49] The account here is based on the lengthy testimony of eight Maris, including the three dreamers. GAKO, f. 237, op. 131, d. 1283, ll. 115–1190b.; Andrievskii, "Dela o sovershenii," pp. 540–41; and RGIA, f. 797, op. 3, d. 12654, l. 22.

nature of the gathering and noted that the Maris dispersed from the prayer site without showing any desire to "violate the general tranquillity." He pointed also to the actual content of the Mari prayer, which had included requests for help in paying taxes and for the well-being of "the White Tsar."[50] Thus the investigator concluded that "even their prayers . . . show the simplicity of their disposition, an understanding of the Sovereign which is in conformity with loyal subjecthood [*vernopoddanost'*], and a concern for the payment of taxes."[51] In short, pagan proclivities notwithstanding, these were essentially good subjects.

The governor of Viatka province was more skeptical of the whole enterprise and supported the use of more decisive action. Noting that a "great number" of Maris had come to participate in the gathering "even from other provinces," he suggested that the dreamers "had aroused even more superstition" among Maris for their own personal enrichment, through the money they collected for the purchase of livestock for the sacrifice. Since the dreamers' greed and readiness to exploit Maris' "simplicity and superstition" could cause further gatherings in the future, tending toward "the violation of tranquillity," he suggested prosecuting the dreamers, "with the goal of [ensuring] that in the future they do not engage in fraud and thus attract people from other places."[52] Thus the governor, while convinced of the Maris' "simplicity" generally, was suspicious of the dreamers themselves and worried about the potential consequences of such gatherings in the future.

Informed by the Synod's Chief Procurator of "the importance of this event," the Emperor exhibited somewhat greater leniency. He decreed that in bringing Maris back to Orthodoxy, "out of condescension for their simplicity, these people should in no way be persecuted and they should be handled with extreme care."[53] This order, as we shall see, was to serve Maris as a powerful weapon in mobilizing opposition to missionaries' activities. As regards the dreamers, Nicholas decided against prosecution, ordering instead that if they were sufficiently young and able to travel, they should be brought to St. Petersburg for questioning. Thus in late March 1829 the three dreamers were gathered up and brought to the imperial capital for interviews with a senator and the Emperor himself.[54] Nicholas appears to have been genuinely interested in understanding the reasons for the gathering and

---

[50] GAKO, f. 237, op. 131, d. 1283, l. 1; and Andrievskii, "Dela o sovershenii," pp. 540–41. The "White Tsar" was a reference to the Russian Emperor.

[51] Cited in Andrievskii, "Dela o sovershenii," p. 540. The Maris in Tsarevokokshaisk district had evidently also prayed for the Sovereign and his family (NART, f. 1, op. 1, d. 112, l. 360b.).

[52] Cited in Andrievskii, "Dela o sovershenii," p. 541.

[53] RGIA, f. 797, op. 3, d. 12654, l. 12. See also Andrievskii, "Dela o sovershenii," p. 538.

[54] Two of the dreamers were evidently young. Tokmetev was sixty years old, but because he was healthy and knew some Russian, he was brought to St. Petersburg as well.

in treating Maris fairly in accordance with what he understood to be their potential for guilt.

In St. Petersburg, the dreamers succeeded in convincing the Emperor of their "simplicity and superstition." They explained that many Maris had abandoned paganism for a period of two or three years and had made a sincere effort to adhere strictly to Orthodox prescriptions, but that then poverty and agrarian crisis drove them to conduct pagan prayers once again. The dreamers then proceeded to make several accusations against the local clergy, explaining that priests did not visit them with the cross, did not admit them into their homes, and in general held their Mari parishioners in contempt. Most damaging were the accounts of local clergy's excessive monetary demands and their insistence on performing certain indispensable rites only *en masse*. While it was perhaps tolerable to baptize infants ten at a time, the clergy's concern for efficiency had horrible consequences in the case of burials:

> [Priest Andrei Darovskii] does not bury Cheremis in a timely fashion but instead collects a few, ten, and sometimes many more bodies in the cellar, and for a long time until [the burial] keeps the bodies, which are eaten by worms and mice, so that sometimes when they are taken out of the cellar [there is] an infectious stench, and the bodies are not only disfigured, but sometimes only bones are actually buried; and for this rite he takes between ten and forty rubles for each body.[55]

Such stories horrified the interviewing senator, and Nicholas charged Moscow Metropolitan Filaret (Drozdov) with appointing a special priest for the purposes of "enlightening" the three dreamers, so that they might return to Viatka province and spread Orthodoxy among their fellow Maris. The dreamers were transferred to Moscow where they spent several months under the instruction of A. Pokrovskii. Pokrovskii reported that the dreamers were attentive to his teachings, but that they displayed only limited intellectual capacity and knowledge of Russian and had begun to worry about the condition of their households and families. Since in Viatka province there were other Maris who had "sufficient knowledge of the Russian language," Filaret sent Pokrovskii to accompany them back to their villages in the summer of 1829.[56]

The bishop of Viatka, Kirill (Bogoslovskii-Platonov), meanwhile defended his local clergy and claimed that even the "elders" of the Mari gathering had testified that the two local priests, Darovskii and Il'ia Anisimov, attended to all their religious needs and had not oppressed them in any way. Echoing the Viatka Governor, Kirill concluded that the immediate cause of the gathering

[55] RGIA, f. 797, op. 3, d. 12654, ll. 28–33. Chuvash parishioners had raised similar complaints against their clergy in the late eighteenth century. See N. V. Nikol'skii, *Khristianstvo sredi chuvash Srednego Povolzh'ia v XVII–XVIII vekakh: Istoricheskii ocherk* (Kazan, 1912), p. 162.

[56] RGIA, f. 797, op. 3, d. 12654, ll. 40–41.

"was the vision, allegedly seen, or, as one should almost undoubtedly suggest, slyly thought up" by the three dreamers. But the real reason for such gatherings, Kirill argued, was the "hereditary impenitence" of the Maris, as fathers sternly ordered their children to continue homage to their old gods. He therefore suggested appointing four missionaries for the two districts most heavily populated by Maris (Urzhum and Iaransk) and opening a school in each parish for Mari children. The Synod agreed to these suggestions, and thus the mission in Viatka diocese was born.[57]

Pokrovskii himself traveled widely in Urzhum district, received "unanimous" promises from Maris to abandon their "delusions," and "converted" 1,524 persons. Prince Devlet-Kil´deev, the police chief in Urzhum district who accompanied Pokrovskii in his missionary work, reported a standard pattern in Mari responses to this missionary activity. At each canton board, Mari peasants were gathered for discussions. At first, they were almost always resistant, arguing that they did not reject the church, but that "they cannot abandon these ancient pagan rituals, because they have been performed by their fathers and grandfathers and so on." When Pokrovskii explained to them "all the holiness of the Greco-Russian faith and God's punishment for those who withdraw from the church," the Maris proved more amenable: "After much consultation among themselves, they unanimously admitted their delusions, exculpating themselves by their ignorance and incomprehension, and [declared] that they are sincerely glad that the Great Sovereign has ordered that they be taught the true faith." They agreed to go to church, to observe the church's rules, and not to perform any more pagan rituals in the forest.[58]

Pokrovskii's journal contains somewhat greater detail concerning the ways in which Maris understood the sojourn of their three dreamers in St. Petersburg and Moscow.[59] In August 1829 Pokrovskii arrived in Makarovo, whose residents "were the crudest and most superstitious of the whole district." They nevertheless listened "with the greatest curiosity and attentiveness," as Pokrovskii related that he had taught the three dreamers "the Russian faith" and that they had now become good Christians. But the reaction was hardly what Pokrovskii had hoped for. "In response to this a cry rose up, which according to the translator was a general cursing of the

---

[57] Ibid., ll. 37–50. Kirill's conclusions were based on Darovskii's reports and the investigation conducted by two archpriests. GAKO, f. 237, op. 131, d. 1283, ll. 81–830b., 121–210b.

[58] Citations in Andrievskii, "Dela o sovershenii," p. 544. Devlet-Kil´deev was an unlikely missionary assistant since he was, in fact, a Muslim. Thus while Pokrovskii praised him as a zealous associate and he even received an award for his efforts, the governor was in the end forced to transfer him to a nearby Russian district (Nolinsk), since Maris "do not see in him an example for Christianity, for he himself belongs to the Mohammedan faith" (RGIA, f. 797, op. 3, d. 12654, l. 233; and GAKO, f. 237, op. 133, d. 1385, ll. 4–40b.).

[59] A small portion of the journal has been published: "Vypiska iz zhurnala Missionera sviashchennika A. Pokrovskogo," *Khristianskoe chtenie* 2 (1835): 97–106.

three dreamers." Later Pokrovskii was informed by the Russian peasants accompanying him (who spoke Mari):

> that in great bitterness the Cheremis had not at all expected this from their dreamers: they had expected that the latter would solicit for them imperial assent to conduct all pagan holidays and sacrifices in the forest, but the opposite had occurred: "[the dreamers] themselves accepted the Russian faith and became Russians [*sdelalis' russkimi*]; they acted as betrayers, deceivers, traitors. Get them out of our village! And out of the Cheremis land altogether!"

Pokrovskii acted quickly to counteract this interpretation of what had occurred in St. Petersburg and Moscow. He gathered all the relatives of the dreamers and stood them beside him and addressed the crowd with these words:

> Good and wise Cheremis! You are unjustly angry with your three fellow-villagers. . . . Instead of being angry with them, you should love, honor, and respect them as intelligent people who have seen the Great Sovereign, the Synod, and the Senate. You must now help them. They endured much woe on your behalf and encountered much hardship. They cried a lot, and I alone at times consoled them; at times I cried along with them: and indeed, how could one not cry! They left their homes, their wives and children, relatives and friends, and their fields, meadows, and livestock. They lived in a foreign and distant land for almost half a year!

As a result of this display, "the relatives of the dreamers began to sob, and the people were moved." At this point, the police chief questioned the dreamers in front of the crowd about their trip to St. Petersburg and Moscow. They recounted how they had seen the Tsar and the imperial family, ministers, the Senate, and the Tsar's palace; in Moscow they saw holy cathedrals, the bodies of saints, the Kremlin, and "the big bell." When Pokrovskii asked whether they had accepted the "Russian faith," the dreamers responded in the affirmative—"we believe in the one true God, in three persons, who created the heaven and the earth"—and read a short creed, several prayers, and the Ten Commandments.[60]

Pokrovskii expended much effort to make this set of interchanges a performance. He spoke to the crowd and presented the dreamers on a porch, which constituted a kind of stage. He evidently sought to invest this meeting with maximum drama, since he kept the dreamers hidden from the spectators until the most "propitious" moment and had even requested ahead of time, before leaving Moscow, that the dreamers "not be able to consult with their fellow Cheremis prematurely."[61] Pokrovskii's subsequent account

[60] RGIA, f. 797, op. 3, d. 12654, ll. 115–17; and GAKO, f. 237, op. 133, d. 1385, l. 9. Responses were given in Russian and then translated into Mari.

[61] Cited in Andrievskii, "Dela o sovershenii," p. 543.

confirms that choreographing the dreamers' first contact with local Maris was indeed fundamental to his success. He was able to turn the dreamers' own suffering—their long stay "in a foreign and distant land"—to the advantage of Christianity. He was thus able to strengthen the resolve of the dreamers themselves, who went on to render immeasurable aid, especially by informing Pokrovskii of the "harmful schemes" that were secretly circulating among Maris.[62] But while these theatrics could help to produce certain very powerful representations, Pokrovskii was not entirely able to control their meaning, and later on Maris used precisely these events to contest the claim that the mission truly enjoyed the Emperor's sanction.

As with the Tatars in 1827–30, the activities of missionaries consisted above all in securing non-Russians' written rejection of their previous faiths. The dynamics here seem to have been fairly similar to those in the encounter with the Tatars. Initially resistant to the idea of rejecting animism, the Maris finally agreed when it became clear that they would have no peace otherwise. The struggle between Pokrovskii and the Maris became one of securing the latter's acknowledgment of their Orthodox status and foreclosing in their minds the possibility of a return to their native faith. But as we shall see, this turned out to be very hard work, as opposition to Pokrovskii's activities began to grow. It would not be long before Pokrovskii, citing the constant travel, incessant shouting and tension, and the disappointments, eventually claimed to be "sick in body and soul" and requested permission to return to Moscow.[63] What, then, were the sources of his frustrations?

The Mobilization of Mari Opposition

By the end of his first trip, as we have seen, Pokrovskii was able to report substantial success and had "converted" almost all the baptized Maris of Urzhum district. These "conversions" consisted of Maris signing promises that they would attend church, abandon pagan rituals, and so on. Not surprisingly, these promises turned out to be rather tenuous, and many Maris disregarded them as soon as it was possible to do so. Pokrovskii, like Svetovidov, was not so naive as to believe that he had altered Maris' religious convictions fundamentally. He expressed great frustration with this "crude, cunning, and ignorant people, who despite the fact that they gave a written promise to abandon their delusions, a few days later, with the appearance of the first trickster, on the words of the first deluder, change their mind, reject their promises, return to their previous uncleanliness, and fall into their previous delusions."[64] Indeed, in contrast to Pokrovskii's first trip to the Viatka

---

[62] Pokrovskii praises the dreamers in RGIA, f. 797, op. 3, d. 12654, l. 1170b. From this point forward, only two of the dreamers are noted. It is not clear what happened to the third.

[63] RGIA, f. 797, op. 3, d. 12654, l. 1230b.

[64] Ibid., l. 123.

region, when the Maris appear to have been discombobulated by his appearance and the return of the dreamers from St. Petersburg, Pokrovskii's subsequent trips, and the activities of other missionaries who had by then been appointed from among local clergy, met with greater resistance. It took some time for locally entrenched interests to recognize the nature of the new intervention and to mobilize against the missionary initiative.

There can be little doubt, as Pokrovskii's account of their reaction to the dreamers' acceptance of the "Russian faith" demonstrates, that Maris were not prepared to abandon their indigenous practices. Most evidence suggests that after the original baptisms of the 1740s and 1750s the church had focused principally on the fulfillment of "Christian obligations," and the clergy had been able to do little more than attempt verbally to dissuade Maris from conducting prayers in the forests. Maris had employed sufficient circumspection in performing these rituals that until the present case local clergy had never actually witnessed such a prayer, even though Maris themselves had at times confessed to pagan "delusions." Thus the priest Darovskii concluded, "This evil among novokreshchenye did not begin now or at any [particular] time, but has continued since long ago, from the time of their paganism."[65] While the authorities drew a fairly clear distinction between baptized Maris and unbaptized ones, on the local level this distinction was blurred, or at least did not have such significance, as their joint participation in animist ceremonies suggests. Mari references to the "Russian believers" (*ruskovery*) in their midst had more to do with the disposition of the individual than with his official confessional status (although *ruskovery* were in almost all cases already baptized). Pokrovskii reported that when he convinced some Maris to repudiate their "delusions" and sprinkled each of them with holy water, Maris referred to this as "their induction [*privedenie*] into the Russian faith."[66] On several occasions they explained that having abandoned their pagan "delusions," they had now become "Russians," and religious authorities themselves referred to Maris' written repudiation of paganism as "conversion" (*obrashchenie*).[67] In short, while Maris construed religious affiliation in terms of actual practice, Russian authorities for the most part took a more bureaucratic view that centered on the fact of baptism.

If Maris were already inclined to maintain their religious practice, they were also encouraged from numerous (and unlikely) quarters to resist the missionaries. Another bad harvest in 1830 provided pagan elders with plenty of ammunition against those who had converted. Interpreting the crisis as God's punishment for their abandonment of the "old faith," these elders "threatened that henceforward more misfortunes were being prepared

[65] GAKO, f. 237, op. 131, d. 1283, l. 1030b.

[66] RGIA, f. 797, op. 3, d. 12654, l. 118.

[67] Thus one meets rather strange, but nonetheless intelligible, expressions like "the conversion of baptized Maris" (*obrashchenie kreshchenykh cheremis*).

by the offended old god, if [Maris] do not turn to him and do not make offerings in the keremet groves as before."[68] Moreover, there were reports that "ancient Russian Christians," or Old Believers, were encouraging Maris to stand firm against the missionaries.[69] Indeed, Pokrovskii reported that in one region where Maris had begun discussing the "old faith," the "seducers" "*to our amazement turned out to be Russian peasants.*"[70] Some local officials also had an interest in upholding Maris' animist inclinations, in order to extract bribes from them for the unimpeded practice of animism. As one missionary reported, the source of Maris' stubbornness in the parish of Upsha was a local rural assessor, who gathered Maris in the village and told them "that everything depends on him, that he is their defender; if they want to remain in the Cheremis faith, they need only collect twenty rubles for him from the whole community, and things will stay as they were before."[71] It was these circumstances that led Pokrovskii to remark with frustration, "A missionary alone, despite all the purity and wholeness of his zeal, cannot act with adequate success *where hindrances come from all sides.*"[72]

Pokrovskii pointed in particular to the problem of former canton scribes, who stirred up all kinds of trouble for personal profit. One former scribe, a certain Ivan Sevriugin (evidently a Russian), was particularly troublesome. A merchant dealing in bast and wood-tar, Sevriugin had developed extensive trade contacts with local Maris and lent them money and even paid their taxes in times of difficulty. As a result, local Maris turned to him for advice and help, and "he has gained their trust to such an extent that his words are considered law." While Sevriugin presented himself as a proponent of the Maris' conversion, Pokrovskii discovered that in fact he was secretly orchestrating their resistance, providing advice about how best to deal with the missionaries. Pokrovskii considered Sevriugin to be the "principal reason" for the unrest he encountered in the village of Makarovo (see below).[73] Though Pokrovskii himself could not explain Sevriugin's actions, his discovery revealed a local network of patronage and influence that stood squarely at cross-purposes to the mission's objectives.

There were even problems emanating from within the religious bureaucracy itself. Some Maris had succeeded in obtaining a copy of the Synodal decree containing the Emperor's order that Maris "should in no way be persecuted and they should be handled with extreme care."[74] Maris of course

[68] Cited in Andrievskii, "Dela o sovershenii," p. 555. See also NRF MarNII op. 1, d. 31, ll. 7–8; and RGIA, f. 797, op. 3, d. 12654, ll. 219–219ob.

[69] RGIA, f. 797, op. 3, d. 12654, l. 221ob.; and Andrievskii, "Dela o sovershenii," p. 556. The details here are obscure.

[70] RGIA, f. 797, op. 3, d. 12654, l. 170 (emphasis in the original).

[71] GAKO, f. 237, op. 132, d. 1463, ll. 5–5ob. Also cited in Andrievskii, "Dela o sovershenii," pp. 552–53.

[72] RGIA, f. 797, op. 3, d. 12654, l. 168 (emphasis added).

[73] NRF MarNII, op. 1, d. 31, ll. 13–14.

[74] Cited in Andrievskii, "Dela o sovershenii," p. 554.

interpreted this order liberally, as constituting permission for them to remain animists, which emboldened them in their dealings with missionaries. When apprehended with a copy of the decree, one Mari explained that he had obtained it "for expensive money from the Viatka Ecclesiastical Consistory."[75] Thus once again, Russian clerks had sold copies of a decree with ambiguous content to non-Russians who used it to strengthen the resolve of their comrades. These "leaks," as should now be clear, constituted a fundamental weakness of tsarist administration in the countryside.

In light of these circumstances, it is hardly surprising that missionaries' work did not go uncontested. In most cases, sources refer vaguely to "stubbornness" and "opposition," without providing specific detail. In one case, for example, Maris answered missionaries "with rude inflexibility and offensive shouting."[76] In the village of Makarovo, Pokrovskii arrived together with Bishop Kirill to find several thousand Maris, both baptized and unbaptized, who had gathered in the village square, yelling "Old faith! Old faith!" No matter how much Pokrovskii and the Bishop tried to admonish and calm them, they continued yelling "Old faith!"[77] At the conclusion of the investigation, moreover, many Maris absolutely refused to confirm their testimony with their signatures. For four days [!], authorities encouraged and cajoled, even bringing in Russian peasants from a nearby settlement to apply extra pressure, but the Maris, while acknowledging that the testimony had been accurately recorded, "could in no way be persuaded to confirm [the testimony] with their *tamgi* or signatures."[78] By making it impossible to legitimize the investigation, this obstinacy brought the whole matter to a grinding halt.[79]

But Maris went further still. In 1830 they sent a representative on behalf of 630 people to Kazan and filed a complaint with Minister of Internal Affairs A. A. Zakrevskii, who was in that city in connection with the outbreak of cholera there. Evidently drawing on their knowledge of the Emperor's earlier decree, they complained that they had been subjected to

[75] Cited ibid., p. 555.

[76] RGIA, f. 797, op. 3, d. 797, l. 170. Four Maris were arrested at this time. They evidently were put in prison on the basis of a new provision enacted in 1829, calling for the exile of anyone caught spreading "pagan false prophecy or other pagan and seductive suggestions." Cited in Andrievskii, "Dela o sovershenii," p. 549. Andrievskii has no further information on their fate, but a number of Maris later complained that they had been thrown in prison, which suggests that these four were subsequently released.

[77] RGIA, f. 797, op. 3, d. 12654, ll. 170–71. Pokrovskii later related that Sevriugin was most likely behind this display of opposition.

[78] *Tamgi* were small signs indicating clan derivation and ownership. The signatures referred to here were *rukoprikladstva*, whereby a literate person guided the hand of an illiterate person. On the significance of *tamgi*, see P. D. Shestakov, "Byt cheremis Urzhumskogo uezda," *Tsirkuliar po Kazanskomu uchebnomu okrugu* 16 (1866): 127; S. K. Kuznetsov, "Ostatki iazychestva u cheremis," *Izvestiia Imperatorskogo Russkogo Geograficheskogo Obshchestva* 21, 6 (1885): 464–66.

[79] GAKO, f. 237, op. 131, d. 1283, ll. 98, 121–23. As far as I know, Maris *never* agreed to authenticate the testimony, thus divesting the findings of their legitimacy.

"oppressions" by Devlet-Kil'deev and missionaries in Urzhum district, including Pokrovskii. They requested permission to conduct pagan rituals and asked that measures be taken to restrain missionaries from interfering in their prayers. They also claimed that they had been bullied into signing the promise to observe Christianity without really understanding its content. During an investigation, the Maris elaborated further, underscoring that the baptized among them had been subjected to "persecution" for their performance of pagan rituals, and the unbaptized for their refusal to accept Christianity. Some claimed that they had been beaten, others that they had been thrown in prison, some that they had been threatened with conscription.[80] While the actions taken by Devlet-Kil'deev to ensure proper respect for missionaries and to punish the unbaptized accused of seducing the baptized perhaps stretched the limits of the permissible, it seems likely that what Devlet-Kil'deev understood to be an appropriate use of authority for the promotion of Christianity appeared to Maris themselves— armed with the Emperor's decree—to be excessive and arbitrary "persecution."[81] In any event, while this complaint did produce an investigation and contributed to Devlet-Kil'deev's transfer to another district, the petition was otherwise rejected.

Like their counterparts working among baptized Tatars, Pokrovskii and the new missionaries struggled with only partial success to convince Maris that the mission actually enjoyed the Emperor's sanction. Even as Pokrovskii labored, rumors began to circulate that the old faith "is not offensive to the Sovereign, and that the dreamers were neither in St. Petersburg nor Moscow but only in Viatka."[82] Similarly, elders and fortune-tellers were assuring Maris

> that the old faith is known to the Sovereign, and that he approves of it and that when he dismissed the dreamers from St. Petersburg he gave them a decree to maintain the old faith, written in golden letters, but they, having become drunk, lost it in Moscow, and that I [Pokrovskii], having found it, hid it and have converted them to the Russian faith so that when all the Cheremis convert, then their old god will kill them all, and we will take all their belongings and return to Moscow.[83]

Other missionaries encountered similar rumors, while the police chief concurred that it was essential "to remove from [the Maris] the harmful seducers and to assure [them] that their conversion to the church is the will of the Sovereign Emperor, *which they do not believe at the present time*."[84] The

---

[80] I unfortunately do not have the original petition but merely a digest of its contents.

[81] Devlet-Kil'deev attempted to justify his actions, but the Governor was forced to conclude that his actions "superseded gentleness and voluntary persuasion" and therefore produced bad relations between himself and the Maris (RGIA, f. 797, op. 3, d. 12654, ll. 225–33).

[82] Ibid., l. 1220b.

[83] Ibid., ll. 1250b.–26.

[84] Cited in Andrievskii, "Dela o sovershenii," p. 545 (emphasis added).

Maris' appropriation of the Emperor's decree calling for circumspection demonstrates how a directive designed for internal bureaucratic use, disengaged from this original context, acquired new meanings and authorized actions very different from those originally envisioned.

Here again, the cohabitation of baptized with unbaptized in the same villages generated significant problems, for while those Maris who remained unbaptized did indeed have the right to practice animism, even the baptized contended "that they are permitted to maintain [the old faith] and that no one can prohibit that."[85] As the priest Darovskii bitterly complained, novokreshchenye "bend the indulgence of the law to corroborate [their assertions] and, what is more, incorrectly interpreting the toleration of all faiths in Russia, consider their own delusions completely permitted as well."[86] Maris even argued that the "Sovereign himself cannot change [our] faith" (which in light of the law code was an essentially accurate statement).[87] The very presence of unbaptized Maris, enjoying the right to practice paganism in accordance with the empire's laws, only deepened the impression that the state and the Emperor looked upon paganism favorably and were not partial to Maris' conversion. Eager to obtain sanction for their indigenous practices, Maris were either unwilling or unable to reconcile the tension between the toleration of non-Orthodox faiths and the privileging of Orthodoxy.

Pokrovskii was nonetheless determined to demonstrate in dramatic fashion the Emperor's patronage of the mission. Evidently based on his request, the Synod requested that the dreamers be rewarded "with caftans from the office of His Imperial Majesty."[88] Two expensive and beautifully embroidered caftans were sent to Pokrovskii, who deployed them in subduing the Maris in Makarovo. Having himself put on one caftan, he gave the other to one of the dreamers, who was then put "on an elevated place" for all to see. Then,

> having gone into the middle of this violent crowd, [Pokrovskii] directed all his efforts to explaining to them that the Sovereign Emperor was very pleased by the report of their abandonment of the old faith, and that as a sign of His good will toward the Cheremis people, he was pleased to send these two expensive caftans. Upon the conclusion of this discussion, the police chief took the rewarded [dreamer] and led him along the rows of Cheremis, ordering [them] to render him honor with bows and congratulations.

The result of this display was profound, as the Maris then approached Pokrovskii to receive his benediction. "At this time amazement and confusion

[85] GAKO, f. 237, op. 131, d. 1283, l. 82.

[86] Ibid., l. 81ob.

[87] RGIA, f. 7970p. 3, d. 12654, l. 124. The law stated, "The predominant [Orthodox] church does not allow itself even the least forceful means in the conversion of non-Christians [*inovernye*] to Orthodoxy, and does not threaten those of them who do not wish to join" (*SZ* [1832], vol. 14, article 73).

[88] RGIA, f. 797, op. 3, d. 12654, ll. 1130b.–14.

were clearly visible on their faces; they all stood motionlessly in one place in silence, confusion, and fear: and in this position they remained until deep into the night."[89]

Yet while Pokrovskii's dramatic presentation of these caftans appears once again to have produced a profound impression on the Mari population, the event was soon being interpreted in an entirely different way. Writing many years later, a missionary related contemporary Mari claims that these caftans had been conferred on the dreamers by the Emperor as a way of thanking Maris for their pagan prayers on his behalf. "From that time, the fame of the prayers in [the village] Kuprian-Sola spread throughout the entire Cheremis world, attracting worshipers from all over"—to such an extent that local Russians referred to Kuprian-Sola as "the Cheremis Jerusalem."[90] Ironically, then, the attempt of authorities to invest the project of Maris' Christianization with the powerful imagery of imperial benefaction in the long run actually created a new center of paganism in the region, invested with the legitimacy originally intended for the mission itself.

Something similar occurred with the petition submitted to the minister of internal affairs. Escorted back to their villages under guard, the Mari petitioners "had no trouble presenting their case as proof of special attention to them of Mr. Minister and set out for the villages with news of the reception given to them. . . . And even today [1838] hope for success has not gone out for everybody." Thus the Maris presented the escort back to their villages, which was presumably designed to ensure that they caused no further trouble, as a sign of the special favor that their case enjoyed with higher authorities. As late as 1837 one petitioner was still using a copy of this petition to promote the "old faith."[91] In short, both the caftans and the petitions confirm that, as with certain other spectacles engineered by tsarist authorities for the purposes of governing the populace, the connotations emanating from these displays were never entirely fixed and could always be invested with alternative meanings very much contrary to the intended ones.[92]

In the end, however "simple" Maris may have appeared to outsiders, they seem to have negotiated the demands made of them with considerable acumen. Given the language barrier and their relative isolation from the Russian world, Maris exhibited a keen ability to exploit the tensions in imperial

[89] The whole account is taken from RGIA, f. 797, op. 3, d. 12654, ll. 170–71 and is alluded to briefly in Andrievskii, "Dela o sovershenii," p. 555. Though the prose here is in the third person, the account was probably written by Pokrovskii himself.

[90] A. Odoev, "Po povodu iazycheskikh zhertvoprinoshenii u cheremis-khristian," *VEV* 24 (1897): 1201–2.

[91] RGIA, f. 796, op. 118, d. 73, ll. 1–2, 520b.–53.

[92] For a discussion of this issue concerning corporal punishment, see Abby M. Schrader, "Containing the Spectacle of Punishment: The Russian Autocracy and the Abolition of the Knout, 1817–1845," *Slavic Review* 56, 4 (1997): 613–44. On the propensity of peasants (in this case Russian) to "misunderstand" Tsarist legislation, see David Moon, *Russian Peasants and Tsarist Legislation on the Eve of Reform: Interaction between Peasants and Officialdom, 1825–1855* (London, 1992).

ideology and practice in their search for satisfaction. The rumors they for-mulated successfully reconciled and unified elements of the state's perspec-tive with their own aspirations and fears. However much these rumors ap-peared as "silly lies" to outsiders, in fact they made a great deal of sense in terms of Maris' own understanding and experience, and in terms of the gov-ernment's own pronouncements and actions.

The Problem of Local Clergy

Both of the cases in this chapter demonstrate that accusations against the local clergy served as an important safety valve for novokreshchenye once the possibility of more direct forms of protest disappeared. This was one of the principal defenses erected by the Mari dreamers in St. Petersburg and by the Tatar petitioners when confronted by missionaries. Usually, non-Russians did not make such accusations initially but fell back on them when pushed into a corner, and this usually helped to absolve them of full re-sponsibility for their "delusion." The government itself was quick to assume the worst about the clergy. Before any investigation into the causes of the Mari gathering, the Synod's Chief Procurator immediately commissioned Bishop Kirill to find out whether the gathering had not occurred "due to the negligence or some other fault of the local clergy."[93] The Synod more gener-ally attributed the sorry religious state of the non-Russian converts to "the inadequate activity of the local clergy, who are not sufficiently prepared for the special circumstances of this service."[94] Given the low opinion of the parish clergy already held by the central authorities, non-Russians' accusa-tions of corruption and negligence were almost sure to fall on fertile soil.

And indeed, the clergy's qualifications were in many cases dismal. Investi-gations in the aftermath of the Tatar petitions revealed that only seven of forty-three priests in the affected region had actually completed the seminary course.[95] In Tsarevokokshaisk district, the Consistory's records showed that the local Orthodox clergy were so "unreliable" for service in Mari parishes that they were all subsequently transferred to other locations.[96] Frequently accused of laxness, drunkenness, extortion, or worse, parish clergy were in a poor position to exert any positive influence on non-Russian parishioners.

But the pressures faced by parish clergy—from both their superiors and their parishioners—were often intense, as the case of Andrei Darovskii demonstrates. Compelled by a sense of obligation to report in detail about the pagan gathering in Urzhum district, Darovskii subsequently added a lengthy analysis of the reasons for Maris' attachment to paganism, in which

[93] RGIA, f. 797, op. 3, d. 12654, l. 100b.
[94] RGIA, f. 797, op. 3, d. 12652, l. 20b.
[95] See Mozharovskii, *Izlozhenie*, p. 135.
[96] RGIA, f. 797, op. 3, d. 12647, ll. 12–16.

he underscored the cohabitation of baptized Maris with pagans, "the complete coarseness of these unhappy superstitious people in their previous Cheremis customs," and the almost total absence of books in Mari.[97] Yet instead of thanking Darovskii for his efforts, ecclesiastical investigators demanded that he explain how and when he had learned about these pagan tendencies, what he had done to combat them, and why he had not reported them earlier.[98] Implicit in this inquiry was the assumption that if he had been doing his job properly, paganism would not be a problem in the parish, and that his failure to report earlier constituted an effort to hide his poor performance.

This was only the beginning of Darovskii's woes. While the dreamers accused him in St. Petersburg of making excessive monetary demands on his parishioners, Maris in his parish filed a more formal complaint, in which they recounted these same accusations and called for Darovskii's transfer.[99] Darovskii rejected the complaint as "completely false," refuted each of the accusations in turn, and argued that the parishioners were just trying to get back at him for his exposure of their pagan prayer. He added that the petition, allegedly filed on behalf of 233 persons, had in fact been illegitimately constituted. Further inquiry revealed that indeed several Maris had been included on the complaint without their knowledge, while the signatures (*tamgi*) on the complaint were conspicuously neat (signing neatly was something "which Cheremis are in no way able to do").[100] Despite his astute defense of his position, and despite his exoneration by the investigators, Darovskii's original report about the gathering had created so much "bitterness" among his parishioners that authorities decided to transfer both him and his colleague Anisimov to other parishes.[101] Subsequently, Maris abandoned their complaint, remarking that Darovskii had "driven us to bitterness" when he exposed their pagan prayer, but that "we no longer have any claims against him" since "he has been transferred out of our parish."[102] Such, in short, was Darovskii's reward for having done his priestly duty. Given this experience, it is hardly surprising that other priests were reluctant to initiate cases against their parishioners.

Though in Darovskii's case the key issue was his role in exposing the pagan prayer, in most cases antagonisms were the result of economic contradictions inscribed in parish life. Yet there was some disagreement over the

---

[97] GAKO, f. 237, op. 131, d. 1283, ll. 72–73, 81–83.

[98] Ibid., ll. 101–2. Darovskii and his fellow priest Il'ia Anisimov actually demonstrated that their actions were in accord with existing decrees, emphasizing that they had indeed reported the gathering when they discovered it but were unable to report on earlier gatherings because they had never witnessed any.

[99] GAKO, f. 237, op. 132, d. 52, ll. 1–10b.

[100] Ibid., ll. 7–11, 21. Whether or not the *tamgi* can be considered "neat," it is certainly suspicious that they all appear to have been written in the same hand.

[101] GAKO, f. 237, op. 131, d. 1283, ll. 1460b., 154.

[102] GAKO, f. 237, op. 132, d. 52, ll. 30–320b.

degree to which purely economic factors were truly the cause of such antago-nisms. An investigation of Tatar parishes in 1828 found that although the collection of *ruga* (fixed support) "always entails great inconvenience and even offensive unpleasantries for both the [church] servitors and the parish-ioners," the cause of such difficulties was usually poor harvests and the gen-eral poverty of the parishes rather than the "stubbornness" of baptized Tatars. The Kazan Consistory disagreed, concluding that in fact all the parishes had more than the established minimum number of parishioners (1,200) necessary to ensure adequate material support for the clergy. The Consistory thus concluded that the collection of *ruga* was so difficult "probably because the priests of those villages, who were uneducated, were not able to win over the parishioners through love."[103]

In any event, clergy at times took energetic steps to protect their economic interests. Not long after his arrival, Pokrovskii was already calling for satis-factory salaries for the church servitors of seven Mari parishes, in order to protect Maris from the "excessive" demands of "self-interested" priests, and advocated transferring suspected priests if necessary.[104] In fact, Pokrovskii suspected that many of the difficulties he encountered among Maris had, re-markably, been instigated by the Orthodox clergy itself. Specifically, when Pokrovskii began to suggest that more churches were needed in the Mari re-gion, rumors spread among the native population that local residents would be required to pay for this construction. As Pokrovskii explained, "malevo-lent people," "and more than likely, the clergy, are trying to frighten the Cheremis with various rumors that the new churches and prayer houses will be constructed at the expense of Cheremis, that they will be resettled from parish to parish, and that they will be completely forbidden to slaughter sheep and other animals."[105]

The clergy's defense of its interests was reasonable enough, given the eco-nomic structure of the parish. Dependent on their parishioners, they felt threatened by any attempt to reorganize parishes in ways detrimental to their economic interests. As Gregory Freeze has shown, obtaining and hold-ing a good clerical position was perhaps the central problem for the clergy, especially beginning in the 1780s or so.[106] The religious instability generated by Pokrovskii's activity became, among other things, an economic struggle between parish clergy and Mari parishioners. Perhaps making a virtue of necessity, baptized Maris argued that their "conversion" by Pokrovskii freed them from the obligation of paying *ruga* to their priests, since among

---

[103] RGIA, f. 796, op. 108, d. 595, ll. 193–207.
[104] RGIA, f. 797, op. 3, d. 12654, ll. 131, 168. It is unclear what role Pokrovskii had in Darovskii's transfer.
[105] Ibid., l. 172.
[106] See Gregory L. Freeze, *The Russian Levites: Parish Clergy in the Eighteenth Century* (Cambridge, Mass., 1977), esp. pp. 107–46, which documents an intense struggle for clerical positions in the late eighteenth and early nineteenth centuries.

Russian peasants *ruga* had been replaced by voluntary contributions, or emoluments: "Now [Maris], having converted (by their expression) to the Russian faith, based on the example of Russians reject *ruga* payments, saying that they are now already Russians."[107] If nothing else, "conversion" thus offered Maris the possibility of liberation from the burden of *ruga*. Hence Maris understood *ruga* as something that non-Christians paid to the Orthodox clergy, an obligation that should be removed when they "became Russians."

The problem, as Pokrovskii noted, was that Maris "have not yet become used to contributions for church rituals and to voluntary payments made out of zeal."[108] Without the discipline imposed by *ruga* payments, it was not clear that Maris would actually support their clergy at the appropriate level. Local clergy realized the financial threat posed not only by Mari attempts to renounce *ruga* prescriptions but also by the construction of new churches and the establishment of new parishes, which threatened to reduce the support base of the existing parishes. Since new parishes and "conversion" were bad for clerical business,[109] the clergy spread various rumors in order to derail the missionary effort. While new Mari churches were established by 1836, this construction and the support of the clergy subsequently depended on a special state subsidy. These antagonisms persisted, dissuading some non-Christians from accepting baptism.

Although the secular state undoubtedly regarded religious deviance with great seriousness, the Orthodox church did most of the work in dealing with the "apostasy" and "delusion" considered here. The Emperor was, of course, involved, as were secular officials at the local level, who accompanied missionaries in the field to enhance their authority. By all indications prince Devlet-Kil´deev made an important contribution to the missionary work in Viatka diocese, albeit one that was resented by many of the affected Maris. But the state entrusted this work principally to ecclesiastical officials and applied secular law only to the few baptized Tatars who refused to renounce their petitions. Otherwise, deviant *novokreshchenye* were confronted with "admonitions" or, in the case of more recalcitrant baptized Tatars, incarceration in a monastery until they "repented."

Novokreshchenye's opposition to the church's efforts to impose religious discipline contained an element of defiance—for example, when Maris chanted "Old faith!" and refused to sign their testimony. But on the whole, non-Russians remained decidedly deferential in protesting against the missionary intrusion. Petitions were filed in both of the cases considered here,

---

[107] RGIA, f. 797, op. 3, d. 12654, l. 131.

[108] Ibid.

[109] It should be stressed here that *new baptisms* were probably welcomed by the parish clergy, since they expanded the parish support base. The problem here was that these were essentially *reconversions*, which Maris used to *lessen* their obligations toward the clergy.

and novokreshchenye appear to have believed that their aspirations could be satisfied through such supplication. Yet they were not equally deferential to all representatives of authority. Baptized Tatars remained reluctant to renounce their petitions until they were certain that the central government had indeed rejected them. Missionaries' statements were recognized as legitimate only to the extent that they were seen to reflect the true disposition of the central government, and above all the Emperor. The same was true for baptized Maris, although in this case we are fortunate enough to get a glimpse—frustrating in its brevity, to be sure—of alternative networks of authority and patronage that stood at cross purposes with those officially established for the purposes of promoting "Christian enlightenment." Clearly, the imperial regime had great difficulty communicating its will to the non-Russian population in such a way that it could not be subverted or translated into forms utterly at odds with its original purposes.

3   Mission and Baptism

Aside from Muslims, most non-Russians in the Volga-Kama region were baptized into Orthodoxy in the eighteenth century. Hence we focused initially on "apostasy" and "delusion" in the late 1820s, the events that led to the formation of Orthodox missions in the region. Even so, the missions to "reinforce" baptized novokreshchenye in Orthodoxy were expected also to promote the baptism of those "who have not yet come to know Christianity."[1] Many thousands of pagans and over a million Muslims in the region remained unbaptized, and their presence served as a great source of "seduction" for novokreshchenye, especially in mixed villages.[2] The state and the church thus desired the conversion of these remaining non-Christians not only for itself, but also because it would presumably ameliorate the "religious condition" of novokreshchenye communities as a whole. But under what circumstances did non-Christians actually abandon their earlier confessional status and formally join the Orthodox community? What were the principal inducements to accept this formal transfer of confessional identity, and what were the major obstacles to it? How often did new baptisms actually occur, and what were their consequences? In short, what place did baptism occupy in the confessional politics of the region?[3]

[1] RGIA, f. 797, op. 3, d. 12652, l. 1.
[2] This problem is highlighted in GAKO, f. 237, op. 131, d. 1283, l. 147; RGIA, f. 797, op. 5, d. 20775; and RGIA, f. 381, op. 44, d. 23503, l. 10b.
[3] In this chapter my concern is with conversion in the narrow sense, the formal transfer of confessional status through baptism. I do not address the question of whether the converts were actually believing Christians, were it even possible to ascertain this on the basis of existing sources.

74

Missions Established

By the mid-1830s, based on a combination of the Emperor's directive and the initiative of some local churchmen, formal missions had been established in Kazan, Viatka, and Simbirsk provinces. In approving the Synod's appointment of Filaret (Amfiteatrov) as the new archbishop of Kazan in February 1828, the Emperor instructed the new hierarch "to travel quickly to the diocese to eliminate the difficulties concerning novokreshchenye which have recently arisen in Kazan diocese."[4] It was thus Filaret who authored the missionary statute for Kazan diocese, which called for three missionaries. In Viatka diocese, the Mari mission appeared as a response to the animist prayer considered in chapter 2. With the Synod's blessing, four priests continued their work (principally in Iaransk and Urzhum districts) after Pokrovskii returned permanently to Moscow. The establishment of the Mari mission in turn induced Iosif Stefanov, an archpriest in Glazov district of Viatka diocese, to propose a mission for Udmurts as well. His proposal called for one missionary in each of four districts (Glazov, Malmyzh, Elabuga, and Sarapul) and was approved by the Synod in 1830.[5] Finally, a mission in Simbirsk diocese emerged in 1836, with two missionaries.[6]

To a large degree, each of these missions was a distinct and separate enterprise that communicated with the others only to a limited degree, which suggests that there was a strong sense of territorial jurisdiction on the part of the ecclesiastical authorities. Indeed, it was precisely the creation in 1832 of a Simbirsk diocese independent of Kazan diocese that necessitated the establishment of the Simbirsk mission, subordinate directly to the Synod in St. Petersburg.[7] The internal structure of these different missions was nonetheless similar. The basic model in each case was itinerary, whereby missionaries traveled about the areas under their jurisdiction, aided local clergy in encouraging non-Russians to abandon their "delusions," and proposed baptism to the unconverted. Novokreshchenye were considered "reinforced" in the faith when they signed statements to the effect that they "renounce forever their rituals and superstitious sacrifices and commit

---

[4] Cited in A. Mozharovskii, *Izlozhenie khoda missionerskogo dela po prosveshcheniiu kazanskikh inorodtsev s 1552 po 1867 goda* (Moscow, 1880), p. 134.

[5] RGIA, f. 796, op. 110, d. 793, ll. 1–270b.

[6] RGIA, f. 796, op. 116, d. 172; and RGIA, f. 796, op. 129, d. 1867.

[7] RGIA, f. 796, op. 116, d. 172, ll. 1–110b. The creation of Simbirsk diocese brought the region into conformity with a decree of 1803 calling for the boundaries of provinces and dioceses to coincide, but this creation was more immediately the result of the baptized-Tatar apostasy of 1827, as a result of which Filaret complained about the excessive size of Kazan diocese. See *Materialy dlia istorii Russkoi tserkvi: Pis'ma Vysokopreosviashchenneishego Filareta, Mitropolita Kievskogo i Galitskogo k Kirillu Arkhiepiskopu Podol'skomu*, appendix to *Pravoslavnyi sobesednik* (1876): 31, 41, 53; and "Kazanskaia eparkhiia i ee predely (Tserkovno-istoricheskii i geograficheskii ocherk)," *Pravoslavnyi sobesednik* 2 (1896): 317–26. Kazan diocese before 1832 included vast tracts on both sides of the Volga river, territory that would later compose Kazan, Simbirsk, and Samara dioceses.

themselves to go to church for prayer and to fulfill all Christian obligations voluntarily."[8] Missionaries were, of course, expected to file regular reports on their activities.[9]

Yet there were some differences among the missions as well. Those who served in Viatka diocese were usually parish clergy who knew some Mari or Udmurt, while in Kazan diocese missionaries were monastic clergy who sometimes did not know local languages and had previously had less regular contact with non-Russian parishioners.[10] Moreover, the Kazan mission placed a greater emphasis on marshaling the supervisory resources of the diocesan hierarchical structure, making the clergy itself the object of scrutiny as much as novokreshchenye. Ecclesiastical superintendents (blagochinnye) were to verify journals kept by the parish clergy twice a year "not only to scrutinize the behavior of the parish clergy but thoroughly to make note of their abilities and inabilities." These superintendents were themselves in turn subject to supervision by those appointed as missionaries, who were required to submit journals to the archbishop. Without exaggerating the contrast, one can say that the Viatka missions exhibited somewhat fewer authoritarian strains. Here missionary manuals left many of the details "to the prudence of the missionaries themselves" and envisioned a more cooperative and integrated relationship between missionary and local clergy.[11] On the whole, the Viatka missions were more nuanced, more cognizant of conditions in the village and the need to establish and develop trust, and more apt to rely on missionaries themselves to make the right choices. Still, whether monastic or white clergy, missionaries usually were of the clerical elite: they were often archpriests rather than village clergy, and many of them were already superintendents before becoming missionaries.

Significantly, although the attempt by baptized Tatars to revert to Islam had been central to the establishment of the missions, the new institutions focused comparatively little attention on this group. If the Viatka Consistory created missions specifically for Maris and Udmurts, none was established for baptized Tatars, at least until much later in 1881.[12] Likewise, the concern

---

[8] GAKO, f. 237, op. 131, d. 1282, l. 74.

[9] RGIA, f. 797, op. 3, d. 12652, ll. 17–23; RGIA, f. 796, op. 109, d. 1552, ll. 1–11; GAKO, f. 237, op. 131, d. 1283, ll. 169–76; and RGIA, f. 796, op. 110, d. 793, ll. 1–27. The major points of the proposal for Kazan province were published in Mozharovskii, Izlozhenie, pp. 165–76; and as "Instruktsiia missioneram Preosviashchennego Filareta, byvshego Arkhiepiskopa Kazanskogo," in Pravoslavnyi sobesednik 2 (1865): 35–40.

[10] Notably, Filaret had requested the establishment of a missionary institute as part of his original proposal, but the Synod, apparently balking at the expense of such an institute, rejected this request. Several missionary historians, writing later, suggested that this rejection condemned the Kazan mission to ineffectiveness, since Filaret had intended to rely on monastic clergy only until more qualified missionaries could be trained. Mozharovskii, Izlozhenie, pp. 177–78; and V. Zeletnitskii, "Ocherki missionerskoi deiatel'nosti nekotorykh kazanskikh arkhipastyrei," Pravoslavnyi blagovestnik 5 (1901): 301–4.

[11] RGIA, f. 796, op. 110, d. 793, ll. 6–150b. (citation from 150b.); and GAKO, f. 237, op. 131, d. 1283, ll. 169–76.

[12] GAKO, f. 811, op. 1, d. 207, l. 1; and ibid., d. 239, l. 1.

in Simbirsk diocese was principally with Chuvash, despite the presence there of many Muslims and at least a few thousand baptized Tatars.[13] In Kazan diocese, Archbishop Filaret also emphasized the need to work among Chuvash, the largest and most concentrated group of baptized non-Russians in the province.[14] Filaret concluded in 1833 that if most of the diocese's non-Russians (including Kräshens) were reliable Christians or at least amenable to proselytism, then novokreshchenye Tatars "offer little hope that they will accept the word of God." He accordingly requested that the mission continue its work among non-Tatars, while adopting a policy of resettlement of the "stubbornly deviating" novokreshchenye Tatars.[15] This suggestion was adopted, and thus by the 1830s the missions appear to have worked among novokreshchenye Tatars only where they were settled near other baptized non-Russians and belonged to the same parishes.

Moreover, secular authorities eventually instructed the church to avoid missionary work among Muslims. Almost as soon as missionary activity began in Simbirsk province in the mid-1830s, Muslims there became apprehensive that the government was preparing to baptize them all by force. The Ministry of Internal Affairs concluded that the church's representatives, "though animated with laudable fervor, have not always followed the rules of appropriate caution, which are indispensable in so delicate an affair as the conversion of non-Christian peoples, and especially Muslims, known for their attachment to their religion."[16] In order to calm the local population, the DDDII ordered the Simbirsk governor in 1836 to announce to Muslims in the name of the Emperor "that in accord with the rules of religious tolerance adopted by the government, their freedom of conscience will never be violated and that the government did not nor can have the intention of forcing them to change their faith, for that would be against the teaching of Christianity." Furthermore, the DDDII concluded that however desirable the conversion of non-Christians, "in light of the fanaticism of Muslims, it seems most opportune to focus predominant attention on idolaters." If for some reason the church felt compelled to send missionaries among Muslims, "then it is necessary, at the very least, *to avoid any appearance that this is being done by the directive of the government*, and not by the personal [initiative] of priests devoted to the faith."[17] Given its commitment to upholding the Christian status of novokreshchenye, the state was thus required to walk an almost impossibly fine line between making a strong enough impression on baptized novokreshchenye to keep them lodged in the "bosom"

[13] RGIA, f. 797, op. 5, d. 20775; and RGIA, f. 796, op. 116, d. 172. The Simbirsk missionaries also worked among Mordvins, but the latter group was almost universally regarded as being only marginally distinguishable from Russian peasants in terms of their Orthodox religiosity.
[14] RGIA, f. 797, op. 3, d. 12652, ll. 9–23.
[15] RGIA, f. 796, op. 109, d. 1552, ll. 253–55.
[16] RGIA, f. 821, op. 11, d. 11, l. 107.
[17] Ibid., ll. 106–13 (emphasis added).

of the church, on one hand, and not agitating excessively those formally recognized as Muslims on the other.

The state's fear of agitating Muslims was one reason missionary activity was so weak in Orenburg province, even though there were more pagans there than in any other province (over fifty thousand in the mid-nineteenth century). The state's control of the area east of the Kama river had always been rather tenuous, and the activities of the Kontora in the eighteenth century never extended to this territory. The Pugachev rebellion of 1773–75 had been especially disruptive in this region, and unrest appeared again among Muslim and pagan state peasants in 1834–35, based on rumors that they were to be transferred to court-peasant status and / or converted to Christianity.[18] Few organized missionary efforts were undertaken until 1848, when the Emperor, struck by the number of "idolaters" under the jurisdiction of the Ministry of State Domains (MGI), called on the minister to promote their conversion to Christianity. After much discussion, the Synod instructed fifteen priests to begin missionary work among the pagans in the vicinity of their parishes in early 1854, just after the outbreak of the Crimean War. The Muslim population, according to reports of the secular administration, saw in this new activity "merely the beginning of the conversion to Christianity of all non-Christians," and spread rumors "that the Turkish war was begun because the government intends to exterminate the Mohammedan faith and convert all Tatars to Christianity."[19] Whatever the currency of these rumors, the missionary activity was quickly terminated, and despite the efforts of the bishop of Orenburg to revive this work once the war was over, secular officials were extremely reluctant to endorse anything more than the creation of a few schools for the region's pagans. Indeed, the commander of the Bashkir military host was willing to countenance narrowly circumscribed missionary activity among pagans "only if the missionaries do not concern themselves with Mohammedans and in each instance declare openly that they require nothing of the latter, since the Mohammedan religion is tolerated by the government."[20] As late as the 1870s, the Orenburg governor-general resisted efforts to establish in Ufa a committee of the Orthodox Missionary Society for fear of agitating the region's Muslims.[21] In short, the circumstances in Orenburg province de-

---

[18] On the Pugachev rebellion in the region, see I. M. Gvozdikova, *Bashkortostan nakanune i v gody krest′ianskoi voiny pod predvoditel′stvom E. I. Pugacheva* (Ufa, 1999). On the unrest in 1834–35, see *Ocherki po istorii Bashkirskoi ASSR*, vol. 1, part 2 (Ufa, 1959), pp. 93–110; N. M. Druzhinin, *Gosudarstvennye krest′iane i reforma P. D. Kiseleva* (Moscow, 1946), 1:224–44; and RGIA, f. 821, op. 11, d. 11. Although there was no attempt at this time to convert non-Christians, many peasants were in fact being transferred between the Ministry of State Domains (with jurisdiction over state peasants) and the Crown Department (with jurisdiction over court peasants) at about this time. The rumors were therefore not without foundation.

[19] TsGIARB, f. I–11, op. 1, d. 560, l. 6; and RGIA, f. 796, op. 129, d. 1542, l. 2510b.

[20] TsGIARB, f. I–11, op. 1, d. 560, l. 129.

[21] "Pravoslavnoe Missionerskoe Obshchestvo," *Pravoslavnyi blagovestnik* 20 (1894): 158–59. Such a committee was finally established only in 1879.

manded that the state promote Orthodoxy with much greater circumspection than was the case in the more western provinces.

Such, then, was the basic structure of the several missions of the region by the 1830s. Each diocese, with the exception of Orenburg, had two or more missionaries entrusted with the task of "reinforcing" novokreshchenye and promoting conversion among non-Christians. Novokreshchenye Tatars quickly became identified as a special problem, while the state made clear that missionaries should avoid making any attempt to convert Muslims—or, indeed, doing anything that could possibly appear to Muslims as such an attempt. Pagans, therefore, became the principal object of the missionaries' conversion work.

Inducements and Obstacles to Baptism

Both church and state regarded baptism as an irreversible act. Drawing on the writings of holy fathers and on church directives prohibiting the renunciation of Christianity, the civil law stated, "Both those born into the Orthodox faith and those who are converted to it from other faiths are prohibited from abandoning it and accepting a new faith, even a Christian one."[22] But the sanctity of baptism required also that the ritual be performed with the necessary preparations and without force, so as to ensure that the desire "to accept baptism" was genuine. Ascertaining the genuineness of the candidate's desire to convert constituted an important aspect of the baptismal ceremony, at least in principle.[23] Existing civil law made clear that "the predominant church does not allow itself the slightest coercive means in the conversion of people of other faiths to Orthodoxy, and in no way threatens those who do not wish to join [Orthodoxy]."[24]

Already in the eighteenth century the church instituted a number of safeguards designed to ensure that baptisms were performed properly. When non-Russian complaints began to appear in the wake of the mass conversions in the 1740s, the Synod required local religious authorities to collect "written voluntary petitions" from those desiring baptism and to confirm that the candidates had been adequately instructed in the essentials of Christianity.[25] Such petitions were retained in the nineteenth century and formed part of a bureaucratic process surrounding baptism. Petitions were filed either in person or by mail with the diocesan bishop, who then requested information from civil authorities about the candidate. A local priest was then charged with performing the baptism, which occurred only after the

[22] *SZ* (1832), vol. 14, article 40.
[23] For a full description of the sacrament of baptism, see Amvrosii, "Tainstvo kreshcheniia po chinu pravoslavnoi tserkvi," *Strannik* (1864): 1–50.
[24] *SZ* (1832), vol. 14, article 73.
[25] *PSZ* I, vol. 13, no. 9825 (1750).

candidate had given a promise "of strict and lifelong observance of the Christian faith."[26] The candidate's instruction in Christianity was supposed to continue for forty days prior to baptism, with an exception in the case of life-threatening illness.[27] This process was instituted not only to ensure that the candidate was sincere in his acceptance of the faith but also to prevent excesses by local clergy and other officials—whom, as many church directives suggest, church hierarchs did not always trust to demonstrate proper judgment. The new missionaries were invested with the authority to baptize without going through this complex process.

Along with baptism came a number of material benefits (*l'goty* or *vygody*), the most significant of which were lifetime freedom from military service and a three-year tax exemption. Until 1866, non-Christians could also be freed from prosecution in the case of lesser crimes (or have sentences lightened in the case of more serious ones), and at least until 1837, converts even received cash payments and clothes after baptism.[28] Supposedly, as one author wrote, the Christian faith "does not allow any mercenary motives [*korystnykh vidov*] in its acceptance and therefore does not allow the use of such means for the conversion of nonbelievers."[29] But the idea of using material encouragements to promote conversion was not without its supporters, who offered a series of arguments to justify this practice. Pointing to the measures of Ivan the Terrible, the law code of 1649, and the directives of Peter the Great and his immediate successors, they argued that the use of benefits "has been observed in Russia since olden days" (*izdrevle*) and added that conversion would be attractive only if the material position of converts was superior to that of nonconverts.[30] Most importantly, defenders recognized that for "simple" and "ignorant" people, some material encouragement was required in order to overcome their inability to recognize the superiority of Christianity.

These sentiments received their clearest expression in Orenburg province, where officials regarded more direct forms of missionary work as potentially

---

[26] RGIA, f. 796, op. 126, d. 213, ll. 54–540b.; Amvrosii, "Tainstvo kreshcheniia," 15.

[27] In 1864 the State Council added the provision that those younger than fourteen years of age could not be baptized without the written consent of their parents or guardians. Those between the ages of fourteen and twenty-one (majority) could be baptized without their parents' permission, but only after a six-month period of instruction in Christianity (*PSZ* II, vol. 36, no. 37709 [1864]).

[28] On the establishment and implementation of material benefits, mostly in the eighteenth century, see Mozharovskii, *Izlozhenie*, pp. 41–44, 50; E. A. Malov, *O novokreshchenskoi kontore* (Kazan, 1878), pp. 35–36; Andreas Kappeler, *Rußlands erste Nationalitäten: Das Zarenreich und die Völker der Mittleren Wolga vom 16. bis 19. Jahrhundert* (Cologne, 1982), pp. 270–87. The tax exemption was confirmed in 1826 (*PSZ* II, vol. 1, no. 409 [1826]), and the exemption from military service was confirmed in the 1831 recruitment regulation (Elise Kimerling Wirtschafter, *From Serf to Russian Soldier* [Princeton, 1990], p. 13). On the elimination of privileges for converts in criminal cases, see RGIA, f. 1405, op. 63, d. 4952.

[29] "O sposobakh obrashcheniia inovertsev k Pravovere," *Pravoslavnyi sobesednik* 1 (1858): 473.

[30] Ibid.

dangerous. The bishop of Orenburg stated quite openly in 1853 that "idolaters can be more conveniently stimulated to religious acceptance of the saving Christian faith by means of material encouragements."[31] Likewise, a parish priest who had just baptized over a hundred pagans contended: "In the beginning one must win over pagans to the acceptance of the Christian faith through benefits and the promise of special protection, and only then can one explain the virtue of the Christian faith. Captured by the privileges, they understand the virtue of the Christian faith quite well."[32] The governor of Ufa wrote in 1857 that instead of relying on missionaries it would be better to ascertain "through which material privileges one may act upon pagans, so that they, not understanding the truths of the holy faith, will perceive the considerable benefit for themselves of sympathizing with the acts of the clergy and of yielding to exhortations that are intelligible to them in neither word nor meaning."[33] In short, one had to cultivate an inclination among pagans to consider conversion before they could realistically be expected to accept Christianity on its spiritual merits. To be sure, some would become critical of the use of material benefits to attract converts. The Ministry of Finance, too, understandably opposed the use of direct cash payments, which were eliminated in 1837, and rejected a proposal of the MGI to extend special privileges enjoyed by Jewish and Kalmyk converts to the peoples of the Volga-Kama region.[34] But many missionaries, clergy, and officials continued to view material benefits as a perfectly legitimate, perhaps indispensable, means of promoting conversion.

Whereas such benefits may have attracted some non-Christians to Orthodoxy, numerous other factors repelled non-Christians from baptism. Given their sense of dependence on the keremet and other indigenous spirits, on one hand, and the discipline and claims to exclusivity central to Orthodoxy, on the other, pagans understandably exhibited a reluctance to convert. As pagans, unencumbered by various "Christian obligations," they in fact enjoyed substantial religious freedom. Sources from later in the century make clear that they could still participate in many rituals of the Orthodox church and could incorporate Orthodox practices into their lives, if they so desired.[35] Thus pagans venerated certain icons, invited priests into their homes, and even attended church at times. In short, free to synthesize from their

[31] RGIA, f. 796, op. 129, d. 1542, l. 1720b.

[32] RGIA, f. 796, op. 122, d. 1014, l. 50b.

[33] TsGIARB, f. I–11, op. 1, d. 560, ll. 510b.–52.

[34] On the elimination of cash rewards, see *PSZ* II, vol. 12, no. 10135 (1837); and RGIA, f. 796, op. 118, d. 1806. On the Ministry of Finance's opposition to the extension of special payments, see RGIA, f. 383, op. 12, d. 11870.

[35] See, for example, Evgenii Popov, "Cheremisskaia missiia," *Permskie eparkhial'nye vedomosti* 5 (1874): 53; and "Kreshcheno-tatarskie shkoly v Kazanskom uchebnom okruge v 1870 godu," *VEV* 24 (1871): 492. M. A. Reisner notes the relative freedom that pagan status entailed in *Gosudarstvo i veruiushchaia lichnost': Sbornik statei* (St. Petersburg, 1905), pp. 217–20.

indigenous traditions, Christianity, and even Islam, pagans could enjoy the best of these different religious worlds.

Insofar as baptism imposed on converts the obligation of supporting parish clergy, the whole issue of *ruga* (fixed support) and emoluments created another strong disincentive to accept baptism. When asked about conversion, one Chuvash stated quite directly, "I would convert, but your priests take much *ruga* and oppress their parishioners. Maybe I'll convert right before my death." The behavior of Chuvash "sorcerers" (*iomzi*) provided a clear contrast: "They do everything for us, give us advice, but do not haggle, and we thank them, some with a grivna, others with two kopecks, [and] they take everything and do not ask for more."[36] If pagans felt incapable of abandoning indigenous forms of veneration even after their acceptance of Christianity, their baptism would lead to their incurring the costs of *both* Orthodoxy *and* paganism—that is, the costs of supporting clergy *and* of providing animals and goods for sacrifice. Although in 1849 the Kazan chamber of the MGI tried to secure at least a temporary exemption from *ruga* for those who converted, this proposal was ultimately unsuccessful.[37]

Furthermore, material benefits themselves often created difficulties and ironically even hindered the promotion of Christianity. Benefits did not always accrue in a timely fashion, and new converts sometimes filed complaints that they had not been given their benefits years after their baptism. Difficulties usually had their origin in bureaucratic confusion of one form or another.[38] But whatever the reason, converts felt deceived by missionaries who had promised them benefits and were thus subjected to ridicule by their unbaptized neighbors. One religious superintendent reported in 1828 that he had talked a village of Udmurt pagans into accepting baptism on the basis of the tax break, but after only one baptism had been performed, "the other pagans, having heard from their canton scribe that the indicated benefit from the Emperor was allegedly not being fulfilled by the secular government, and that my promise to fulfill that benefit was false, announced that they were abandoning their intention to accept holy baptism."[39] A missionary in Urzhum district related that the sluggish dispensation of benefits "produces great grumbling and complaining about me on the part of Cheremis, and coming to me in the church or in my home they call me a cheat, on ac-

---

[36] RGIA, f. 383, op. 3, d. 2332, l. 110b. For accounts of similar sentiments, see also NART, f. 4, op. 84, d. 70, ll. 1–3; E. V–n, "Soobrazheniia o sposobakh k uspeshneishemu privlecheniiu nekreshchenykh inorodtsev k vere Khristovoi dlia sviashchennikov Kazanskoi eparkhii," *Pravoslavnyi sobesednik* 1 (1871): 66.

[37] RGIA, f. 381, op. 44, d. 23503.

[38] GAKO, f. 237, op. 140, d. 1626, ll. 34–340b.; GAKO, f. 237, op. 134, d. 19; GAKO, f. 237, op. 147, d. 183; NART, f. 4, op. 75, d. 11; RGIA, f. 796, op. 117, d. 1303; RGIA, f. 383, op. 18, d. 23612; RGIA, f. 796, op. 118, d. 1806; RGIA, f. 381, op. 44, d. 23503; RGIA, f. 796, op. 117, d. 1264; RGIA, f. 383, op. 18, d. 23612; and RGIA, f. 796, op. 117, d. 1303.

[39] P. N. Luppov, ed., *Materialy dlia istorii khristianstva u votiakov v pervoi polovine XIX veka* (Viatka, 1911), p. 188. Two Udmurts did agree to be baptized nonetheless.

count of which I enjoy little trust with them."[40] As a consequence of the difficulties in processing claims for benefits, potential converts, "convinced by real-life experience of the difficulty and uncertainty of receiving benefits, do not wish to hear when missionaries refer to them."[41] It was, of course, ironic that measures designed to attract non-Christians to Orthodoxy should in many cases wind up repelling them instead.

Yet another problem was that converts tended to draw the ire of their fellow villagers when they converted. In Orenburg province, where the vast majority of animists were still officially pagan, "It is well known that all non-Russians who leave or have left their faith lose all favor among their former co-religionists; the latter look upon the former as apostates and traitors [and] try to inflict on them all kinds of trouble and avoid all contact with them."[42] Another official concurred that baptized pagans "serve as the object of ridicule and contempt of their pagan fellow villagers. Their situation is not in the least attractive and cannot induce [others] to follow their example."[43] Given that religious affiliation was, throughout Russia, the most basic source of communal identity, these perspectives are hardly surprising. They also suggest why many non-Christians were willing to consider conversion only as a collective matter. As the bishop of Simbirsk wrote of unbaptized Chuvash, "Nowhere do they allow anyone to listen to Evangelical preaching individually; but arriving as a group [*sovokupno*] and considering themselves not responsible for their deviations, at the first voice of one or two of their elders they immediately leave, not allowing anyone to stay behind and listen further to the preaching that has begun."[44] This sort of collectivism may also explain the claim, made over and over by non-Christians in different contexts, that they would be willing to convert if there were an order to that effect from the "higher authorities" or the Sovereign, presumably because this would compel *everyone* to convert (at least in a given locale), and each individual would thereby be absolved of personal responsibility for the act.

Finally, at least as regards some of the region's inhabitants, there was the problematic relationship between conversion and privileged social status. The authors of the law providing the core benefit of the three-year tax break were careful to ensure that baptism would not erase the personal tax benefits enjoyed by those with a privileged social status, such as Bashkirs and Teptiars. Thus documents indicate clearly that Bashkirs who had been baptized retained their exemption from all taxes in accordance with their previous status. Likewise Teptiars, after enjoying the three-year tax break

---

[40] GAKO, f. 237, op. 140, d. 1626, l. 34.

[41] RGIA, f. 796, op. 117, d. 1303, l. 1; and RGIA, f. 797, op. 3, d. 12654, l. 303.

[42] TsGIARB, f. I–11, op. 1, d. 560, l. 230b.

[43] Ibid., l. 520b. See also F. Zemlianitskii, "Neskol′ko slov po povodu iazycheskikh sueverii cheremis Tsarevokokshaiskogo uezda," *IKE* 8 (1871): 249.

[44] RGIA, f. 796, op. 116, d. 172, l. 26.

resulting from baptism, went back to paying only the reduced poll tax that was one of their principal privileges.[45] Nonetheless, baptism *did* require the exclusion of Bashkirs and Teptiars from their previous social status (e.g., *iskliuchenie iz bashkirskogo zvaniia*) into the state peasantry, the urban class (*meschchane*), or even the Cossacks. It was precisely for this reason that no Bashkir or Teptiar could convert without the permission of the Orenburg military governor. This exclusion from the ranks of a privileged estate, even with the personal retention of tax privileges, of course dissuaded Bashkirs and Teptiars from converting, because they lost other privileges associated with their status and were now expected to resettle in a Christian community. Moreover, any children born *after* their baptism would belong to the new unprivileged estate in all respects.[46] In short, for Bashkirs and Teptiars conversion to Orthodoxy represented a kind of social demotion.

In light of these various obstacles, it is hardly surprising that baptisms did not occur frequently or in large numbers. For example, having visited over one hundred Udmurt settlements in 1831, one missionary could report only five baptisms.[47] Another missionary in Simbirsk province in 1847 reported only twelve baptisms (one Muslim and eleven pagans) after two months of work.[48] In general, in the 1830s and 1840s Kazan, Viatka, and Orenburg dioceses averaged fewer than two hundred new baptisms of pagans per year (and these averages are skewed by a few remarkable cases of mass baptism treated below), in some years recording as few as nine conversions. At mid-century substantial pockets of pagans remained, principally in the districts of Chistopol (Kazan province), Urzhum and Malmyzh (Viatka province), and above all Belebei and Birsk (Orenburg province).[49]

Moreover, many of the baptisms that did occur were clearly mercenary in motivation. Many non-Christians agreed to baptism, by all indications, only to receive the material privileges listed above. In 1828 Udmurt pagans made no secret about their motivations when they signed a statement stating that they "wish to accept holy baptism provided that upon completion of [the baptism] the appropriate authorities be informed concerning the granting of the three-year benefit from the collection of state taxes and obligations."[50] Non-Christians also used baptism in order to terminate court cases. In 1830 one Mari accepted baptism while under investigation for an unspecified

[45] For the law, see *PSZ* II, vol. 1, no. 409 (1826). Examples of Bashkir and Teptiar conversion in the mid-1830s include TsGIARB, f. I-2, op. 1, dd. 3353, 3665, 3666, 3853, 3863, 3888, 3905, 5752, and 5994. Bashkirs were predominantly Muslim, but there were many pagans among Teptiars.

[46] These issues are addressed in a lengthy report whose authorship is not indicated, apparently written in 1854, in TsGIARB, f. I-11, op. 1, d. 560, ll. 61–900b.

[47] RGIA, f. 796, op. 110, d. 793, l. 400b.

[48] RGIA, f. 796, op. 129, d. 1867, l. 50b.

[49] RGIA, f. 796, op. 129, d. 1542, ll. 160b., 290b., 77–79. A survey of the holdings of the MGI in 1849 revealed 8,698 pagans in Kazan province; 8,134 in Viatka province; and 53,071 pagans in Orenburg province. These data reflect only those pagans who were state peasants.

[50] Luppov, *Materialy*, p. 281.

crime. His son and daughter also agreed to baptism and immediately requested their tax break, citing their family's poverty.[51] Likewise, several of the Bashkir candidates for baptism were under arrest when they expressed their willingness to convert.[52] The director of the Kazan chamber of the MGI reported that "only recruitment, which is so burdensome in their conception, and fear of punishment for crimes compel [pagans] to accept the Christian religion." He added that Tatars in particular, "having accepted the Christian faith more for personal gain than out of conviction concerning the religion's superiority, and not having learned its dogmas beforehand, little by little deviate from Orthodoxy and as a consequence have become complete apostates."[53] In general, the authorities considered Muslims more likely than others to accept baptism exclusively for material gain and in one report claimed that they sometimes sought baptism more than once using different names in order to receive benefits several times.[54]

In some cases, baptism seems to have offered the opportunity for a spouse to leave an undesirable marriage. In 1838 a recent Mari convert requested the right to remarry, citing his wife's refusal to accept baptism as well as the fact that she was six years his senior and had not been living in his home for a half-year. His wife also wanted to end the marriage, allegedly because he had converted and had baptized their son without consulting her. Although in this case the baptism itself ostensibly emerged as the issue of contention between husband and wife, the evidence suggests that there were other issues involved and that the husband perhaps used baptism to precipitate the divorce. Indeed, after confirming that the wife refused to convert, the Viatka Consistory dissolved the marriage and granted the husband the right to remarry.[55] Another newly baptized Mari made a similar request in 1836, explaining that his wife, seventeen years his senior, was blind. The wife concurred, noting that she was unable to do any housework. She planned to move in with her daughter, also a pagan, and made no claims on her husband's freedom to remarry. Again, convinced of the wife's refusal to convert, the Consistory dissolved the marriage.[56] In another case, an Udmurt husband, after having been baptized together with his wife in 1834, took a new bride with the latter's permission. But if in this case the couple sought to end their marriage through conversion, they made the mistake of both being baptized, which left their previous, pagan marriage in legal force. As a result, the husband was compelled to dismiss his new bride and to sanctify the

---

[51] GAKO, f. 237, op. 133, d. 1403, ll. 4–40b., 7. This baptism also gave the father the opportunity to enter a new marriage, since his previous wife was dying and would not agree to conversion.

[52] TsGIARB, f. I–2, op. 1, d. 5752, ll. 1–10b., 39–390b.

[53] RGIA, f. 381, op. 44, d. 23503, l. 1; and RGIA, f. 797, op. 19, d. 42689, l. 1.

[54] RGIA, f. 796, op. 126, d. 213, ll. 540b.–55. Multiple baptism had been common in the eighteenth century.

[55] RGIA, f. 796, op. 119, d. 115, ll. 1–4.

[56] RGIA, f. 796, op. 119, d. 987, ll. 1–3.

original marriage by Orthodox rite.[57] In these cases, it was notably the husband—in each case considerably younger than his wife—who desired a new spouse and evidently converted for the purpose of making this possible. While the precise motivations here remain obscure, one can safely assert that the conversion of one spouse (though emphatically *without* the baptism of the other) created at least the possibility of ending a previous marriage.[58]

In short, given the advantages of pagan status and the burdens of Orthodox affiliation, it appears that baptism became an attractive option to non-Christians primarily in the context of specific circumstances—poverty, prosecution for certain minor crimes, military recruitment, or problematic family relations. This is not to say that the resulting converts were entirely indifferent to Orthodox spirituality or steadfastly opposed the incorporation of Christian practices into their lives. Nor is it to deny that the formal transfer to Orthodox religious status represented a potentially important step toward the conscious acceptance of "Christian truths" in the longer term. But conversion was unlikely to be a purely spiritual affair as long as the state chose to invest baptism with a series of decidedly secular consequences. The government's rhetoric about baptism was clearly at odds with its own practices. Nowhere was this tension more clearly revealed than in cases of mass baptism.

Lingering Habits: Mass Baptism and Coercion

Mass baptism had been characteristic of the Kontora's activity in the mid-eighteenth century. But while the practice of inducting non-Christian communities wholesale into Orthodoxy for the most part ended with the Kontora's closing in 1764, a few such cases did occur in the nineteenth century. A brief consideration of three cases—the only ones on such a scale, to my knowledge—exposes a number of tensions in prevailing conceptions of religious affiliation and authority.

The first case involves the estate of Countess Anna Orlova-Chesmenskaia along the left bank of the Volga in Simbirsk province, where over three thousand Chuvash pagans were baptized in 1829–30. In this case, the Countess herself, concerned "not just with the material well-being of her peasants, but also with their moral improvement," seems to have played a key role in gaining the assent of her serfs to baptism.[59] Thus her stewards went about the

---

[57] GAKO, f. 237, op. 142, d. 43.

[58] Nicholas Breyfogle similarly finds the desire for de facto divorce to have been a cause for conversion among Russian sectarians in Transcaucasia. See his "Heretics and Colonizers: Religious Dissent and Russian Colonization of Transcaucasia, 1830–1890" (Ph.D. diss., University of Pennsylvania, 1998), pp. 292–94.

[59] See the account by A. Ivanov, "Grafinia Anna Alekseevna Orlova-Chesmenskaia, kak revnitel′nitsa khristianskogo prosveshcheniia inorodtsev-chuvash," *Chteniia v Imperatorskom Obshchestve Istorii i Drevnostei Rossiiskikh* 207, 4 (1903): 62–67 (quote from p. 64); and

estate "inclining" their Chuvash charges to accept Christianity. (There is unfortunately no detailed information about these efforts.) Having been baptized, in some cases by Kazan Archbishop Filaret himself, the converts received not only their tax break and exemption from military service but also direct cash payments from the government and a small silver coin each from the archbishop.[60] At the consecration of a stone church constructed for the new converts in 1834, the Countess gave out still more gifts of cash and clothing. It is hardly surprising, in light of this bonanza, that old-timers in the early twentieth century told about this event "with tender emotion."[61] Nor were the estate's stewards, as the principal agents behind the conversions, left without reward. One received a gold medal, and this example of "monarchical kindness" induced other stewards to apply their energies toward the conversion of all Chuvash on the estate (and to request further rewards for their efforts).[62] Though the details here remain obscure, presumably the material dimensions of the act and the authority of the Countess and her stewards over their serfs went a long way in securing the agreement of Chuvash to receive baptism.

Coercion evidently occupied a more prominent place in another large-scale baptism that occurred in Birsk district of Orenburg province in the mid-1840s. Here the instigators were local representatives of the MGI, which had only recently established a chamber in Orenburg province for the administration of the many state peasants there. Since its creation under the impetus of P. D. Kiselev in 1838, the MGI had been undertaking a multifaceted program of reform throughout Russia that included the establishment of parish schools for state peasants, the promotion of measures for agricultural improvement, and the advancement of standardized plans for the "correct" construction of villages and homes. The MGI viewed the religious and moral foundations provided by Orthodoxy as central to its project of ameliorating peasant life, and it therefore supplied schools with books of "Christian good conduct," sought to ensure the material well-being of the clergy, and aided in the construction of churches. The Ministry also instructed its local subordinates to ensure peasants' respect for clergy, to prevent them

---

idem, "Iz istorii khristianskogo prosveshcheniia chuvash Samarskoi gubernii," *Pravoslavnyi blagovestnik* 11 (1900): 127–28. These were secularized church lands that the Orlovs had received from Catherine II in 1768.

[60] Men over fifteen years of age received twenty rubles, ten kopecks; women older than twelve received five rubles, thirty kopecks; children received correspondingly less, though males always received more than females (RGIA, f. 796, op. 110, d. 767, ll. 27–29). Direct cash payments to converts were ended in 1837 (RGIA, f. 796, op. 118, d. 1806). A brief eyewitness account of eight hundred of these baptisms, by a certain Gustav Fokht, is cited in Mozharovskii, *Izlozhenie*, pp. 184–85 (originally published in *Pribavleniia k Kazanskomu vestniku* 1 and 10 [1830]).

[61] Ivanov, "Grafinia," 66.

[62] RGIA, f. 796, op. 110, d. 767, ll. 67–68.

from attending drinking houses until after church services, and in general to enforce religious morality in the villages.[63]

Because of the Ministry's reformist energy and its emphasis on the role of Orthodoxy, its local representatives were eager to draw pagans, whose "ignorant way of life is without argument a consequence of their crude and paltry religion," into the Christian faith.[64] And this eagerness met with its most striking success in Birsk district of Orenburg province in 1845. As a provincial newspaper recounted, the MGI district chief [*okruzhnoi nachal'nik*] N. Bludarov, accompanied by several assistants and a priest, "gradually gaining the trust of the Cheremis, finally succeeded, through the strength of convictions, in shaking their obdurate superstition. At first only a few, then a large number, and finally by whole villages, [Cheremis] decided to accept the Christian faith, and in 1845, on the clergy's lists, there appeared up to nine hundred new Christians."[65] Noting that the conversions were due "primarily to the efforts and good management" of Bludarov, and eager to incite similar zeal among other district chiefs, the Orenburg chamber of the MGI requested a reward for him from St. Petersburg.[66] A new church was constructed and was blessed by the bishop in a large ceremony involving various local officials and over three thousand participants, at which the new parishioners received crosses and icons. The new converts agreed to the destruction of a sacred grove near their villages where they had previously gathered for animist sacrifices.[67]

Shortly after the baptisms, however, certain members of the newly converted community sent a petition to the minister of state domains, explaining that Bludarov and his assistants, through torture, beatings, and threats of exile to Siberia, had forced Maris into accepting baptism. As a subsequent petition explained in greater detail, Bludarov's group, "at first having gotten the old folks drunk on alcohol and promising to give them a monetary reward, tried to talk us into accepting the Christian faith." Later, Bludarov, with a contingent consisting of his assistants, a priest, Russian peasants, and baptized Maris, visited small villages at night and by means of various

[63] On these many projects, both among non-Russians and more generally, see "Obozrenie upravleniia gosudarstvennykh imushchestv za poslednie 25 let (1825–1850)," *Sbornik Imperatorskogo Russkogo Istoricheskogo Obshchestva*, vol. 98 (St. Petersburg, 1896), 468–98; S. A. Kniaz´kov, "Graf P. D. Kiseleva i reforma gosudarstvennykh krest´ian," *Velikaia reforma* (St. Petersburg, 1911), 2:209–34; RGIA, f. 383, op. 7, d. 6109, parts a, b, and v; RGIA, f. 383, op. 9, dd. 7741, 7743, 7752, and 7772; and *SZ* (1842), vol. 2, esp. articles 1117, 1118, 1119, 1122, 1142, 1148, 2932, and 2954.

[64] Such was the characterization of the director of the MGI's Orenburg chamber (RGIA, f. 796, op. 126, d. 213, l. 920b.).

[65] "O kreshchenii cheremis Birskogo uezda," *Orenburgskie gubernskie vedomosti* 43 (1846): 518. See also the account in V. M. Cheremshanskii, *Opisanie Orenburgskoi gubernii v khoziastvenno-statisticheskom, etnograficheskom i promyshlennom otnosheniiakh* (Ufa, 1859), pp. 182–83.

[66] RGIA, f. 383, op. 8, d. 6977, ll. 4–40b.

[67] Ibid., ll. 117–170b.

threats and coercion managed to convert "many in various villages, in all around six hundred souls and even more."[68]

However eager to promote Orthodoxy, the Ministry in St. Petersburg demanded an explanation from its subordinates, adding that "however desirable the conversion of non-Christians to the Christian religion [may be], *no forceful measures whatsoever should be allowed*." The Governor of Orenburg province, too, requested the bishop to report "whether the Cheremis were brought into the Christian faith by their own desire, or by the order of the local authorities."[69] Church officials later admitted that "the means of action was not in accordance with the laws," and even officials who openly denied the petitioners' claims agreed that "some irregularities" had occurred.[70] The Synod itself was deeply skeptical of the whole affair and charged the bishop to investigate whether or not the converts had accepted Christianity "with heartfelt inclination." Local clergy were to be reminded that "rushed conversion to Christianity, not based on conviction, not only does not benefit the church, but on the contrary harms it, by bringing ruinous examples of apostasy, and by requiring the assistance of civil authorities and measures of severity and punishment, which do not accord with the peaceful paths by which the church attains its goals of salvation."[71] Although the Maris' complaint was never actually vindicated—all the "converts" were required to accept their new Christian status—it did precipitate a lengthy investigation and probably helped to prevent a collective baptism of much larger dimensions, since the central authorities enjoined their local subordinates to exercise greater circumspection in the future. Still, the apparent abuses that the investigation revealed were disregarded in order not to compromise the sanctity of baptism itself.[72] Once performed, baptism simply could not be reversed.

In the following decade a similar case developed among Chuvash court peasants (serfs of the imperial family), who were under the jurisdiction of the Crown Department. This department had an ethos remarkably similar to that of the MGI—indeed, the former's policies served as a model for the latter's reform projects—and its attitude toward its non-Russian dependents, mostly Mordvins and Chuvash, was similar as well.[73] Allotting funds for the construction of nine new churches among Chuvash in Buinsk district, the

[68] Ibid., ll. 23–24.

[69] Ibid., l. 3 (emphasis in the original); RGIA, f. 796, op. 126, d. 213, ll. 250b.–26.

[70] RGIA, f. 796, op. 126, d. 213, ll. 40, 930b.

[71] Ibid., l. 64.

[72] I have considered this investigation and the whole affair at greater length in "Baptism, Authority, and the Problem of *Zakonnost'* in Orenburg Diocese: The Induction of Over 800 'Pagans' into the Christian Faith," *Slavic Review* 56, 3 (1997): 456–80.

[73] In the 1820s–1830s, the Department acquired extensive holdings in the Middle Volga region, so that by 1850 almost 36% of its 800,000 peasant dependents were in Simbirsk province. On court peasants generally, see *Istoriia Udelov za stoletie ikh sushchestvovaniia, 1797–1897*, 3 vols. (St. Petersburg, 1901); and V. A. Bogoliubov, "Udel'nye krest'iane," in *Velikaia reforma* (St. Petersburg, 1911), 2: 234–54.

Department remarked that those novokreshchenye, "in comparison to other peasants of the crown bureaucracy, [are] in a very bad condition, and the reason for this is their laziness, deep-rooted prejudices, and superstitions, their very untidy way of life, and their ruined morality." Their habit of drinking heavily in conjunction with their "idolatrous rituals . . . is without doubt one of the principal reasons for their poverty." Christianity, needless to say, was indispensable for their moral and material improvement.[74] In 1857 the chairman of the Crown Department noticed that some of its Chuvash dependents were still officially pagans, and he therefore instructed his subordinates in Simbirsk province to encourage their conversion to Orthodoxy. From Simbirsk, local chiefs (*golovy*) accordingly received a remarkable directive calling on them to take "the most active measures" for the pagans' conversion, "using, to incline and admonish those pagans, all wisdom, which, while not violating the lawful order, would *without fail* have complete success in making them Christians and compelling them to fulfill the rules of the Christian faith. The [local] chief is informed that success in this important matter will bestow on him particular distinction, for which he will not remain without reward from the authorities."[75] Shortly thereafter, the Simbirsk office reported that one thousand pagans had been baptized (leaving only forty-nine holdouts in its jurisdiction). But, as in Orenburg province a decade earlier, Chuvash quickly filed a complaint, in this case to the minister of internal affairs, in which they wrote: "For several centuries we and our ancestors, living under the protection of the laws of our most merciful Emperors were not coerced into accepting the Orthodox faith." But now, canton chiefs (who in many cases were themselves baptized Chuvash) had come to their villages with a priest and a few helpers "to baptize us all, if not voluntarily, then by force," using the following method: "seeing a person coming out of his home, [and] having grabbed him, they bring him to a chamber and baptize him there." Many Chuvash had thus abandoned their homes and gone into hiding, some of them across the border in Kazan province.[76]

The Simbirsk office countered that the accusation amounted to "just a lie," and that neighboring Muslim Tatars had encouraged the plaintiffs to file their bogus complaint.[77] But Chuvash continued to file petitions over the course of 1858–59, contending that the forceful measures continued. A secret inquiry revealed that local authorities had indeed compelled Chuvash to

[74] RGIA, f. 796, op. 119, d. 255, ll. 1–2.

[75] Cited in E. A. Malov, *Missionerstvo sredi mukhammedan i kreshchenykh tatar* (Kazan, 1892), p. 198. The emphasis appears to have been added by Malov.

[76] RGIA, f. 821, op. 133, d. 428, ll. 1–10b., 14–15, 17; and RGIA, f. 515, op. 8, d. 2120, ll. 1–6, 10–16ob., 24–24ob. The missionary E. A. Malov heard a similar account from local informants (*Missionerstvo*, pp. 197–98).

[77] Indeed, those Chuvash who desired to confess Islam were among the most active in protesting the conversion campaign with petitions. RGIA, f. 515, op. 8, d. 2120, ll. 15–16ob., 37–37ob., 50–51, 54–55, 63–63ob.

show up and at least listen to the missionary, which was standard and legitimate practice. Yet the inquiry was also compelled to allow that coercion had perhaps been involved in the baptisms themselves. But here, too, the authorities refused to give the petitioners satisfaction on the basis of this admission, because—stated baldly—"the act of baptism, entered into the registries, cannot be reversed."[78] In short, even when non-Russian complaints were fully justified, imperial authorities could not admit this fact, or at least act on it. To do so would be to invite chaos, officials believed. Given their "ignorance" and "simplicity," the mass of rural non-Russians were bound to misconstrue the acknowledgment of excess in one particular case as a general authorization of apostasy. Although non-Russians were the losers in such instances, it is worth highlighting that officials themselves were essentially prisoners of a dynamic that was in large measure beyond their control.

In none of these three cases of mass baptism did missionaries play any significant role. In each instance secular authorities took the lead in promoting baptism, though for various reasons. If Countess Orlova-Chesmenskaia's promotion of baptism reflected her concern for the moral improvement of her dependents, then in Simbirsk province the very presence of pagans in the Crown Department's holdings constituted a source of embarrassment crying out for rectification. In Orenburg province, meanwhile, baptism offered officials of the newly established MGI, charged with executing an interventionist reform program in a culturally diverse region, a way of prying open indigenous communities and governing them more effectively.[79] In each case, the authority enjoyed by stewards and officials over their dependents make it difficult, if not impossible, to distinguish persuasion from compulsion (although if the petitions filed by unhappy converts contain any truth, the issue of coercion is clear enough). In any event, ecclesiastical figures were marginal in these cases, performing the sacrament after others had prepared the ground.

Yet despite the apparent application of coercion—to one degree or another—in each of these cases, at least some of the new converts seem to have accepted their baptism with equanimity. On Orlova's estate, in fact, we have no evidence that Chuvash opposed the baptisms. An eyewitness to some of the baptisms wrote that the new converts parted with the Archbishop ("their enlightener") with great sorrow, took communion "with the greatest reverence," and prayed "with zeal" in the mobile Cossack church that was temporarily installed in the vicinity of their villages.[80] By all indications, the event retained a distinctly positive valuation among those who could recollect it. In Orenburg province, if a number of Maris contested the legitimacy of their baptism by Bludarov and his associates, others were prepared to

[78] RGIA, f. 821, op. 133, d. 428, ll. 17–170b.
[79] This is my argument in "Baptism, Authority, and the Problem of *Zakonnost'*," esp. pp. 476–77.
[80] Cited in Mozharovskii, *Izlozhenie*, pp. 184–85.

testify that no one had been subjected to any compulsion.[81] In Simbirsk province, too, the evidence suggests that complaints were filed by a minority—those with aspirations to adopt Islam, who realized that they would never be able to do so if baptized—and that many of the local chiefs who carried out the directive were themselves baptized Chuvash. It was in no small measure the divisions *within* these indigenous communities that allowed the authorities to assert with confidence—even in the face of compelling evidence to the contrary—that the complaints had arisen not because of actual abuses but rather because of instigation by external agents, whether Muslim Tatars or "malevolent zealots of paganism." In short, different villages and even individuals seem to have regarded the question of baptism differently, with the result that some pagans required only a small push to secure their acquiescence, while others would submit only after the deployment of considerable force.

The latter group tenaciously filed petitions exposing the circumstances leading to their baptism. These petitioners were nonetheless careful to phrase their discontent in highly deferential terms, portraying themselves as good subjects, appealing to the sentiments of the Emperor or specific ministers, and referring to both the law and a tradition of religious toleration as the foundation for their complaints. The Mari petitioners made quite clear that they were prepared to submit to baptism if they could ascertain that this was indeed the will of the sovereign or the "higher authorities." The proxy for the Mari petitioners, Shamatbai Shumatov, explained how he and several of his comrades "set out to ascertain in legal places whether it was true that they were forcing us to accept the Christian faith in accordance with a directive from the Sovereign Emperor, but in the city nobody knew anything about this." Concluding that the actions of MGI district chief Bludarov lacked legitimacy and should therefore be overturned, Shumatov ended his petition with the following statement: "If I, Shumatov, hear either a directive from the higher authorities or a command from the Sovereign Emperor, then I am prepared to obey and will even try to persuade other peasants of other villages to accept the Christian faith, *for this I expect from Your Honor a most gracious directive.*"[82] Although one can see in such statements a calculated and even disingenuous effort to emphasize submission in order to exploit the good Tsar myth to maximum effect, they also reflect an awareness of the existing provisions on tolerance and the prohibition on the use of force for conversion, coupled with an acknowledgment of the authority of the Emperor and the "higher authorities" to initiate legislative change. This approach was potentially fruitful insofar as the conversion campaign undertaken by local officials of the MGI and the Crown Department, to judge by the available evidence, did violate existing law and procedure. Unknown to

---

[81] RGIA, f. 383, op. 8, d. 6977, ll. 14–19.
[82] Ibid., ll. 23–25, 132 (emphasis in the original).

the Mari and Chuvash petitioners was the degree to which the *fact* of baptism trumped any and all other concerns.

The cases here suggest that even when baptism represented a traumatic and violent experience for non-Christians, it was by no means without its advantages. Aside from the material incentives already discussed, we might note that baptism offered new converts the possibility of receiving protection from powerful local figures. Countess Orlova's patronage was clearly demonstrated in her generous dispensation of gifts to converts at the consecration of the new church. In the case of one prominent Chuvash pagan who had initially refused to convert, the Countess even agreed to serve personally as his godmother at his baptism and then granted him three hundred desiatins of land.[83] In the other cases, officials sought to achieve a certain reconciliation with the new converts and to represent their patronage symbolically through food and wine. Thus the Mari converts, after the consecration of their new church, were treated to food and drink, while the pagans present (who had apparently been bullied into attending the consecration) were explicitly excluded.[84] Chuvash in Simbirsk province, likewise, were evidently offered drink immediately after their conversion.[85] Perhaps the clearest example comes from yet another case in Orenburg province, when 157 pagans had been induced to accept baptism under the influence of another local MGI district chief. When all the new converts had returned from the river in which they had been baptized, the district chief, "holding in his hand a glass of simple wine, congratulated them on their acceptance of holy baptism, and having drunk the glass, he kissed all of them, young and old, *and said that he would be their protector.*"[86] He thus established a kind of covenant with the new converts, whereby they would receive "protection" and special treatment. In each case, the advantages of this "protection" and patronage were at least implicit, if not obvious, while those who refused to accept baptism could presumably expect further trouble.

Also prominent in all three cases is the role played by rewards for secular authorities. The Russian law code contained explicit provisions for rewarding those responsible for the conversion of over one hundred people with the order of St. Anne.[87] On the estate of Countess Orlova, several stewards were clearly enticed to convert more Chuvash in order to receive recognition and perhaps a gold medal. Bludarov in Orenburg province was at least recommended for a reward (though it is not clear whether he actually received one) specifically with the goal of encouraging such zeal on the part of his col-

[83] Ivanov, "Grafinia," 66.

[84] RGIA, f. 383, op. 8, d. 6977, ll. 117–18; "O kreshchenii," 519.

[85] Malov, *Missionerstvo*, p. 197.

[86] RGIA, f. 796, op. 122, d. 1014, l. 4 (emphasis added). This was the account of the priest who performed the baptisms.

[87] The law originally provided this award for those who converted "a significant number of people," which in 1829 the Emperor defined as being more than one hundred persons (*PSZ* II, vol. 4, no. 3348 [1829]).

leagues. In Simbirsk province local chiefs were explicitly promised "distinction" and "reward" if they could succeed in baptizing the pagans in their jurisdiction. In principle at least, each local official or steward fortunate enough to have pagans in his jurisdiction enjoyed a remarkable opportunity to prove his capacities to his superiors, who were almost always receptive to such efforts as long as they did not violate the established legal order too blatantly.

In focusing on material benefits, social status, and the apparent abuse of authority, I do not mean to expunge spiritual and moral concerns from the process of baptism. Such concerns are, however, almost entirely absent in the historical record. We lack the kinds of conversion narratives that several historians have uncovered in the case of Russian sectarians and Baptists, which show us the deep spiritual issues that such converts confronted and attempted to resolve through conversion.[88] Considering those narratives against the issues that have emerged in our account, one might be inclined to view conversions in the Volga-Kama region with a certain cynicism, to suggest that they were somehow "not genuine." No doubt, the official church's own focus on the spiritual dimension of baptism makes it difficult to accept that these were fully legitimate baptisms even by the standards of the day.

In this particular historical context, however, and especially for those situated at the intersection of these different religious worlds, baptism signaled something other than a change in religious consciousness on the part of the convert. For communities that still regarded religious affiliation primarily as a collective matter, the idea of religious "conviction" was by all indications too individualistic to serve as the predominant factor in the determination of one's confessional allegiances. Baptism for many thus served as a kind of safety valve—a last resort when pagans or Muslims were confronted with conscription, extreme poverty, or criminal prosecution. For local secular officials, baptism offered a way to establish more effective control over subordinates. For the local parish clergy, entrusted with the task of ensuring that the desire to be baptized was genuine and spiritually motivated, even the questionable induction of non-Christians into Orthodoxy could be seen as a first step in a longer process of religious acculturation. Viewed from this perspective, no conversion, no matter how worldly in motivation, was entirely devoid of a potentially larger spiritual significance. Even the central authorities, while looking askance at some of the practices of their local subordinates, made it clear that religious conviction was not the central issue in baptism by steadfastly refusing to reinstate non-Christian status even when recent converts explicitly stated that they did not want to be Christians. Although the central authorities generally refrained from promoting baptism through coercion and demanded explanations when unhappy converts filed

---

[88] See, for example, Heather Jean Coleman, "The Most Dangerous Sect: Baptists in Tsarist and Soviet Russia, 1905–1929" (Ph.D. diss., University of Illinois, 1998), chapter 2.

petitions of protest, they were usually prepared to accept the consequences after coerced baptisms had occurred, especially if the protesters could be made to submit. At the very least, baptism placed some kind of moral authority over pagans, who otherwise had no recognized clergy through whom the state might confidently transmit the basic moral values of hierarchy and obedience that lay at the foundation of the traditional order.[89] Even as baptism rhetorically involved revelation and new consciousness, its greater significance lay in the new social relationships that were created through it.

Still, it should be emphasized that—whatever the combination of spiritual conviction, material encouragement, and even coercion—on the whole, new baptisms occurred with relative infrequency in the nineteenth century, especially since the largest group of non-Christians (Muslims) were for the most part exempt from missionary overtures, and the state remained apprehensive about having missionaries operate in Orenburg province, where most pagans actually resided. Accordingly, novokreshchenye—those already baptized—remained the principal object of the missions' work.

[89] In the absence of a clergy, there was no coherent system for registering births, marriages, deaths, and other vital statistics among pagans. The administrative confusion that arose over pagan marriages is addressed in RGIA, f. 821, op. 133, d. 428, ll. 5–9, 59–670b., 104–10; and RGIA, f. 821, op. 10, d. 779, ll. 1–25.

4   The Limits of Missionary Intervention

However desirable the baptism of pagans in the region, novokreshchenye nonetheless remained a much larger problem for church and state alike. They vastly outnumbered pagans, and both their poor grasp of "Christian truths" and their animist and Islamic recidivism offended Orthodox sensibilities and challenged the church's authority. This recidivism was all the more distressing given that most novokreshchenye communities had been Orthodox, at least formally, for close to a century by the 1830s. At the core of the new missions' concerns was therefore the task of imposing religious discipline on wayward novokreshchenye and devising ways to deepen their attachment to Orthodoxy.

Although the church adopted different strategies to achieve these goals, and although it largely avoided the problem of both Muslims and baptized Tatars, its missionary work frequently encountered obstacles and difficulties, particularly in its early years. The church continued to lack qualified candidates for clerical service, and the translation of religious texts into native languages raised a whole series of problems. Laws on religious toleration forced missionaries to tread carefully in their attempts to discipline novokreshchenye while also respecting the religious rights of pagans. Perhaps most significant was the Emperor's injunction to treat pagan recidivism as "a fruit of ignorance and age-old prejudice" requiring "spiritual admonition" rather than prosecution,[1] which helped fuel non-Russians' defiance and prevented local officials from taking the more "urgent" measures that many of them considered necessary. Throughout the 1830s–1840s, therefore, many novokreshchenye continued to perform animist rituals, rendered

[1] P. N. Luppov, *Vzgliad Imperatora Nikolaia I na mery k utverzhdeniiu votiakov v khristianstve* (Viatka, 1906), p. 5.

only partial deference to missionaries, and to a degree "indigenized" Orthodoxy by forcing authorities into compromises that diluted Christian concepts and practices in native cosmologies.[2]

Novokreshchenye's "Religious Condition"

Indications of the weakness of non-Russian attachments to Orthodoxy arose even prior to the Tatar apostasy and Mari gatherings in 1827–28.[3] But it was really only when missionaries began their work that a clearer picture of novokreshchenye's "religious condition" began to emerge. That picture was far from encouraging from the church's standpoint. In addition to sacrificing animals in sacred groves and venerating keremets, novokreshchenye were supposedly inclined to heavy drinking during their animist rituals. In one case Udmurts, "having been distracted by the unbaptized Cheremis and Tatars who live in their village, spent the last three days of Holy Week in drunkenness." In another instance an Udmurt even died during a pagan prayer because of his "excessive use of *kumyshka* and beer." The church viewed such drunkenness not just as foolishness and immorality, but as "open scorn for the Holy regulations of the Orthodox church." Clergy therefore requested that nearby unbaptized villagers, who were accused of deliberately conducting pagan holidays to interfere with Christian ones, be restrained by the secular authorities.[4]

Furthermore, clergy reported that their Mari parishioners "almost never" went to church and "consider our efforts to persuade and remind them to be an insult, and for this reason alone raise complaints against us."[5] Similarly, novokreshchenye often ignored important Orthodox sacraments, hiding newborn children from clergy to prevent their baptism or disregarding Orthodox marriage and living in "debauched cohabitation" (*bludnoe sozhitel'stvo*). Because parishioners married off their daughters at young ages without the knowledge of parish clergy, "illegal cohabitation among Votiaks and Cheremis, in spite of all the admonitions of parish priests, does not

[2] On the question of "indigenization," I draw on Gauri Viswanathan, *Outside the Fold: Conversion, Modernity, and Belief* (Princeton, 1998), esp. pp. 39–43; and on the issue of syncretism, see Rosalind Shaw and Charles Stewart, eds., *Syncretism / Anti-Syncretism: The Politics of Religious Synthesis* (London, 1994).

[3] See, for example, the case of a remarkable Mordvin "false prophet" in 1808–10 in my "Armed Defiance and Biblical Appropriation: Assimilation and the Transformation of Mordvin Resistance, 1740–1810," *Nationalities Papers* 27, 2 (1999): 247–70.

[4] RGIA, f. 796, op. 118, d. 73, ll. 165ob.–66; RGIA, f. 797, op. 5, d. 20775; RGIA, f. 1473, op. 1, d. 15, l. 447; and RGIA, f. 797, op. 5, d. 20785, l. 3. See also Aleksandra Fuks's description of a Mari wedding in *Zapiska Aleksandry Fuks o chuvashakh i cheremisakh Kazanskoi gubernii* (Kazan, 1840), pp. 226–27.

[5] NRF MarNII, op. 1, d. 43, ll. 45–46. See also P. N. Luppov, ed., *Materialy dlia istorii khristianstva u votiakov v pervoi polovine XIX veka* (Viatka, 1911), p. 184; and Petr Denisov, *Religioznye verovaniia chuvash: Istoriko-etnograficheskie ocherki* (Cheboksary, 1959), p. 260.

cease, and their ancient habit of taking girls and widows of their own accord [*samovol'no*] and living with them as spouses without marriage does not end."[6] In defense, novokreshchenye often claimed that they had been unable to consecrate the marriage because their priest demanded an exorbitant sum to perform the rite—accusations that the clergy, of course, denied vehemently. In some cases religious authorities returned the young girls in question to their parents and placed them under the strict supervision of the parish priest. In other cases, because illegitimate children had already appeared, the marriage was sanctified by Orthodox rite and the children baptized.[7]

Novokreshchenye also ignored confession and communion, two essential "Christian obligations." While in some cases floods and other natural conditions were to blame, authorities admitted that parishioners' failure "is sooner due to their indolence, although during visitations [by the missionary] they were repeatedly told about the necessity and benefit of these sacraments." When a missionary suggested that clergy be sent out to confess novokreshchenye in their own villages, the bishop of Viatka responded that this "would mean giving these people occasion to forget about the [parish] church entirely." Instead, the guilty parties were ordered to bow down ten times in the presence of the canton chief before the Icon of the Savior for each year they had missed confession.[8]

Missionaries identified women as a particular problem. Because women tended to be religiously conservative, they had "a very great, and consequently very harmful, influence on Cheremis families." As Viatka Bishop Kirill contended in 1830, "Newly converted Cheremis of the male sex, who are not yet sufficiently consolidated in Orthodoxy, hearing each day harmful advice and requests about the old faith from their wives, and heeding the suggestions, orders, and even curses of their mothers, could easily return to their earlier paganism."[9] Women's stronger attachment to paganism derived in part, it seems, from the church's focus on heads of households and the assumption that the latter's familial authority would ensure the Christianization of the rest.[10] It also appears that women's sphere of activity was decidedly more domestic than men's, and women were thus less likely to know Russian. Though several missionaries proposed focusing special attention

---

[6] Luppov, *Materialy*, p. 106; and GAKO, f. 237, op. 139, d. 1759, l. 2.

[7] GAKO, f. 237, op. 134, d. 204; GAKO, f. 237, op. 135, d. 1146; and RGIA, f. 796, op. 118, d. 73, ll. 225–250b.

[8] GAKO, f. 237, op. 139, d. 1749, ll. 1–2, 13–14.

[9] RGIA, f. 797, op. 3, d. 12654, ll. 221–22. In the 1890s ethnographers continued to note that women remained favorably disposed to animism and would sometimes perform pagan offerings without their husbands' knowledge. See N. Troitskaia, "Cheremisy Arbanskoi volosti," *IOAIE* 11, 1 (1893): 82.

[10] The original missionary charter in Viatka province required that missionaries obtain promises to observe Christianity only from the heads of household (RGIA, f. 796, op. 110, d. 793, l. 14).

on women, little appears to have been done in this regard before the 1860s or so. Yet women were not always the most religiously conservative, and in some cases they were cited for their readiness to fulfill confession and their zealous attendance at church.[11]

In their dealings with Orthodox authorities, novokreshchenye insisted that their attachment to paganism was essentially beyond their control. They explained that they had promised their fathers to uphold the "old faith" and were thus under an obligation to continue performing these rituals.[12] To this they added simply that it was too dangerous to defy native spirits, positing that they would all perish if they failed "to live in the old way."[13] Thus, while one group of novokreshchenye Udmurts listened attentively to a missionary and "even became inclined to fulfill the will of the authorities and to affirm themselves within the Christian faith," they were nonetheless unwilling to abandon animism and especially the keremet, "saying everywhere in many voices: that they cannot abandon the faith and law of their elders; that it is impossible to leave the keremet, which will destroy every last one of them if they do."[14] On numerous occasions novokreshchenye justified their performance of animist rituals as a response to bad agricultural conditions: excessive rain, drought, or pestilence among their livestock, which they interpreted as punishment for their failure to supplicate native spirits.[15] Missionaries recognized that for novokreshchenye to abandon animism was no small matter. As one wrote, "Paternal traditions, which are especially agreeable to [Maris] because they released them from all fasts and permitted debauched living and other indecencies, were more valuable to them than anything on earth. To part with them forever: that meant for them to make the most important sacrifice in life, to change their nature, to be reborn."[16]

The Problem of Missionary Authority

The missions proved to be a challenge not just to novokreshchenye but also to parish clergy. Missionaries were specifically instructed to find out whether parishioners had any "claims" (*pretenzii*) against their clergy.[17] For lacking knowledge of their parishioners' language, a number of parish priests lost their posts or were transferred to others, in one case "with the

---

[11] RGIA, f. 796, op. 123, d. 1216, l. 570b.; and RGIA, f. 796, op. 129, d. 1867, l. 20b.
[12] GAKO, f. 237, op. 132, d. 1463, l. 4; RGIA, f. 797, op. 3, d. 12654, l. 230b.; and RGIA, f. 796, op. 123, d. 1216, l. 650b.
[13] RGIA, f. 796, op. 118, d. 73, l. 190.
[14] RGIA, f. 796, op. 110, d. 793, ll. 39–390b.
[15] In one case, for example, a pagan ritual was undertaken in response to disease that decimated 90% of parishioners' livestock (RGIA, f. 796, op. 123, d. 1216, l. 43).
[16] GAKO, f. 237, op. 132, d. 1463, l. 100b.
[17] NART, f. 7, op. 72, d. 27, ll. 2–28; A. Odoev, "Stranichka proshlogo (Istoricheskie nabroski)," *VEV* 7 (1901): 367.

deprivation of all the movable and immovable possessions I have rightfully acquired over the course of twenty years."[18] In some cases priests contested a missionary's report, arguing that it was the product of "very rushed passage" through the parish, or that they in fact knew the languages of the parishioners or that the latter spoke sufficient Russian.[19] The truth of these claims is virtually impossible to ascertain, but more than once local priests, faced with the prospect of losing their parish after an unfavorable missionary report, rather suddenly claimed sufficient command of the local languages. Occasionally, local priests received recognition and reward based on a good missionary report.[20] But it appears that in many cases, as the priest Sergei Nurminskii recalled from his childhood, that the arrival of a missionary "had no effect whatsoever on either the clergy or non-Russians, except fear."[21]

In these conditions, priests were, of course, eager to present their parishes as positively as possible. They tried to highlight the good religious condition of parishioners, noting only isolated cases of "idolatry," "superstition," or "stubbornness." On closer inspection, of course, many of these assertions turned out to be inaccurate, and even missionaries themselves sometimes engaged in such deceit. In 1838 the report of a missionary in Iaransk district that the Maris in his jurisdiction "all zealously confess Christianity" was contradicted by the bishop's own survey of the area a short time later, which revealed that "in many settlements" villagers tenaciously maintained their "old faith."[22] Fortunate clergy learned ahead of time that a missionary would visit them, which gave them an opportunity to bring their parishes into order, as Nurminskii recounted:

> For example, a missionary comes to village N. The priest learns about this beforehand and hurries to the district police chief in the city: "Thus and so, dear sir, please help me, and I will pray to God for you. . ." At the same time he tries to gain the police chief's favor by offering what he can. The police chief promises to help. . . . Just before the arrival of the missionary, the police chief hurries to the parish and, having gathered the parishioners in the church, firmly demands complete silence under threat of terrible reprisal. Furthermore, he sends his agents to the place where the parishioners will gather [for the missionary]. The parishioners are quiet and pray zealously in the church. The missionary sees this and reports to his superiors, who consider the matter and decide to reward the priest of village N. for the healthy and zealous execution of his duties.[23]

[18] Luppov, *Materialy*, pp. 180–82.
[19] Ibid., pp. 180–82; and NART, f. 4, op. 1, d. 3659.
[20] For example, a priest in Sviiazhsk district was cited for his tireless efforts among baptized Tatars. NART, f. 4, op. 66, d. 74.
[21] S. Nurminskii, "Inorodcheskie prikhody," *Pravoslavnoe obozrenie* 12 (1863): 253.
[22] RGIA, f. 796, op. 118, d. 73, l. 51.
[23] Nurminskii, "Inorodcheskie prikhody," 253 (ellipses in the original). For another case, see NART, f. 7, op. 91, d. 108.

Increasingly—especially in Kazan province—missionary reports became very standardized, offering merely a generic hierarchy of Christianization, according to which Mordvins occupied the top rung, Chuvash and Maris exhibited somewhat greater "delusions," and novokreshchenye Tatars often did not bother attending church even when missionaries visited.[24]

In defining the relationship of its missionaries with local secular authorities, the church was faced with two broadly contradictory needs. On one hand, it sought to protect its sphere of influence and resist secular intrusions. Thus, when the Viatka governor in 1834 proposed the establishment of a special committee for more effective coordination of the mission, with representatives from both the secular and religious bureaucracies, Bishop Nil (Isakovich) flatly dismissed the committee as superfluous and intrusive: "In its essence, the matter of conversion to the Christian faith and reinforcement within it directly concerns the servitors of the church, and its direction toward a happy end belongs predominantly to the religious jurisdiction, and not to the civil."[25] On the other hand, missionaries depended on the secular authorities to demonstrate that their activities actually enjoyed imperial sanction. Indeed, religious authorities more often complained about secular officials' failure to respond to their requests than about their undue interference. Thus A. Pokrovskii, the first missionary sent to Mari settlements in 1829, accused the Viatka governor of failing to fulfill the actions requested of him—for example, the destruction of sacred Mari groves.[26] Another missionary encountered a similar response when he sought the aid of the canton chief, who not only refused to fulfill his request to knock down an Udmurt sacred hut, but, as the missionary reported, even defended the Udmurts and "said to me some rather offensive words."[27] Secular officials were sometimes unwilling to persecute non-Russians for what they viewed as harmless fun, but what the church viewed as dangerous and anti-Christian.[28]

More damaging still to the mission's success were personal antagonisms between missionaries and local officials. We have already seen how Pokrovskii encountered resistance from some Maris who had been assured by a local police official that they could remain pagans. A more dramatic conflict began in 1835, when a missionary accused the Iaransk district police chief of allowing Maris their old practices and even inciting them to submit a petition to St. Petersburg. In the contradictory testimonies that followed, the secular and religious bureaucracies defended their respective subordinates, until everyone finally agreed that further publicity of the matter "may weaken success in the conversion of pagans to the Christian faith and destabilize those who have already converted." Only after a year had

---

[24] Examples of such reports include NART, f. 4, op. 1, dd. 2390 and 4345.
[25] RGIA, f. 796, op. 115, d. 165, ll. 7–10. The Synod fully supported Nil's conclusion.
[26] RGIA, f. 797, op. 3, d. 12654, l. 1710b.
[27] Luppov, *Materialy*, p. 186.
[28] RGIA, f. 796, op. 117, d. 1454; and NART, f. 2, op. 1, d. 2218.

passed was Bishop Nil able to report that Maris had "calmed down."[29] In 1839 another missionary accused a police official of having incited baptized Udmurts to file charges of extortion against him.[30] Although they recognized the need for a unified front with respect to novokreshchenye, senior government officials were not always able to prevent their subordinates from drawing novokreshchenye into their personal disputes.

Native reactions to missionary intrusions varied from village to village and above all situationally. Some non-Russians "readily" listened to missionaries' discourses about "the Russian faith" with a certain curiosity. One missionary reported that Maris in one settlement changed clothes and met him with bread and salt, while others accepted him "with kindness and readiness to listen."[31] In some cases local parishioners even complained about others in their villages, who, "secretly executing their earlier rituals, force them to do the same," and requested that measures be taken to reduce the influence of local pagan neighbors.[32] Notably, some parishioners located an extraordinary distance from their parish church showed themselves receptive to Orthodoxy, while certain villages along major roads, with greater exposure to Russians, were demonstrably hostile to missionary overtures and even made use of their knowledge of Russian to defend their traditions "with eloquent expressions." In one such case a missionary asked rhetorically, "Considering the good manners of the residents and their use of pure Russian language, who would think that these Russians by speech [*po narechiiu rusaki*] are pagans."[33]

The principal concern of missionaries initially was to secure from novokreshchenye pledges "that they forever renounce their rituals and superstitious sacrifices and promise to go to church for prayer and fulfill all Christian obligations voluntarily."[34] Novokreshchenye were to confirm statements prepared by missionaries by attaching their *tamgi*, small personal marks of identity that were used by non-Russians of the region in place of signatures. Typically, after giving such promises, novokreshchenye were anointed with oil and had their homes and livestock sprinkled with holy water—a set of rituals that they understood to constitute their "induction into the Russian faith." The missionaries themselves referred to the extraction of these promises explicitly as "conversion," even though the vast majority of the villagers were already formally Christian. While some reports suggest that such promises were

---

[29] RGIA, f. 796, op. 116, d. 891 (citations from ll. 60b., 200b.); and RGIA, f. 796, op. 118, d. 73, ll. 550b.–56.

[30] RGIA, f. 796, op. 120, d. 1631.

[31] GAKO, f. 237, op. 132, d. 1463, ll. 8, 24.

[32] RGIA, f. 796, op. 118, d. 73, l. 149; and NART, f. 4, op. 75, d. 11.

[33] GAKO, f. 237, op. 132, d. 1463, l. 460b. On distant villages, see Odoev, "Stranichka proshlogo," 375–76.

[34] GAKO, f. 237, op. 131, d. 1283, l. 174; and GAKO, f. 237, op. 136, d. 354, l. 2.

collected from novokreshchenye with relative ease,[35] as a rule the more detailed the account, the more conditional and equivocal the provision of these signatures appears to have been. In some instances, even those who in principle agreed to the missionaries' propositions refused to confirm their promises with *tamgi*. Their principal concern, according to missionaries, was that after providing *tamgi*, "they will be considered to be in the Russian faith" (*stanut schitat´ ikh v russkoi vere*)."[36] Apparently, novokreshchenye feared that signing such statements would make their legal status as Christians entirely irrevocable and that they would thereby forfeit any opportunity of remaining in the "old faith." There may also have been fundamental doubts about what the promises actually entailed and whether they perhaps were not quite what missionaries represented them to be. In any event, missionaries were in some cases forced to leave non-Russian villages without having obtained residents' *tamgi*.

On the whole, novokreshchenye were skeptical of the mission's legitimacy and openly doubted that it actually enjoyed the imperial sanction that it claimed. A Mari informant for one missionary explained the reasons for his compatriots' stubbornness as follows:

> They say, "why are they trying to talk us into accepting the Russian faith, but they are not trying to talk the Votiaks and the Chuvash, who also go into the forest to pray, like we do, into maintaining it[;] and Russian sectarians not only do not go to church, but do not even accept priests into their homes," [and the informant] said on top of this, that some Russians are telling them that it is not allowed to compel them with force to accept the Christian faith.[37]

Indeed, at this moment (1829), the mission among Udmurts and Chuvash had not yet begun, sectarians continued to constitute a bad example for novokreshchenye to the extent that they rejected the official church, and the legal prohibition on the use of force in matters of conversion was solidly in effect. In short, the prevailing circumstances gave novokreshchenye good reason to doubt that the mission constituted a legitimate enterprise.

Accordingly, they often demanded documentation authorizing the missionaries' activities. "Read us a decree from the Sovereign Himself," said one group of Maris, "and we will abandon the Cheremis faith."[38] This request put missionaries in a difficult spot, since the decree with which they were equipped, although reflecting the will of the Emperor, had actually

---

[35] For example, the missionary Stefanov in the first few months of the Udmurt mission breezed through his jurisdiction with remarkable speed, visiting two or three villages a day in November and October 1830. He collected *tamgi* from heads of household in each village and managed to baptize close to 150 people. See RGIA, f. 796, op. 110. d. 793, ll. 43–114 and P. N. Luppov, *Khristianstvo u votiakov v pervoi polovine XIX veka* (Viatka, 1911), pp. 267–68.

[36] Quoted in Odoev, "Stranichka proshlogo," 390.

[37] GAKO, f. 237, op. 132, d. 1463, ll. 53–530b. Quotation marks added for clarification.

[38] Ibid., ll. 22, 45.

been issued by the Viatka Ecclesiastical Consistory. Thus the paper had little effect, and novokreshchenye dismissed it as "unfounded" (*pustyi*) or "not important because it is not printed."[39] In such cases the missionary was reduced to arguing "that in this affair there is no need for a special imperial directive, because without the will of the Sovereign Emperor we would not dare take up such a public and important affair."[40] The missionary Polikarp Kuvshinskii was particularly quick to learn his lesson and made the decree, along with "proper commentary on it," the starting point of his discussions.[41] Likewise, when a missionary commission was assembled for surveying Iaransk district in 1833, the Consistory made it a specific point of calling on local secular and religious officials to prepare the ground by impressing on Maris that the commission's activity represented the will of the Sovereign. Even so, local clergy reported that their efforts had no real effect: their parishioners "don't believe anyone—neither us nor the missionary—thinking that their conversion involves not the imperial will of the Sovereign Emperor but the religious superintendent, who wishes to receive honor and reward."[42]

Instead of recognizing the "will of the Sovereign" inscribed in the mission, novokreshchenye claimed imperial sanction for their own purposes. On numerous occasions baptized Maris justified their animist practice with reference to an alleged decree from the Tsar granting them permission to perform native rituals. When a local priest confronted an animist gathering in Iaransk district, one baptized Mari responded "with a great temper, 'we have a decree, by which no one is allowed to prohibit us from maintaining the previous habit.'" Called in to admonish these Maris, the missionary was presented with the decree and an explanation that parishioners had received it from their compatriots in neighboring Urzhum district. When the missionary pointed out that their alleged decree did not in fact contain the permission that they claimed it did, the Maris responded, "We don't know, but when it is read to us, we hear that one may pray in the forest and make offerings." The decree itself had a stamp from 1842, but the writing was "deliberately spoiled," and it lacked an official number and copyist.[43] In short, someone had obtained a piece of paper of marginally official appearance and was using it to promote paganism among Maris. Such rumors arose frequently and were difficult to extinguish, precisely because they reflected the aspirations of most novokreshchenye. In 1837 clergy in Urzhum district discovered more "papers," consisting of a decision of the Viatka court on

[39] Ibid., ll. 38ob., 39ob. It was true that only printed copies of the law were valid, and Maris may have understood the decree in these terms. See David Moon, *Russian Peasants and Tsarist Legislation on the Eve of Reform: Interaction between Peasants and Officialdom, 1825–1855* (London, 1992), p. 12.

[40] GAKO, f. 237, op. 132, d. 1463, l. 22.

[41] Ibid., l. 47ob.

[42] Odoev, "Stranichka proshlogo," 364, 366, citation from 371–72.

[43] RGIA, f. 796, op. 123, d. 1216, ll. 64ob.–66.

pagan rituals, receipts from the Kazan post office concerning a petition to the Emperor, and the petition to Minister of Internal Affairs A. Zakrevskii that had been filed and rejected seven years earlier. Villagers explained that two Maris were ordering them to live in the old faith on the basis of these documents.[44] Chuvash peasants, too, refused to take communion in 1836 on the basis of rumors about a similar tsarist decree.[45]

In general, novokreshchenye latched onto anything that could possibly be construed as official permission to perform paganism. When an article describing Udmurt rituals appeared in *Viatka Provincial Gazette*, in which it was stated that priests were allowing Udmurts to consume horse meat (which was prohibited by Orthodoxy), Udmurts took this as permission for them to perform these rituals. "And this is not surprising, for the article was read at the canton board together with other announcements from the authorities, and, moreover, in it were repeated twice the words: they [priests] allow them a few pagan habits and allow them to roast and eat horse during the summer holiday."[46] Thus an attempt to admonish Udmurts to abandon the consumption of horse meat in fact seemed to suggest to them that the clergy approved of this practice. Similarly, in the 1850s an MGI official made the mistake of telling Chuvash that their faith was the most ancient and that they, in doing *chuki* (a form of sacrifice), were doing what Abraham and other "saints" had done. As a result, even two decades later, "This idea firmly established itself in Chuvash heads and at present is often presented by Chuvash as a most forceful argument." Thus clergy in this parish found themselves with the difficult task of explaining the theological differences between Chuvash and Old-Testament sacrifices.[47] In general, as novokreshchenye became more familiar with biblical history, they presented their own animist practices as Old-Testament traditions, calling them "faith of Adam" or "faith of Abraham" (*vera Adamova ili Avramova*).[48] Here, in short, was a way for non-Russians to invest their traditions with biblical sanction without submitting to Orthodox authority.

Perhaps some of novokreshchenye's ostensible exhibitions of loyalty and "naive monarchism" constituted merely a "public transcript," disingenuously presented to mask more consciously oppositional aspirations.[49] Yet the intentions of the Emperor and the central government could hardly have

---

[44] RGIA, f. 796, op. 118, d. 73, ll. 1–2.

[45] Denisov, *Religioznye verovaniia chuvash*, p. 259.

[46] Luppov, *Materialy*, pp. 83–84.

[47] "Besedy s chuvashami o vere khristianskoi," *IKE* 3 (1879): 72.

[48] See, for example, "Selo Sernur, Urzhumskii uezd," *Viatskie gubernskie vedomosti* 84 (1882); Iakob Koblov, "Kreshchenie 48 chelovek iazychnikov cheremis v prikhode Bol. Musherani, Tsarevokokshaiskogo uezda," *IKE* 9 (1902): 402; and Uchastnik-nabliudatel´ (pseud.), "Episkop na iazycheskom mol´bishche u cheremis," *VEV* 19 (1901): 981. These claims may also have been made under Islamic influence.

[49] See James C. Scott, *Domination and the Arts of Resistance: Hidden Transcripts* (New Haven, 1990).

appeared indisputable to novokreshchenye in the countryside. As we have seen, the Emperor ordered in 1828 that "out of condescension for their simplicity, [novokreshchenye] should in no way be persecuted."[50] Beginning in 1837, the Emperor issued a series of directives in specific cases, involving both Maris and Udmurts, in which he reiterated that the "ignorance" of novokreshchenye dictated that "spiritual" methods should be used rather than persecution. This trend culminated in 1842 with a general instruction to governors that, even while preventing the performance of pagan rituals, "in such cases they should appeal to the diocesan authorities," who in turn would instruct the parish clergy "to try with all means to substitute prayers established by the church for pagan rituals."[51] Thus, in spite of the general trend in these years toward the criminalization of religious dissent, Nicholas was inclined to construe pagan deviance as a matter of "ignorance" best handled without prosecution by secular authorities. It is not difficult to imagine that with such directives in circulation, novokreshchenye would be skeptical at best of the authority of local officials, in particular religious ones. Even if founded on a certain willful suspension of disbelief, the rumors and "misunderstandings" resonated with sentiments contained in state directives and laws.[52]

The prevailing interpretations among novokreshchenye were often immensely effective in mobilizing opposition. In general, missionaries faced a range of resistance strategies, ranging from dissimulation to outright threats. In a number of cases, novokreshchenye simply refused to show up when summoned, even though they were obligated at least to listen to the missionary's preaching. Alternatively, a village might purposely conceal half of its members, and then refuse to agree to anything on the pretext that only part of their community was present.[53] Nor could missionaries necessarily keep novokreshchenye in place once they had been gathered. When Pokrovskii approached a group of Maris, they declared that they already had their "own old faith," and they "began to disperse and even run away with shouts."[54] Similarly, in Simbirsk province Chuvash simply ran away from a missionary, and secular authorities were unable to retrieve them.[55] In the village of Upsha, Maris listened attentively to admonitions and were even anointed with oil, when "suddenly, like timid sheep having unexpectedly seen a predatory wolf running towards them, [they] ran out of the temple and hid wherever they could."[56] This pattern was repeated on numerous oc-

---

[50] RGIA, f. 797, op. 3, d. 12654, l. 12.

[51] Cited in Luppov, *Vzgliad*, pp. 5, 18.

[52] In seeing a combination of manipulation and belief, I concur with the interpretation of Moon, *Russian Peasants*, esp. pp. 165–81.

[53] GAKO, f. 237, op. 132, d. 1463, l. 240b.

[54] A. Pokrovskii, "Vypiska iz dnevnika missionera sviashch. A. Pokrovskogo," *Khristianskoe chtenie* 2 (1835): 99.

[55] RGIA, f. 769, op. 129, d. 1867, l. 5.

[56] GAKO, f. 237, op. 132, d. 1463, l. 40b.

casions: having been gathered, novokreshchenye would "suddenly" (and usually "with shouting") scatter, and often missionaries had no choice but to move on to the next settlement.[57]

On other occasions, novokreshchenye responded to missionaries with "caustic mockery" or even ignored them altogether: Udmurts in one settlement, "not paying any attention [to the admonitions], sat and conversed among themselves and smoked their pipes."[58] Alternatively, novokreshchenye could simply cause such a ruckus as to render any efforts at preaching futile. Drawing on the model of the parishioners in Makarovo, many Maris simply yelled "old faith!" or "*ogem, ogem, ogem*"! (I don't want [to convert]), while Udmurts shouted "*udlo*" (it is impossible [to convert]).[59] In some cases missionaries were confronted with "such words that cannot be written."[60] They complained that it was often extremely difficult to calm novokreshchenye to the point where they could conduct a discussion, and frequently there was nothing to do but to wait until their aggravation had run its course. Naturally, these confrontations took their toll on missionaries, as one ruefully remarked: "Akh! how sorrowful it was to look at the resistance and stubbornness of these superstitious ones! How hard it is to work among them!" This missionary decided to leave this village, lamely proposing to parishioners that they could have two weeks to finish up all their pagan festivals, at which time he would return. Not surprisingly this offer was rebuffed,[61] and it is indicative of the futility of the enterprise that the missionary would even propose such a scheme.

Missionaries were at pains to break through the tremendous wall of solidarity that characterized indigenous religious attachments. With some isolated exceptions, novokreshchenye were willing to agree to missionary propositions only collectively, "when every one of them to the last person decides on this."[62] Thus individuals justified their rejection of admonitions as a matter of their subordination to the collective, and even those ostensibly willing "to convert" postponed their ritual induction (*tamgi*, anointment, and holy water) for fear of retribution from their neighbors. Novokreshchenye could be seen preparing for a session with the missionary: "they constituted private gatherings, at which they decided to defend sternly their idolatry and [arranged] so that no one would dare express agreement with any of the admonitions."[63] Nor did novokreshchenye construe the collective simply in terms of their own villages but instead took a much broader

[57] Ibid., ll. 130b., 38; Odoev, "Stranichka proshlogo," 368–69.

[58] Luppov, *Khristianstvo*, p. 291.

[59] Odoev, "Stranichka proshlogo," 383; GAKO, f. 237, op. 132, d. 1463, l. 120b.; and Luppov, *Khristianstvo*, p. 291.

[60] Quoted in Odoev, "Stranichka proshlogo," 370. See also GAKO, f. 237, op. 132, d. 1463, l. 390b.

[61] GAKO, f. 237, op. 132, d. 1463, l. 14.

[62] RGIA, f. 796 op. 118, d. 73, l. 113.

[63] GAKO, f. 237, op. 132, d. 1463, l. 39. See similarly Luppov, *Khristianstvo*, p. 292.

view, arguing that they would agree to submit only when the residents of neighboring cantons and even districts did so as well. Parishioners watched attentively to see what would happen in other villages and were highly susceptible to the boasting and encouragement of those who had already resisted missionaries successfully.[64] When a group of novokreshchenye Maris in Iaransk district were told by a missionary to cease their offerings and prayers in the forest, they responded: "let those in Urzhum district cease first, and then we will, too."[65]

Resistance could also involve threats and violence. One priest in Iaransk district reported that some Maris responded with "rudeness" to his exhortations, and one in their midst told him, "I thought I already taught you, and I'll teach you even more, not to come to our parish."[66] A Mari in one village not only refused to listen to the missionary but drove both him and the accompanying priest out of his home.[67] Most dangerous of all was to confront novokreshchenye in the midst of animist rituals, when "they are insolent to the point of fury."[68] It was during these encounters that the greatest violence occurred, and some clergy and officials escaped harm only through luck. This was the case for one priest and the village elder who attempted to break up a Mari gathering in Urzhum district. When they appeared at the site, they heard Maris yell, "Scare them away with sticks; we must tie the priest to a tree and beat him with clubs, and kill the elder." As the priest explained, only darkness allowed them to hide from the agitated Maris.[69] Some clergy made the unwise decision to proceed to the site of animist rituals with an icon procession, which "instead of the expected reverence towards these Holy things and respect for the clergy, produced among the Cheremis beastly severity. As the priests began the prayer, from the Cheremis came a headlong and almost violent attack on the icon-bearers."[70] At another site, Maris defended their gathering from an icon procession using red-hot stakes, damaging an icon and injuring its bearer in the process.[71] Many secular officials tried to avoid confronting novokreshchenye over the issue of animism by, for example, claiming "to be busy with important business."[72] They understood that while Maris generally refrained from open and violent resistance to the authorities, animist rituals were so sacred to them that to interfere was dangerous.

Despite these examples of tenacious opposition, it should be emphasized that many novokreshchenye were willing to go to church and to fulfill

[64] This phenomenon is visible numerous times in GAKO, f. 237, op. 132, d. 1463.
[65] RGIA, f. 796, op. 123, l. 1216, l. 66.
[66] RGIA, f. 796, op. 118, d. 73, l. 1650b.
[67] Ibid., l. 86.
[68] Luppov, *Materialy*, p. 116.
[69] RGIA, f. 796, op. 123, d. 1216, ll. 86–87.
[70] Ibid., l. 630b.
[71] RGIA, f. 796, op. 130, d. 965, ll. 1–5.
[72] RGIA, f. 796, op. 118, d. 73, l. 76.

certain obligations but became upset principally when they were asked to abandon their animist traditions. Some even claimed that they "pray to God in our own way and in the Russian way," with evident hope that this would satisfy their interrogators.[73] At issue, then, was not the practice of Christianity as such but the prohibition on animist traditions that Orthodox status entailed. When missionaries succeeded in securing novokreshchenye's acquiescence, the latter accepted holy water enthusiastically, even requesting the rite for themselves, their homes, and their livestock. Although the reasons for this enthusiasm are not entirely clear, I suspect that it derived from their fear of retribution from native spirits for having openly violated the sacred vow they had given to their parents and ancestors and the belief that the Russian God, through holy water, might be able to offer them protection.

Broader Measures of "Reinforcement"

Besides dispatching missionaries, church and state adopted other measures designed to "reinforce" novokreshchenye in Christianity. One was to construct new churches in order to reduce the physical size of the largest parishes.[74] Another was to promote greater contact and even intermarriage between Russians and non-Russians. Pokrovskii was the first to promote this strategy, when he proposed that the government produce a directive "so that Cheremis take in wedlock Russian girls of good upbringing and honest life, at least two or three for each village, for in this way not only their future tribe but fellow members of the family and even neighbors might in the closest and most simple way learn the Orthodox religion and Christian life." Russian men, meanwhile, were to be encouraged to wed Mari women: "In this way such mutual rapprochement and kinship would serve to deepen the means for spreading Christianity among the Cheremis."[75] These encouragements were to be accompanied by a more directed program of resettlement, whereby one household of Russian peasants would be settled in each Mari village "for the supervision of Cheremis' conduct and for teaching them all Christian habits." Unbaptized Maris, meanwhile, were to be resettled to "special places," separate from the baptized.[76] Missionaries made similar

---

[73] GAKO, f. 237, op. 132, d. 1463, l. 40. See also A. Andrievskii, "Dela o sovershenii iazycheskikh zhertvoprinoshenii kreshchenymi inorodtsami Viatskoi gubernii," in *Stoletie Viatskoi gubernii, 1780–1880: Sbornik materialov k istorii Viatskogo kraia* (Viatka, 1881), 2:569.

[74] RGIA, f. 796, op. 119, d. 255; and RGIA, f. 796, op. 118, d. 73, ll. 4–26. In one case a Mari village was located 110 versts (almost eighty miles) from its parish church! (Odoev, "Stranichka proshlogo," 377.) In some cases secular ministries (e.g., the Crown Department) or even private merchants provided funds for church construction. See *Istoriia Udelov za stoletie ikh sushchestvovaniia, 1797–1897* (St. Petersburg, 1901), 2:294–97; RGIA, f. 383, op. 16, d. 21143.

[75] RGIA, f. 797, op. 3, d. 12654, ll. 222–220b.

[76] Ibid., l. 1310b.

recommendations for Udmurts by encouraging local clergy to bring no-vokreshchenye and Russians "to the extent possible into religious and carnal kinship."[77] This proposed policy suggests that Russian authorities shared none of the apprehensions about miscegenation apparent in empires ruled from Western Europe.[78]

The settlement of Russian families among Maris never occurred, however. The Synod acknowledged that it could not actually require anyone to enter such marriages, and neither Maris nor Russians appear to have been interested in the prospect.[79] Although they were sometimes willing to accept Russians if the state provided land, in general Maris "always try to distance themselves from [Russians] and avoid all interaction with them."[80] More immediately, since rumors about the cost of constructing the churches had already upset Maris, Pokrovskii suggested putting off the implementation of the resettlement policy "until the complete calming of minds."[81] But even when the missionary Iosif Stefanov found an Udmurt settlement in which the male members of ten households had Russian wives in 1831, he was nevertheless forced to report that "they still do pagan prayers called *kurbany*."[82] The presence of Russian spouses in non-Russian villages by no means guaranteed that animist practices would cease.

Indeed, Russians were not always the model that religious authorities hoped they would be. In Iaransk district, one of the most ardent pagans turned out to be a "pure-blooded Russian," who evidently had been adopted by a Mari family in childhood and raised as an animist.[83] Stefanov discovered, "to the shame of Christians," that Russians were on occasion the stewards of sacred groves and tents and that sectarians "through various actions and divulging gradually cool the faith in these children and naturally incline them toward paganism."[84] In particular, Russian sectarians and Old Believers, who represented a serious problem for the official church in the Volga-Kama region, were frequently more hostile to Orthodox authority than were non-Russians, and were accused by the Bishop of Viatka of giving the latter

---

[77] Luppov, *Materialy*, p. 61.

[78] For a discussion of miscegenation in Dutch colonial holdings, see Ann L. Stoler, *Race and the Education of Desire: Foucault's History of Sexuality and the Colonial Order of Things* (Durham, 1995), esp. pp. 43–46, 105–7.

[79] RGIA, f. 797, op. 3, d. 12654, l. 223.

[80] RGIA, f. 797, op. 5, d. 20785, l. 3; P. Shestakov, "Byt cheremis Urzhumskogo uezda," *Tsirkuliar po Kazanskomu uchebnomu okrugu* 16 (1866): 127.

[81] RGIA, f. 797, op. 3, d. 12654, l. 1680b.

[82] Luppov, *Materialy*, p. 191. *Korban* is the Tatar word for sacrifice or offering.

[83] Odoev, "Stranichka proshlogo," 389. One observer noted in 1902 that it was not uncommon for Russians with large families to give "extra children" to others—"even Cheremis"—to raise. See N. Kibardin, "Iz nabliudenii inorodcheskogo missionera nad cheremisami," *VEV* 15 (1902): 808. On the epistemological crisis precipitated by such examples of reverse assimilation, see Willard Sunderland, "Russians into Iakuts? 'Going Native' and the Problem of Russian National Identity in the Siberian North, 1870s–1914," *Slavic Review* 55, 4 (1996): 806–26.

[84] Luppov, *Materialy*, p. 60.

the "stubborn idea" of maintaining the old faith.[85] Even Russian officials did not always inspire non-Russians to a more purely Christian life. Bishop Nil complained in 1836 that novokreshchenye Maris and Udmurts "are thoroughly seduced, seeing that the rural police officials acting in their midst, being Russians, openly use meat during fasts. With such examples all exhortation to observe the fasts remains ineffective."[86]

Recognizing the need for more effective church servitors in non-Russian parishes, religious authorities in Viatka diocese also initiated a program of educating Mari boys at the Viatka ecclesiastical seminary.[87] But this policy, too, encountered numerous obstacles in practice. While the program was ideally to be based on the voluntary agreement of Mari parents, religious authorities admitted that most Maris did not wish to relinquish their children for study. Thus Bishop Kirill acknowledged that the sudden induction of a large number of young Maris for study "may provoke grumbling among these half-savage people." He thus suggested taking only ten boys initially, and then five more every two years until there were thirty in all.[88] Despite this soft-pedaling, however, some parents complained that their sons had been taken without their permission, to which the Synod responded (in one case) that a request for one child's return could not be satisfied, "for in that case not only would the effort expended up until now on his education be wasted, but there would be the danger of his seduction, and an example would be given to other unbaptized Cheremis to burden the authorities with similar requests."[89] In 1836 the authorities began to take only children from poor families, who might see some material benefit in having the seminary provide for the child, and orphans, who essentially had no one to protest on their behalf. This, the government hoped, would not only minimize "unpleasant sensations" but might also serve as "obvious proof of the government's concern."[90] But the government wanted also to avoid producing the impression that such schooling was a particular burden on Christians. Thus from the start the Synod made the curious proposal of beginning

[85] Ibid., p. 90. For similar statements, see also ibid., pp. 194, 200. On the presence of religious dissenters, see RGIA, f. 797, op. 5, d. 20785, l. 30b.; and *Polnoe sobranie postanovlenii i rasporiazhenii po vedomstvu Pravoslavnogo ispovedanii Rossiiskoi Imperii*, 5th series, vol. 1 (Petrograd, 1915), no. 275.

[86] RGIA, f. 796, op. 117, d. 1345, l. 3. On the problem of disciplining Russians as part of a larger missionary project in the late nineteenth century, see also Robert Geraci, "Going Abroad or Going to Russia? Orthodox Missionaries in the Kazakh Steppe, 1881–1917," in *Of Religion and Empire: Missions, Conversion, and Tolerance in Tsarist Russia*, ed. Robert Geraci and Michael Khodarkovsky (Ithaca, 2001), pp. 274–310.

[87] RGIA, f. 797, op. 3, d. 12654, ll. 241–42. The Crown Department made a similar proposal for Chuvash in 1838 (RGIA, f. 796, op. 119, d. 255, l. 2).

[88] NART, f. 10, op. 1, d. 3343, ll. 1–2. In 1867 Viatka diocese had fifty-seven "Mari parishes," by which presumably was meant parishes with a significant number of Mari parishioners (RGIA, f. 796, op. 148, d. 290, l. 20b.).

[89] RGIA, f. 796, op. 123, d. 258, ll. 21–23. The Synod did, however, impress on its local subordinates the need to exercise greater care in selecting children.

[90] Ibid., l. 4.

"predominantly with pagan children," taking Christians only subsequently, so that Maris could see in this action an effort of the government "to educate their ethnicity in general, and not a particular [effort] imposed on Christians."[91] Most of the pagan children drafted into the Viatka school were eventually baptized, which, of course, did little to encourage pagan parents to agree to this scheme.

One of the more remarkable aspects of the school and seminary was the mortality rate of the Mari pupils: by 1855 fifteen of the fifty-two students had died.[92] There was thus a kind of sad irony when one of two fathers petitioning for their sons' return was informed that his child was now dead, while the second was assured that the authorities were taking good care of *his* child.[93] Cognizant of the high mortality rate, the Synod's Educational Board complained that in the selection of pupils insufficient attention had been paid to their "physical constitution."[94] Most of the remaining students demonstrated little success in their studies, and by 1855 the Seminary had expelled fourteen of them, arguing that their failure derived from Maris' "natural stupidity [*tupost*]." By 1867 another seven students had been expelled.[95] In fact, the Seminary made all kinds of efforts to promote the boys' success—from appointing a special tutor and freeing them from difficult classes like mathematics, to housing them in a separate room with special supervision. But the Mari pupils, "living in one room, on account of their unsteadiness [*shatkost*], not only do not encourage one another towards good but even seduce one another into performing pranks."[96]

For all the difficulties, the Synod was nonetheless determined to place some of the pupils in clerical positions and thus to ensure that the project was not a complete waste. Thus, while one student's "coarseness and extreme laziness" had rendered his study "completely unsuccessful," he had studied for twelve years and had received enough education, according to the Bishop, "for the first level of clerical service." This was too much for the Synod, but in another case it agreed that four Mari students, slated for exclusion from the Seminary for laziness and poor academic performance— but not for "crude ingrained vice" or criminal behavior—could be given positions as sacristans, the lowest and unordained clerical rank.[97] By 1855 the Mari students had produced two priests, four deacons, and six sacristans. Of these, however, only one priest and two deacons were serving satisfactorily

---

[91] RGIA, f. 797, op. 3, d. 12654, l. 242; and GAKO, f. 237, op. 133, d. 1384, ll. 1–3.

[92] RGIA, f. 796, op. 133, d. 2091, l. 70b.

[93] RGIA, f. 796, op. 123, d. 258, ll. 6, 23. The circumstances behind some of the deaths, involving various illnesses, are covered in RGIA, f. 802, op. 1, dd. 8609, 9230, and 11081.

[94] RGIA, f. 796, op. 133, d. 2091, l. 12.

[95] RGIA, f. 796, op. 148, d. 290.

[96] RGIA, f. 796, op. 123, d. 258, ll. 26–28.

[97] RGIA, f. 796, op. 133, d. 2091, ll. 3–5.

by the church's standards.[98] Faced by what he saw as the students' incorrigible disobedience, natural stupidity, inclinations toward disorder and drunkenness, and above all incapacity for learning, the bishop began to question the whole enterprise, suggesting that instead of teaching Maris to be clergy, the Seminary ought to be teaching Russian seminary students the Mari language (which indeed began in 1856). The decisive blow for the Synod came with reports that the Mari graduates serving in clerical posts did not even enjoy the respect of fellow Maris and were therefore incapable of having any influence on them. By the late 1850s the project had collapsed, and non-Russian clergy would appear in substantial numbers only in the early twentieth century.[99]

The religious authorities also hoped to make Christianity more accessible to native parishioners through translations of basic religious works, but this effort, too, ran into considerable difficulties. The tremendous variation in regional dialects limited the geographic scope of each particular translation, and there was a dearth of specialists fluent enough in native languages to render accurate and canonically sound translations. In these years, translators generally opted for a word-for-word approach, which grossly violated patterns of indigenous grammar and syntax and thus rendered many of the translations completely unintelligible. Moreover, completed translations often went unpublished for years because there was no one competent to verify them. In addition, there were problems of acquisition and distribution. In 1832 the Synod published a number of basic catechisms in Chuvash, meadow-Mari, and highland-Mari. But the number of copies printed (1,200, 100, and 100, respectively) was hardly adequate even for Kazan diocese. Thus the missionary Amvrosii reported in 1838 that because many parishes lacked religious primers and the parish clergy made no independent effort to teach the parishioners in their own language, "novokreshchenye for the whole year remain without any religious edification."[100]

Financial limitations also played a role. When Udmurt catechisms were finally printed in the late 1840s, parish churches were expected to *purchase* a certain number of copies, based on the parish population, with their own financial resources. Faced with the unlikelihood of being able to sell these texts to predominantly illiterate Udmurts, priests began to petition diocesan authorities to reduce the number of copies they were required to purchase, but the Viatka Consistory, itself having expended large sums on printing the translations, was unwilling to satisfy these requests. In the end, out of financial necessity, the Consistory agreed to a proposal to allow local Russian parishes to buy copies for their archives and for distribution among Russian

[98] Ibid., ll. 7–8. Of the fifty-two Mari students recruited in the years 1829–1855, fifteen died, fourteen were expelled, twelve completed the seminary course, and eleven were studying in a district church school.

[99] RGIA, f. 796, op. 133, d. 2091, ll. 38–43.

[100] NART, f. 4, op. 1, d. 3583, ll. 1–10b.

peasants living near Udmurt settlements. Needless to say, the distribution of catechisms in Udmurt to Russian parishes perverted the whole idea of making these works available to non-Russians.[101] Lacking qualified translators and greater state support that might have further reduced the costs of printing and distribution, the church was able to make translations only a limited part of its missionary effort.

Aside from these purely technical and institutional problems, the very act of translation was perhaps less straightforward than Russian clerics may have supposed. Vicente Rafael's recent analysis of native-language Tagalog religious texts stresses that "some things in Tagalog culture could not be unequivocally restated in Spanish-Christian terms, just as some aspects of the vernacular exceeded the limits that the missionaries sought to set for it." Rafael focuses on the use in native language texts of Castilian terms, whose untranslatability could be reread in different ways by native converts to create a whole range of possible associations having only a tenuous link to the missionary's original message. The use of native terms, similarly, often carried meanings inconsistent with or even contradictory to the Christian idea. The result of this "semantic drift" was that "translation enabled [Tagalogs] to negotiate with Spanish authority and hence to contain its demands."[102]

Although this question merits more specialized inquiry, the effects of translation in Russia were evidently similar. The earliest efforts at translating appear to have been inconsistent in their expression of important Christian concepts. Before published translations, which appeared only in the early nineteenth century, individual priests made choices about whether they would express Christian concepts using Russian words or would employ native equivalents. Non-Russians themselves appropriated Russian words in varying degrees, in some cases using them even when native expressions were by all indications adequate. The result, as one observer noted in the 1870s, was that religious terminology could differ substantially from parish to parish.[103] In some instances, translations maintained Russian terms in the native-language text, such as *Sviatoi Dukh* (Holy Spirit), *Iisus Khristos* (Jesus Christ), and so on. The use of these Russian words opened up "blanks" (Rafael's term), offering natives the possibility of inscribing in those terms their own interpretation.

---

[101] On these early translation efforts, see K. Prokop′ev, "Perevody khristianskikh knig na inorodcheskie iazyki v pervoi polovine XIX veka," *IKE* 33–35 (1904): 1100–1118, 1139–51, 1171–79; P. Luppov, *O pervykh votskikh perevodakh istochnikov khristianskogo prosveshcheniia* (Kazan, 1905); Vasilii Sboev, *Issledovaniia ob inorodtsakh Kazanskoi gubernii* (Kazan, 1856), pp. 163–65; I. G. Ivanov, *Istoriia mariiskogo literaturnogo iazyka* (Ioshkar-Ola, 1975), pp. 20–23; A. Karimullin, *Tatarskaia kniga poreformennoi Rossii* (Kazan, 1983), pp. 234–42; and G. D. Frolova, *Udmurtskaia kniga: Istoriia knigopechataniia, sovremennaia kniga* (Izhevsk, 1982), pp. 8–24.

[102] Vicente L. Rafael, *Contracting Colonialism: Translation and Christian Conversion in Tagalog Society under Early Spanish Rule* (Durham, 1993), quotes from pp. 110 and 208.

[103] F. Zemlianitskii, "Neskol′ko slov o iazyke, kotorym soobshchaiutsia istiny khristianskoi very cheremisam," *IKE* 12 (1871): 370–74.

Whereas these texts were forced to retain Russian terms in many cases, on the whole it seems that early translations and explanatory texts strove to retain as much as possible in the native language, including even the names of such important Christian sacraments and concepts as sin, angel, savior, and baptism.[104] In rendering "God," for example, translations often favored the native equivalent: *Kugu Iumo* in Mari, *Inmar* in Udmurt, *Tora* in Chuvash. From this perspective, Christianity simply became a more complete revelation of the natives' own God; He was the same entity, but now with a son and a new colleague—the Holy Spirit. By placing the pagan *Kugu Iumo* at the apex of Christian theology, translators thereby promoted religious synthesis. Sometimes, translations that employed native-language equivalents for important Christian concepts ran into difficulties. In one case an attempt to render "Holy Spirit" in fact produced "Holy smell," which must have made Christianity seem quite odd to native parishioners. Such translations could not avoid producing impressions beyond those envisaged by translators and missionaries precisely because the referents were either so indeterminate or so culturally specific.

Indeed, evidence from later in the century shows how many Christian figures and concepts were simply integrated into indigenous frameworks and pantheons. Russian saints, for example, constituted a potential analogy for the many native spirits. As one Chuvash explained in recalling his upbringing, "Nicholas the miracle-worker, or an icon with his face on it, is a kind of evil god, equal to an *irikh* or a keremet, only with the difference that Nicholas the miracle-worker is a Russian evil god, and a keremet or *irikh* is a Chuvash one."[105] The ethnographer Vasilii Sboev recalled from his youth that Chuvash would conclude a native prayer, which involved drinking a bucket of beer for each native god, goddess, and keremet, by making the sign of the cross and bowing before an icon; the leader of the prayer would then request "the Russian God" [*vyras Tora*], the Mother of God, the "Godly Angel," and "God Nikolai" (i.e., Saint Nicholas) to save them and be merciful to them.[106] The fact that some Maris understood Jesus Christ to be a *iumo*—the Mari term for god / spirit[107]—suggests just how much "Christian truths" could become entangled in indigenous frameworks and thus invested with profoundly different characteristics and functions.[108] It also suggests that in

---

[104] See, for example, *Nachatki khristianskogo ucheniia ili kratkaia sviashchennaia istoriia i kratkii katekhizis na cheremiskii iazyk lugovogo narechiia, perevedennye v Kazani 1839 goda* (Kazan, 1841).

[105] Cited in Denisov, *Religioznye verovaniia chuvash*, p. 280.

[106] Sboev, *Issledovaniia*, pp. 52–53. Maris also referred to St. Nicholas as "Nicholas-God" (*Mikol'-iumo*).

[107] Maris referred to Jesus as *Kiiushul'-iumo*. See K. M., "Cheremisy Iaranskogo uezda, Viatskoi gubernii," *Russkie vedomosti* 114 (1872): 3.

[108] On the notion of "entanglement" (albeit in a somewhat different context), see Nicholas Thomas, *Entangled Objects: Exchange, Material Culture, and Colonialism in the Pacific* (Cambridge, Mass., 1991).

some parishes a transition from *dvoeverie* (dual faith)—that is, the conscious and deliberate practice of Christianity and paganism by the same person—to a syncretic blending had begun.[109]

Along with the attempt to communicate such "Christian truths" to novokreshchenye, Orthodox authorities sought to assert religious discipline through penance. Novokreshchenye caught in the act of performing animist prayers were often sent off to a monastery for a period of time. This, of course, proved quite detrimental to the household economies of the penitents, who sometimes petitioned for their release. In one instance a Mari, Stepan Anisimov, made such a request to the bishop, noting the disarray into which his household had fallen in his absence. Claiming that he desired "forever to accept and keep the Christian faith," he also expressed his readiness to make a forty-ruble contribution to the monastery. But the monastery's father superior remained skeptical, despite the offered "donation," and noted that Anisimov "has no comprehension of the Christian faith whatsoever," and indeed "knows no prayers or even the name Jesus Christ." Anisimov was nonetheless released a short time later, once he had received basic instruction in Christianity and had renounced "completely and forever paganism and its rituals."[110]

More dramatic were efforts to extirpate indigenous religiosity through the destruction of the sacred groves and special huts and tents (*shalashi* and *chumy*), which served as the foci of animist practice. One missionary explained in 1831 that as long as the groves continued to exist, it would take merely one "insidious scheme" to convert the groves "into a stumbling block and a source of seduction for weak souls." Destroying the groves might also give missionaries a more accurate picture of novokreshchenye's true religious disposition, since "forever bidding farewell to an article of deep veneration, a person cannot avoid revealing his religious thoughts and feelings."[111] The destruction of such sacred sites accordingly became an important dimension of activity among novokreshchenye.[112] In 1829–30 Pokrovskii destroyed a sacred bridge, under which local Maris believed an important keremet lived, as well as a prominent rocky cliff to which local residents ascribed supernatural powers. Moscow Metropolitan Filaret justified Pokrovskii's actions to the Synod by writing, "When this rock is destroyed, the very dull-witted people will

---

[109] That is, I take *dvoeverie* to be a useful term to describe early stages of Christianization, when Christianity and paganism continued to exist as distinct systems of religious practice. See Eve Levin, "*Dvoeverie* and Popular Religion," in *Seeking God: The Recovery of Religious Identity in Orthodox Russia, Ukraine, and Georgia,* ed. Stephen K. Batalden (DeKalb, 1993), pp. 31–52.

[110] GAKO, f. 237, op. 142, d. 237, ll. 10–11, 15–17.

[111] GAKO, f. 237, op. 134, d. 996, ll. 10b.–2.

[112] See, for example, Luppov, *Materialy,* p. 190; Sboev, *Issledovaniia,* p. 123; and RGIA, f. 796, op. 126, d. 213, l. 1060b.

understand that it is not a god, and reference to this event [the destruction] will be beneficial and instructive."[113]

Attempts to enlist non-Russian participation in these acts of destruction typically elicited a lukewarm response at best. Non-Russians, however, did not always oppose the destruction of the groves, registering instead their fear of retribution from native spirits if they themselves participated in this act. As one missionary reported, "The Cheremis said: let whoever wants to destroy [the grove do so], but not they; their arms will not rise for this purpose."[114] Another priest reported that, though Maris refused to participate "out of fear of some misfortune," they attended the burning of the trees and not only did not oppose the priest's actions but "even rejoiced that those boughs would no longer disturb their conscience."[115] Thus for some non-Russians the clergy's actions represented an opportunity for liberation from the power of the keremet. By Maris' understanding, as long as they themselves did not take part in the destruction, they were immune to punishment from the keremet. In other cases, however, local parishioners were more resistant and could see no benefit in the destruction of sacred huts and groves. One missionary reported that Udmurts "paid no attention whatsoever to my explanations and exhortations. When I said to them that they should voluntarily break down the hut, they responded to me: 'Not only will we not break it down, but we'll fix it up even better; you have no business in this, we don't know who you are, and we don't want to know you, we have our own priest.' "[116]

The policy of destroying indigenous religious sites ran into the greatest difficulty in regions where some residents were still officially pagans. These residents, according to the law, had the right to perform their own religious ceremonies and therefore to maintain their places of worship, even if baptized residents were settled nearby. The MVD regarded such attempts to restrict legitimate pagan practice as being "in some measure inconsistent with our rules on religious toleration, which have been accepted by the government, and could appear to unbaptized Votiaks as persecution and give them grounds from grumbling and maybe even agitation."[117] Stefanov was thus allowed to destroy huts and tents only in settlements without unbaptized

---

[113] Cited in S. K. Kuznetsov, "Poezdka k drevnei cheremiskoi sviatyne, izvestnoi so vremen Oleariia," *Etnograficheskoe obozrenie* 1 (1905): 147. The destruction of the cliff known as Chembulat is also covered in RGIA, f. 797, op. 3, d. 12654, ll. 169, 175, 212. Spanish missionaries engaged in similar destructive practices in their attempt to eliminate idolatry among Indian converts. See Kenneth Mills, "The Limits of Religious Coercion in Mid-Colonial Peru," *Past and Present* 145 (1994): 104–11.

[114] N. V. Nikol'skii, ed., *K istorii khristianskogo prosveshcheniia cheremis v XIX v.* (Kazan, 1915), p. 44.

[115] RGIA, f. 796, op. 108, d. 1850, l. 560b.

[116] Luppov, *Materialy*, p. 185.

[117] GAKO, f. 237, op. 151, d. 2064, l. 34. This was the MVD's position as recounted by the Bishop of Viatka.

Udmurts; in two mixed settlements, however, the huts were the collective property of local community, and therefore, "due to the stubbornness of pagans and the novokreshchenye's lack of courage," the huts and tents remained "unabolished."[118] At times, secular authorities simply refused to sanction confrontational measures, because, as the MGI argued, "in affairs concerning faith, excessively severe measures, instead of eliminating delusions, only strengthen them."[119] Even the Synod admonished diocese authorities in 1844 for requesting the destruction of a sacred Mari grove, noting that

> people, having barely had their eyes opened from the darkness of idolatry, limited in all their understandings, cannot suddenly abandon those prejudices and superstitions, into which they were born. . . . [R]estrictive and stern measures can only irritate, tear at the very beginning the union of love and trust between new children of the church and pastors, [and] hinder the successes of preaching on others, who still stagnate in idolatry.[120]

There were likewise attempts to combat the influence of "seducers" and "debauchers"—that is the various "sorcerers," "fortune-tellers," and "false prophets." These figures frightened their fellow villagers with prophecies of the punishments they would incur for abandoning their beliefs, asserted that all change was for the worse, and even that the Tsar knew about their indigenous beliefs and approved of them.[121] We unfortunately have little information on these figures, since they bore no outward marks of distinction and their activities were almost always surreptitious. Moreover, Russian authorities were inclined to consider as "sorcerers" virtually anyone who used his or her influence to promote animism and to oppose missionary efforts. Though several missionaries requested that the activities of "sorcerers" be prohibited and that the violators of this prohibition be exiled from local communities,[122] such a policy was never openly adopted, not least because "sorcerers" were simply so difficult to identify with any certainty. Sometimes, when an offender was identified or apprehended, he or—often enough—she would be sent to a monastery until a satisfying display of "repentance" had been made. In 1840 this was the fate of one Chuvash woman who was accused of "inclining various baptized Chuvash people to the idolatrous faith and performing fortune-telling for them." Having repented "with visible grief," and having promised to abandon such activities in the future, she was eventually released.[123] An Udmurt woman received a harsher sentence of twenty-five strokes with a birch rod, plus an undisclosed term of penance for recom-

---

[118] Luppov, *Materialy*, p. 190.

[119] RGIA, f. 797, op. 14, d. 33778, ll. 1–2.

[120] Nikol'skii, *K istorii*, p. 46.

[121] RGIA, f. 797, op. 3, d. 12654, l. 1250b.

[122] The missionary Anisimov made this recommendation after encountering difficulties among Udmurts (RGIA, f. 796, op. 110, d. 793, l. 40).

[123] NART, f. 1, op. 2, d. 294.

mending a pagan sacrifice through fortune-telling.[124] But like the attempt to destroy sacred groves, efforts to restrain "wizards" could not be so easily sustained in areas of mixed settlement. The MGI contended that the government could not actually prohibit such activity altogether but could only forbid *baptized* non-Russians from being "fortune tellers" and require that these figures be elected openly through official resolution of the local community.[125] Here again, then, the church's desire to ameliorate the Orthodox religiosity of non-Russian parishioners ran up against the state's commitment to at least a basic level of religious tolerance, even for pagans.

Not all local authorities were in favor of this "soft line." In one case from 1836, Bishop Nil of Viatka, having already sentenced the principal mentor of an Udmurt animist prayer to internment in a monastery for a two-month term of "repentance and admonition," was reluctant to accept the Emperor's subsequent order that the authorities limit themselves "to only spiritual admonition." Forced to reconsider his original sentence but convinced that Udmurts' "coarseness and obduracy" rendered hopeless "typical measures of admonition," Nil reinterpreted the internment as a matter of "edification" rather than punishment and was thus able to secure the Emperor's acquiescence to the Consistory's decision.[126] In general, while stereotypes of "stupidity" and "simplicity" enjoyed wide currency, officials closer to novokreshchenye on the ground were more likely to believe that the situation required "urgent" and "decisive" measures and a more prosecutorial style, precisely because non-Russians were inclined to misconstrue condescension as a license to do as they wished.[127] It was difficult to find an appropriate balance between deference in matters of faith and the need to make a forceful impression on non-Russians.

As time passed—and especially as the Emperor's "humane" view of novokreshchenye's "ignorance" softened the official line against pagan recidivism—the authorities found themselves making greater compromises. The Emperor's call for "substituting" Orthodox prayers for pagan rituals helped ensure that Christianity, instead of replacing indigenous outlooks wholesale, was inserted into existing frameworks of understanding, thereby facilitating religious syncretism. Christian prayers became the functional equivalents of indigenous prayers—for example, when a religious superintendent suggested "a service with holy icons in the open field" as a substitute for pagan sacrifices at the time of sowing.[128] Similarly, the Synod wrote to Viatka,

---

[124] GAKO, f. 237, op. 136, d. 600, l. 1.

[125] RGIA, f. 796, op. 127, d. 694, ll. 2–4.

[126] Luppov, *Vzgliad*, pp. 3–8.

[127] See Luppov, *Vzgliad*, p. 14, and Paul W. Werth, "Baptism, Authority, and the Problem of *Zakonnost'* in Orenburg Diocese: The Induction of Over 800 'Pagans' into the Christian Faith," *Slavic Review* 56, 3 (1997): 472–76.

[128] *Materialy dlia istorii Russkoi tserkvi: Pis'ma Vysokopreosviashchenneishogo Filareta, Mitropolita Kievskogo i Galitskogo k Kirillu Arkhiepiskopu Podol'skomu*, appendix to *Pravoslavnyi sobesednik* (1876): 37.

chiding the religious authorities there for wanting to destroy sacred groves and calling on them "to explain [to parishioners] that the church has prayers, by which [Christians] solicit abundance of the fruits of the earth; to invite them to such prayers; and to expect further success from the grace of God."[129] It was as if the church was saying to novokreshchenye: we have our own ways (more effective ones) for securing material well-being. A direct equivalence was thus established between "superstitious sacrifices" and "holy sanctifying and edifying rituals of our church."[130]

This idea of substitution can also be seen in Pokrovskii's proposed construction of small prayer houses, or chapels, in villages located especially far from their parish church. These houses were to contain icons and serve as the focal point for local Christian practice, and clergy were expected to perform at least three services at these sites annually. The goal of these houses as replacements for native religious practice was explicit, for Pokrovskii identified important points in the agricultural cycle (before sowing and before and after harvest) as the time for Christian prayers, "because Cheremis precisely at this time constantly conduct their [pagan] offerings."[131] In 1838 Bishop Neofit (Sosin), too, promoted such prayer houses "for the attraction of Udmurts to Christian prayers instead of to pagan [*vorozhudnye*] offerings" and in instances when the clergy was unable to deflect Maris from pagan offerings.[132] These prayer houses resembled the huts and tents that were the foci of native religiosity, and there is evidence that they were treated as such by native parishioners—so much so, in fact, that one missionary later argued that local chapels had become rivals to proper churches and should therefore be closed.[133]

The need for compromise also generated disagreement about whether native celebrations were inherently of "pagan" character, thereby requiring abolition, or whether they simply constituted nonreligious festivals. Often, it was the secular authorities who were reluctant to ascribe an anti-Christian character to native festivals. In 1836 a missionary reported that baptized Tatars in Viatka province had engaged in *Akaiashka*, a ritual involving the offering of bread, salt, beer, and other produce to the land to secure a more bountiful harvest, followed by contests in horsemanship. The police official sent to investigate the matter concluded that "there is nothing illegal or tempting [in this ritual]," and the Governor agreed that the matter be

---

[129] Nikol'skii, *K istorii*, p. 47.

[130] *Materialy dlia istorii russkoi tserkvi*, p. 37.

[131] RGIA, f. 797, op. 3, d. 12654, ll. 129–30. The Synod approved of Pokrovskii's suggestion by ukaz in 1830, and by 1833 thirteen prayer houses had been constructed among Maris in Viatka diocese (ibid., l. 256). These houses and chapels were promoted in other dioceses as well (RGIA, f. 796, op. 116, d. 172, l. 28; and RGIA, f. 797, op. 5, d. 20775, l. 3).

[132] Luppov, *Materialy*, p. 92; RGIA, f. 796, op. 118, d. 73, l. 68.

[133] RGIA, f. 796, op. 110, d. 793, l. 40. Even among Russians chapels could rival proper churches, at least according to higher church authorities. See Vera Shevzov, "Chapels and the Ecclesial World of Prerevolutionary Russian Peasants," *Slavic Review* 55, 3 (1996): 585–613.

dropped. But Bishop Neofit countered that "in this ritual, performed for the request of abundance, *there is nothing Christian.*" Anything *non*-Christian, by implicit logic, was *anti*-Christian and indeed even diabolical.[134] Sometimes the clergy themselves adopted more lenient attitudes. In 1838 Viatka Bishop Nil, noting an apparent rise in Maris' fulfillment of Christian obligations, wrote that native offerings "often have nothing religious [in them] and in their essence are nothing more than popular rural fun or carousing, accompanied by milk rituals [?] of one sort or another, based on the traditions and habit of old." If these activities were not construed as "pagan" tendencies, he argued, then "the condition of the novokreshchenye would appear brighter . . . and the stubborn zealots of pagan antiquity would surely soften, having seen that Christianity does not prohibit popular celebratory customs and the joys of life."[135] Although such latitude was on the whole rare (particularly from a bishop), some figures clearly considered it unwise for the church to adopt attitudes that prohibited all indigenous practices. In any event, non-Russian habits and practice were not in any objective sense either "pagan" or even "religious" but had to be given significance as such, either by non-Russians themselves or, more frequently, by Russian observers.[136]

Even a more tolerant attitude required that boundaries of the permissible be defined. In one instance a priest actually participated in an Udmurt animist ritual, considering himself successful to the extent that he was able to introduce icons and to bless the animals awaiting sacrifice with holy water. He justified his act by writing,

> In my opinion it would be unwise to deny them [Udmurts] altogether in this admixture of pagan ritual with church [ritual], to the extent that by this prohibition one would produce in their minds, weak in Christian faith, a tangible dissatisfaction; one would for the future take away from them their disposition for prayers, conducted by true Christians in the fields, which has appeared among them for the first time; one would halt rapprochement of this kind with the church, even if superficial, at its first step; children cannot be removed from their mothers' breasts suddenly.

[134] RGIA, f. 796, op. 117, d. 1454, ll. 4–7 (emphasis added); Pokrovskii, "Vypiska iz dnevnika," 103; Luppov, *Materialy*, pp. 218–19. Such diabolization of native beliefs was common on the part of European missionaries overseas. See, for example, Mills, "Limits of Religious Coercion," 94–95; and two recent articles by Birgit Meyer, "Beyond Syncretism: Translation and Diabolization in the Appropriation of Protestantism in Africa," in Stewart and Shaw, *Syncretism/Anti-Syncretism*, pp. 45–68; and "Modernity and Enchantment: The Image of the Devil in Popular African Christianity," in *Conversion to Modernities: The Globalization of Christianity*, ed. Peter van der Veer (New York, 1996), pp. 199–230.

[135] RGIA, f. 796, op. 118, d. 73, ll. 53–54.

[136] Here I draw on the observations of Stewart and Shaw, *Syncretism/Anti-Syncretism*, pp. 19–22, and of Talal Asad in *Genealogies of Religion: Discipline and Reasons of Power in Christianity and Islam* (Baltimore, 1993), pp. 27–54. Both of these treatments stress that particular practices, utterances, and dispositions must be identified (and authorized or condemned) as "religion" or "deviation" by some person or institution with the power to do so.

The Synod sternly rejected this approach by transferring this priest from his original, wealthy parish to a less prosperous one.[137] But lest this priest's compromise appear unique, we should consider that the missionary Stefanov asserted in 1851 that Udmurts' rituals were losing their pagan significance, because now "clean" animals were being used (rather than those that the church prohibited the Orthodox to consume, like horses), and because the animals slated for sacrifice were now being blessed either through the prayer of a priest or through a prayer at home before holy icons.[138] Clerical participation in pagan rituals seems not to have been an irregular occurrence.

In considering the strategies adopted in the 1830s and 1840s, we see that the mission was limited by significant structural and ideological constraints. Financial limitations hindered a more effective educational policy and the regularization of the clergy's financial position with respect to their parishioners. The absence of persons fluent in both Russian and non-Russian languages impeded the translation effort. The government's view of pagans as essentially "ignorant" rather than malevolent led to limits on the use of police influence that many missionaries deemed necessary to convince non-Russians of the mission's authority. And the government's commitment to basic religious tolerance in many cases prevented religious authorities from eliminating important foci of pagan belief and practice. Increasingly, religious authorities found themselves making strategic compromises, ones that allowed novokreshchenye to "domesticate" and in some sense neutralize Orthodoxy and to subordinate it to their own needs.[139]

Following the Emperor's directives of 1837–42, reports of pagan gatherings and interaction between missionaries and novokreshchenye fall off somewhat, making it more difficult to assess the situation in the 1850s or 1860s. Evidently novokreshchenye became better at hiding their pagan activities and succeeded in regularizing their dealings with missionary institutions. In some parishes, moreover, novokreshchenye's "religious condition" (as defined by the church) evidently *was* improving, though not without the curious kinds of syncretism that we have identified here. In any event, the missions, as they had been created in the 1830s, were scaled back or allowed to terminate around mid-century. The Viatka missions continued into the twentieth century,[140] but their activities seem to have become more limited

---

[137] Luppov, *Khristianstvo*, pp. 383–87, citation from p. 384; and Luppov, *Materialy*, pp. 177–80.

[138] Luppov, *Materialy*, pp. 204–5.

[139] On this notion of "domestication" by colonial subjects of alien religious and cultural beliefs, see Viswanathan, *Outside the Fold*, p. 41.

[140] Iosif Stefanov, the author of the project for the Udmurt mission in 1830, served until 1876. S. Kreknin, *Votiaki Glazovskogo uezda i kratkii ocherk khristianskoi missii sredi nikh* (Viatka, 1899), pp. 35–38.

and programmatic, and in 1855 the number of missionaries in Urzhum district was reduced from two to one.[141] Although the Synod created special missionary divisions at the Kazan Ecclesiastical Academy in 1854, these were, initially at least, a scholarly enterprise above all and did not involve any active proselytism. The archbishop of Kazan thus reported in 1862 that "the mission in Kazan diocese in reality no longer exists."[142] As we shall see, ideas about missionary strategy and methods were undergoing important changes at this time, but these need to be understood in terms of broader shifts in Russia at mid-century.

[141] RGIA, f. 796, op. 136, d. 308.
[142] RGIA, f. 796, op. 442, d. 52, l. 18.

5 Changing Conceptions of
Difference, Assimilation, and Faith

Beginning in 1830, imperial authorities sought in an organized and concerted fashion to "reinforce" novokreshchenye in Orthodoxy and to combat "pagan deviations" and apostasy. But the standards by which they judged converts and the ways in which they marked non-Russians as distinct from Russians were undergoing considerable change in these decades. Even as confessional status remained central to both the administration of the empire and to the taxonomies by which imperial authorities classified the empire's diverse population, officials and, increasingly, publicists began also to employ a newer taxonomy rooted in language and ultimately ethnic origins. This shift can be traced in changing terminological usage, more specifically in the expansion of the term *inorodtsy* ("aliens," literally "those of other origin") from its initial referents in Siberia to the non-Russians of the Volga-Kama region, who had so far been collectively classified principally in religious terms. Related to this shift were more frequent references to *obrusenie* (Russification), which suggest that many officials had now begun to envision a more thorough cultural assimilation that went considerably beyond Christianization. Accordingly, missionaries offered novel arguments about the ways in which non-Russians' internalization of Christian values would facilitate the process of Russification and instill in them a sense of civic-mindedness (*grazhdanstvennost'*) that many secular officials saw as crucial to their meaningful participation in the new order. "Faith," in this scenario, became less a matter of fulfilling religious obligations, accepting legal ascription, and recognizing the church's authority than one of belief and religious conviction.

These new orientations were part of a larger transformation in Russia known as the Great Reforms of the 1860s. Serf emancipation, judicial reform, the introduction of new forms of local self-government (zemstvos), and the elimination of numerous particularistic social categories placed many people in the empire on a more equal footing in relation to the state (even as certain basic social distinctions remained in place). For these and other reasons considered below, the regime began to identify more closely with the Russian people specifically. Indeed, even as officials remained largely committed to the ideal of a composite state, the regime also began to aspire to create a more thoroughly unified and efficient polity, a project that inevitably acquired certain national overtones. Officials were in effect forced to confront the question: What kind of political entity *was* the Russian empire? As I argue, the turn toward a national model—however partial and hesitant—required the definition of "alien" elements and contributed to the elaboration of more modern colonial ideologies. Yet these shifts were only partial, and these new layers of signification did not obliterate the old. In this sense, Russia from this point became a strange hybrid that drew simultaneously on several models of state organization: a traditional, dynastic, composite state; an emerging (incomplete) national state; and a modern colonial empire.

From Novokreshchenye to Inorodtsy

To understand these newer modes of conceptualizing cultural difference, we must go back briefly to the early modern period. At that time, non-Russians of the Volga-Kama region were often referred to as specific tribes or were labeled by their religious confession or social status: for example, *tatarove*, *cheremisy*, *mordva*, *magometane* (Mohammedans), *idolopoklonniki* (idolaters), *teptiari*, and so on.[1] Before the eighteenth century and the transfer of most tribute-paying peoples of the region to state-peasant status, these designations were simultaneously linguistic, confessional, and social. For example, *cheremisy* (Maris) were presumed to be "idolaters," were understood to speak their own language, and had a specific legal social status in relation to the state. As Gregory L. Freeze has written, the social structure of pre-Petrine Russia "consisted of numerous, small groups and lacked collective terms for legal aggregation." The existence of nearly five hundred separate social categories underscores "the peculiar, fragmented structure of medieval Russian society."[2] At this time the term *inovertsy* ("those of other faith") probably came closest to serving as a general term for non-Russian peoples.[3]

---

[1] Michael Khodarkovsky, "'Ignoble Savages and Unfaithful Subjects': Constructing Non-Christian Identities in Early Modern Russia," in *Russia's Orient: Imperial Borderlands and Peoples, 1700–1917*, ed. Daniel R. Brower and Edward J. Lazzerini (Bloomington, 1997), p. 14; and S. V. Sokolovskii, "Poniatie 'korennoi narod' v Rossiiskoi nauke, politike i zakonodatel'stve," *Etnograficheskoe obozrenie* 3 (1998): 76.

[2] Gregory L. Freeze, "The *Soslovie* (Estate) Paradigm and Russian Social History," *American Historical Review* 91 (1986): 14.

[3] Andreas Kappeler, *Rußlands erste Nationalitäten: Das Zarenreich und die Völker der Mittleren Wolga vom 16. bis 19. Jahrhundert* (Cologne, 1982), p. 356. In Siberia, however, the terms *tuzemtsy* (natives, "people of those lands") and *inozemtsy* (foreigners, "people of other

This older system of classification began to change in the eighteenth century. The transfer of tribute payers to state-peasant status beginning in 1719 served to eliminate the sense of socio-legal difference attached to ethno-linguistic designations, for now many non-Russians had the same privileges and obligations as Russian state peasants.[4] Furthermore, the mass conversion of non-Russians in the mid-eighteenth century created a large pool of non-Russian Christians, which rendered "inovertsy" inadequate as a term for designating non-Russians. Thus there appeared a tripartite taxonomy of mutually exclusive categories: Orthodox Christians (Russians), novokreshchenye, and inovertsy. Implicit in this distinction between novokreshchenye and full-fledged Orthodox Christians was a recognition of the former's liminal position, even after several generations, at the edge of the Orthodox community. To be sure, on some level the state presumed, with good reason, that conversion to Orthodoxy was part of a process of cultural assimilation. Especially at the elite level, many non-Russians had been integrated into the Russian ruling class through conversion.[5] Yet latent doubts about the transformative power of baptism persisted, so that the *origins* of a convert, especially if he was one of a group of neophytes that had been inducted into Orthodoxy wholesale, remained an important part of his ascriptive identity and underscored his tenuous connection to Orthodox status. Thus the term novokreshchenye served as a basic category to describe converts and even their descendants for decades after their baptism.[6]

Moreover, this term seems to have served simultaneously as a religious distinction and a social one, for it was used in opposition to both "Orthodox Christian" and "peasant" (*krest'ianin*), which itself signified a baptized person. Official documents typically used the term "novokreshchen" (singular) where one would expect the term "peasant," often with an ethnic referent for clarification—e.g., *novokreshchen iz cheremis* (lit., a new convert from the Cheremis). Andreas Kappeler contends that non-Russians were re-

lands") encompassed all indigenous non-Russians (Sokolovskii, "Poniatie 'korennoi narod,' " 76; Yuri Slezkine, *Arctic Mirrors: Russia and the Small Peoples of the North* [Ithaca, 1994], esp. pp. 42–43), though the term *inovertsy* could also be used in these contexts.

[4] On the tax reform, see Kappeler, *Rußlands erste Nationalitäten*, pp. 245–91; and E. V. Anisimov, *Podatnaia reforma Petra I: Vvedenie podushnoi podati v Rossii, 1719–1728 gg.* (Leningrad, 1982), esp. pp. 179–89. Bashkirs and Teptiars were the exception in this regard, because they continued to represent distinct social groups as much as (or even more so than) ethno-linguistic ones.

[5] At the same time, of course, many also entered the ruling class *without* conversion to Orthodoxy. Indeed, Kappeler stresses that the existence of a multiethnic and multiconfessional elite was one of the defining characteristics of the Russian empire. See Andreas Kappeler, *Rußland als Vielvölkerreich: Entstehung, Geschichte, Zerfall* (Munich, 1992) pp. 134–38.

[6] Khodarkovsky makes this point in "'Ignoble Savages,'" pp. 18, 20–21. The notion that a convert's origins in one or another community trumps his or her own profession of religious conviction is a central theme in Gauri Viswanathan's exploration of conversion in colonial India, *Outside the Fold: Conversion, Modernity, and Belief* (Princeton, 1998), esp. pp. 75–117.

ferred to as "peasants" (*krest´iane*) by the second half of the eighteenth century, presumably because many of them were baptized.[7] But even in the 1820s at least one priest suggested that baptized Maris "no longer be called novokreshchenye, but peasants."[8] Moreover, because novokreshchenye status could in certain contexts confer privileges, non-Russians themselves were sometimes eager to uphold the distinction. Baptized Udmurts in one instance insisted on calling themselves novokreshchenye "so as not to be deprived of the right they have received to brew *kumyshka* [an indigenous alcoholic drink] for domestic use."[9] In short, the term novokreshchenye operated as a kind of hybrid social and religious category that allowed both the state and indigenous communities to signify that the latter were formally Christian, yet still distinct from full-fledged Orthodox Christians.

The terminology of difference was to evolve further in the second quarter of the nineteenth century, but to understand how this occurred we need to turn briefly to Siberia. For it was there that the term inorodtsy made its debut in official usage in the Siberian "Statute on Administration of Inorodtsy" of 1822.[10] Indeed, Yuri Slezkine suggests that the term appeared in part due to a growing discrepancy between official religious status on one hand and tax status and behavior on the other. Wholesale conversions in Siberia "resulted in the creation of a substantial group of Christians who were indistinguishable from pagans" and who continued to pay tribute instead of being exempted from it. But in contrast to the term novokreshchenye, which upheld a fundamental distinction between the baptized and the unbaptized, the designation inorodtsy encompassed *all* non-Russian Siberians, regardless of their religious confession. This designation also implied that natives, while previously redeemable through baptism, had become "congenital and apparently perennial outsiders" by the early nineteenth century.[11]

This marking of difference with reference to origins, regardless of religious status, should be understood in terms of new romantic conceptions of nationhood that were making their way into Russia at the time of the statute's composition. Indeed, the neologism *narodnost´* (nationality), which

---

[7] Kappeler, *Rußlands erste Nationalitäten*, p. 357.

[8] GAKO, f. 237, op. 131, d. 1283, ll. 820b.–83. This was Andrei Darovskii.

[9] "Istoriko-statisticheskaia zapiska o sele Sviatitskom v severo-zapadnoi chasti Glazovskogo uezda," *Viatskie gubernskie vedomosti* 41 (1851): 345. Udmurts, as a tribe, had been granted a special right to brew this drink, and these novokreshchenye evidently believed that they would no longer be considered Udmurts if they were regarded as full-fledged Orthodox Christians.

[10] *PSZ* I, vol. 38, no. 29126 (1822). Khodarkovsky and Sokolovskii contend that this term appeared well before the nineteenth century, but neither offers any specific examples of its use before 1822 or indicates where precisely the term was applied. Limiting myself to the Volga-Kama region, I concur with Kappeler and John Slocum, who argue that the term gained broad currency only in the mid-nineteenth century (Kappeler, *Rußlands ertse Nationalitäten*, p. 481; and John W. Slocum, "Who, and When, Were the *Inorodtsy*? The Evolution of the Category of 'Aliens' in Imperial Russia," *Russian Review* 57, 2 [1998]: 176).

[11] Slezkine, *Arctic Mirrors*, p. 53.

conveyed these romantic conceptions, was making its appearance almost simultaneously with the elaboration of the statute. Developing since the second half of the eighteenth century, these notions found more explicit articulation among Russian romantics of the early nineteenth century.[12] While the term *narodnost'* was adopted principally with reference to the Russian nationality (as a way of differentiating Russia from the West), at its root was the idea that *each* people had its own national character and spirit, revealed in its language, songs, ballads, and religious beliefs.[13] As Nathaniel Knight has argued about this concept in the early practice of nationalist ethnography in Russia, "Rather than viewing peoples collectively and comparatively, the nationalists looked to each nation as a unique entity unto itself and sought to capture the particular essence of national life through a study of the creative expression of the common people."[14]

From this perspective, the creation of an administrative category of inorodtsy in the Siberian Statute was rooted in a recognition that native Siberians' fundamental distinctiveness made it unrealistic to expect them to develop along Russian lines in the immediate future. Although Mikhail Speranskii and G. S. Baten'kov, the principal authors of the statute, envisioned a kind of gradual and voluntary development in the direction of Russian social and cultural forms ("organic Russification," in Marc Raeff's terms), underlying the statute was the conviction that laws should reflect the spiritual character of the people in question, as well as local history, ethnography, and climatology.[15] Although there was a hierarchy implicit in the statute—the Siberian natives were viewed as childlike—the administrative provisions relied on the idea that each people had its own spirit, its own life cycle, and implicitly, therefore, its own way forward. One of the more remarkable features of the statute, as Slezkine has noted, is that it provided no timetable for the native population's eventual assimilation and offered no real route by which they might cease being inorodtsy and become something else.[16] Difference here was construed as organic, and the adoption of the term inorodtsy was in part a product of this romantic view of nations.

Only gradually was the term inorodtsy applied to the non-Russians of the Volga-Kama region. Nowhere have I encountered it in documents originating

[12] On the appearance of this term, see Nathaniel Knight, "Ethnicity, Nationality and the Masses: *Narodnost'* and Modernity in Imperial Russia," in *Russian Modernity: Politics, Knowledge, and Practices*, ed. David Hoffmann and Yanni Kotsonis (New York, 2000), pp. 41–64.

[13] On the roots of this development in the eighteenth century, see Yuri Slezkine, "Naturalists versus Nations: Eighteenth-Century Russian Scholars Confront Diversity," in *Russia's Orient*, pp. 27–57; idem, *Arctic Mirrors*, p. 85.

[14] Nathaniel Knight, "Constructing the Science of Nationality: Ethnography in Mid-Nineteenth Century Russia" (Ph.D. diss., Columbia University, 1994), p. 84.

[15] Marc Raeff, *Siberia and the Reforms of 1822* (Seattle, 1956), pp. 112–28. This outlook was inscribed also in a companion statute on Siberian Kazakhs in 1822. See Virginia Martin, *Law and Custom in the Steppe: The Kazakhs of the Middle Horde and Russian Colonialism in the Nineteenth Century* (London, 2000).

[16] Slezkine, *Arctic Mirrors*, pp. 80–92.

before the 1820s; and its usage becomes more frequent only by the late 1840s and truly pervasive only in the 1860s. An isolated reference occurs in 1823, just a year after the approval of the Siberian Statute, when the Committee of Ministers used the term with regard to Tatars, Chuvash, and Maris in the Volga region.[17] Synodal officials combined materials from the Kazan and Tobol'sk missions of 1830 in a single file under the heading "On the Discussion of the Holy Synod about Sending Missionaries to Kazan and Tobol'sk Dioceses for the Conversion of Inorodtsy to Orthodoxy," even though only the documents on Tobol'sk province actually make reference to inorodtsy.[18] Even an 1841 ethnographic description of Kazan province, which offered ample opportunity to use the term inorodtsy, did not actually do so.[19]

The first repeated use of the term in Kazan province came only in the mid-1840s, when the Ministry of State Domains (MGI) attempted to establish special schools for pagans and Muslims to complement those already established for the Orthodox. In this context, documents refer to *inorodcheskie shkoly* (schools for inorodtsy) and "cantons and communities of these inorodtsy."[20] Still, the term had clearly not yet been universally accepted, and its specific referents remained ambiguous. At times officials retained more cumbersome phrases, such as "state peasants of Mohammedan faith or pagans," while local officials in Viatka province did not use the term inorodtsy at all, classifying the inhabitants first by ethnicity, and then within each ethnicity by faith.[21] Moreover, the term was at this point being used as a synonym for inovertsy, rather than for non-Russians more generally, since *baptized* non-Russians were under the jurisdiction of the regular state-peasant schools and were therefore not under separate discussion. Statistics assembled by the Kazan chamber of the MGI broke the population down into three categories that were presumably designed to be mutually exclusive: Russians, novokreshcheny, and inorodtsy.[22] Only as the deliberations on the schools continued did the term inorodtsy begin to be used more broadly to designate non-Russians rather than just non-Christians. Minister P. D. Kiselev called on "inorodtsy boys" to attend the Orthodox parish schools, while acknowledging that Muslims and pagans would have to be dealt with separately.[23]

Over the course of the 1850s the term inorodtsy was used more frequently as a shorthand for non-Russians regardless of faith. The term gained wider currency in ethnographic accounts in the 1850s, including a special volume

---

[17] NRF MarNII, op. 1, d. 43, l. 34.

[18] RGIA, f. 796, op. 109, d. 1552, covering the years 1828–37. It is not clear when the title of the file was actually composed.

[19] "Etnograficheskoe opisanie Kazanskoi gubernii," *Zhurnal MVD* 39 (1841): 350–410.

[20] RGIA, f. 383, op. 7, d. 6109a, ll. 91, 122ob.

[21] RGIA, f. 383, op. 7, d. 6109b, ll. 22–23.

[22] The Siberian Statute itself seems to have used the terms inovertsy and inorodtsy indiscriminately at times, even though they referred to two different sets of people (albeit with much overlap).

[23] RGIA, f. 383, op. 7, d. 6109b, ll. 11–11ob.

of *Ethnographic Anthology* that the Russian Geographic Society devoted to inorodtsy in 1858.[24] Soon inorodtsy were being mapped, counted, and given history—all explicitly as inorodtsy.[25] The term gained a pervasive currency in the 1860s in connection with educational reforms in the Volga-Kama region and had clearly begun to encompass non-Russians of *any* religious affiliation.[26] P. D. Shestakov, curator of the Kazan educational district, identified the following groups as inorodtsy under his jurisdiction in 1867 (by their prerevolutionary appellations): Tatars, Bashkirs, Kirgiz, Besermians, Mordvins, Chuvash, Cheremis, Votiaks, Permiaks, Zyrians, Voguls, Meshchers, Kalmyks, Latvians, Estonians, and Germans.[27] The report divided these inorodtsy into five groups, based on their "degree of obrusenie and their inclination for the Christian faith."[28] By this time non-Russians of all religions had clearly become inorodtsy. Religious affiliation remained salient, but even where the term inovertsy would surely have been more concise, authors sometimes used "unbaptized inorodtsy" (*nekreshchenye inorodtsy*).[29]

Meanwhile, those who were previously novokreshchenye now became, depending on the context, simply "peasants" or specifically "baptized [*kreshchenye*] inorodtsy." Indeed, the term novokreshchenye for the most part disappeared in the reform era as a social category, along with the many terms designating particularistic estates that had punctuated the region's social map and had now been largely collapsed into a single "peasant" category: *lashmany*, various peasant categories (state, crown, and manorial),

---

[24] S. M. Mikhailov, *Trudy po etnografii i istorii russkogo, chuvashskogo i mariiskogo narodov* (Cheboksary, 1972); V. A. Sboev, *Issledovaniia ob inorodtsakh Kazanskoi gubernii* (Kazan, 1856); V. M. Cheremshanskii, *Opisanie Orenburgskoi gubernii v khoziaistvenno-statisticheskom, etnograficheskom i promyshlennom otnosheniiakh* (Ufa, 1859); Petr Keppen, *Ob etnograficheskoi karte Evropeiskoi Rossii* (St. Petersburg, 1852); and *Etnograficheskii sbornik*, no. 4 (1858). For more on the role of the Geographic Society in the study of non-Russians, see Nathaniel Knight, "Science, Empire, and Nationality: Ethnography in the Russian Geographical Society, 1845–1855," in *Imperial Russia: New Histories for the Empire*, ed. Jane Burbank and David L. Ransel (Bloomington, 1998), esp. pp. 128–31.

[25] Keppen, *Ob etnograficheskoi karte*; M. Laptev, *Materialy dlia geografii i statistiki Rossii, sobrannye ofitserami General'nogo shtaba: Kazanskaia guberniia* (St. Petersburg, 1861). P. I. Keppen, *Khronologicheskii ukazatel' materialov dlia istorii inorodtsev Evropeiskoi Rossii* (St. Petersburg, 1861); and Nikolai Firsov, *Inorodcheskoe naselenie prezhnego Kazanskogo tsarstva v novoi Rossii do 1762 goda i kolonizatsiia zakamskikh zemel' v eto vremia* (Kazan, 1869).

[26] Slocum, "Who, and When, Were the *Inorodtsy*?" 185.

[27] Germans were included as a kind of special case. The report concluded that there were 4,223,035 inorodtsy in the district, or 4,476,590 "with Germans."

[28] P. D. Shestakov, "Soobrazheniia o sisteme obrazovaniia inorodtsev, obitaiushchikh v guberniiakh Kazanskogo uchebnogo okruga (Predstavlenie popechitelia Kazanskogo uchebnogo okruga Ministerstvu Narodnogo Prosveshcheniia ot 3 dekabria 1869, no. 369)," RGIA, Khranilishche pechatnykh zapisok, folder 3103.

[29] E. V–n, "Soobrazheniia o sposobakh k uspeshneishemu privlecheniiu nekreshchenykh inorodtsev k vere khristovoi," *Pravoslavnyi sobesednik* 1 (1871): 50–72. Compare this title to an earlier text (1858) on the same subject: "O sposobakh obrashcheniia inovertsev k Pravovere," *Pravoslavnyi sobesednik* 1 (1858): 451–82.

and to a degree Bashkirs and Teptiars.[30] It was perhaps the broad standardization of social identity associated with the Great Reforms—the elimination of a large number of particularistic social categories in favor of a simpler social taxonomy—that facilitated the ascendancy of newer epistemologies of difference.

If not entirely neutral, the term inorodtsy initially lacked the deeply pejorative connotation characteristic of terms used in the West to designate the other, such as "savage" and "barbarian." Rather, as Knight argues, inorodtsy at this point "denoted an all-encompassing 'other' free from any gradations of hierarchy." At least in the 1840s and 1850s (and perhaps later), the field of Russian ethnography did not adopt paradigmatic conceptions involving stages of development or "civilization" to any significant degree. In using the term inorodtsy, "Russians placed the emphasis on [non-Russians'] generic 'otherness' rather than their specific cultural identity and varying levels of development."[31] Petr Keppen, in his efforts to map and count non-Russians, applied the term not only to the Finnic and Turkic tribes of the eastern portion of the empire, but also to Estonians, Finns, Germans, Swedes, and Jews.[32] The term could be used in entirely relative ways to include even Russians themselves. In 1854 the Bishop of Simbirsk wrote that Chuvash in his diocese "shun interaction with inorodtsy," by which he seems simply to have meant that they avoided contact with anyone who was not Chuvash.[33] Non-Russian authors (or at least authors of non-Russian origins), such as Spiridon Mikhailov (a Chuvash), Sergei Nurminskii (a Mari), and Petr Keppen (a German), themselves used the term without visible reservation and were in fact among the earliest to do so.[34] While Russians were undoubtedly convinced of their own cultural superiority—especially with respect to the peoples of the empire's east—the term inorodtsy itself did not baldly signify such hierarchy, as its extension to decidedly European peoples suggests. It was only later, in the early twentieth century, that the term became derogatory and even polemical.[35]

What, then, is the significance of the fact that novokreshchenye became (or were becoming) baptized inorodtsy? In one sense, the significance seems to be quite limited. If, as novokreshchenye, non-Russian Christians were

---

[30] After their transfer to civilian rule in 1863 Bashkirs retained the distinction of being recognized as the owners of land they used (*votchinniki*).

[31] Knight, "Constructing the Science," pp. 340–41. Boris Mironov concurs that the term inorodtsy "did not convey anything belittling or insulting." Mironov, *Sotsial'naia istoriia Rossii (XVIII–nachalo XX v.)*, vol. 1 (St. Petersburg, 1999), p. 32.

[32] Keppen, *Ob etnograficheskoi karte*, esp. pp. 29–40; and idem, "Ob inorodcheskom, preimushchestvenno nemetskom naselenii S.-Peterburgskoi gubernii," *Zhurnal MVD* 32 (1850): 181–209.

[33] RGIA, f. 802, op. 6, d. 17303, l. 1.

[34] See the works by Mikhailov and Keppen cited above, as well as S. Nurminskii, "Inorodcheskie prikhody," *Pravoslavnoe obozrenie* 12 (1863): 243–63; and "Inorodcheskie shkoly," ibid. (1864): 201–26.

[35] Slocum, "Who, and When, Were the *Inorodtsy*?" 185–90.

discursively situated at the margins of the Russian Orthodox world, then they remained there even once they became baptized inorodtsy. Both designations signified simultaneously inclusion and exclusion: formal incorporation through baptism, yet recognition of the partial and provisional nature of that incorporation through reference to either the novelty of the conversion or to ethnic origins. To be sure, non-Russians *could* become full-fledged Russians and Orthodox Christians eventually, as many "Russian" surnames of obviously non-Russian origins testify. But one may also exaggerate the degree to which conversion offered "a fast track to assimilation," even for elites.[36] In medieval Russia, one's origins were by no means irrelevant, even after conversion. After the conquest of Kazan in 1552, distinctions between Russian provincial servitors and the Turkic novokreshchenye elite continued to be sharply observed. The latter were long affiliated with other Kazan service Tatars who remained Muslim, and only later did they blend into the Russian elite.[37] Likewise, converted Turkic families in Novgorod were distinguished from the main body of servitors and made different economic choices from their Russian counterparts long after conversion.[38] And if this was the experience of elite converts, who were comparatively small in number and had greater opportunities for integrating themselves into Russian society, it was even more the case for lower-class converts, who had been baptized *en masse* and who were usually slow to abandon their previous religious practices. There was certainly no "fast track" here.[39]

But the shift from novokreshchenye to inorodtsy was ultimately much more than just a semantic shift, for it implied that the process of assimilation and incorporation was now to occur along somewhat different lines and was to extend beyond the realm of religious confession alone. If previously the state's goal was that non-Russians become better Christians, as its focus on baptism and the problems of religious deviance suggests, then the goal now became "Russification" in a much more extensive and explicit sense. No doubt, Orthodoxy remained linked to this goal, but its exact relationship to broader processes of cultural change became somewhat less certain. Nor was it clear that Christianization would produce with the requisite speed the transformations that many officials now desired. In short, just as the Great Reforms raised a series of questions about the relationship of state to society, the nature of the Russian peasantry, the place of law in society, and so on, they also raised crucial questions about how non-Russians, both in the

[36] This is Khodarkovsky's phrase ("'Ignoble Savages,'" p. 18).

[37] Valerie Kivelson, "The Effects of Muscovite Colonial Rule on Kazan's Non-Russian Population: The First Fifty Years, 1552–1602" (unpublished paper, Stanford University, 1985), pp. 10–11.

[38] Janet Martin, "The Novokshcheny of Novgorod: Assimilation in the Sixteenth Century," *Central Asian Studies* 9, 2 (1990): 13–38.

[39] Khodarkovsky himself draws a key distinction between elite and common converts ("'Ignoble Savages,'" p. 14).

Volga-Kama region and more generally, actually fit (or should fit) into the larger society.

National Minorities or Colonial Subjects?

As with the term inorodtsy, references to obrusenie began to appear with much greater frequency in bureaucratic correspondence by the 1860s. Catherine II had used the intransitive verb *obruset'* as early as 1764, to mean centralizing and unifying the Empire's administrative and legal structure, and Nicholas I used the noun *obrusevanie* with regard to Congress Poland with much the same meaning in 1835.[40] But however much officials in this earlier period sought to promote a deeper acquaintance among non-Russians with Russian language and outlooks, this enterprise was still not one that proceeded under the banners of obrusenie and "fusion" (*sliianie*), as it would by the 1860s. To be sure, Minister of Education Sergei Uvarov could speak of the need in the 1830s to coopt Polish youth and "to smooth over those sharp characteristic traits that differentiate Polish from Russian youth and . . . to bring them closer to Russian concepts and morals, to transfer to them the general spirit of the Russian people." And he could also refer to the desirable "rapprochement" (*sblizhenie*) of Jews with the Christian population.[41] But one would search in vain to find in the Nikolaevan age the ambitious aim that the curator of the Kazan educational district articulated for educational reform in 1869: "The final goal of the education of all inorodtsy, living within the boundaries of our fatherland, should without argument be [their] obrusenie and fusion with the Russian people."[42] Although the actual meaning of the term "fusion" remained unspecified, clearly the implied level of assimilation was much greater in the 1860s than it had been previously. Officials now began to point to the supposed "alienation" [*otchuzhdennost'*] of non-Russians from things Russian as a matter of utmost significance. As Minister of Education Dmitrii Tolstoi wrote in 1867, "Inorodtsy remain to this day in the same ignorant condition as they were a few centuries ago and, moreover, in the most complete alienation

[40] Edward Thaden, ed., *Russification in the Baltic Provinces and Finland, 1855–1914* (Princeton, 1981), p. 7. Alishev quotes Catherine as writing of borderland provinces that they should "by the easiest available measures be brought to the point that they will russify and will cease looking to the forest like a wolf" (S. Kh. Alishev, *Istoricheskie sud'by narodov Srednego Povolzh'ia, XVI–nachalo XIX v.* [Moscow, 1990], p. 246). Catherine here was presumably referring to the Russian saying, "However much you feed a wolf, it will still look to the forest" (*skol'ko volka ni kormi, on vse v les gliadit*). I thank Elizaveta Zueva for pointing out this connection.

[41] Quoted in Cynthia H. Whittaker, *The Origins of Modern Russian Education: An Intellectual Biography of Count Sergei Uvarov, 1786–1855* (DeKalb, 1984), pp. 191, 193. On Uvarov and the Jews, see Michael Stanislawski, *Tsar Nicholas I and the Jews: The Transformation of Jewish Society in Russia, 1825–1855* (Philadelphia, 1983), pp. 59–69.

[42] Shestakov, "Soobrazheniia," p. 20.

from the Russian element. Nevertheless, the gradual enlightenment of inorodtsy and their rapprochement with the Russian people constitutes a task of the very greatest political significance in the future."[43]

Why had this matter now become so urgent? Broadly speaking, Russia's defeat in the Crimean War made clear to leading officials, as well as to many in Russian society, that the country had to modernize more quickly and aggressively in order to remain competitive in the international arena. Because the nation-state was showing itself to be the most effective model for the organization and mobilization of a society's resources—a principle that was being confirmed at this time by the national unification of Italy, Rumania, and Russia's most important neighbor, Germany—it is not surprising that some officials began to look to the model of a unified national state.[44] These tendencies had by no means been entirely absent under Nicholas I. His government undertook several measures designed to centralize and to integrate his realms: the incorporation of the Uniate church into the Orthodox, the replacement of Lithuanian and Polish laws by the Russian imperial law code, the transfer of Ukrainian Cossacks to state-peasant status, and the abolition of the Jewish kahal (the executive agency of Jewish communities).[45] But these tendencies always remained deeply qualified by Nicholas' continuing commitment to a non-national imperial model and to the principle that any reform be limited. Nor, for the most part, did these policies have a significant ethnic or linguistic dimension; they were principally administrative and institutional in nature. The Great Reforms represented a much more extensive overhaul of state institutions and existing social structure, which could not fail to have significant implications for non-Russians. As the legal historian Alexander Gradovskii wrote, "It is not difficult to notice that as soon as Russia took the first steps on the path toward the equalization of social status [*k uravneniiu soslovii*] and toward the development of personal and public liberty, the idea of nationality as the foundation and standard of policy made significant progress."[46]

Sviatoslav Kaspe has stated the problem succinctly and effectively: "Even so moderate a democratization as the Great Reforms inevitably had to render more urgent the question of the nature—national or imperial—of the

---

[43] *Sbornik postanovlenii Ministerstva Narodnogo Prosveshcheniia*, vol. 4 (St. Petersburg, 1867), no. 172, p. 415.

[44] Indeed, Elena Vorob´eva stresses that in this period one sees more frequent references to state unity and the idea of a "unified state" (*edinoe gosudarstvo*). See her "Musul´manskii vopros v imperskoi politike Rossiiskogo samoderzhaviia: Vtoraia polovina XIX veka–1917 g." (cand. diss., Institute of Russian History, St. Petersburg, 1999).

[45] See Kappeler, *Russland als Vielvölkerreich*, pp. 204–7, as well as Thaden, *Russification*, pp. 15–24; Stanislawski, *Tsar Nicholas I*, pp. 123–27; and Zenon E. Kohut, *Russian Centralism and Ukrainian Autonomy: Imperial Absorption of the Hetmanate, 1760s–1830s* (Cambridge, Mass., 1988).

[46] Quoted in Sviatoslav Kaspe, "Imperskaia politicheskaia kul´tura i modernizatsiia v Rossii: Peremeny vtoroi poloviny XIX veka" (paper presented at the conference "Empire and Region: The Russian Case, 1700–1917," Omsk, 1999).

Russian state system under renovation."[47] The state's partial dismantling of the system of social hierarchy that lay at the foundation of the old imperial orientation suggested that the regime, willy-nilly, would take a substantial step in the direction of the national model. In effect, Russia's further modernization and liberalization implied the adoption of a model of a national state—a more thoroughly integrated, if still not ethnically homogeneous entity.[48] It needs to be stressed that this did not necessarily mean the adoption of brutal and heavy-handed policies of cultural Russification. But to the extent that Russians were now being identified as the "core population" (*korennoe naselenie*) and even the "ruling population" (*gospodstvuiushchee russkoe naselenie*), the new orientation *did* represent a potential threat to non-Russians, who were in danger of being reduced to the status of ethnic and confessional minorities.

The Polish insurrection of 1863 was a seminal event in the state's reorientation along these lines and can indeed be regarded as a major turning point in the empire's history. Construed by officialdom as a traitorous "mutiny" (*miatezh*), the insurrection contributed to a climate of counter-reform already developing in the mid-1860s, and cast into doubt the loyalty of other ethno-religious groups.[49] In response to the insurrection, the regime took a number of steps that represented a significant departure from traditional policies. In contrast to its long practice of ruling through local elites, the state focused its repression on the Polish nobility, who were understood to be the leaders of the insurrection, and even sought to foster antagonism among the peasantry against their landlords while implementing emancipation in Poland in 1864. The state also retreated from its policy of cooperation with recognized non-Orthodox clergy by attacking the Catholic church in Poland.[50] Although these measures were not without precedent, they had a much greater national and cultural dimension than, for example, the state's repression of the 1830 Polish insurrection, which was more administrative and institutional in character. There continues to be debate about the degree to which the state initiated a conscious policy of cultural and linguistic Russification after 1863, but there can be no doubt that state policy was now

[47] Kaspe, "Imperskaia politicheskaia kul'tura," p. 11. See also Charles Robert Steinwedel, "Invisible Threads of Empire: State, Religion, and Ethnicity in Tsarist Bashkiriia, 1773–1917" (Ph.D. diss., Columbia University, 1999), pp. 93, 101–14.

[48] As Geoffrey Hosking has written, "Probably the Russian government had no alternative but to pursue some kind of Russification policy in an era when economic growth required greater administrative unity and coordination, and when national solidarity was establishing itself as a paramount factor in international relations and in military strength" (Geoffrey Hosking, *Russia: People and Empire, 1552–1917* [Cambridge, Mass., 1997], p. 397).

[49] Theodore R. Weeks, *Nation and State in Late Imperial Russia: Nationalism and Russification on the Western Frontier, 1863–1914* (DeKalb, 1996), pp. 94–96; W. Bruce Lincoln, *The Great Reforms: Autocracy, Bureaucracy, and the Politics of Change in Imperial Russia* (DeKalb, 1990), p. 168; and S. Frederick Starr, *Decentralization and Self-Government in Russia, 1830–1870* (Princeton, 1972), pp. 256–60.

[50] Kappeler, *Russland als Vielvölkerreich*, pp. 208–9.

directed toward the "weakening of the Polish element," which in practice meant strengthening the Russian. This orientation served also to effectuate a reconfiguration of geographical space along national-confessional lines. Most dramatically, the designation "Poland" was simply eliminated from official usage in favor of "Vistula land" [*Privislinskii krai*]. Officials began also to act on the long-held proposition that the western provinces—that is, the area adjacent to the former Kingdom of Poland and inhabited primarily by Lithuanians, Belorussians, Ukrainians, and Jews—had been Russian and / or Orthodox from the oldest times. It was, of course, the government's self-appointed task to make this "fact" clear to the local population through the energetic promotion of Russian language and culture at the expense of alternatives.[51] It should be stressed that similar policies did not extend to other portions of the empire, or did so only considerably later, and we should therefore be careful not to exaggerate the scale of the shift.[52] But it seems beyond dispute that there had been a key change in the ways that many officials and segments of Russian society regarded their state.

By the 1860s, moreover, this shift led to the emergence of a more coherent and explicit ideology of imperialism, especially in relation to Russia's eastern territories. Monika Greenleaf has noted that already in the early nineteenth century Russian elites had begun to fortify their sense of association with Europe by participating in discourses of Orientalism. With regard to the Amur region, Mark Bassin has identified a strong sense of imperial mission that emerged in the 1840s and culminated in the late 1850s and early 1860s. This vision suggested that Russians were uniquely qualified, given their location between East and West, to bring European civilization and enlightenment to the peoples of Asia. Similarly, Thomas Barrett contends that the capture of the rebel Shamil in the North Caucasus in 1859 after almost thirty years of warfare represented a clear demonstration of Russia's westernness and a comforting confirmation of the notion that Russia had a role to play in the march of civilization. Finally, Russia's conquest of Central Asia in the 1860s seemed to offer a clear example of the victory of civilization and prosperity over barbarity and fanaticism, and thus reinforced Russia's European status still more.[53] The fact that Russia now found

---

[51] Ibid., pp. 210–11. On Ukraine specifically, see A. I. Miller, *"Ukrainskii vopros" v politike vlastei i russkom obshchestvennom mnenii (vtoraia polovina XIX v.)* (St. Petersburg, 2000), which shows that the government was able to do far less than its own pronouncements might suggest.

[52] Kappeler, *Russland als Vielvölkerreich*, pp. 211–15; Thaden, *Russification*, pp. 27–28; idem, *Russia's Western Borderlands, 1710–1870* (Princeton, 1984), pp. 144–68, 236; John Doyle Klier, *Imperial Russia's Jewish Question, 1855–1881* (Cambridge, 1995), pp. 145–58; and Tuomo Polvinen, *Imperial Borderland: Bobrovnikov and the Attempted Russification of Finland, 1898–1904*, trans. Steven Huxley (London, 1995).

[53] Monika Greenleaf, *Pushkin and Romantic Fashion: Fragment, Elegy, Orient, Irony* (Stanford, 1994); Mark Bassin, *Imperial Visions: Nationalist Imagination and Geographical Expansion in the Russian Far East* (Cambridge, 1999), esp. pp. 37–68 and 182–205; Thomas Barrett, "The Remaking of the Lion of Dagestan: Shamil in Captivity," *Russian Review* 53 (1994):

itself faced with "fanatical" Muslims (and could therefore assign itself the task of subordinating them to reason and civilization) established it as a functional equivalent of other colonial European powers, who had their own Muslim "fanatics" to deal with.[54] Russia thus began to participate much more consciously in a larger European project of modern colonialism. In the context of educational reform in the 1860s, one publicist could write,

> If in general it is characteristic for a state, in which one people, by its numbers and its historical significance, decisively prevails over all alien elements, to aspire to their complete merging with the element that constitutes its main strength, then such an aspiration for Russia with respect to the inorodtsy of her eastern outskirts is an obligation that is doubly holy: assimilating these inorodtsy to its predominant nationality, the Russian state would simultaneously fulfill its calling as a Christian and European-educated power and would render a true service both to the Christian church and to the matter of general civilization.[55]

Similarly, the historian Stepan Eshevskii, having identified Russia's "predominant Russo-Slavic element" as "European," could conclude in 1857 that "each step forward of the Russian *narodnost´* at the expense of other tribes is a victory for Europe."[56] That Russians now viewed their imperial project as essentially a Europeanizing one is underscored by the fact that educators studied British and French school policies in India and Algeria before drawing up the 1870 statute on education of non-Russians.[57]

This new colonial orientation can be seen in the organization of missionary work as well. The state had long understood itself to be a promoter of civilization in its realms and at times promoted the conversion of non-Christians to Orthodoxy. But by the 1870s missionary work was undertaken, at least ostensibly, in the name of the Russian people and even with their participation. The key institution in this regard was the Orthodox Missionary Society established through the initiative of Moscow Metropolitan Innokentii in 1870 (after the failure of a similar society in St. Petersburg in the 1860s). Though subordinate to the Holy Synod, the Society was created as a nonstate institution that would draw, in the spirit of the times, on

---

353–66; and Adeeb Khalid, *The Politics of Muslim Cultural Reform: Jadidism in Central Asia* (Berkeley, 1998), pp. 15–16, 50–53.

[54] Patricia M. E. Lorcin, *Imperial Identities: Stereotyping, Prejudice, and Race in Colonial Algeria* (London, 1995), pp. 53–75; and David Edwards, "Mad Mullahs and Englishmen: Discourse in the Colonial Encounter," *Comparative Studies in Society and History* 31 (1989): 649–70.

[55] "K voprosu ob ustroistve uchilishch dlia inorodcheskikh detei Kazanskogo Uchebnogo Okruga," *Zhurnal MNP* 134, 3 (1867): 79.

[56] S. V. Eshevskii, "Missionerstvo v Rossii," in *Sochineniia S. V. Eshevskogo* (Moscow, 1870), 3:670. This article was also published in *Zhurnal MNP* 135 (1867): 58–90.

[57] *Sbornik postanovlenii MNP*, vol. 4 (St. Petersburg, 1867), p. 415.

the participation of Russian society. The Society's principal purpose was to acquaint Russians with missionary activity in the empire—above all in Siberia—and to enlist their support for this enterprise. The organization accordingly began publishing the journals *Missionary* (*Missioner*, 1874–79) and later *Orthodox Bearer of Good News* (*Pravoslavnyi blagovestnik*, 1893–1917) and encouraging the establishment of local committees in all the empire's provinces.[58]

The details of the Society's work are beyond the scope of this book.[59] My point here is that its participants considered it the task of the Orthodox Russian people to spread their faith among the empire's benighted non-Christians. One supporter stressed the necessity of making the St. Petersburg society "popular and national" (*popularnoe i narodnoe*), adding even that the term "missionary" should be jettisoned because it was foreign (it had come "through Rome") and therefore "does not instill trust in the Russian people."[60] For similar reasons—and to become financially solvent—the Society in Moscow placed much emphasis on establishing as many local committees as possible and on publicizing news of missionary work both in print and through sermons in parish churches. Count A. V. Bobrinskii, a member of the Society's board, complained in 1875 that several dioceses had no local committees even though they had "a native Orthodox Russian population [*korennoe pravoslavnoe russkoe naselenie*] which is therefore capable of relating to the missionary cause with just as much love" as had Russians in other dioceses.[61] The bishop of Perm, speaking at the opening of the Society's Perm Diocesan Committee, also saw missionary work as a task for the Russian people:

> I submit that Russian Orthodox Christians do not need to look to the example of other Christian states of Europe, from which proselytes go in great numbers to the American deserts and across the burning sands of Africa and to the maritime states of Asia, China and Japan to proclaim the Gospel to the wild Americans, the Negroes, or those who revere Brahma and Mohammed. . . . The Russian heart does not sympathize with the spread of the faith of Christ any less.[62]

[58] See "Pravoslavnoe Missionerskoe Obshchestvo," *Pravoslavnyi blagovestnik* 20 (1894): 149–59. Between 1877 and 1893 *Moskovskie tserkovnye vedomosti* carried the society's materials in a special missionary section. On the St. Petersburg society, see RGIA, f. 796, op. 145, d. 1134.

[59] But see Yuri Slezkine, "Savage Christians or Unorthodox Russians? The Missionary Dilemma in Siberia," in *Between Heaven and Hell: The Myth of Siberia in Russian Culture*, ed. Galya Diment and Yuri Slezkine (New York, 1993), pp. 15–31; and Andrei A. Znamenski, *Shamanism and Christianity: Native Encounters with Russian Orthodox Missions in Siberia and Alaska, 1820–1917* (Westport, Conn., 1999).

[60] *Missionerskoe Obshchestvo v 1866: Vzgliad na ego proshedshee, nastoiashchee i budushchee* (St. Petersburg, 1867), p. 9.

[61] Quoted in "Pravoslavnoe Missionerskoe Obshchestvo," p. 152.

[62] Quoted in Evgenii Popov, *Ob userdii k missionerskomu delu* (Perm, 1874), p. 9.

He accordingly called on church servitors and laymen, people of all ranks and calling, men and women to contribute in any way they could. The spread of Orthodoxy had now become a task for the entire Russian people. Particularly given the Siberian and Asian focus of the Society's work, these perspectives reflected a new colonial consciousness, according to which the Russian Orthodox population represented the empire's "core," while everybody else, to one degree or another, represented its periphery.[63]

Viewed in this context, the broader significance of the term inorodtsy becomes apparent: it was a conceptual tool for a changing state and society to define who constituted the "core population" of the empire and who made up the residual. John Slocum has skillfully described the broadening of the term's application, from its original referents in Siberia to the inhabitants of Central Asia, to Jews, to the peoples of the Volga region, and eventually—principally for polemical purposes—to virtually all the empire's non-Russian groups: "The term originally meant to designate the empire's most radically different 'others' had come to signify an insurmountable barrier of difference separating Eastern Slavs [who were all considered to be Russians on religious grounds] and all other inhabitants of the empire."[64] "Inorodtsy" always marked particular groups as alien to some putative core population—a core population that had rarely, if ever, been identified clearly as such before.

But if, as Slocum argues, the term eventually was to signify "insurmountable" difference, I would argue that this was not yet the case in the period of the Great Reforms. For at this stage, it seems to me, the concern was not merely to ascertain who was Russian and who was not, but also—and perhaps more important—to determine which groups could realistically be expected to participate in a process of national construction, and which would be excepted from this project.[65] By the 1860s "inorodtsy" seems to have been used to signify *both* "national minorities" (those understood to be different from Russians but amenable to assimilation) and "colonial subjects" (those who were so different and / or uncivilized that they should be administered in a particularistic fashion). Thus state officials could energetically promote obrusenie among some inorodtsy, such as the smaller Finnic groups, while refusing to incorporate others even into the state's system of social classification—for example, the native populations of Central Asia.

[63] Societies were central to the colonial missions launched from western European states in Africa and Asia. See for example T. O. Beidelman, *Colonial Evangelism: A Socio-Historical Study of an East African Mission at the Grassroots* (Bloomington, 1982); John and Jean Comaroff, *Of Revelation and Revolution*, vol. 1: *Christianity, Colonialism, and Consciousness in South Africa* (Chicago, 1991); and vol. 2: *The Dialectics of Modernity on a South African Frontier* (Chicago, 1997); Peter Van Rooden, "Nineteenth-Century Representations of Missionary Conversion and the Transformation of Western Christianity," in *Conversion to Modernities: The Globalization of Christianity*, ed. Peter van der Veer (New York, 1996), pp. 65–88; and Antony Copley, *Religions in Conflict: Ideology, Cultural Contact, and Conversion in Late-Colonial India* (Delhi, 1997).

[64] Slocum, "Who, and When, Were the *Inorodtsy*?" 189–90.

[65] Kaspe makes this point very effectively ("Imperskaia politicheskaia kul'tura," p. 30).

Similarly, the state could extend to *some* provinces with substantial non-Russian populations the major institutions of the Great Reforms—for example, zemstvos and the judicial reform—while postponing or indeed rejecting their introduction to other non-Russian provinces, especially those further from the center.[66] The regime never fully adopted the national model and continued to place great emphasis on dynastic loyalty and social distinction, so that the imperial landscape remained uneven. I would argue nonetheless that the attempt to draw such distinctions—identifying a core and periphery—was an important aspect of the Great Reforms.

The Volga-Kama region was one of the places where this division proved especially difficult to establish. If we attempt to classify the peoples here as either national minorities or colonial subjects, it is difficult to avoid the conclusion that they were both at once. To some extent, this was probably true of all the empire's non-Russian peoples. Nonetheless, important lines were being drawn. Missionaries and state officials increasingly came to regard Muslims in the region as intractably alien, unassimilable, and ultimately hostile to Christianity and the Russian state. Simultaneously, most officials maintained hope that the Finnic peoples and Chuvash could be assimilated, as long as the state adopted the appropriate policies.[67]

Thus, even as state officials continued to espouse older conceptions of dynastic loyalty and to emphasize social distinctions that in principle encompassed the entire state, alternative orientations were now beginning to appear, as a result of both the state's own promotion of change in the context of the Great Reforms and the challenges presented by non-Russians (most importantly, in Poland and the western provinces). The appearance of a modern ideology of colonialism represented a corollary to the new aspirations of creating a national state, since not all the empire's far-flung and diverse territories could realistically be included in a project of national construction. Accordingly, while all those distinct from "the core population of the empire" (Russians) would gradually be labeled inorodtsy, only some of those inorodtsy would actually be considered objects for assimilation.

Confession, Assimilation, and Belief

The spread of the concepts inorodtsy and obrusenie suggests a certain demotion of religious confession as a marker of difference in the Russian

[66] Kappeler, *Russland als Vielvölkerreich*, p. 227. Jörg Baberowski traces the differential implementation of the 1864 judicial reform in *Autokratie und Justiz: Zum Verhältnis von Rechtstaatlichkeit und Rückständigkeit im ausgehenden Zarenreich, 1864–1914* (Frankfurt am Main, 1996), pp. 339–427. For the most part, Kazan, Simbirsk, and Viatka provinces were treated as part of the state's central provinces, while Ufa province lagged slightly behind, receiving zemstvos a decade later. Orenburg province received zemstvos only in 1912.

[67] Kappeler likewise notes that in Transcaucasia, the Christian peoples became the object of Russification, while the Muslims did not (*Russland als Vielvölkerreich*, p. 218).

empire. As contemporary discussions about obrusenie make clear, Orthodoxy was clearly *not* an indispensable tool of governance in the minds of all
officials and educators. In establishing a new school system for the non-
Russian population, officials explicitly recognized that obrusenie for certain
peoples—Muslim Tatars in particular—would have to occur without the
help of Orthodoxy, since there was no possibility of attracting them to institutions in which Orthodoxy played a visible role. Instead, imperial administrators planned to make language the main vehicle for obrusenie, by introducing Russian language classes into Tatar schools and eventually requiring
mullah-teachers to have some knowledge of Russian.[68] In writing to the
Chief Procurator of the Synod, Archbishop Antonii of Kazan emphasized
that local missionaries' efforts to translate religious texts into indigenous
languages were not intended to develop a complete non-Russian literature
"with which inorodtsy could be satisfied and not have after that a need to
study the Russian language, [because this] would be contrary to the main
goal of establishing schools among inorodtsy and teaching them literacy—
that is, their gradual obrusenie." Rather, missionaries would publish "only
those books in inorodtsy languages that contain the most necessary elementary ideas, especially religious-moral ones, . . . to render them capable of further education, which will then in general occur in inorodtsy schools in the
Russian language."[69] In this formulation, translation could proceed only if
it represented no obstacle to the project of obrusenie.

Missionaries thus found themselves making the argument that Christianization's principal benefit was its contribution to larger processes of assimilation and civilizing. E. A. Malov wrote in 1866, trying to gain state support for
missionary work: "One or another religion, confessed by a given people or
tribe, can, by its essence and character, present favorable or unfavorable conditions for the internalization by that tribe of education and civic-mindedness
[*grazhdanstvennost*]. The example of European peoples without argument
accords to Christianity in this regard the best and highest significance."[70]
Non-Russians' internalization of Christian values would render them amenable to the sensibilities that secular authorities considered essential in the reform era. In a similar fashion, the bishop of Perm in 1872 listed numerous

[68] *Sbornik Postanovlenii MNP*, vol. 5 (St. Petersburg, 1872), p. 760. For a broad consideration of these questions, see Isabelle Teitz Kreindler, "Educational Policies Toward the Eastern
Nationalities in Tsarist Russia: A Study of Il´minskii's System" (Ph.D. diss., Columbia University, 1969), pp. 169–70; Robert Paul Geraci, "Window on the East: Ethnography, Orthodoxy,
and Russian Nationality in Kazan, 1870–1914" (Ph.D. diss., University of California, Berkeley,
1995), pp. 110–84.

[69] RGIA, f. 796, op. 149, d. 102, ll. 40b.–5.

[70] E. A. Malov, "Statisticheskie svedeniia o kreshchenykh tatarakh Kazanskoi i nekotorykh
drugikh eparkhii, v volzhskom basseine," *Uchenye zapiski Kazanskogo universiteta*, no. 3
(1866): 313. Such a formulation was not entirely new. Officials like Uvarov and Kiselev had
likewise contended in the 1830s that Christianity and "civic-mindedness" were inherently
linked, the former constituting the purest manifestation of the latter. See Whittaker, *Origins of
Modern Russian Education*, esp. pp. 205–6, and Stanislawski, *Tsar Nicholas I*, p. 66.

benefits "for our Fatherland here on earth" that would appear once non-Christian peoples both "among us" and at the empire's periphery "become sons of the Orthodox church":

> Then in place of the unbridled arbitrariness of wild passions, to which unenlightened people usually submit, there will appear law and legality; instead of rapaciousness and pillage, to which people alien to Christian civilization are inclined, respect for the fellow man's property will come into force, and the laws of both state and family will become inviolable; instead of interminable wars, as there are among the various tribes of barbarous peoples, there will emerge peace and tranquillity; instead of vagrant and uncoordinated life will appear life attached to a permanent place, and there will appear order in family and public life. The cross and the Gospel bring with them all these worldly blessings.[71]

Most famously, perhaps, the lay missionary N. I. Il'minskii asserted that Orthodoxy could play a crucial role in promoting Russification among inorodtsy: "As soon as an inorodets has internalized Orthodoxy consciously and with conviction, with his mind and heart, he already has become Russified" (*on uzhe obrusel*).[72] In all these cases, missionaries and clerics were intent on emphasizing the contribution that they could make to the fulfillment of the secular government's larger goals.

The more explicit association between Orthodox Christianity, on one hand, and Russification and "civic-mindedness," on the other, also contributed to the appearance of new standards for measuring "faith." If non-Russians' internalization of Orthodoxy was to provide all the benefits that missionaries claimed, then that internalization had to be genuine and thorough. Accordingly, by the 1860s clerics began to focus much more of their attention on the *convictions* of baptized non-Russians, rather than on external markers of confessional belonging. To grasp this transition, we need to return to the eighteenth century, at which time Russian authorities had construed religion above all as "law" (*zakon*)—a set of rules and prescriptions governing behavior, worship, rites, hygiene, and appearance. Documents speak of persons belonging to "the Muslim law" or "the Christian law." (It remained unclear whether or not paganism constituted "law.")[73] In this way, religion for imperial authorities constituted above all a matter of "law" and ascription; the putative believer's convictions were less important than whether he or she submitted to the religious authority of the clergy. The

---

[71] Quoted in Popov, *Ob userdii*, pp. 9–10. Perm diocese itself had many non-Christians, including almost 89,000 Muslims, almost 13,000 "idolaters," roughly 300 "fire-worshippers" (*ognepoklonniki*), and even 250 Jews (ibid., p. 3).

[72] Quoted in A. N. Grigor'ev, "Khristianizatsiia nerusskikh narodnostei, kak odin iz metodov natsional'no-kolonial'noi politiki tsarizma v Tatarii," *Materialy po istorii Tatarii*, fasc. 1. (Kazan, 1948), p. 262.

[73] For example, a decree of 1750 referred to the conversion "of nonbelievers of the Mohammedan law and of idolaters, who have no law" (*PSZ* I, vol. 13, no. 9825 [1750]).

principal concern of both state and church was to ensure the submission of deviates and apostates to the authority of the church by having them sign statements promising to abandon "Mohammedanism" and "delusions."

Central to this older conception was also the performance of prescribed rituals, the assumption of the appropriate external appearance, the proper display of designated religious objects (such as crosses and icons)—in short, *orthopraxy* as opposed to *orthodoxy*.[74] This is not to deny that ritual represented a way for believers to express and maintain their religious beliefs, nor to suggest that the church was entirely indifferent as to what its adherents actually believed. My point is not to separate ritual and faith in some artificial sense but rather to underscore the *relative significance* of external display vis-à-vis internal conviction in church and state's conception of what constituted religious affiliation.

In this context the experience of "old-convert" Tatars, or Kräshens, is particularly revealing. We unfortunately have woefully little information about Kräshen communities prior to the appearance of apostasy among some of them in the years after 1866 (and even then, the situation in communities unaffected by apostasy remains largely unknown to us). Kräshens were generally considered good Christians, so that in 1830 Kazan Archbishop Filaret contended that they were reasonably well "reinforced" in Orthodoxy, and he therefore did not recommend that the new mission devote any particular attention to them.[75] By contrast, the young Malov would claim in 1865 that if apostasy had not yet occurred among Kräshens, then this was principally because of "the vitality of their ancient, dogmatic religious conceptions and rituals" (i.e., paganism) and *not* because of any affinities they felt for Christianity.[76] Similarly, in 1875 the missionary Mikhail Mashanov was severely disappointed to learn how much his expectations that Kräshens "differ from Russians only by their language and clothing" had been misplaced.[77] Until clerics with new standards of religiosity emerged to cast a critical eye on converts' "religious condition," Kräshens were considered to be sufficiently Christian by the standards of the day, presumably because they fulfilled all the obligations required of them by ecclesiastical authorities with only minimal "deviation." Malov's observation in 1865 was essentially correct: it took outright "apostasy"—that is, the *open* rejection of even the formal requirements of Orthodoxy—for Kräshens to earn any real attention from ecclesiastical authorities.[78]

[74] I adopt this distinction from Clifford Geertz, "'Internal Conversion' in Contemporary Bali," in *The Interpretation of Cultures* (New York, 1973), p. 177.

[75] RGIA, f. 797, op. 3, d. 12652, l. 160b. Kräshens make their way into documents of the Nikolaevan period in large measure to the extent that they were settled near more problematic novokreshchenye Tatars (above all in Chistopol district).

[76] E. A. Malov, "Prikhody starokreshchenykh i novokreshchenykh tatar v Kazanskoi eparkhii," *Pravoslavnoe obozrenie* 17 (1865): 450.

[77] Mikhail Mashanov, *Religiozno-nravstvennoe sostoianie kreshchenykh tatar Kazanskoi gubernii Mamadyshskogo uezda* (Kazan, 1875), p. 5.

[78] Malov, "Prikhody," 451. What precisely was going on at the parish level remains unclear.

Indeed, Malov's work demonstrates nicely the transition toward faith-as-belief that I have in mind. Having completed the Kazan Academy in 1862, Malov wrote a series of articles on the history of Orthodox mission and state policy toward Islam.[79] Central to this work was a forceful criticism of earlier missionary methods—mechanical "admonitions," resettlement, and so on—for being too "external" and "official," for attempting merely to demonstrate the illegality of apostasy, rather than "strengthen[ing] the internal bond between the baptized-Tatar apostates and the Christianity they had accepted." It was now time, Malov contended, to focus on the *convictions* of baptized Tatars, on the nature of their "internal bond" with Christianity—to abandon "forceful" and "external" measures in favor of "purely spiritual ones."[80] To be sure, Malov was hardly indifferent to external manifestations of religious affiliation. But the explicit contrast he drew between the "internal" and the "external" suggests the appearance of a more faith-based, perhaps even individualized, notion of confessional affiliation.

Ideas about what constituted "conversion" accordingly changed. If the missionaries of 1830 gauged conversion by whether or not novokreshchenye signed statements promising to abandon indigenous traditions, then already by 1850 Il′minskii dismissed this standard with scorn. The earlier missionaries considered it to be a "very great success," he wrote with irony, "when they managed, in one way or another, to take from a few Tatars signatures for the fulfillment of Christian rites, although these signatures *did not in the least vouch for the sincerity of conversion.*" Il′minskii doubted the effectiveness of itinerant missionaries, because "a person's religious convictions, naturally, cannot change quickly as a result of merely verbal admonitions."[81] As late as 1858, an instructional text for clergy openly supported the use of material benefits in promoting baptism, while later commentaries would identify this practice as a major source of apostasy and pagan recidivism.[82] Whereas imperial authorities had been largely indifferent to the nature of the baptisms that produced these very questionable Christians—the important matter was *the fact* of their baptism rather than *how* precisely it had occurred—later observers looked more deeply into this question, almost always concluding that the methods behind the original conversions were

---

[79] Most important were a series of works in the mid- to late 1860s: "Prikhody"; *Pravoslavnaia protivomusul′manskaia missiia v Kazanskom krae v sviazi s istoriei musul′manstva v pervoi polovine XIX veka* (Kazan, 1868); and "O tatarskikh mechetiakh v Rossii," *Pravoslavnyi sobesednik* 3 (1867): 285–320; 1 (1868): 3–45.

[80] "Malov, "Prikhody," no. 18, 294; no. 17, 451.

[81] NART, f. 10, op. 1, d. 5964, l. 170b., 180b. (emphasis added).

[82] On the promotion of material benefits, see "O sposobakh obrashcheniia inovertsev k Pravovere," 473. For a criticism of material benefits, see Ivan Katetov, "Obzor pravitel′stvennykh i tserkovnykh rasporiazhenii, kasaiushchikhsia obrashcheniia v khristianstvo tatar-mukhammedan (XIII–XVIII vv.)," *Strannik* 8 (1886): 565–91, esp. 588–91. Note that the state did away with important material incentives for conversion in the mid-nineteenth century (RGIA, f. 796, op. 118, d. 1806; and RGIA, f. 1405, op. 63, d. 4952).

dubious, to say the least. But these methods were dubious—and this is the key point—only by the newer standards that were now being adopted.

Broadly speaking, this shift can be attributed to two principal factors. First, apostasy itself vividly demonstrated the limits of the older standards. As long as baptized non-Russians feared the consequences of apostasy, the old standards were sufficient to keep the edges of the Orthodox community reasonably firm, even when spiritual commitments to Christianity remained weak. But once the situation became demonstrably fluid in the 1860s, and the true intentions of the Emperor were once again cast into doubt, it became clear that only an "internal" commitment to Orthodoxy would allow baptized non-Russians to resist the temptations of apostasy. Second, aspirations in the reform period to create a more inclusive civil order that would draw on the initiative of the empire's population and entrust them with crucial responsibilities of administration and justice required that subjects no longer merely submit passively to the dictates of secular and ecclesiastical authorities but instead actively engage in the reform and improvement of the empire. This active engagement could not be created by simply gathering *tamgi* or through force. As Malov wrote, "At the present time, in light of the newly arising civil changes in our fatherland and even partly of political calculations, forceful measures in the matter of faith and conscience are being abandoned."[83] Faith was no longer to be just a matter of constituting difference and securing subordination to authority, but was now more explicitly to help shape a virtuous populace for a transformed imperial Russian polity.

Still, even as many recognized the significance of religious conviction, hardly anyone in this period was prepared to allow non-Russians' self-definitions to determine their religious status. Such a moment came only in 1905, and even then it was significantly conditioned by provisions designed to defend the church's predominance. Most officials seem to have implicitly agreed with Malov's contention that formal Christian status was the indispensable precondition for Christian enlightenment and therefore could not be negotiated.

It is crucial not to exaggerate the scale of the shifts I have described here. Many of these "new" outlooks and practices clearly had significant precedents, especially in the period of Nicholas I. Likewise, older conceptions— the dynastic and non-national character of the empire, the role of religion as a crucial sign of cultural identity, the state's refusal to accept its subjects' expressions of religious confession as decisive in all cases—persisted, to one degree or another, until the end of the old regime. And as Richard Wortman has shown, the monarchy began to identify with the Russian people explicitly only in the reign of Alexander III (1881–94).[84] But with all these caveats

[83] Malov, "Prikhody," 451.

[84] Richard S. Wortman, *Scenarios of Power: Myth and Ceremony in Russian Monarchy*, vol. 2: *From Alexander II to the Abdication of Nicholas II* (Princeton, 2000), pp. 161–95, 235–70.

in place, we may nonetheless posit a series of important shifts in the way the state marked cultural difference, the ways in which both officials and members of educated society understood their polity, and the criteria that many people employed for measuring religiosity and confessional affiliation. The Great Reforms and the Polish insurrection of 1863 were crucial to these shifts. But at this point we need to return to the confessional politics of the Volga-Kama region itself. For it was in 1866—in the very midst of the Great Reforms and in the immediate aftermath of the Polish insurrection—that apostasy reappeared on a grand scale and helped crystallize many of the developments described here.

6   The Great Apostasy of 1866

The Great Reforms and the Polish insurrection of 1863 were both critical to a broad, though still partial, reconceptualization of the nature of the Russian Empire and of non-Russians' place within it. Non-Russians in the empire's east had, by the 1860s, become inorodtsy ("aliens"), in contrast to the "core population of the empire" (Russians), and many Russian elites now saw a clear "civilizing mission" for Russia, akin to the "missions" that other European states had conferred on themselves. The goal of Russifying non-Russians emerged as part of these larger processes of change in mid-nineteenth century Russia, but the urgency that officials and publicists began to attach to this project in the Volga-Kama region was also the product of a massive movement of apostasy that appeared in Kazan province in the mid-1860s. By the end of the decade, over ten thousand baptized Tatars had again filed petitions requesting recognition as Muslims.[1] Coming shortly after the Polish insurrection and coinciding with a rise in revolutionary activity and an assassination attempt on Emperor Alexander II, this violation of imperial law and church authority made a deep impression on officials and missionary activists. Virtually, all the novokreshchenye communities that had been forced back into Christianity in the late 1820s now broke with that religion decisively and in most cases permanently. Moreover, the apostasy subsequently spread across the Volga and Kama rivers into eastern Kazan, southern Viatka, and northwestern Ufa provinces.[2] Some "old convert" Tatars (who had otherwise been considered reasonably good Christians) and in mixed areas even Udmurts and

---

[1] By the mid-1870s there were close to twelve thousand apostates. See Ia. B. [E. A. Malov], "Otpadenie kreshchenykh tatar ot pravoslaviia," *Missioner* 11 (1874): 114–15. The Kazan governor counted fourteen thousand apostates in 1883, though, he noted, many were children and infants (RGIA, f. 821, op. 8, d. 743, ll. 162–162ob.).

[2] Ufa province was created out of Orenburg province in 1865.

Chuvash joined the larger movement and renounced Orthodoxy in favor of Islam. These developments illustrated with alarming clarity the profound weakness of the church's hegemony in the region and presented officials with the disturbing possibility that the bulk of the region's non-Russian population—baptized and unbaptized alike—might fall victim to this "Mohammedan" rival before the project of obrusenie could achieve success.

"Deviation" and Resettlement (1830s–1850s)

The year 1866 saw the most dramatic rejection of Orthodoxy, but "deviation" had in fact been developing less obtrusively ever since novokreshchenye Tatars agreed to abandon their petitions in the late 1820s. Having been categorized by authorities as "deviates" (*uklonivshiesia*) from Orthodoxy for their refusal to fulfill "Christian obligations," baptized Tatars across the Volga in southeastern Kazan province had tenaciously resisted efforts to return them to the "bosom" of the church. It was the state's decision in the early 1860s to call a temporary retreat from its persecution of these "deviates" that provided the spark for a new movement of apostasy.

In 1827 rumors that baptized Tatars could receive official recognition as Muslims generated a flood of petitions in settlements along the right bank of the Volga. Although quelling these rumors proved difficult, authorities were able to convince the petitioners that their aspirations would not be satisfied, and by most accounts, these novokreshchenye went on to fulfill their "Christian obligations" without openly raising the issue of Islam again until 1865. But as Kazan Archbishop Grigorii (Postnikov) remarked in 1849, "deviation" among baptized Tatars across the Volga, in Spassk and Chistopol districts of Kazan province, "occurred gradually, remains to the present day, and is very difficult to bring to an end."[3] Here baptized Tatars rejected Orthodoxy somewhat more cautiously than their counterparts in 1827. They focused on practicing Islam to the extent possible but not on seeking Islamic status outright for the time being. Indeed, many practiced Islam secretly, using various tricks to avoid detection by missionaries: they concealed their Christian names or called themselves "by various Tatar names at once"; they hid among Muslim Tatars to escape resettlement, constructed their own makeshift mosques, and served as mullahs for one another. The disposition of these Tatars was discovered largely, it would appear, because of the introduction of a new statute for ecclesiastical consistories in 1841, which dictated that all parishioners failing to attend confession and communion for more than two or three years should be reported to the diocesan authorities

[3] RGIA, f. 796, op. 125, d. 1518, l. 83.

and, if necessary, to civil authorities.[4] It was for this reason that so many new reports of "deviation" (*uklonenie*)—the failure or refusal to fulfill "Christian obligations"—began to appear in 1843. By 1844 missionaries had identified 4,448 Tatar "deviates," which led one missionary to speak of "a general revolt against the church by the novokreshchenye Tatars of Spassk and Chistopol districts."[5]

Recognizing the negative influence of Muslims on baptized Tatars, authorities began to push for the resettlement of "deviates" to Russian settlements, or at least to areas where there were no Muslims. Already in the aftermath of 1827, authorities had resettled some of the most stubborn apostates (in some cases even sending them to Siberia), and by 1837 a policy of resettlement—usually within the confines of Kazan province itself—had been adopted, so that over the next few decades some "deviates" found themselves transferred to new communities.[6] Although the goal of this policy was ostensibly to create the conditions necessary for the "enlightenment" of the "deviates," it was above all its punitive dimensions that made their mark on its intended objects. In an effort to avoid resettlement, "deviates" petitioned the Tsar, noting that through resettlement they would be deprived of much of their property, and that even local Russians had testified that they were truly Muslims. After resettlement they related that they had not actually received parcels of land in their new villages, so that "they are required to return to their previous places of residence in order to sow grain."[7] In one case, authorities accidentally resettled the wrong Tatar but decided to leave him in his new home because, they argued, he was likely to have deviated into Islam eventually anyway![8] Even after years in new settlements, baptized Tatars petitioned for return to their homelands, usually in vain.[9]

Baptized Tatars often defied the resettlement order simply by remaining in their original villages as laborers employed by Muslims or went on to lead "vagrant lives." Some "deviates" slated for resettlement never arrived in their new districts, presumably having absconded during the process. When Tatars did remain in their new settlements, arguments soon developed

---

[4] *PSZ* II, vol. 16, no. 14409 (1841), articles 17 and 279; *SZ* (1842), vol. 14, article 28. See also David W. Edwards, "The System of Nicholas I in Church-State Relations" in *Russian Orthodoxy under the Old Regime*, ed. Robert L. Nichols and Theofanis George Stavrou (Minneapolis, 1978), pp. 154–69.

[5] RGIA, f. 796, op. 125, d. 1518, l. 15; and NART, f. 4, op. 77, d. 116, l. 1230b. Though the two terms were to some degree used interchangeably, "deviation" seems to have represented a lesser degree of rejection than "apostasy" (at least in the minds of imperial observers).

[6] These resettlements are described in some detail by E. A. Malov, "Prikhody starokreshchenykh i novokreshchenykh tatar v Kazanskoi eparkhii," *Pravoslavnoe obozrenie* 17 (1865): 460–67. In a few cases, deviates were resettled to neighboring provinces (RGIA, f. 796, op. 143, d. 1398, ll. 32–340b.).

[7] RGIA, f. 797, op. 5, d. 20749, ll. 7–10; and RGIA, f. 797, op. 5, d. 20749, l. 43.

[8] RGIA, f. 796, op. 130, d. 1521, ll. 16–17.

[9] For example, one group, resettled in 1840, sought to return in 1874 but was denied (RGIA, f. 821, op. 8, d. 778).

between them and indigenous residents over land allotments, tax obligations, and so on.[10] Thus the resettlement process, while imposing tremendous hardships on "deviates" and creating all kinds of disorders, did virtually nothing to convince them to abandon their protest. By 1848 the MVD's
Secret Committee on Schismatics, which had been entrusted with handling
the problem of Tatar "deviation," agreed with the MGI's recommendations
to end the resettlement policy and pin its hopes on the missionary divisions
soon to be created at the Kazan Ecclesiastical Academy.[11]

Without romanticizing the struggle of the "deviates," one can hardly deny
that the imperial authorities became virtually powerless in the face of this
sustained resistance. Over the course of decades, clergy admonished and cajoled the "deviates" (often with the help of the police), while a paper correspondence of astounding dimensions made its way into both central and
regional archives. But in almost all cases, clergy reported that their "admonitions" had no effect whatsoever and that the "deviates" categorically
refused to abandon their aspirations to be Muslims. Even the prospect of Siberian exile, while initially making a strong impression on the "deviates,"
failed to frighten them a short time later. Indeed, "deviates" made clear that
they were not afraid of any punishment whatsoever, "*because the sun is
everywhere the same*, and if they receive any punishment, they will bear it
for Mohammed."[12] Detectable in the official reports is a growing sense of futility, as clergy seem to have abandoned all but the most formal attention to
the task of admonition out of sheer frustration.

What triggered the apostasy of 1866, however, was the state's adoption of
more extreme measures in the mid-1850s followed by its renunciation of
those measures a short time later. In 1841 a group of 114 "deviates" and
their families were resettled from Spassk to Mamadysh district. Because they
stubbornly resisted all "admonitions," in 1855 the Secret Committee on
Schismatics ordered that special measures be adopted against them: unbaptized children were to be taken from their parents into foster care; women
who had married after their resettlement were encouraged to sanctify the
marriage with the Christian rite; if they refused, they were to be separated
from their husbands and returned to their original families. In 1856 these
measures were extended to a larger group of 1,721 apostates.[13] The apos-

---

[10] RGIA, f. 796, op. 125, d. 1518, l. 23; NART, f. 4, op. 72, d. 12, ll. 25–26; RGIA, f. 797,
op. 15, d. 35644, ll. 49–50; and RGIA, f. 796, op. 130, d. 1521, l. 21. Many of these problems
are also covered in Malov, "Prikhody," esp. no. 18 (1865): 288–95.

[11] RGIA, f. 797, op. 15, d. 35644, ll. 50–53. On the transfer of the issue of Tatar apostasy
to the Committee's jurisdiction, see *Sobranie postanovlenii po chasti raskola* (St. Petersburg,
1858), 2:682; and RGIA, f. 821, op. 11, d. 11, l. 113. This committee also handled some cases
of pagan "delusion," as well as certain questions concerning the Uniates before their "reunion"
with Orthodoxy in 1839 (RGIA, f. 1473, op. 1, d. 53; and RGIA, f. 1473, op. 1, d. 15, ll.
570b.–59, 164–65, 2530b.–54, 392–920b., 447–480b.).

[12] Cited in Malov, "Prikhody," 470 (emphasis in the original).

[13] RGIA, f. 821, op. 11, d. 36, l. 74.

tates decisively resisted these measures, however. They filed complaints with the MGI that the authorities were taking their wives and children from them for the purposes of converting them forcibly. Authorities who attempted to take the children met resistance "that went to such a point, that they [Tatars] refused to hand over their children for baptism and declared that in the case of further insistence, *they would kill either themselves or the official who had come to take their children and slaughter the latter* [the children]."[14] The MGI, considering these measures "extremely onerous" for the Tatars and inconsistent with both religious doctrine and its own aspirations for "legality and humaneness," requested that the measures introduced in 1855 be halted until the government had the opportunity to assess the activities of the Anti-Muslim Missionary Department at the Academy, which had been opened in 1854. The MVD, faced with the impending emancipation of serfs in the empire, agreed that in light of the "decisive resistance" and the questionable nature of the original baptisms the measures against these two groups should be halted, as was done in 1861 and 1865, respectively.[15]

This decision by no means represented a capitulation to the desires of the "deviates" to be officially Muslims. It was, rather, a tactical retreat that the government felt compelled to make in light of the complex situation of the early 1860s. Not surprisingly, however, "deviates" saw it all rather differently. In particular, a Tatar, Galim Samigulov, was easily able to present the government's retreat as a positive response to the many petitions that he had submitted to St. Petersburg on behalf of his village in Chistopol district throughout the late 1850s. Samigulov in effect demonstrated that persistence and repeated petitions would eventually lead to success, and he was later identified as a major instigator of the 1866 apostasy and the author of many of the petitions submitted at that time.

The Apostasy's Outbreak

The apostasy of 1866 should be viewed against the backdrop of a dynamic and uncertain atmosphere in the mid-1860s. The emancipation of serfs in 1861, followed by the emancipation of crown peasants in 1863 and state peasants in 1866, demonstrated that substantial change in the tsarist order was possible. It was hardly unreasonable for baptized Tatars to conclude that religious reform might be forthcoming. Tatars also found grounds for apprehension, however. The elimination in 1859 of *lashmany* as an estate category agitated its Tatar members, who had previously been exempt from military service and now interpreted the call for them to provide recruits as the beginning of a harsher government policy toward Muslims that would

[14] RGIA, f. 821, op. 8, d. 739, l. 13 (emphasis in the original).
[15] RGIA, f. 821, op. 11, d. 36, ll. 76–770b.

culminate in their baptism.[16] In his travels in early 1866 the missionary E. A. Malov discovered that Tatar villagers were similarly interpreting a recent fire ordinance, which called for the doors on churches and mosques to open outward, as part of a plan to convert mosques gradually (and imperceptibly) into churches.[17] At least a few Tatar families were worried enough about these rumors to request permission to resettle in the Ottoman Empire.[18] Thus for Tatars the mid-1860s were a time of both hope and fear.

The government, meanwhile, was extremely apprehensive that rural inhabitants would misunderstand the parameters of the peasant emancipation. Indeed, local authorities had decided to leave the emancipation statute untranslated into Tatar, "to avoid confusing and incorrect interpretations by the Tatar population."[19] The government's fears about such "misunderstandings" were soon justified by events among Russian peasants elsewhere in Kazan province. In the village of Bezdna, peasants claimed to have found in the emancipation statute the *volia* (freedom) they were looking for, and authorities were forced to fire into crowds of peasants who gathered to hear this interpretation and refused to disperse.[20] This unrest was followed by a requiem among students of Kazan University and the Ecclesiastical Academy for the fallen peasants, and in 1863 authorities discovered a radical conspiracy at the university to foment peasant insurrection, if necessary by using a false manifesto from the Tsar.[21] Faced with these challenges, provincial authorities were perhaps reasonable to regard any disturbance with great apprehension.

The apostasy itself began when word about the termination of measures against the residents of Chistopol district began to reach other baptized Tatars. Sent by the Kazan Ecclesiastical Consistory to Sviiazhsk, Tetiushi, and Buinsk districts in late 1865 and early 1866, Malov found many villagers who were convinced that the Emperor had issued a law allowing baptized Tatars to profess Islam. Villagers informed Malov that "A Chistopol Tatar

---

[16] NART, f. 1, op. 2, d. 2111, ll. 1–2, 7, 47.

[17] E. A. Malov, *Missionerstvo sredi mukhammedan i kreshchenykh tatar: Sbornik statei* (Kazan, 1892), p. 190.

[18] Many reports of such plans to resettle turned out to be false (NART, f. 1, op. 2, d. 2111, ll. 20, 39, 44), but there was at least one such petition, filed on behalf of 104 persons, and the missionary Malov found evidence in 1866 that indeed several Muslim *ishans* (or Sufi teachers) had encouraged Tatar villagers to resettle in Turkey. See *Materialy po istorii Tatarii vtoroi poloviny XIX veka*, part 1: *Agrarnyi vopros i krest'ianskoe dvizhenie, 50–70-kh godov XIX v. Tatarskaia ASSR* (Moscow, 1936), p. 213; and Malov, *Missionerstvo*, p. 203.

[19] *Materialy po istorii Tatarii*, pp. 108–9.

[20] These events are discussed in Daniel Field, *Rebels in the Name of the Tsar* (Boston, 1989), pp. 31–111.

[21] On the requiem, see Gregory Freeze, "A Social Policy for Russian Orthodoxy: The Kazan Requiem of 1861 for the Peasants of Bezdna," in *Imperial Russia, 1700–1917: Essays in Honor of Marc Raeff*, ed. Ezra Mendelsohn and Marshall Shatz (DeKalb, 1988), pp. 58–75. On the "Kazan conspiracy," see Franco Venturi, *Roots of Revolution: A History of the Populist and Socialist Movements in Nineteenth-Century Russia* (Chicago, 1960), pp. 303–15.

told us that he filed a petition for permission to maintain the Mohammedan faith and that he received permission." Rumors also related that petitions would be accepted only before the beginning of the new year (1866), which put great pressure on baptized Tatars to reject Orthodoxy before it was too late.[22] By all indications, this "Chistopol Tatar" was none other than Galim Samigulov, who was now spreading the word that he and his fellow villagers had been left in peace after many efforts to attain Muslim status.

In January 1866 a police official received a tip concerning the whereabouts in Kazan of some of the instigators. A raid uncovered nine Tatars (including Samigulov) from five different districts who had been writing petitions and copying correspondence between the Commission of Petitions and the St. Petersburg police chief, evidently for distribution to baptized Tatar villages.[23] Though these Tatars were arrested and the papers confiscated, they were released shortly thereafter, and in any event other copies of internal governmental correspondence made their way into the countryside. The police chief in Tsivil'sk district, for example, reported that baptized Tatars came to him with petitions for the Tsar and "a copy, written illiterately on stamped [i.e., official] paper, as was visible, by some Tatar, of a correspondence between the Kazan provincial authorities and Mr. Minister of Internal Affairs, concerning the petition of baptized Tatars from several villages in Chistopol and Spassk districts about permission for them, 1,721 souls, to convert from Orthodoxy to Mohammedanism."[24] Baptized Tatars had obtained a copy of this correspondence, probably directing the governor to end the measures introduced in 1855, and were copying and distributing it. Such correspondence fueled rumors, virtually impossible to suppress, that there existed a law allowing baptized Tatars to return to Islam if they so desired.

Apostasy usually took the following form: village gatherings agreed to apostatize and elected representatives to travel to Kazan to mail petitions to the Tsar. Parishioners then went to their local priest or canton board and announced that they would no longer fulfill Orthodox obligations and that the priest need not come to their village.[25] Because the 1861 emancipation statute, which was extended to state peasants in 1866, accorded a significant degree of self-government to local peasant communities, baptized Tatars seem to have considered these actions sufficient to constitute "official" apostasy. The rejection of Orthodoxy was usually accompanied by the shaving of heads (in the case of men) and the adoption of Muslim dress, especially skullcaps.[26] This visible alteration constituted an act of profound symbolic

[22] Malov, *Missionerstvo*, pp. 178–79.

[23] RGIA, f. 821, op. 8, d. 759, ll. 6–7. See also Malov, *Missionerstvo*, p. 213.

[24] RGIA, f. 821, op. 8, d. 759, ll. 6–100b. Petitioners submitted a similar paper in Sviiazhsk district (NART, f. 1, op. 3, d. 228, l. 1).

[25] RGIA, f. 821, op. 8, d. 759, ll. 1–4.

[26] E. A. Malov, "Ocherk religioznogo sostoianiia kreshchenykh tatar, podvergshikhsia vliianiiu magometanstva," *Pravoslavnyi sobesednik* 3 (1871): 247, 252.

significance, dramatically representing the apostates' espousal of Islam and in some cases virtually justifying their apostasy. Indeed, some baptized Tatars pointed to their appearance as if that in itself constituted their right to be Muslims: "I am of the Tatar faith: here are my Tatar clothes, my short hair, and Tatar hat."[27]

The spread of the movement was swift and alarming, beginning most rapidly among novokreshchenye along the right bank of the Volga river, where apostasy had already occurred in 1827.[28] After completing his trip to this region, Malov wrote to Chief Procurator Dmitrii Tolstoi that "the apostasy movement, like an epidemic, is getting stronger and stronger. If things stay this way, then not only will all the novokreshchenye apostatize into Mohammedanism, but the majority of old converts of Kazan, Laishevo, and Mamadysh districts will begin to vacillate greatly."[29] By the summer of 1866 apostasies were being reported northeast of Kazan, and by early 1867 the new archbishop, Antonii (Amfiteatrov), reported that he was "almost constantly" receiving reports "about new seductions of baptized Tatars into Mohammedanism by tens and families, and the same threatens whole villages and cantons."[30]

Each village that apostatized exerted a profound influence on those around it. Near the village of Kansar (Mamadysh district) baptized Tatars and Udmurts of several neighboring villages "are inclined to apostatize into Mohammedanism, and they are looking at the village Kansar and are saying: if its residents apostatize from Orthodoxy then they will too."[31] Perhaps the central site in the apostasy was the village of Kibiak-Kozi (Laishevo district), whose residents were among the first to announce their apostasy. Many neighboring parishioners came there "for consultation," and baptized Tatars and Udmurts invoked the Kibiak-Kozi villagers on numerous occasions as justification for their own apostasy. Even fifteen years later baptized Tatars considering apostasy consulted the residents of Kibiak-Kozi and were inspired by the rumor that its "agitators," who had been exiled in 1866, were now returning.[32]

The government's first reaction was to reject the petitions as unequivocally as possible. As the influential lay missionary N. I. Il′minskii wrote early in the apostasy, "This decision should not be secret or ministerial but rather ceremonial and tsarist" (*torzhestvennoe i tsarskoe*).[33] Malov, based on his travels, argued that "only when the higher authorities announce clearly and decisively the illegality and impossibility of their solicitations to go over to

---

[27] GAKO, f. 811, op. 1, d. 51, l. 40b.; and "Poezdka glavnogo missionera Viatskoi eparkhii v inorodcheskie prikhody v kontse 1871 g.," *VEV* 16 (1872): 360.

[28] RGIA, f. 821, op. 8, d. 759, ll. 95–99.

[29] Ibid., l. 190b.

[30] Ibid., l. 220; and NART, f. 4, op. 98, d. 34, l. 1.

[31] NART, f. 4, op. 101, d. 11, ll. 230b., 75.

[32] RGIA, f. 821, op. 8, d. 759, l. 300b.; NART, f. 4, op. 101, d. 11, l. 85; and Iapei Babai [E. A. Malov], "O kreshchenykh tatarakh: Iz missionerskogo dnevnika," *IKE* 20 (1891): 626.

[33] RGIA, f. 821, op. 8, d. 759, l. 16.

Mohammedanism—then, and only then, will the possibility to begin instilling them with the truth and divinity of the Christian faith open up."[34] The Department for the Religious Affairs of Foreign Faiths (DDDII), under the MVD, took this advice and called on the Kazan governor to inform baptized Tatars that their petitions "can never be considered by the government and that those suggesting the contrary are deceiving them and are exploiting their trust."[35] Eventually Vice-Governor Emel'ian Rozov, joined by Il'minskii as translator, set out for baptized Tatar villages to announce the rejection. Fluent in Tatar and an expert on Islam, Il'minskii had a decisive influence in the affair, as he in large measure composed the reports that Rozov submitted to the governor and to the DDDII.[36]

The diocesan authorities meanwhile unimaginatively called on parish priests to offer "the most thorough admonitions" to their parishioners and to explain "all the falsity of the Mohammedan faith." The church also dispatched Malov to trans-Volga districts, as we have seen, and he subsequently spent several weeks in the villages of Elyshevo and Apazovo in late 1866.[37] Vasilii Timofeev, himself a baptized Tatar and a close associate of Malov and Il'minskii, was later dispatched on similar expeditions. As the apostasy developed, the Ecclesiastical Consistory ordered religious superintendents to file monthly reports on the state of affairs in their respective locales.[38] But it was clear that the church could do painfully little without secular assistance. As one local newspaper asserted rather baldly in the early stages of the crisis, "Parish clergy, without the assistance of the government, can accomplish nothing in this affair, however well they may know the Tatar language and the Mohammedan law, and however much zeal they may have for the conversion of those who have gone astray."[39]

While parish clergy harangued the apostates with "thorough admonitions," Vice-Governor Rozov and his entourage traveled around Kazan province in the summer and fall of 1866. But despite their exhortations, the vast majority of the petitioners categorically refused to return to Orthodoxy, making claims with which we are now quite familiar. They contended that they were waiting for a response to their petitions, though some once again signaled their willingness to return to Orthodoxy should the government reject their petitions.[40] Some accused their local clergy of corruption or of

[34] Malov, *Missionerstvo*, p. 185.

[35] NART, f. 1, op. 3, d. 231, l. 6.

[36] See Il'minskii's letter to Chief Procurator K. P. Pobedonostsev in *Pis'ma Nikolaia Ivanovicha Il'minskogo k Ober-Prokuroru Konstantinu Petrovichu Pobedonostsevu* (Kazan, 1895), p. 135.

[37] RGIA, f. 821, op. 8, d. 759, l. 400b. Malov published accounts of the first trip in *Missionerstvo*, pp. 166–242, and the second in "Ocherk," serialized in *Pravoslavnyi sosbesednik* 3 (1871): 234–55, 397–418; 1 (1872): 62–78, 124–39, 237–50, 377–405; 2 (1872): 38–78.

[38] NART, f. 4, op. 98, d. 9.

[39] *Sovremennyi listok* 24 (23 March 1866).

[40] NART, f. 1, op. 3, d. 231, l. 22.

entering them falsely in parish registers. Many claimed that they had never been Christians, that they had virtually no knowledge of the Christian religion, and that they wanted to practice Islam because it was the religion they knew and understood. The main problem, as Governor N. Skariatin reported to the MVD in August, was that the petitioners were convinced "that this rejection [as announced by Rozov] came not from the Sovereign Emperor, but from the local provincial authorities." Paralyzed by their lack of authority, Rozov and others stressed the need to return the *original* petitions with documentation to prove they had been rejected by central authorities.[41] Even this had virtually no effect on the mood of the petitioners. When Rozov informed 710 heads of households of Tetiushi district who were congregated at central locations for the announcement, only 1 signed for his family that they would respect the Tsar's will and practice Orthodoxy. All the rest decisively refused, aside from a small group that wavered even though its sympathies obviously lay with Islam.[42]

While the government identified various causes for the apostasy, Rozov and local officials focused above all on the "instigators" and began to press for their immediate exile. The principal concern thus became one of separating the leaders of the movement from their supposedly hapless followers. The newspaper *Sovremennyi listok* accurately reflected the thinking of many officials when it editorialized:

> It is necessary above all to separate those baptized Tatars who can be called Christians according to their religious convictions (if not reinforced in Christianity), from those Christians of the Tatar tribe who are in fact enemies of Christ's faith. Otherwise it follows that a comparatively insignificant portion of baptized fanatics of Mohammedanism, supported by the unbaptized, through their influence will attract the majority of those who are baptized but not yet reinforced in the holy faith.[43]

Priests and others indeed reported that when such "instigators" had been put in prison temporarily at the beginning of the crisis, the remaining baptized Tatars had begun to fulfill their Christian obligations once again. The release of these "agents," in contrast, had profoundly reinforced the idea that apostasy was not in fact illegal. For this reason, in August 1866 the governor of Kazan was already calling for the administrative exile of instigators, without further investigations or judicial proceedings.[44] Archbishop Antonii also called for "harsh measures," and his requests were relayed to the MVD by Chief Procurator Tolstoi, who declared ominously that if the instigators

---

[41] N. I. Il'minskii, ed., *Kazanskaia tsentral'naia kreshcheno-tatarskaia shkola: Materialy dlia istorii khristianskogo prosveshcheniia kreshchenykh tatar* (Kazan, 1887), pp. 280–81, 290.
[42] NART, f. 1, op. 3, d. 231, ll. 218ob.–21.
[43] *Sovremennyi listok* 24 (23 March 1866).
[44] Il'minskii, ed., *Kazanskaia tsentral'naia*, p. 289.

were not removed "without delay," then "the Mohammedan movement will take such dimensions that the government will consequently not be in a position to stop it."[45] Rozov, presumably following Il'minskii, articulated more dramatically what was at stake: "Considering that it would not be healthy or in character for an Orthodox State like our Fatherland to allow the strengthening and multiplication of a population confessing a faith that by its unity and nature will always hinder the merging of Mohammedans with the mass of the Russian people, it is necessary to take energetic measures to terminate the present movement and to prevent future ones."[46]

What followed was a lengthy correspondence among various government agencies on the relative merits of administrative and judicial proceedings.[47] While judicial proceedings required substantial evidence to prosecute but could involve rather severe punishment, administrative measures required merely that civil authorities identify troublemakers and remove them quickly by exile to Siberia.

The criminal code identified two potentially adjudicable acts in each case of apostasy. In the first place, article 185 of the code provided that apostates from any Christian confession to a non-Christian faith were to be turned over to religious authorities "for admonitions and persuasion" and could be deprived of their rights and property, and even lose their children to temporary guardianship, until they returned to Christianity. Article 184 of the code ascribed a higher degree of criminality to those attempting to lure Christians into non-Christian religions "through instigation, seduction, and other means," depriving such people of all rights and sentencing them to hard labor in exile for a period of eight to ten years, or twelve to fifteen years if their instigation had involved coercion.[48] Through the concept of "seduction" (*sovrashchenie*), the law drew a clear distinction between instigators, who were supposedly conscious of their guilt, and the "seduced," who allegedly lacked criminal intent and required only admonition.[49] Accordingly, "seducers" were actually punished, while the "seduced" simply endured certain deprivations until they capitulated.

In practice, enforcing these laws presented substantial difficulties. First, the law required rather higher standards of evidence for the successful prosecution of such cases. But officials complained that Tatars' "resourcefulness

---

[45] RGIA, f. 821, op. 8, d. 759, l. 180.

[46] NART, f. 1, op. 3, d. 231, ll. 238–380b.

[47] The tension between these approaches was a defining feature of the Russian legal system. See Richard S. Wortman, *The Development of a Russian Legal Consciousness* (Chicago, 1976); and Laura Engelstein, *The Keys to Happiness: Sex and the Search for Modernity in Fin-de-Siècle Russia* (Ithaca, 1992), esp. pp. 17–127.

[48] *Ulozhenie o nakazaniiakh ugolovnykh i ispravitel'nykh* (St. Petersburg, 1866), articles 184 and 185.

[49] According to V. N. Shiriaev, this notion of "seduction" was a unique feature of Russian criminal law. See his *Religioznye prestupleniia: Istoriko-dogmaticheskii ocherk* (Iaroslavl, 1909), p. 377.

and cunning," involving bribery, witness tampering, and the intimidation of baptized Tatars by apostates and Muslims, hindered effective prosecution and necessitated the abandonment of many cases.[50] Even figures whom the administration regarded as obvious "instigators" had their cases dropped due to lack of sufficient evidence. Most notably, Galim Samigulov, whom local authorities identified as being at the vortex of instigation, was freed entirely from judicial proceedings.[51] In general, as one district police chief explained, baptized Tatars "like the judicial ceremony, [because] one always finds a possibility there of emerging from the water dry, of dragging the case out for a long time, and during this time remaining free and having the opportunity to agitate."[52]

Moreover, some officials harbored reservations about the applicability of articles 184 and 185 in such cases of apostasy. While acknowledging that seduction of baptized Tatars by Muslims constituted a violation of the law, these officials rejected the notion that the mass of apostates themselves could actually be divided into groups of "instigators" and "seduced," since they were all officially Orthodox. Under these circumstances article 184 was "very harsh and even unfair," since the ostensible "seducers" merely expressed the general mood among baptized Tatars.[53] Others, like Minister of Internal Affairs P. A. Valuev, were skeptical that one could ascribe criminal motivations to the mass of baptized Tatars under prosecution. If the apostasy had involved Russians who had long been Orthodox, "then obviously, in such a case, the seducers and seduced alike would be subject to the full harshness of the law, without leniency." But the reports indicated that the prevailing circumstances—baptized Tatars' kinship with Muslim Tatars, their inability to understand Russian, and the weak influence of the Orthodox clergy—"did not allow the population the possibility of establishing themselves in Orthodoxy."[54] The Kazan Chamber of State Domains concurred that "religious education and inculcation of Christian ideas among the baptized Tatars was always slipshod, and one cannot blame Tatars themselves for this."[55] Thus some officials doubted that what they were observing could actually be considered apostasy in the sense that the law code intended, precisely because so many baptized Tatars had never been Christians in anything but the most formal sense.

Finally, the large number of apostates greatly complicated the task of handling cases successfully. One official rhetorically asked whether it was possible to submit almost eight thousand people to religious exhortation and to

---

[50] RGIA, f. 821, op. 8, d. 763, ll. 29–31; and NART, f. 1, op. 3, d. 229, ll. 53–540b.

[51] RGIA, f. 821, op. 8, d. 780, l. 100b. Samigulov was eventually convicted, however, based on his own admission of guilt in the writing of petitions and his service as acting mullah in his village (RGIA, f. 821, op. 8, d. 763, l. 76).

[52] NART, f. 1, op. 3, d. 228, l. 140.

[53] RGIA, f. 821, op. 8, d. 763, l. 420b.

[54] Ibid., ll. 119–190b.

[55] RGIA, f. 821, op. 8, d. 759, l. 700b.

deprive them of their rights until they embraced Orthodoxy.[56] The governor of Simbirsk province likewise held that this law was not appropriate to large masses of people and thus "cannot make any impression on them whatsoever."[57] Evidence suggests that the verdicts that did result from court cases were at best partially carried out.[58] In some cases, it was simply dangerous to attempt to admonish apostates as provided in the law, as they increasingly challenged Orthodox clergy.[59] Over the course of the 1870s, clergy in many cases abandoned attempts to persuade apostates to return to Orthodoxy, leaving them without any real punishment or edification. In short, existing law was ill-suited for handling apostasy to Islam on such a grand scale.[60] Those who opposed the use of judicial measures did recognize that something needed to be done to reinstate order; they favored the exclusive use of administrative exile, which had already begun as these discussions continued.[61]

Yet not everyone was prepared to abandon the judicial route so readily. Some argued that distinguishing "seducers" from "seduced" was not as difficult as others made it out to be. Others noted that if the judicial route threatened to convict too many people, then the administrative, with its focus on instigators, would leave the rest without any prosecution whatsoever. Meanwhile, Governor N. Skariatin of Kazan, in contrast to those more sympathetic to baptized Tatars, argued that the apostates' activities could not be ascribed to "simple-minded ignorant error" (*prostodushno-nevezhestvennoe zabluzhdenie*) but involved a healthy dose of deceit and "Muslim intolerance." And because any lightening of punishment would be construed as permission to transfer to Islam freely, only the continuation of judicial measures would convince the petitioners of the illegality of their actions.[62]

The principal advantage of "administrative-repressive" measures was that they allowed the authorities to act quickly and decisively, without meticulous regard for evidence. As a local police chief wrote in favor of this approach, "Whoever truly turns out to be harmful for social peace is immediately exiled without being charged and the disorder ceases."[63] Such extralegal measures were usually construed not in punitive terms but as a form of "protection" for baptized Tatars from insidious "seduction" and in general as a way of creating more propitious conditions for their deeper acceptance of Orthodoxy. As the MVD asserted, the goal "is not so much the

[56] RGIA, f. 821, op. 8, d. 763, ll. 540b.–55.

[57] RGIA, f. 821, op. 8, d. 780, ll. 60b., 10; and RGIA, f. 821, op. 8, d. 763, ll. 120–21.

[58] RGIA, f. 821, op. 8. d. 774, ll. 39–400b. This refers above all to verdicts under article 185. Over twenty people were exiled to Siberia.

[59] RGIA, f. 796, op. 172, d. 2667, l. 140; RGIA, f. 796, op. 167, d. 2271, l. 350b.; and RGIA, f. 821, op. 8, d. 794, l. 1450b.

[60] Ia. B. [Malov], "Russko-gosudarstvennyi vzgliad na otpadenie inorodtsev-khristian v mukhammedanstvo," *Tserkovnyi vestnik* 23 (1876): 10.

[61] RGIA, f. 821, op. 8, d. 763, ll. 120–21.

[62] Ibid., ll. 60b., 90b., 42–430b., 89–94.

[63] NART, f. 1, op. 3, d. 228, l. 140.

application of harsh punitive measures to the defendants, as it is *the suppression of the emerging movement through the removal* of the principal instigators from their place of residence, for the elimination of the harmful influence on the mass of baptized Tatars."[64]

Although the MVD came out strongly in favor of the exclusive application of administrative measures, the Committee of Ministers decided to retain the judicial route until the judicial reforms of 1864 could be implemented in the Volga area, which occurred in 1870. Thus in the late 1860s two separate routes, judicial and administrative, continued to coexist. In fact, the minister of justice noted the benefits of this dual system of prosecution and saw no real barriers to its continuance, for "administrative measures could be allowed as supplementary, precisely in those cases when in considering the case the court cannot find sufficient evidence to recognize the defendants as guilty."[65] Between the two systems of prosecution, then, all the truly guilty parties would be dealt with.

Eventually 21 people were sentenced to hard labor, 20 to prison terms, and 260 to religious exhortation along with their families. But even as the court cases were in progress, baptized Tatars began to petition the MVD for a more rapid conclusion to the affair and to contest their original arrest. They argued that they had long sat in prison unaware of the status of their cases, that they had been selected by the luck of the draw to represent their villages, and that therefore they should not be locked up while those who sponsored them remained free. Their arrest had been based entirely on the bogus testimony of local priests that they were baptized, and now their households and families were falling into ruin while they sat in prison.[66] In response to these complaints, the MVD argued that those sentenced to hard labor should simply be exiled to Siberia immediately. In the case of lesser verdicts, the MVD argued, the defendants should be released because of all the time they had already spent in prison.[67] The Committee of Ministers agreed, and in October 1869 the Ministry of Justice ended its prosecution. All those in prison were released and placed under police surveillance.[68]

The result of this decision was, predictably, a resurgence of apostasy, as baptized Tatars in other locales became convinced that the local authorities had no real basis for preventing their return to Islam. As one religious superintendent reported in late 1869, apostates claimed that many Tatars, "though they were convicted and sat in jail for apostasy from the Christian faith, have now been released and live freely as Muslims." And Archbishop Antonii concluded that "the main reason for the new repetitions of apostasy

[64] RGIA, f. 821, op. 8, d. 763, l. 161ob. (emphasis in the original).
[65] Ibid., ll. 95–95ob.
[66] Ibid., ll. 142–420b., 185–90, 203–6, 208, 222.
[67] Ibid., l. 161ob. The MVD based itself on articles 135 and 153 of *Ulozhenie o nakazani-iakh*, which stated that under certain circumstances authorities could petition the Tsar for the lessening of sentences.
[68] RGIA, f. 821, op. 8, d. 763, ll. 207–9; and RGIA, f. 821, op. 8, d. 743, l. 820b.

is the failure to punish the earlier apostates," who were now free to disseminate the claim "that the authorities who judged them have allowed them to stay in Mohammedanism."[69] In large measure, local religious authorities and missionary activists were left to their own devices to combat this second wave. Indeed, Kazan Archbishop Antonii complained in 1875 about the government's lax attention, adding that Tatars were now convinced that the government did not really care about the state of Orthodoxy in the Kazan region.[70]

On the whole, the imperial administration was deeply divided in its efforts to deal with the apostasy. While some clearly recognized the need to act decisively, others were skeptical of harsh measures. Most notably, the governor of Simbirsk asked, "would it not be better to let the poor Tatars believe as they think proper, and would not tolerance instead of persecution diminish the fanaticism and perhaps the spread of the prohibited religion itself?"[71] Similarly, some local investigators repeatedly released supposed instigators for lack of real evidence against them.[72] This revolving door of arrest and release deeply compromised the government's ability to counteract the apostasy, for baptized Tatars, "seeing that one authority paralyzes the others . . . of course came to the conviction that the law does not prevent them from renouncing Orthodoxy at all and that the police official, the canton board, and the priest completely illegally hinder their aspirations to go over to Mohammedanism."[73] Already in 1866 Il'minskii complained that once "instigators" had been released, "our administration, with its enslavement to paper and bureaucracy [*pri svoei bumazhnoi i kantseliarskoi zakabalennosti*] was unable to round up and stop these propagandists again, and they effectively made use of the time."[74]

Reasons for Apostasy

As we have seen, authorities identified "instigation" and "seduction" by a small number of "fanatics" as the immediate source of the apostasy. Noting that all the petitions were "in essence a direct imitation of that petition which Galim Samigulov filed in 1856," Vice-Governor Rozov concluded that the whole apostasy "is a general affair, gradually developing from a single source, namely, Samigulov and his helper Abdiushev."[75] But as much as malevolent "instigators" stood at the center of the state's conception of

---

[69] Ibid., ll. 238–39, 268.
[70] RGIA, f. 821, op. 8, d. 743, l. 610b.
[71] RGIA, f. 821, op. 8, d. 759, l. 242.
[72] Il'minskii, ed., *Kazanskaia tsentral'naia*, p. 296.
[73] NART, f. 1, op. 3, d. 231, ll. 63–630b. For an inquiry into the acts of one investigator, see NART, f. 13, op. 1, d. 945.
[74] NART, f. 968, op. 1, d. 8, l. 610b.
[75] Il'minskii, ed., *Kazanskaia tsentral'naia*, pp. 306–7.

the developing movement, the authorities were nonetheless compelled to contemplate the deeper causes of the apostasy. Paying greater attention to the environment in which baptized Tatars lived, the government discovered that almost every circumstance promoted closer affinity with Islam.

While Orthodox clerics tended to assert that baptized Tatars had only limited knowledge of Islam, thereby confirming the significance of "instigation," such assertions seem to have implied only formal, and indeed "correct," knowledge of Islam. In fact, baptized Tatars' religious knowledge was extensive but took particular forms. The missionary Mikhail Mashanov found in 1875 that baptized Tatars could recite a tremendous number of legends rooted in Islam, and Agnès Kefeli has recently underscored the breadth of this popular knowledge, which was based on songs and Sufi textbooks.[76] Orthodox clerics' focus on formal Islamic knowledge blinded them to the knowledge of popular Islam that already prevailed in the village. Even where they had little or no direct tutelage from Muslims, apostates knew enough to construct their own mosques, to bury their dead by Islamic rite, and to serve as mullahs for one another.

Perhaps the biggest problem remained baptized Tatars' cohabitation with Muslims, which exposed them to Islam through the mosques and schools that invariably existed in every village. Baptized Tatars often sent their children to these schools, since this represented the only opportunity for them to gain literacy in any language. Even Russian clerics were forced to admit, with notable rue, that "literacy among Tatar Muslims is developed incomparably more strongly than among Russians and Orthodox [Christians] in general."[77] Given this cohabitation and Islam's remarkable institutional presence, it was hardly surprising that in some locales "baptized Tatars in no way differ from unbaptized."[78] Cohabitation also rendered baptized Tatars susceptible to "Mohammedan propaganda," which could include virtually all dealings of Muslims with baptized Tatars. As Rozov recounted in his report, "Muslims, especially women, on every possible occasion impress their religion on baptized Tatars, and other inorodtsy as well, its sham divinity and [the idea] that it leads directly to paradise; and on those baptized Tatars who do not wish or do not decide to apostatize from the church, Muslims act through ridicule and profanity of Russian holy things."[79]

The spread of apostasy was also aided by kinship ties and business dealings among different groups of baptized Tatars. In particular, women from

---

[76] Agnès Kefeli, "Constructing an Islamic Identity: The Case of Elyshevo Village in the Nineteenth Century," in *Russia's Orient: Imperial Borderlands and Peoples, 1700–1917,* ed. Daniel R. Brower and Edward J. Lazzerini (Bloomington, 1997), pp. 271–91; and idem, "L'Islam populaire chez les Tatars Chrétiens Orthodoxes au XIXe siècle," *Cahiers du monde russe* 37, 4 (1996): 409–28.

[77] RGIA, f. 821, op. 8, d. 743, l. 21 (Archbishop Antonii).

[78] NART, f. 1, op. 3, d. 231, l. 39.

[79] Ibid., ll. 228–280b.

villages whose residents had already apostatized often came to other villages through marriage and thereby encouraged further apostasy. Malov found that in Elyshevo, once baptized Tatars had actually decided to abandon Orthodoxy, they rejected marriage with baptized Tatars who remained Christian.[80] In effect, authorities began to realize that the baptized-Tatar countryside was made up of a web of interrelationships in which no single settlement could be isolated effectively from the others. The apostasy in Kibiak-Kozi arose in part because the villagers there "have connections" with baptized Tatars in Chistopol district, where there were already many apostates who "almost from very childhood drink up the poison of Mohammedan delusion."[81] From this perspective, the prevention of apostasy in each village was of the utmost significance.

Baptized Tatars were also increasingly drawn into broader social and economic networks in which Muslims were predominant. By mid-century, most Tatar peasants were unable to make ends meet based exclusively on agricultural pursuits, and baptized Tatars, too, were forced to engage in cottage industries and migrant labor. Each year many adult men left their villages and crossed the Kama river into Ufa, Orenburg, and Samara provinces where for several months they sold their wares or worked in factories and other establishments.[82] To the chagrin of Orthodox observers, during this time they lived with Muslims and "pick up Mohammedanism."[83] As one priest explained, based on baptized Tatars' own testimony, "engaging in tailoring in the homes of unbaptized Tatars, in no way can they confess the Christian faith, and living almost constantly in Tatar villages, from a young age they have become used to Mohammedanism, and thus there is no way they can be Orthodox Christians in the future."[84] Thus baptized Tatars' implication in larger economic systems in which their clients and customers were Muslims encouraged them to reject the practice of Christianity.

---

[80] Malov, "Ocherk," *Pravoslavnyi sobesednik* 1 (1872): 125. For more on women's role in sustaining apostasy, see Agnès Kefeli, "Une note sur le rôle des femmes tatares converties au Christianisme dans la réislamisation de la Moyenne-Volga, au milieu du XIXe siècle," in *L'Islam de Russia: Conscience communautaire et autonomie politique chez les Tatars de la Volga et de L'Oural depuis le XVIIIe siècle*, ed. Stéphane A. Dudoignon, Dämir Is'haqov, and Räfyq Möhämmätshin (Paris, 1997), pp. 65–71.

[81] RGIA, f. 821, op. 8, d. 759, l. 31; NART, f. 4, op. 98, d. 9, ll. 44–45; and GAKO, f. 811, op. 1, d. 51, l. 20b.

[82] This was true above all for Tatars of Kazan, Laishevo, and Mamadysh districts, where land was in especially short supply. See N. A. Khalikov, *Zemledelie tatar Srednego Povolzh'ia i Priural'ia, XIX–nachala XX v.* (Moscow, 1981), pp. 17–19; and Iu. G. Mukhametshin, *Tatary-kriasheny: Istoriko-etnograficheskoe issledovanie material'noi kul'tury, seredina XIX–nachalo XX v.* (Moscow, 1977), pp. 27–28, 52–55. Khalikov estimates that by the 1880s in Laishevo district 91–94% of the population was engaged in rural industry.

[83] Malov in RGIA, f. 797, op. 35, otdel 2, d. 289, l. 2; and NART, f. 4, op. 98, d. 9, ll. 710b.–72.

[84] NART, f. 4, op. 98, d. 9, l. 101. For more on migrant labor in / from Kazan province, see N. N. Vecheslav, "Kustarnye i otkhozhie promysly v Kazanskoi gubernii," *Izvestiia Imperatorskogo Russkogo Geograficheskogo Obshchestva* 11, 4 (1875): 290–95.

Furthermore, such migrant artisans constituted the wealthier and more influential social segment in baptized-Tatar villages.[85] Baptized Tatars who did not engage in such trade were perhaps more likely to maintain ties with Christianity, but they were also less likely to command wealth and influence. One cannot escape the impression from many sources that in the Tatar countryside Christianity was a religion of the poor, which is not surprising since poor villagers were most likely to resort to baptism in return for tax breaks. Church servitors from one village noted the "dependent relationship of poor baptized Tatars to rich unbaptized [Tatars] of the same village and even to mullahs, in whose service they occasionally were."[86] Although Soviet scholarship tended to exaggerate the degree to which baptized Tatars' religious aspirations merely reflected Muslims' economic predominance in the village, the associations of Islam with prosperity were by no means irrelevant.[87]

Nor did the example set by local Russians do much to endear Christianity to baptized Tatars. As Tatar parishioners in one village explained, "Russians don't like us. They all curse us or laugh at us, but Muslims accept us tenderly and gently teach us their faith."[88] Il'minskii concurred that "Russian simple people view baptized Tatars with scorn," and another missionary wrote, "As the ruling people, Russians always looked at the inorodtsy of Russia as people standing lower than themselves." Even where baptized Tatars and Russians got along, the latter made no effort to explain Christianity; they felt that it did not matter which religion a person confessed, as long as he or she led a good life.[89] Nor did Russians set an attractive aesthetic example, for as Timofeev wrote, baptized Tatars "are disposed towards Mohammedanism by the external cleanliness and order that Mohammedans observe in mosques, with which they compare the unwashed condition in which Russians and Christians in general appear in church."[90]

Complaints against the parish clergy and deeper inquiry into the causes of apostasy revealed that the economic burden of being Christian remained central to baptized Tatars' discontent. Tatar parishioners cited "the strain of [paying] the priest's income, which seems to them to be extortion," and complained in one case that their priest was rude, oppressive, and "incredibly greedy."[91] Others openly declared, "We did not apostatize from Christianity because we believed that the Tatar faith was better, but because of [the priest's]

[85] M. A. Mashanov, *Religiozno-nravstvennoe sostoianie kreshchenykh tatar Kazanskoi gubernii Mamadyshskogo uezda* (Kazan, 1875), pp. 53–55.

[86] NART, f. 1, op. 3, d. 228, l. 162ob.

[87] See I. L. Morozov, "Ekonomika tatarskoi poreformennoi derevni i massovoe dvizhenie tatarskogo krest'ianstva v Tatarii 50–70-kh gg. XIX v.," in *Materialy po istorii Tatarii*, esp. pp. lii–liii.

[88] V. Timofeev, "Poezdka v prikhody kreshchenykh tatar po povodu poslednikh otpadenii v magometanstvo," *Pravoslavnoe obozrenie* (1872): 486.

[89] RGIA, f. 821, op. 8, d. 743, l. 95ob.; Mashanov, *Religioznoe-nravstvennoe sostoianie*, pp. 35–45. Note the reference to Russians as the "ruling people."

[90] NART, f. 4, op. 101, d. 11, l. 86ob.

[91] Ibid.; NART, f. 1, op. 3, d. 228, l. 186; and GAKO, f. 811, op. 1, d. 99, l. 300b.

requisitions."[92] When a newspaper correspondent asked baptized Tatars in Otary in 1874 why they had gone over to Islam, they answered: "We have no money with which to pay the priest for religious rites. . . . [But] one doesn't have to pay the mullah a lot. . . The mullah himself ploughs; he has his own grain."[93] Some baptized Tatars claimed that they paid money to the clergy to be left in peace, and local landlords confirmed that the clergy had allowed all kinds of abuses and that "there was a time when at the Consistory priests intensely solicited appointment to baptized-Tatar parishes, considering these parishes to be more profitable."[94] Yet while clergy apparently engaged in some excesses, their legitimate functions also antagonized parishioners. Timofeev found in one parish (Chura) that the local priest,

> as a zealous person who strictly executes his priestly duty, persistently requires the fulfillment of established regulations during weddings: that there is no relation [between groom and bride], that announcements be made in the church, that the groom and bride know prayers or at least be able to make the sign of the cross, and that they fast and take communion. But the parishioners are used to a lively wedding, without hindrances. And they look on the demand of lawful formalities as oppressive arbitrariness and extortion.[95]

Particular antagonism arose with regard to funerals, since Tatar parishioners found onerous the Orthodox requirement that Christians wait three days to bury dead relatives.[96] One of Timofeev's discussions with baptized Tatars was interrupted when an apostate yelled, "And so? Is a priest allowed to trade in the bones of a dead person?"[97]

In general, as Orthodox clerics delved deeper into the movement, they found more reasons for the desire of baptized Tatars and others to be Muslims. Women and girls were concerned about rumors that the government was intending to force them to dress like Russians, while Udmurt parishioners declared their preference for Muslim fasting, "because it allows [one] to eat horse meat, which they now eat, and which, living and working together with Tatars, they cannot avoid."[98] Religion in the countryside thus represented not so much a set of theological propositions as a whole cultural ensemble involving clothing, food, language, and so on.

[92] Timofeev, "Poezdka," 485.

[93] E. Osviannikov, "'Otpadshie' tatary," *Kazanskii birzhevoi listok* 85 (26 October 1875): 2–3.

[94] NART, f. 1, op. 3, d. 231, l. 224. This testimony was excluded from the published version of this report in *Kazanskaia tsentral'naia*, probably due to Il'minskii's support for the rural clergy and his desire not to discredit them publicly.

[95] NART, f. 4, op. 101, d. 11, l. 87. Other priests likewise remarked that they were being accused simply because they demanded proper observance of Christian rules (ibid., l. 19).

[96] Nikolai Krylov, "O povodakh k ukloneniiu v magometanstvo kreshchenykh tatar i drugikh khristian-inorodtsev v povolzhskom krae," *Missioner* 44 (1877): 353–58.

[97] Timofeev, "Poezdka," 480.

[98] NART, f. 1, op. 3, d. 231, l. 138; and NART, f. 4, op. 101, d. 11, l. 190b.

Nonetheless, despite the recognition that many baptized Christians were Christians in name only, the authorities could not bring themselves to grant the freedom to choose a religious affiliation for two principal reasons. First, the law quite simply prohibited apostasy, and a combination of habit and deference to the Emperor's exclusive legislative authority made it impossible to consider any exceptions to this provision. Second, even those highly critical of the mission's past efforts nonetheless considered formal Christian status to be a fundamental starting point for Christian "enlightenment." Malov stated this argument most directly already in 1865, on the eve of the mass apostasy: "While baptized Tatars remain Christians, even if only in name, and at peace, if only ostensibly, with the church, there is still hope of bringing them to their senses and affirming them in Christianity, whereas after their official apostasy into Mohammedanism, their conversion to Christianity will be as difficult as that of present Mohammedans."[99] Baptized Tatars were to gain nothing merely by articulating their religious preferences; on the contrary, they would have to wrench recognition as Muslims from imperial authorities, a process that continued until 1905 but was most intense in the late 1860s.

Exit Strategies

In their petitions and conversations, baptized Tatars made several arguments that they thought might resonate with higher authorities. Some claimed that they had never been Christians, whatever their official status, and that the local priest "calls us baptized arbitrarily."[100] Others acknowledged that they were baptized but cited the nature of their conversion and the fact that they simply had no knowledge of Orthodoxy. One group concluded that "it is better for us to be Tatars [Muslims], than baptized but ignorant of the Christian religion."[101] They were "unable to pray to God in the Orthodox way" or to pray for the Tsar and "the authorities."[102] Some explained that they were not sure whether they had been baptized or not. As investigations began and "instigators" were arrested, baptized Tatars protested their wrongful subjection to prosecution and insisted that there really was a law allowing them to practice Islam.

Though some petitioners were forceful and demanded that they be left in Islam, most invoked an image of the Tsar as a fatherly and gracious figure who would grant the petitioners their wishes. As one baptized Tatar de-

[99] Malov, "Prikhody," 451.
[100] RGIA, f. 821, op. 8, d. 759, l. 135; NART, f. 1, op. 3, d. 231, l. 116; and Malov, "Ocherk," *Pravoslavnyi sobesednik* 1 (1872): 77.
[101] NART, f. 4, op. 98, d. 9, l. 72.
[102] NART, f. 4, op. 101, d. 11, l. 1; and Il'minskii, ed., *Kazanskaia tsentral'naia*, p. 307.

clared, "Our Sovereign is gracious: he allows seventy-seven religions in his state, and it is not possible that he has not allowed us to practice the Mohammedan faith."[103] Samigulov and some of his comrades wrote to the Tsar from prison after their arrest: "Defend us and forgive [us;] You are our single and compassionate Father; we are your loyal slaves; we pray for Your health and [the health] of Your entire August home."[104] The petitioners were quick to exploit the parental image of the Tsar when they told officials that they "consider the Sovereign Emperor to be a father and mother, and just as parents fulfill earnest requests of their children, restated many times, the Sovereign, under their further pleading, will finally satisfy their requests."[105] Reportedly, baptized Tatars believed that the Tsar actually *wanted* them to practice Islam and had sent them Muslim skullcaps. Others applied this same motif to the central government more broadly, noting that the government "would long ago have rejected the machinations of the priest," if it were aware of the injustice of the clergy's claims and the resulting investigations.[106] They generally emphasized that they had no desire to stir up trouble, that they fulfilled all their obligations, diligently paid their taxes, and so on.[107]

The petitions were "legalistic" also in that they drew on a discourse of religious tolerance and reform. One noted that the Tsar "gave freedom to the serfs from slavery, [gave] the schismatics the freedom to live by their old faith. Condescend to us as well, whose fathers were baptized not by [their] will; give us the freedom to live according to the Mohammedan faith . . . and at the very least do not order that our children be forcibly baptized."[108] Indeed, baptized Tatars viewed their situation as analogous with that of the Old Believers, for "Russians found [their own] old faith, and we also want to be in the old [faith]."[109] As one apostate explained to Malov, "Look, even among you there are people of the old faith. They maintain the Christian law but don't go to church. And we, too, now want to maintain our old, Mohammedan faith, and we won't go to church."[110] One baptized Tatar, who had served in the military in St. Petersburg, pointed not only to the Old

[103] RGIA, f. 821, op. 8, d. 759, l. 233.

[104] RGIA, f. 821, op. 8, d. 766, l. 32.

[105] NART, f. 1, op. 3, d. 231, ll. 221–210b.

[106] RGIA, f. 821, op. 8, d. 759, l. 135ob.

[107] See, for example, Malov, "Ocherk," *Pravoslavnyi sobesednik* 1 (1872): 77; NART, f. 1, op. 3, d. 231, l. 6; and RGIA, f. 821, op. 8, d. 759, l. 135ob.

[108] RGIA, f. 821, op. 8, d. 759, l. 19. See NART, f. 1, op. 3, d. 228, l. 1, in which a petition also made reference to the freedom secured by schismatics.

[109] RGIA, f. 821, op. 8, d. 759, l. 4. Kräshens here were evidently referring to a number of provisions in the late 1850s and early 1860s designed to improve the lot of Old Believers. See Peter Waldron, "Religious Toleration in Late Imperial Russia," in *Civil Rights in Imperial Russia*, ed. Olga Crisp and Linda Edmondson (Oxford, 1989), p. 110. Though actually quite minor, these measures evidently promoted the *idea* of greater religious freedom.

[110] Malov, *Missionerstvo*, p. 178.

Believers, but to Catholics and Protestants as well.[111] These numerous references suggest that provisions for religious tolerance were well known in the countryside.

On the whole, government officials were not impressed by the "legalistic" nature of the requests. Vice-Governor Rozov in particular dismissed them as a dubious attempt "to place their case on a legal footing." Local Muslims' negative view of Orthodoxy is well known, he wrote, and their claim to want to pray for the Tsar "is obviously made with the goal of showing that they are not opponents of the Tsar's will, and of attracting to their case the gracious attention of the Sovereign Emperor and the Russian government."[112]

As the authorities attempted to pry baptized-Tatar communities apart into "instigators" and "agents," on one hand, and the hapless "seduced," on the other, baptized Tatars insisted that apostasy was a product of their collective aspiration. As one baptized Tatar declared during the investigation in Kibiak-Kozi, "No one induced us to file the request [petition], but rather everyone suddenly took it into their heads to do so."[113] Various authorities described how difficult it was to determine who was "truly" responsible. Rozov noted that each apostate "completely denies the participation of Galim Samigulov and other instigators, which has been corroborated by full inquiry of the police and other evidence."[114] As much as possible, baptized Tatars tried to make the apostasy their own, perhaps because they believed that arguments about religious tolerance would thus be more effective, perhaps also because testimony against an instigator would almost surely result in his exile or conviction. To a degree, they were also simply afraid of being totally isolated by refusing to apostatize. As one group declared, their apostate relatives "cannot come and visit us, because their arrival attracts the suspicion that they are trying to return us to Mohammedanism. We have remained alone. And so we have come to you to announce that we want to live in the old faith."[115]

Baptized Tatars were clearly aware that the government would be hard-pressed to punish them all and thus made special efforts to present a unified front. They tried to incline their Udmurt counterparts toward Islam by noting "they can't put everyone in prison,"[116] and in Kibiak-Kozi apostates categorically refused to be questioned individually. When the investigator ordered that the residents be interrogated separately, "the peasant gathering

---

[111] NART, f. 4, op. 101, d. 11, l. 52. Specifically, an order in 1865 unofficially released parents in mixed Orthodox-Lutheran marriages from the obligation of baptizing and raising their children in the Orthodox faith. In 1874 the government ceased persecuting Lutheran pastors for administering rites to Estonian and Latvian peasants, who had converted to Orthodoxy in the 1840s. See Edward C. Thaden, "The Russian Government," in Thaden, ed., *Russification in the Baltic Provinces and Finland, 1855–1914* (Princeton, 1981), p. 45.

[112] Il'minskii, ed., *Kazanskaia tsentral'naia*, pp. 307–8.

[113] NART, f. 13, op. 1, d. 943, l. 310b.

[114] Il'minskii, ed., *Kazanskaia tsentral'naia*, p. 299.

[115] NART, f. 4, op. 101, d. 16, l. 330b.

[116] NART, f. 4, op. 101, d. 11, ll. 210b., 96.

responded that they would never allow this," and that he should question them collectively. When the investigator turned to the nearest peasant and asked his name, "the gathering ordered him to be silent."[117] At least one priest noticed this trend and made a point of admonishing each household individually. Another noted during an investigation that baptized Tatars "have all been instructed by somebody and argued among themselves about how and what to testify."[118] In the village of Elyshevo, apostates were angry that one in their midst had informed Vice-Governor Rozov who the "leaders" of the apostasy were: "If you hadn't revealed them, then they would not have interrogated us 'one at a time,' but would have asked everybody together. . . . But when he [Rozov] started to ask us one at a time, we didn't know what to say."[119] One priest visited a new-convert woman and tried to dissuade her from apostasy, but she replied: "I'll look to the village community [*mir*]; I don't want to act alone." Despite all the priest's efforts, this woman simply responded "as the *mir* does, so do I."[120] The collective village mentality even crossed ethnic lines. In one mixed Udmurt-Tatar village, an Udmurt explained his apostasy by saying that "one cannot remain alone in the Orthodox faith in the village."[121]

If baptized Tatars were inclined to behave as collectives, this was in part because the government chose to treat them as such. In some instances, the action of local authorities actually galvanized baptized Tatars and promoted apostasy among those who might otherwise have been less inclined to take such a step. As the archbishop remarked, based on the report of a parish priest, the local canton board had composed lists of apostates which included *all* residents of each village, without determining the inclinations of each parishioner individually. This approach

> gave also those who had not declared themselves deviates the incorrect understanding and perception that they—as entered on the lists in an undifferentiated fashion together with deviates—will be subject to general prosecution for deviation, and therefore, deceived and instigated by others, [they] decided to stand in one indivisible mass, which, as their agents assured them, will be difficult [for the authorities] to manage. They think that as a whole mass they will not be held accountable to the law before the court and, out of necessity, will be shown mercy and will be left to their convictions.[122]

This solidarity was extremely effective: where the community stood firm, the authorities truly had no way of dealing with such a mass.

---

[117] NART, f. 13, op. 1, d. 943, l. 12; and NART, f. 1, op. 3, d. 231, ll. 1300b., 3150b.–16.
[118] NART, f. 1, op. 3, d. 231, l. 103.
[119] This conversation was reported by a baptized Tatar to Malov, in "Ocherk," *Pravoslavnyi sobesednik* 3 (1871): 239.
[120] NART, f. 4, op. 101, d. 11, ll. 27–29; and RGIA, f. 821, op. 8, d. 767, l. 63.
[121] NART, f. 4, op. 101, d. 11, l. 20.
[122] NART, f. 1, op. 3, d. 228, ll. 160–600b.

In some cases, baptized Tatars reverted to the tested strategy of feigned ignorance, as one priest discovered on several occasions. When he confronted his apostate parishioners, he received the following response: "we are illiterate, I am old, I'm deaf, and so on, and a few were completely silent." When he read a prayer in Tatar, "they all tried to escape either through silence, inability to understand, and, allegedly, lack of knowledge of their language."[123] One frustrated missionary reported how an apostate "responded to all my admonitions in Tatar, as if not understanding Russian," even though the local priest insisted that he knew Russian quite well. Another apostate explained "I don't know any Russian," even though "that Tatar spoke Russian fluently and satisfactorily."[124] Here was a textbook case of passive resistance.

Baptized Tatars increasingly challenged the authority of clergy and local officials. As one group declared to the district police chief, "We will believe in the rejection [of our petition] when we are shown the Tsar's [i.e., official] paper at peasant gatherings, or when our envoy tells us."[125] The baptized Tatars of Kibiak-Kozi not only refused to be questioned individually but declared that "they would give responses only *if the investigator were to show them the order to question them.*"[126] In another area a local police official was insulted by a Tatar merchant who made clear the limits of his authority: "You will never get anything your way. Even the vice-governor, traveling around Tatar villages with Cossacks, achieved nothing, and you alone, a local police official, where are you going to butt in? Your reports, as before and always, will have no effect at all."[127] Other police officials faced similar resistance at times. As the movement progressed and the government's measures proved largely ineffective, many apostates became emboldened and openly insulted local officials.

Nor was the priests' position any more enviable. When the Committee of Ministers instructed local clergy in 1868 to act through persuasion instead of turning to the police, local priests lost even more credibility in the eyes of their parishioners and were deprived of virtually any leverage over them.[128] Apostates' confidence accordingly grew, and relations between priest and parishioners became more hostile. One priest reported that earlier his parishioners "received me somehow more simply, more cordially, more trustingly. . . . But today those same Tatars came across not only as uncordial to me but even

---

[123] NART, f. 4, op. 98, d. 9, ll. 81, 76ob.

[124] GAKO, f. 811, op. 1, d. 51, l. 5.

[125] NART, f. 1, op. 3, d. 228, l. 48ob.

[126] NART, f. 13, op. 1, d. 943, l. 315ob. Emphasis in the original. The investigator added, "Given such decisive resistance of the peasants, I definitely could not conduct the investigation" (l. 316).

[127] NART, f. 1, op. 3, d. 229, l. 29.

[128] RGIA, f. 821, op. 8, d. 743, ll. 750ob.–76, 820ob.; and RGIA, f. 797, op. 39, otdel 2, stol 3, d. 93.

hostile."[129] Confrontations became increasingly direct, and priests claimed there was danger of physical violence. Archbishop Antonii noted that Malov and Timofeev, by going to the apostates, risked exposure "not only to various unpleasantries and privation, but even danger to their lives."[130] At Easter in 1870 clergy visited a baptized Tatar village with icons but were greeted by a crowd of novokreshchenye who declared that they would not accept them, and one in particular, "when we went up to his home, was prepared to fight and yelled with excitement."[131] In another case, apostates became so agitated that the priest found it necessary "not only to abandon exhortation but . . . to get out of the village for fear of losing my life."[132] In Kibiak-Kozi, apostates threatened their priest explicitly, saying, "*You, little father, don't come to us in the village, or we'll knock your block off.*"[133] As configurations of authority changed in the countryside—as direct oversight by the MGI over state peasants ceased; as the emancipation created a climate of greater possibility; as the new judicial statute created new standards of evidence—apostates were emboldened by their success and felt less compelled to exhibit the deference they had shown earlier.

The Limits of Apostasy

On closer inspection, the movement actually appears less monolithic than some accounts would have us believe. Although apostasy had a broad, indeed almost universal, appeal among novokreshchenye Tatars, confusion and uncertainty gripped many other communities when apostasy became a real possibility, partly because there were risks in openly renouncing Orthodoxy, but also because in some cases their religious allegiances remained in flux. As the possibilities for apostasy grew, baptized Tatars found themselves forced to choose sides, and given the ambiguous situation of many starokreshchenye, or Kräshens,[134] at the crossroads of Islam, Christianity, and animism, it is hardly surprising that some of them were not at all certain what to do.

There was tremendous pressure on baptized Tatars to join the apostasy. Muslims and apostates encouraged them to reject Orthodoxy with offers of help and protection, and with arguments that by embracing Islam they would remain true to their ancestors and compatriots.[135] To this encourage-

---

[129] NART, f. 4, op. 98, d. 34, l. 120.

[130] "Izvlechenie iz otcheta Vysokopreosviashchennego Antoniia, Arkhiepiskopa Kazan-skogo, o sostoianii Kazanskoi eparkhii za 1872 goda," *IKE* 16 (1873): 512.

[131] NART, f. 4, op. 101, d. 16, l. 6.

[132] NART, f. 4, op. 101, d. 11, l. 107.

[133] NART, f. 1, op. 3, d. 231, l. 64 (emphasis in the original).

[134] Because the discussion here pertains predominantly to "old converts," I refer to Kräshens in this section.

[135] See, for example, S. Danilov, "Vospominaniia starokreshchennogo tatarina iz ego zhizni," *Strannik* 3 (1872): 8–31; and GAKO, f. 811, op. 1, dd. 7, 51.

ment apostates and Muslims often added a sustained critique of Christianity, which they dismissed as superstition or a mere collection of rituals. They referred to Christianity as the "devil's faith" (*shaitan dine*) and church as the "devil's home" (*shaitan öyö*); and they criticized the Trinity as polytheism, the veneration of icons as idolatry, and the divinity of Christ as a sham.[136] Muslims and apostates ridiculed those who resisted apostasy and maintained Christian affinities, calling them "black Kräshens" (*kara Kräshen*) or even "ruined" (*buzulgan*) and using the terms Kräshen and *chukyngan* (baptized) as profanity.[137] In the decentralized countryside created by the peasant reform, moreover, Muslims and apostates made use of their status as majorities in many cantons to burden baptized villagers with various restrictions and impositions to coerce them into apostasy.[138] One priest reported that "complaints by the Orthodox [Tatars] about the offenses of the apostates strew forth with an unbearable tone," while Vice-Governor Rozov reported that in Elyshevo, "families wishing to remain in Orthodoxy were coerced by force and threats to sign the petition."[139] Timofeev, in particular, catalogued a litany of abuses carried out against Kräshen women who were unwilling to join their husbands in apostasy and against the elderly, who were reluctant to embrace such a radical step; apostates would circumcise even grown children ("from which there have been not only illnesses but deaths as well"). There was also fighting between groups of Kräshens and apostates over religion.[140] These sources are one-sided, and Kräshens may well have retaliated in ways that went unreported. But to the extent that the apostates had a vested interest in getting as many to join them as possible—the larger the number of apostates, the more impotent the government—it

---

[136] NART, f. 10, op. 1, d. 5964, l. 13; GAKO, f. 811, op. 1, d. 282, l. 2; Malov, *Missionerstvo*, p. 70; R. Daulei, "Kreshchenye tatary i tatary-mukhammedane," *Pravoslavnyi blagovestnik* 7 (1900): 298; N. P. Ostroumov, "Zametka ob otnoshenii magometanstva k obrazovaniiu kreshchenykh tatar," *Zhurnal MNP* 161, 6 (1872): 94; N. I. Il′minskii, "Izvlechenie iz proekta 1849 g. o tatarskoi missii," in Petr Znamenskii, *Na pamiat′o Nikolae Ivanoviche Il′minskom: K 25-letiiu Bratstva sv. Guriia* (Kazan, 1892), pp. 326–27; P. Znamenskii, "O kreshchenykh tatarakh derevni Bol′shoi Arniash′," *Zhurnal MNP* 137 (1868): 351. Allen Frank has found in Islamic manuscripts that some Muslims even doubted whether Othodox Christians could really be considered monotheists (personal communication, July 2000).

[137] Il′ia Sofiiskii, "O keremetiakh kreshchenykh tatar Kazanskogo kraia," *IKE* 24 (1877): 687–88. Islam and those associated with it were considered to be white. For discussions of this black / Christian v. white / Muslim distinction, see Daulei, "Kreshchenye tatary," 293; Malov, *Missionerstvo*, p. 187; Lev Pavlov, "Byt kreshchenykh tatar Ufimskoi gubernii, Menzelinskogo uezda," *Pravoslavnyi blagovestnik* 16 (1900): 350; and GAKO, f. 811, op. 1, d. 282, l. 2.

[138] Although some baptized Tatars, and especially old converts, tended to live separately in their own villages, they often constituted minorities in their respective cantons, with the result that Muslims and apostates often controlled institutions of local self-government.

[139] RGIA, f. 796, op. 205, d. 621, ll. 31–32, 45–45ob.; and NART, f. 1, op. 3, d. 231, l. 1370b.

[140] RGIA, f. 821, op. 8, d. 763, l. 83. For other accounts, see RGIA, f. 797, op. 52, otdel 2, stol 3, d. 188, ll. 1–2; Danilov, "Vospominaniia"; and Malov, "Ocherk," *Pravoslavnyi sobesednik* 1 (1872): 127.

hardly seems strange that they should have exerted a great deal of pressure on those who had not yet apostatized.

Evidence suggests that much of conflict occurred along generational lines, whereby the most enthusiastic proponents of apostasy were young adults eager to break from the authority of their parents. The older generation remained reluctant to abandon Christianity, however meager their knowledge of that religion, while the children who began to attend new Christian schools established in some of the most vulnerable settlements in the late 1860s exhibited stronger ties to Orthodoxy. As a result, a kind of generational sandwiching occurred, whereby the very young and the very old exhibited stronger ties to Christianity, while the young-adult population became apostates. One young boy told Timofeev how his family was essentially coming undone, as his parents had gone over to Islam and were cursing and beating him. His parents, he explained, "have lost their tempers, and in the family only we two, Grandfather and I, remain [in Christianity] . . . Grandfather cries almost every day." Another old man likewise recounted that he had remained Christian, while his entire family had apostatized and now cursed him and laughed at him and refused to feed him and take care of him.[141] In Viatka province, baptized Tatars who agreed to return to Orthodoxy brought their children to be baptized, "but cannot

Baptized-Tatar parishioners leaving their church in the village of Elyshevo, Mamadysh district, Kazan province, probably in the early twentieth century. RGIA, f. 835, op. 4, d. 72, photograph #4.

[141] RGIA, f. 821, op. 8, d. 763, ll. 292–93, 296–960b.

convince the adults in their families to return to Orthodoxy."[142] Timofeev concluded that baptized-Tatar young adults, with little or no instruction in Christianity and ever more interaction with Muslims, had come to represent "a kind of specific party in the village" and "*very brazenly and persistently ridicule their children and their parents*, who have just begun to obtain an understanding of Christianity."[143]

A few of those who joined the apostasy seemed less than certain about the step they had taken. In spite of tremendous opposition on the part of nearby Muslims, a religious superintendent in Sviiazhsk district was nevertheless able to return 263 apostates to Orthodoxy and to perform eleven new baptisms in 1867.[144] Even in Kibiak-Kozi, one of the centers of apostasy, some families agreed to return to Orthodoxy.[145] On several occasions baptized Tatars apostatized, returned to Christianity, and then apostatized again. As clergy and officials discovered, no Kräshen statements about their religious sympathies necessarily expressed more than momentary dispositions. Much of this zig-zagging was geared toward securing the best possible circumstances for apostasy and backing down when necessary. As a police official noted concerning a number of ostensibly repentant apostates being held in prison, "They and their families all wanted to join the Orthodox church once again, but not based on conviction, no! They hoped to save themselves from the expected exile."[146] Yet I would argue that it was precisely through the testing of the limits and the discussions among themselves and with clergy that baptized Tatars decided who they were and who they wanted to be—at least for the moment. As Agnès Kefeli has argued in her recent discussion of the apostasy in Elyshevo, to assume that all Kräshens wanted to go to Islam obscures the fact that they were faced with a real choice.[147] The reality of that choice is underscored by the fact that many decided against apostasy, even if they were never quite sure of themselves.

Indeed, a large segment of the Kräshen population did not apostatize, sometimes even when the majority in their own villages did. Kondratii Filippov, for example, remained the only Kräshen in the village of Elyshevo in Christianity in 1866. Pointing to his twenty-five years of military service, he recounted how apostates

> would call me to the peasant gathering and would tell me to agree with them; otherwise they wanted to take land from me and drive me out of the village. I

[142] GAKO, f. 811, op. 1, d. 51, l. 7.

[143] RGIA, f. 821, op. 8, d. 763, l. 294 (emphasis added); and NART, f. 4, op. 101, d. 11, l. 84.

[144] RGIA, f. 821, op. 8, d. 766, ll. 14–17, 54–65. This success was remarkable in that it occurred on the right bank of the Volga, where the apostasy was much more decisive than elsewhere. His greatest success was in the village Azbaba (Sviiazhsk district), which was one of the very few villages on the right bank in which baptized Tatars outnumbered Muslims (146 versus 48).

[145] Malov, "Ocherk," *Pravoslavnyi sobesednik* 2 (1872): 69.

[146] NART, f. 1, op. 3, d. 228, l. 1380b.

[147] Kefeli, "Constructing an Islamic Identity," pp. 271–72.

always said to them one thing: "I will remain alone and *will not give in* for anything. For the land I served the Sovereign for twenty-five years, and I pay you what is required of me; and if you are going to drive me out, all the same I won't listen to you. If the Sovereign orders me to leave your village, then I will resettle; but you will not be able to drive me out."[148]

Other Krāshens held out with equal determination. A baptized Tatar in Sviiazhsk district described how he was in danger of being removed from the village "because I do not agree to go over to Mohammedanism and as a literate person hinder them [the apostates]."[149] There were whole communities and cantons where apostasy seems not to have had much appeal, especially among Krāshens in the districts where Kazan, Viatka, and Ufa provinces met. In Viatka province, only a small portion (about 5 percent) of the Krāshen population declared apostasy openly, while several communities expressed their desire to open schools with Christian instruction and Orthodox clergy as teachers.[150] Although apostasy did begin to appear in Ufa province in the early 1880s,[151] the majority of the sizable Krāshen community in Menzelinsk district remained formally Christian, as did groups in Mamadysh and Chistopol districts of Kazan province.[152] Precisely because these communities did not apostatize, we have very little information about them. But it would seem that they constituted the core of the Krāshen community, which had historically had only tenuous connections to the Islamic world and had developed a significant sense of particularity vis-à-vis Muslims. Subsequent missionary interventions, based on the promotion of native clergy and the extensive use of native languages in liturgy and religious instruction, strengthened this particularism, helping to produce a Krāshen ethnic identity, rooted in Orthodoxy, that lasted into the 1920s and in fact up to the present.[153]

Although in some instances defiant, on the whole apostates continued to be deferential in their efforts to gain formal Muslim status. We will never know the degree to which petitioners actually subscribed to their statements of

---

[148] Malov, "Ocherk," *Pravoslavnyi sobesednik* 3 (1871): 247 (emphasis in the original).

[149] NART, f. 1, op. 3, d. 228, l. 870b.

[150] Statistics from Viatka province in 1886 show only 653 of 12,822 baptized Tatars (about 5%) as apostates, and these were concentrated predominantly in two parishes, Kiryndinskii and Alnashevskii (GAKO, f. 811, op. 1, d. 239, ll. 2–20b.).

[151] RGIA, f. 796, op. 162, d. 1077; RGIA, f. 796, op. 163, d. 1331; and RGIA, f. 821, op. 8, d. 774; op. 8, d. 790.

[152] See, for example, N. V. Nikol´skii, *Kreshchenye tatary: Statisticheskie svedeniia za 1911* (Kazan, 1914); N. I. Vorob´ev, "Nekotorye dannye po bytu kreshchenykh tatar (kriashen) Chelninskogo kantona TSSR," *Vestnik Nauchnogo Obshchestva Tatarovedeniia* 7 (1927): 157–72.

[153] On these developments, see my article, "From 'Pagan' Muslims to 'Baptized' Communists: Religious Conversion and Ethnic Particularity in Russia's Eastern Provinces," *Comparative Studies in Society and History* 42, 3 (2000): 497–523.

submission or truly believed that there was a tsarist law permitting the return to Islam. But we have now seen several times in this book that such rumors usually appeared under circumstances that made them compelling and believable. In the present case, the government's temporary retreat from its hard line on "deviates," the general mood of the reform period, and some limited reform with regard to Old Believers and Lutheran converts to Orthodoxy all contributed to a sense of possibility. Once the prospect of transfer to Islam appeared, and novokreshchenye Tatars began to take this step with apparent success, other communities, many of which stood at the boundaries and intersections of two or even three religious traditions, were confronted with the difficult question: Who *were* they in confessional terms?

Despite the deference that apostates showed in their petitions, the apostasy nonetheless represented a smaller (and admittedly less threatening) version of the Polish insurrection of 1863. Indeed, the new archbishop of Kazan, Antonii, who took up his position in late 1866, had been rector of the Kievan Academy in the late 1850s and the bishop of Smolensk until his transfer to Kazan, and he subsequently made a number of recommendations for dealing with the problem of apostasy based on his experience in the west.[154] Although comparisons were rarely expressed openly, it seems that in the minds of many officials Tatars and Islam became rough analogues to Poles and Catholicism. Each of these combinations represented a powerful and formidable rival to Russian Orthodoxy, and each threatened to spread and engulf neighboring peoples (Chuvash, Kräshens, and Finnic peoples, on one hand; Ukrainians and Belorussians, on the other).

The apostasy was undoubtedly a great shock for officials in both Kazan and St. Petersburg. Yet it served principally to confirm, in a dramatic fashion, many of the suppositions and suspicions that had already appeared over previous decades. Thus the processes we consider in the next several chapters—the growing vilification of Islam, the appearance of the region's first non-Russian monastery, and the reform of missionary methods associated with Il'minskii—can all be traced back at least to the 1830s–40s, even as the apostasy of 1866 both confirmed them and gave them greater urgency. It is to the first of these processes—the elaboration of new, hostile attitudes toward Islam—that we now turn.

[154] RGIA, f. 821, op. 8, d. 743, ll. 230b.–26.

7 New Discoveries: Islam and Its Containment

In certain respects, the state's relationship with its Muslim subjects had always been tenuous. The state refrained from recognizing a Muslim clerical estate with the rights and privileges equal to those of the Orthodox clergy, while local mullahs were not always willing to conform with state directives. Especially in Orenburg province, officials feared that one measure or another would "agitate" Muslims, which substantially restricted their ability to conduct policy consonant with the state's interests. Nonetheless, through the establishment of a Muslim nobility and more importantly the creation of the Muslim Spiritual Assembly, the state had forged substantial ties of co-operation with Muslim elites and, though it often deferred to the Assembly, was even able to establish itself as an authority in Islamic religious disputes. Muslims increasingly accepted these institutions and the processes that the state had established for the appointment of village mullahs.[1] The relationship between Islam and imperial state, if not perfect, was thus far from hostile or fundamentally antagonistic.

Subsequently, however, this relationship began to deteriorate. By the early twentieth century, officials and some publicists raised a full-fledged "Muslim question" to complement the many other emerging "questions" of the

---

[1] These relationships have been most thoroughly analyzed by Charles Robert Steinwedel, "Invisible Threads of Empire: State, Religion, and Ethnicity in Tsarist Bashkiria, 1773–1917" (Ph.D. diss., Columbia University, 1999); Robert D. Crews, "Allies in God's Command: Muslim Communities and the State in Imperial Russia" (Ph.D. diss., Princeton University, 1999); Danil′ Azamatov, *Orenburgskoe Magometanskoe Dukhovnoe Sobranie v kontse XVIII–XIX vv.* (Ufa, 1999); and Christian Noack, "Russische Politik und Muslimische Identität: Das Wolga-Ural-Gebiet im 19 Jahrhündert," *Jahrbücher für Geschichte Osteuropas* 47 (1999): 525–37.

day (Polish, Jewish, Ukrainian, women's, etc.).[2] By no means was the earlier cooperative relationship dismantled entirely, and much of the deterioration occurred only after 1905, when Muslim deputies joined the liberal opposition in the new State Duma and the Young Turk Revolution created new fears among imperial officials of pan-Islamism and pan-Turkism.[3] Nonetheless, beginning as early as the 1830s–40s, but principally in the period of the Great Reforms and after, officials began to regard Muslims in the region with growing apprehension, seeing in them "fanatics" and stubborn obstacles to the spread of "Russian civilization."

Missionaries, not surprisingly, were at the forefront of this re-evaluation of Islam. They were ever more fearful of the challenge that Islam represented to their work, especially once Kräshens, Chuvash, and Finnic peoples began to join the apostasy. Missionaries also emphasized the dangers that Muslims represented to the state's secular goals in order to induce the government to adopt a more anti-Islamic policy. Although certainly characterized by arrogance and intolerance, missionaries' growing Islamophobia was nonetheless not simply the product of xenophobic ignorance. Rather, their critique of Islam was now acquiring a more scholarly foundation. Based on the proposition that one should know one's foe, missionary activists such as N. I. Il′minskii, E. A. Malov, and their students invested much time and energy in learning eastern languages and trying to understand the behavior of Muslims in terms of Islam's scriptural sources. They conducted their work in a curious institution known as the "Anti-Muslim Missionary Division," which was opened at the Kazan Ecclesiastical Academy in 1854. Although their viewpoints and recommendations were never accepted entirely by the secular government, these missionary orientalists nonetheless created a body of knowledge that entrenched a set of negative assumptions about Muslims in official consciousness.

Islamic Defiance

As Andreas Kappeler has observed, historically there was no unified Russian policy toward all Muslims, since the contingencies and traditions in separate regions, as well as the circumstances of their annexation by Russia, were too

---

[2] Elena Vorob′eva, "Musul′manskii vopros v imperskoi politike Rossiiskogo samoderzhaviia: Vtoraia polovina XIX veka—1917 g." (cand. diss., Institute of Russian History, St. Petersburg, 1999).

[3] Vorob′eva, "Musul′manskii vopros"; M. A. Mashanov, *Sovremennoe sostoianie tatar-mukhammedan i ikh otnoshenie k drugim inorodtsam* (Kazan, 1910); Serge Zenkovsky, *Pan-Turkism and Islam in Russia* (Cambridge, Mass., 1960); Robert Geraci, "Russian Orientalism at an Impasse: Tsarist Education Policy and the 1910 Conference on Islam," in *Russia's Orient: Imperial Borderlands and Peoples, 1700–1917*, ed. Daniel R. Brower and Edward J. Lazzerini (Bloomington, 1997), pp. 138–61; and Diliara Usmanova, *Musul′manskaia fraktsiia i problemy "svoboda sovesti" v Gosudarstvennoi Dume Rossii, 1906–1917* (Kazan, 1999).

diverse for any single approach. Policy was therefore guided above all by a certain "pragmatic flexibility."[4] To be sure, under this rubric could come a destructive assault on Islamic institutions in conjunction with the Kontora's missionary campaign in the 1740s and 50s (see chapter 1). But Catherine II granted Islam tolerance (1773) and institutional recognition (1788), offered Tatars the possibility to regain noble status, and even promoted Islam actively among Kazakhs in order to temper their tendencies toward "willfulness." Tatars served as intermediaries in the government's dealings with Kazakhs, and the activities of Tatar merchants in Central Asia were encouraged by the imperial authorities.[5] By the second half of the eighteenth century, far from viewing Islam as a source of danger to the Russian state, the government regarded it as a useful tool for the pacification of, and expansion into, the steppe and eventually Central Asia.

Observers in the late nineteenth century maintained that this earlier policy reflected the government's fundamental ignorance about Islam. And indeed, whether one ascribes Catherine's approach to Enlightenment sentiment or to political expediency, it seems safe to suggest that it was not based on any particularly deep or extensive knowledge of Islam. To be sure, Catherine aspired to learn more about her non-Russian subjects, including Muslims.[6] But the institutions and personnel that brought greater familiarity with Islam—universities, ethnography, *vostokovedenie* (Orientalism)—were all products of the nineteenth century.[7] Even in the first half of the nineteenth century, the state largely deferred to the Muslim Assembly in the

[4] Andreas Kappeler, "Czarist Policy toward the Muslims of the Russian Empire," in *Muslim Communities Reemerge: Historical Perspectives on Nationality, Politics, and Opposition in the Former Soviet Union and Yugoslavia*, ed. Edward Allworth (Durham, 1994), pp. 141–56. For another sensitive and historicized account, see Aidar Nogmanov, "Evoliutsiia zakonodatel'stva o musul'manakh Rossii (vtoraia pol. XVI–pervaia pol. XIX vv.)," in *Islam v tatarskom mire: Istoriia i sovremennost'*, ed. Stefan A. Diuduan'on [Stéphane Dudoignon], Damir Iskhakov, and Rafik Mukhametshin (Kazan, 1997), pp. 135–47.

[5] Crews, "Allies in God's Command," pp. 279–84; Alan W. Fisher, "Enlightened Despotism and Islam under Catherine II," *Slavic Review* 27, 4 (1968): 542–53; Allen Frank, "Tatarskie mully sredi kazakhov i kirgizov v XVIII–XIX vekakh," in *Kul'tura, iskusstvo tatarskogo naroda*, ed. G. F. Valeeva-Suleimanova (Kazan, 1993), pp. 124–31; Ramil' Khairutdinov, "Tatarskaia feodal'naia znat' i rossiiskoe dvorianstvo: Problemy integratsii na rubezhe XVIII–XIX vv.," in *Islam v tatarskom mire*, pp. 83–101; M. A. Usmanov, "Tatarskoe kupechestvo v torgovle Rossii s vostochnymi stranami cherez Astrakhan' i Orenburg v XVII i XVIII stoletiiakh," *Russian History* 19, 1–4 (1992): 505–13; and Edward J. Lazzerini, "Volga Tatars in Central Asia, Eighteenth–Twentieth Centuries: From Diaspora to Hegemony," in *Central Asia in Historical Perspective*, ed. Beatrice F. Manz (Boulder, 1994), pp. 82–100.

[6] For example, Catherine commissioned the creation of a dictionary of all languages, including those of the empire. See A. Mozharovskii, "Inorodtsy-khristiane Nizhegorodskoi eparkhii sto let tomu nazad," *Nizhegorodskie eparkhial'nye vedomosti* 1 (1886): 11–24, 2 (1886): 10–15.

[7] On the development of these institutions and practices, see S. M. Mikhailova, *Kazanskii universitet v dukhovnoi kul'ture narodov vostoka Rossii* (Kazan, 1991), pp. 196–244; Nathaniel Knight, "Constructing the Science of Nationality: Ethnography in Mid-Nineteenth-Century Russia" (Ph.D. diss. Columbia University, 1994); and Robert Paul Geraci, "Window on the East: Ethnography, Orthodoxy, and Russian Nationality in Kazan, 1870–1914" (Ph.D.

administration of Islam, only gradually introducing certain regulations concerning the election of mullahs to the Assembly, the maintenance of parish registries, and so on.[8] The archives of the Department of Religious Affairs of Foreign Faiths (DDDII), under whose jurisdiction the Assembly came, suggest that the government did comparatively little to ensure observance of these regulations, which officials later contended were not being put into practice.[9] Similarly, before the 1860s no government agency kept track of the large network of Muslim-Tatar schools, which would later constitute a source of tremendous concern for officials.[10] Hence the attention that authorities found themselves paying to Muslims around mid-century was substantially new, thereby allowing us to speak of a "discovery" of Islam.[11]

By the late 1860s some missionaries and officials, chastened by the experience of the 1866 apostasy, looked back on earlier policies and practices with a certain incredulity. In reviewing the state's earlier reliance on Tatars in the Kazakh steppe, Chief Procurator Dmitrii Tolstoi faulted the government for its naive failure to appreciate the "fanaticism" of Kazan Tatars. Almost in disbelief, he asked, "So what did the administration at the time do? It called fanatic Kazan mullahs into the Kirgiz [Kazakh] steppe, which naturally would fanaticize the Kirgiz, attract them to Tatarness [*k tatarstvu*] and draw them away from Russian civilization."[12] E. A. Malov, in his survey of policy toward Tatar mosques, likewise criticized the government's earlier leniency. The removal of local bishops from the process of approving the construction of mosques in 1773 left them without means to protect novokreshchenye communities from the influence of Islam, while the government's establishment of the Assembly and the printing of the Koran only made matters worse. Thus, Malov concluded, the government in the eighteenth century "in no small measure promoted the strengthening of Mohammedanism, by establishing schools, constructing

---

diss., University of California at Berkeley, 1995). Before 1878 there was not even a direct translation of the Koran from Arabic to Russian. See Ia. B. [Malov], "O perevode Korana Gordiia Sablukova," *Pravoslavnyi sobesednik* 1 (1878): 333–52.

[8] For the basic legislation regulating Islam and its institutions in the first half of the nineteenth century, see Nogmanov, "Evoliutsiia zakonodatel'stva," pp. 141–47. On the interactions between state and Assembly that did occur, see Crews, "Allies in God's Command," and Azamatov, *Orenburgskoe Magometanskoe Dukhovnoe Sobranie*.

[9] RGIA, f. 821, op. 8, d. 594, l. 360b. A collection of the Assembly's directives published in 1905 includes only two items from before 1856, although this may also be a reflection of the fact that there was a fire at the Assembly in 1840. See *Sbornik tsirkuliarov i inykh rukovodiashchikh rasporiazhenii po okrugu Orenburgskogo Magometanskogo Dukhovnogo Sobraniia, 1836–1903* (Ufa, 1905).

[10] RGIA, f. 383, op. 24, d. 37141; and RGIA, f. 383, op. 26, d. 40826.

[11] This notion of "discovery" (*otkrytie*) is shared by Nogmanov, "Evoliutsiia zakonodatel'stva," p. 139. See also my "Otpadenie kreshchenykh tatar," *Tatarstan* 1, 2 (1995): 106–11.

[12] D. A. Tolstoi in his introduction to "Arkhiv grafa Igel'stroma," *Russkii Arkhiv* 24, 3 (1886): 342.

mosques at state expense, providing for mullahs," and so on, thereby creating the necessary conditions for apostasy among baptized Tatars in the
nineteenth century.[13]

This re-evaluation of Islam had several sources. First of all, the sustained
resistance to tsarist rule of the mountain peoples in the North Caucasus, under the leadership of Shamil, provided imperial authorities with a graphic
demonstration of Islamic-inspired opposition. While the mountain peoples
were sometimes construed as noble savages, they were also labeled "Muslim
fanatics" because of the explicitly Islamic foundations of their struggle
against Russian forces.[14] The fact that French colonial forces were encountering similar Muslim resistance in Algeria—a fact not unknown to Russian
observers of the Caucasus at the time—presumably helped to confirm the
notion that "fanaticism" represented a general characteristic of Islam.[15] By
1834 the bishop of Simbirsk was using the term "fanaticism" to describe the
particularly stubborn resistance of three apostates and their families to religious edification.[16] In 1836 the MVD used this concept to refer to Muslims
more broadly, arguing that the "general ignorance of Muslims, their fanaticism [*fanatizm*] and irritability" constituted a fundamental barrier to missionary activity among them.[17]

More important locally was the problem of apostasy, which both generated and reflected new concerns. In the aftermath of the apostasy of 1827,
religious and civil authorities paid remarkably little attention to Islam
itself. Although there were directives that local mullahs be forbidden from
attracting baptized Tatars to their mosques, on the whole Islam was treated
as merely a "Mohammedan" variation on a non-Christian theme.[18] No
particular qualities—such as "fanaticism," conspiracy, or dangerous ties
with Central Asia—were yet ascribed to Islam. Malov, writing in the 1860s,
was essentially correct when he remarked that the authorities in earlier
decades "focused their attention on the novokreshchenye Tatars who had

---

[13] Malov, "O Tatarskikh mechetiakh," *Pravoslavnyi sobesednik* 1 (1868): 22; and idem, *Pravo-slavnaia protivomusul'manskaia missiia v Kazanskom krae v sviazi s istoriei musul'manstva v per-voi polovine XIX v.* (Kazan, 1868–70), pp. 1–25.

[14] See the discussion in Uwe Halbach, "'Holy War' against Czarism: The Links between Su-fism and Jihad in the Nineteenth-Century Anticolonial Resistance against Russia," in *Muslim Communities Re-emerge*, pp. 251–76.

[15] Indeed, the use of the term *fanatizm* with regard to Islam was presumably a result of the French usage, though I have not been able to establish this connection conclusively. On Islamic resistance to French forces and the notion of "fanaticism" in this context, see Patricia M. E. Lorcin, *Imperial Identities: Stereotyping, Prejudice, and Race in Colonial Algeria* (London, 1995), esp. pp. 17–34 and 53–75.

[16] RGIA, f. 797, op. 3, d. 12644, l. 170. This is the earliest reference to fanaticism that I have encountered.

[17] RGIA, f. 821, op. 11, d. 11, l. 1120b.

[18] One missionary referred to Islam as "Mohammedan delusion" (*zabluzhedenie*) and "su-perstition" (*sueverie*), as if it were simply a variant of paganism (NART, f. 4, op. 66, d. 30, ll. 1–10b.).

apostatized into Mohammedanism and instructed parish priests to bring their influence to bear on them; Islam, on the other hand, remained in peace."[19]

By the 1840s, Russian authorities began to focus more explicitly on Islam itself, and especially the activities of the Islamic clergy. Missionaries became increasingly inclined to see Muslims and even the Islamic clergy as complicit in "conspiracies" designed to swell the apostasy and thus to limit the government's ability to counteract it.[20] As the Kazan archbishop wrote in 1849, "Among these Tatars, perhaps not without encouragement from the Tatar Muftii living in Ufa [i.e., the head of the Muslim Spiritual Assembly], not a small number of secret mullahs have gotten loose." Such mullahs, by another account, "sow contagion, arouse fanaticism, and operate with such secrecy, that it is impossible to keep track of them."[21] Observers now began to notice vast networks of Tatar schools that allegedly existed for "the arousal of fanaticism."[22] Eventually, by the mid-1860s or so, these activities would be subsumed under the broad and convenient shorthand "Mohammedan propaganda," a staple item in explaining Islam's successes among other non-Russians.

The appearance of non-Tatars, principally Chuvash, among the ranks of the apostates convinced officials that the Islamic community sought not merely to reclaim its putative lost souls (baptized Tatars).[23] If the apostasy were based simply on natural affiliations and the poor performance of Orthodox clergy, authorities argued, then surely Chuvash would have sought to return to paganism, and not to practice Islam. The fact that they, too, now sought Muslim status offered clear proof that Muslims were actively promoting their religion among baptized non-Russians, in clear violation of Orthodoxy's monopoly on proselytism. The mass apostasy of 1866, which also involved Chuvash, Udmurts, and Kräshens, as well as the growing tendency of pagans in Ufa province to seek conversion to Islam, could only provide graphic confirmation of these notions. Where clerics had previously acknowledged the more or less natural attraction of baptized Tatars to Islam due to linguistic affiliations and settlement patterns, they now saw an aggressive and dynamic Islam.

A final set of impulses to rethink Islam concerned the Crimean War. Even before the war began, the war minister complained that Tatars were evading

---

[19] Malov, *Pravoslavnaia protivomusul´manskaia missia*, p. 41.

[20] NART, f. 4, op. 77, d. 116, ll. 131, 173; and RGIA, f. 796, op. 125, d. 1518, ll. 170b., 22.

[21] RGIA, f. 796, op. 125, d. 1518, ll. 220b., 410b. The phrase "secret mullahs" refers to mullahs without official sanction from the Muslim Spiritual Assembly and the appropriate provincial board.

[22] RGIA, f. 796, op. 125, d. 1518, l. 340b.; RGIA, f. 383, op. 24, d. 37141; and RGIA, f. 383, op. 26, d. 40826.

[23] The Kazan archbishop reported the presence of Chuvash among novokreshchenye Tatar apostates as early as 1844 (RGIA, f. 796, op. 125, d. 1518, l. 140b.; and NART, f. 10, op. 1, d. 1655, l. 24).

military service by "imparting to themselves various artificial illnesses, under the pretense of inability [to serve]," with the result that the burden in mixed recruiting districts fell disproportionately on Russians. In response, the authorities created separate recruiting districts consisting exclusively of Tatars and instituted sterner measures against evasion.[24] Meanwhile in Orenburg province the government was forced to abandon its campaign to convert the region's large pagan population when it encountered opposition from nearby Muslims, who feared that their own conversion was imminent. The Crimean War exacerbated these fears, for as one rumor had it, "the Turkish war was begun because the government had the intention of exterminating the Mohammedan faith and converting all Tatars to Christianity."[25] The Crimean War convinced imperial officials that Muslims in Crimea and the Caucasus were a substantial security risk and that the state should seek to "cleanse" sensitive areas of these questionable elements. The result was a tremendous exodus of Muslims—at least half a million—from Russia to the Ottoman Empire.[26] The war thus represented a significant step in the politicization of Islam.

The Anti-Muslim Division and Analysis of Islam

If various forms of Islamic defiance served as a major impetus for a rethinking of Islam, then much of the actual intellectual labor was centered in the Kazan Ecclesiastical Academy, and more specifically in the Anti-Muslim Division established there in 1854. In this regard, Nikolai Il'minskii, a professor at Kazan University and the Ecclesiastical Academy, played a crucial role. Having completed the course of study at the Academy in 1846 with extensive knowledge of the Tatar and Arabic languages, Il'minskii was dispatched to the field in 1848 by the new archbishop of Kazan, Grigorii (Postnikov), to collect information on the religious condition of baptized Tatars. Based on his observations, Il'minskii submitted a project for a "Tatar mission" in 1849, in which he stressed the "formalism," "fanaticism," and "blind obedience to religious authority" of Muslims. "In general [he wrote] Tatars are devoted to their faith to the point of fanaticism, and are

---

[24] RGIA, f. 383, op. 13, d. 14313, ch. 1 (citation from l. 1); RGIA, f. 383, op. 20, d. 28773; and "O merakh k predotvrashcheniiu ukloneniia tatar ot rekrutskoi povinnosti," *Zhurnal MGI* 40, 2 (1855), book 2:2. Similar measures had been introduced among Jews a few years earlier. See Michael Stanislawski, *Tsar Nicholas I and the Jews: The Transformation of Jewish Society, 1825–1855* (Philadelphia, 1983), pp. 13–34.

[25] RGIA, f. 796, op. 129, d. 1542, ll. 237–38 (citation from l. 2510b.). Other reports, however, suggest that Muslims in Orenburg province remained entirely calm (ibid., l. 253; and RGIA, f. 797, op. 97, d. 410).

[26] See Alan W. Fisher, "Emigration of Muslims from the Russian Empire in the Years after the Crimean War," *Jahrbücher für Geschichte Osteuropas* 35, 3 (1987): 356–70.

unquestionably certain of its truth and divinity."[27] The effects of Il'minskii's observations on official thinking were marked. Whereas, prior to Il'minskii's report, Archbishop Grigorii told the Synod that "the apostasy of novok-reshchenye Tatars is above all the sin of the Orthodox clergy itself," then by 1850 he decisively absolved the clergy and reported, "The main reason for apostasy is their [Tatars'] attachment to Mohammedanism and [their] certainty of its divinity."[28]

Il'minskii's intellectual authority was greatly enhanced after he took a trip to the "East" in 1851–54 for the purposes of studying Arabic, Turkish, and Persian, the history of Mohammed, and sources of Islam. The knowledge and books Il'minskii acquired in Cairo and Damascus—he was unable to visit Constantinople because of the outbreak of the Crimean War—in large measure formed the basis for his activities in the Anti-Muslim Division of the Kazan Academy.[29] Il'minskii's linguistic knowledge and his first-hand observation of Islam in the "East" invested his assessments with what Edward Said has called "referential power" and situated him institutionally in such a way that he could disseminate those views effectively.[30] These assessments helped generate an archetypal image of "Muslims" to which Tatars were largely found to conform.

This change in perception had a number of dimensions. First, it shifted the attention of religious authorities from the church's own deficiencies (the parish economy, the behavior of clergy, etc.) to Islam. Il'minskii, for example, identified as one of the principal defects of the 1830 mission that the missionaries "did not know the essence of the Mohammedan faith and thus could not present a good refutation of Mohammedanism."[31] An effective refutation, Il'minskii contended, should be constructed in terms of the logic and criteria of Islam, which he held to be fundamentally different from those of Christianity. "For our proofs and conclusions to be accessible to and binding on Tatars, we cannot use our own Christian suppositions and our own historical data; on the contrary, we need to adopt a Muslim point of view and take as a given their religious views and stories, which for Muslims have

[27] N. I. Il'minskii, "Izvlechenie iz proekta 1849 g. o tatarskoi missii," appendix to Petr Znamenskii, *Na pamiat´ Nikolaia Ivanovicha Il'minskogo: K 25-letiiu Bratstva sv. Guriia* (Kazan, 1892), p. 326.

[28] The first assessment was made in March 1849 (RGIA, f. 796, op. 125, d. 1518, l. 86); the second assessment is undated but, judging from its location within the archival file, appears to come from sometime in 1850 (RGIA, f. 797, op. 15, d. 35644, l. 112).

[29] See Petr Znamenskii, *Istoriia Kazanskoi Dukhovnoi Akademii za pervyi (doreformennyi) period ee sushchestvovaniia, 1842–1870* (Kazan, 1892), 2:356–58; and Il'minskii's reports published in idem, *Na pamiat´:* "Otchet bakkalavra Kazanskoi Dukhovnoi Akademii N. I. Il'minskogo za pervyi god prebyvaniia ego na Vostoke," pp. 338–56, and "Obshchii otchet bakkalavra N. I. Il'minskogo ob ego zaniatiiakh vo vse vremia prebyvaniia na Vostoke," pp. 357–86. I place the term "East" in quotation marks, since the places Il'minskii visited were in fact geographically to the *west* of Kazan.

[30] Edward W. Said, *Orientalism* (New York, 1978), p. 20.

[31] Il'minskii, "Izvlechenie," p. 333.

force and authenticity."[32] This notion of refutation from within was based on the idea that Islam contained many internal "deficiencies and incongruities" that were accessible to those with the linguistic skills and the desire to find them. This, then, became one of the principal tasks of the students in the division, who learned Arabic and Tatar, studied the original texts of Islam, and wrote lengthy treatises with the goal of refuting Islam on its own terms. A number of these papers were subsequently published in a periodical entitled *Missionary Anti-Muslim Anthology*, beginning in 1873.[33]

Second, the perceived attachment of Tatars to Islam lowered the status of polemical approaches to conversion. Il′minskii criticized the missionaries of 1830 for their tendency merely to tell Tatars: "Abandon your Mohammedan delusions! Abandon your foul faith! Mohammed was a fraud, a dog!"[34] The very inability of Tatars to appreciate the deficiencies of their own religion called for their education, "which would develop in them the desire for independent and impartial thinking, would enrich them with healthy understandings of nature and history, and would encourage their respect for authentic evidence."[35] But Il′minskii insisted that this was hard work that required an intimate understanding of values and sensibilities that were alien to Russians. As he contended with frustration in 1870, "Everyone imagines that it is so easy to prove the superiority of the Christian faith over the Mohammedan, that it doesn't cost anything; you sit down, take a pen, and just crank out a multitude of refutations so that all that remains is for another person to speak [those refutations] to a Mohammedan, and the latter remains speechless . . . and as a result agrees to baptism."[36] In general, after having helped initiate critical analysis of Islam for the purposes of its refutation, Il′minskii exhibited fairly limited interest in developing anti-Islamic polemics further, leaving this task to Gordii Sablukov and E. A. Malov.[37]

Third, Tatars now came to be viewed as fundamentally different from the other non-Russians of the Volga-Kama region. Il′minskii criticized comparisons of Tatars with the small inorodtsy of the region, "whose religious teaching is limited to just a few fragmentary and dark legends and who are almost

---

[32] N. I. Il′minskii, "Oproverzhenie Islamizma, kak neobkhodimoe uslovie k tverdomu priniatiiu tatarami khristianskoi very, vsego poleznee mozhet nachat′sia razubezhdeniem ikh v prorocheskom dostoinstve Magometa," in appendix to Znamenskii, *Na pamiat′*, p. 388.

[33] See E. A. Malov, "Neskol′ko slov o neobkhodimosti privolzhskoi protivomusul′manskoi missii," *Dukh Khristianina* (1865): 63–84, in which he stressed that the weakening of Islam's "fanaticism" required learning and education. See also his introduction to the first issue of the *Anthology:* "Svedeniia o missionerskom otdelenii," *Missionerskii protivo musul′manskii sbornik* 1 (1873): ii–xiii.

[34] Il′minskii, "Izvlechenie," p. 333.

[35] Idem, "Oproverzhenie," p. 401.

[36] Otdel Rukopisei Kazanskogo Nauchnogo Biblioteki im. Lobachevskogo, f. 7 (Dnevnik E. A. Malova), l. 102. See also Egor Vinogradov, "Metod missionerskoi polemiki protiv Tatar-mukhammedan," *Missionerskii protivomusul′manskii sbornik* 1 (1873): 17–20. This essay was written when Vinogradov was a student at the Academy in the late 1840s.

[37] Znamenskii, *Istoriia*, pp. 405–11; and Geraci, "Window on the East," pp. 47–49, 89–100.

all baptized." On the contrary, a range of factors made the Tatar people "worthy of more attention from the clergy" than others: their sheer numbers and geographic dispersal; their social diversity (among them were officials, mullahs, merchants, and landlords); and not least their "stubborn disposition" toward Islam and "their internal religious unanimity."[38] Unlike other non-Russians, who lacked a theologically sophisticated basis for rejecting Christianity, Muslims confessed a religion that was expounded in written texts, and they were familiar with major figures of Christian scripture and could therefore offer critical interpretations of Christianity. For example, they dismissed the doctrine of the Trinity as a form of polytheism, and in general, according to Il′minskii, they "scorn the Christian faith," considering it to be "a superstition, not just a dark one, but one that plunges [Christians] into ignorance," in short, "a collection of rituals lacking any meaning whatsoever."[39] Far more formidable religious rivals than the authorities had previously realized, Muslims accordingly merited more consideration than Chuvash, Maris, and Udmurts.

Indeed, one of Il′minskii's more consequential findings—an outgrowth of his service on the Orenburg Frontier Commission in 1858–61—was that many non-Russians were more likely to be assimilated by Tatars than by Russians. Far from being merely stubborn and impregnable, the Muslim community now appeared dynamic and eager to expand. In Orenburg, Il′minskii witnessed the growing penetration of Tatar language, customs, and mores into the Kazakh steppe,[40] and apostasy in Kazan province demonstrated that the same was occurring among Finnic peoples and Chuvash. Accordingly, sources began to refer with increasing frequency to the Islamization of peoples who were historically pagan or (allegedly) only weakly Islamicized.[41] Just as the French in Algeria expended great intellectual effort to demonstrate that the mountain-dwelling Kabyles were superior to, and more amenable to assimilation than, the fanatically Islamic Arab nomads,[42] Russian observers became convinced that those not yet infected with Islamic consciousness (Kazakhs, Chuvash, Finnic peoples, Kräshens) were amenable

[38] NART, f. 10, op. 1, d. 1655, l. 23. Il′minskii was the principal author of this text, but the name of Professor Gordii Sablukov was added to give it greater authority.

[39] NART, f. 10, op. 1, d. 5964, l. 13. See also Il′minskii, "Izvlechenie," pp. 326–27.

[40] See Isabelle Kreindler, "Ibrahim Altynsarin, Nikolai Il′minskii, and the Kazakh National Awakening," *Central Asian Survey* 2, 3 (1983): 99–116. Kreindler suggests that it was the director of the Orenburg Commission, the orientalist V. V. Grigor′ev, who convinced Il′minskii of the danger of Tatar-Muslim hegemony in the steppe. For an interesting evaluation of Grigor′ev that questions the applicability of a Saidian paradigm of orientalism to the Russian case, see Nathaniel Knight, "Grigor′ev in Orenburg, 1851–1862: Russian Orientalism in the Service of Empire?" *Slavic Review* 59, 1 (2000): 74–100.

[41] The notion that Kazakhs were weakly Islamicized is probably misplaced, but so Russians and their Tatar informants believed. See Allen Frank, "Volga Tatars and the 'Islamization' of Muslim Nomads: A Reverse Angle on Russia's 'Civilizing Mission'" (paper delivered at Humboldt University, Berlin, 1996).

[42] Lorcin, *Imperial Identities*, pp. 35–75.

to the government's projects and reasonably good candidates for true Orthodox conversion and Russification. The Volga-Kama region was accordingly identified as the arena of struggle between Islam and Christianity over the peoples who stood between these two cultural forces. As one author contended in an essay on Maris in 1862: "The Cheremis people, as in general the Finnic nations, is more yielding, and, of course, sooner or later will be reborn—either into the Russian or into the Tatar nation. Pagan religion is likewise yielding, it necessarily must give in—either to Christianity or to Mohammedanism."[43] In the emerging struggle between Islam and Christianity the middle ground receded, and a division—or a front—was more clearly drawn through the region. Because of the region's complex settlement pattern, this front was neither straight and nor well-defined geographically, but it was increasingly clear in the Russian imagination nonetheless.

Although Il'minskii became more hostile toward Islam as he grew older, initially he admired much in that religion and even saw important lessons to be learned from it.[44] In his 1849 report he noted the exemplary conduct of Tatar mullahs: they were elected by their own parishes and rarely transferred from one parish to another. They seldom argued with one another, conducted themselves "soberly, solidly, and honestly," and "are never driven to the extreme of requesting money and are considered to be completely unselfish people."[45] Il'minskii also emphasized the many Islamic schools and the high degree of literacy among Tatars. He in particular admired the informal character of the schools, which did not require entrance examinations or certificates; there was no school bureaucracy, and competition among schools, which drew students based on the fame and abilities of the resident mullah, ensured that Tatar medreses offered an education at least as good as that in Russian middle schools. He noted that the Koran and other religious books gained currency among the people without any official tutelage or biblical societies. Such informalities allowed greater educational experimentation, and the schools' freedom from central authority liberated them from stifling rules and regulations.[46] In fact, a number of the principles Il'minskii discussed in these years found realization in the central baptized-Tatar school that he founded in 1863. Finally, the very strength and

---

[43] S. Nurminskii, "Ocherk religioznykh verovanii cheremis," *Pravoslavnyi sobesednik* 3 (1862): 278–79.

[44] A number of scholars, citing Il'minskii's correspondence with Pobedonostsev and the hostile views articulated there, fail to appreciate the more gradual development of his thought. Jean Saussay, for example, quotes predominantly from letters written in the final years of Il'minskii's life, when he was indeed highly intolerant of Islam. Jean Saussay, "Il'minskij et la politique de russification des Tatars, 1865–1891," *Cahiers du monde russe et soviétique* 8, 3 (1967): 404–26.

[45] NART, f. 10, op. 1, d. 5964, ll. 15–16.

[46] " 'Ex Oriente Lux': Odna iz neizdannykh zapisok Nikolaia Ivanovicha Il'minskogo po voprosu ob ustroistve uchebnykh zavedenii," *Pravoslavnyi sobesednik* 1 (1901), esp. 46–52. This article was evidently written in 1862 or 1863, at precisely the time that Il'minskii was devoting greater effort to the question of Christian education of baptized non-Russians.

persistence of Islam had to be acknowledged: "Islam is such a strong and tenacious religiosity that even the English and the Catholics, with all their erudition and wealth, with strong [illegible word] support and consistent perseverance of their missionaries, cannot make any headway against it."[47]

Many of Il´minskii's ideas—and especially the study of Islam using original sources—were put into practice in the Anti-Muslim Division. The study of "missionary languages" had begun at the Academy already in 1845, and several people at the Academy (including Il´minskii) had already been involved for several years in an effort to translate Orthodox liturgical books into Tatar, as commissioned by Emperor Nicholas.[48] But until the formation of the missionary divisions, these languages were studied largely from a philological standpoint, with little accompanying religious or ethnographic focus.[49] It was in the Anti-Muslim Division that Islam was subjected to a more thorough "analysis" and that the Tatar language received as much attention as Arabic. The division served as a site for the development of new ideas about Islam and about the state's relationship to it. Here Il´minskii worked through the ideas that were to become staples not only in terms of attitudes toward Islam but also in terms of the education of almost all non-Russians in eastern European Russia.[50] Here Malov wrote a thesis on the history of Islam in Russia, which served as the basis for his numerous historical works on non-Russian schools, on the eighteenth-century Kontora, and on government policy toward mosques—works that profoundly influenced perceptions of Russia's historical relationship with its Muslim subjects and demonstrated (at least to the satisfaction of their author) that only a stern attitude toward Muslims could prevent the further spread of Islamic influence and "propaganda."[51] And here other figures who would play important roles in the further development of Russia's relationship with Islam and Central Asia until the October Revolution—such as M. A. Mashanov and N. P. Ostroumov—were trained. Through the journal *Orthodox Interlocutor* these figures were able to disseminate their views and thereby helped develop a new consciousness about Islam.[52]

[47] NART, f. 968, op. 1, d. 8, l. 25.

[48] Details of the translation effort are in NART, f. 10, op. 1, d. 3418.

[49] Znamenskii, *Istoriia*, pp. 360–64.

[50] In the same year that the division was closed (1870), Il´minskii's principles for the education of non-Russians, stressing instruction in native languages, were adopted by the Ministry of Education. See Isabelle Teitz Kreindler, "Educational Policies toward the Eastern Nationalities in Tsarist Russia: A Study of Il´minskii's System" (Ph.D. diss., Columbia University, 1969), pp. 67–88.

[51] Malov's thesis was entitled "History of Islam in Russia." In addition to his works cited above, see also *O Novokreshchenykh shkolakh v XVIII veke* (Kazan, 1868); and *O Novokreshchenskoi kontore* (Kazan, 1873).

[52] Even so, this journal ran into financial difficulties in the 1880s, and it was characterized by Archbishop Palladii as consisting of "dry scholarly articles and vast dissertations." See S. Ternovskii, *Istoricheskaia zapiska o sostoianii Kazanskoi Dukhovnoi Akademii posle ee preobrazovaniia, 1870–1892* (Kazan, 1892), pp. 60–63.

Nonetheless, the division was beset by problems, even in the early years of its existence. The Academy's administration was not fully committed to the division and found the extensive attention to Islam unnecessary and even offensive to Orthodox sensibilities. Already in the late 1850s and early 1860s, missionary courses were demoted within the Academy's curriculum, and several of the division's instructors left the Academy in that period. Moreover, only a minority of students chose to pursue anti-Islamic studies because of the perceived difficulty of the languages involved. Few of those who completed the division's program actually went on to become missionaries, since teaching positions in diocesan seminaries offered higher salaries and greater job security.[53] Moreover, in the 1860s the Synod was eager to introduce a standardized statute for all four of the empire's ecclesiastical academies, and the apostasy of 1866 offered a good excuse to eliminate the division. The Synod saw the division's principal goal as being the eventual conversion of Muslims to Orthodoxy, but precisely the opposite was occurring, even though the division had existed for over a decade. It therefore concluded in 1870 that the division "has not achieved the proposed goal—the education of missionaries for the spread of the Orthodox faith among Muslims and Buddhists."[54] The arguments of the division's proponents that its labors with regard to conversion "have been indirect, and not direct," and had consisted "primarily of the analysis of Islam itself and of the study and teaching of the Arabic and Tatar languages," fell on deaf ears, as did Il'minskii's contention that the division's principal accomplishment had been the elaboration of a more effective system for strengthening Christian attachments among baptized Tatars.[55] The division was effectively shut down in 1870, leaving only token opportunities for missionary studies at the Academy.

Although Il'minskii and the division made crucial contributions to developing conceptions of Islam and its place in the broader Russian imperial polity, these new ideas did not become entirely hegemonic. Many churchmen and officials had faith in the power of Christianity itself or in the notions of development and progress, and were therefore unwilling or unable to recognize the internal strength and insularity of Islam. The rector of the Academy and Archbishop Afanasii were loathe to acknowledge the qualities that Il'minskii ascribed to Islam.[56] Later, in 1882, Il'minskii likewise complained that "the society of the intelligentsia, more or less filled with ideas of religious tolerance or religious indifference, is not particularly pained that Mohammedanism is

---

[53] Znamenskii, *Istoriia*, pp. 412–20; NART, f. 10, op. 1, d. 2566; and NART, f. 10, op. 1, d. 2597.

[54] RGIA, f. 796, op. 151, d. 820, l. 11.

[55] NART, f. 10, op. 1, d. 2597 (*listy* are not numbered, and the file is generally in considerable disarray); "Pis'mo N. I. Il'minskogo k Rektoru Kazanskoi Akademii Arkhimandritu Nikanoru (Brovkovichu), 8 sentiabria 1870 g.," *Pravoslavnyi sobesednik* 1 (1910): 114–15; and NART, f. 10, op. 1, d. 25.

[56] See Znamenskii, *Istoriia*, pp. 413–23, 438–40.

prevailing over Orthodoxy."[57] But at least among those most closely involved in the self-appointed task of administering Muslims, reforming their schools, and protecting hapless baptized inorodtsy from them, there emerged a broad consensus about the "fanaticism" and "insularity" of Islam.

Here, again, the reform period was crucial to investing these new representations with greater poignancy and urgency. To the extent that Muslims, and in particular mullahs, supposedly remained "fanatical" and profoundly "ignorant," many observers contended that the government could expect from them only opposition and hostility to its efforts to restructure rural society. Writing with anxiety in 1867, Orenburg Governor-General N. Kryzhanovskii recounted the opposition that mullahs had stirred up to past government initiatives, by which they sought "to keep the population that is related to them by faith in complete ignorance, to develop in them fanaticism, and to impede the penetration into the people of sensible ideas." Whereas the government had previously been required to settle for half-measures, the new institutions of self-government associated with the Great Reforms required "a certain level of intellectual development and living sympathy for public interests. What benefit will there be in such institutions from a crude and ignorant people when it wishes to turn to the instructions of the Koran and Shariat?"[58] Similarly, the first attempts to assess existing Tatar schools in Kazan province in 1861 (with the goal of their eventual reform) revealed that the "fanaticism" of mullahs, the numerical strength of the Tatar population, and the peculiarities of their faith, language, and habits "leave Tatars not only separated from Russian residents but beyond the influence of the administration on their education." Because mullahs made every effort to convince their flocks that everything outside Islam was false and useless, existing Muslims schools "have not brought any benefits for the practical life of the Mohammedan population."[59] These alleged characteristics—Muslim "fanaticism," the insularity of Muslim communities, their "alienation" from the progress and enlightenment that the government was working so hard to promote—all emerged in their most vivid and intractable forms in the context of reform, for it was precisely the reforms that these characteristics threatened so seriously to disrupt.

Curiously, the conquest of Central Asia worsened the situation, for it conjured up a more disturbing imaginative geography. Now, the entire region from Kazan to the (south)east could appear as one single grand mass of Muslims—fanatical, alienated, hostile, and large. This new configuration of religious and imperial space was probably most visibly captured by Orenburg Governor-General Kryzhanovskii in 1867 when he commented that the region from Kazan to the Tian-Shan mountains now represented an "unin-

[57] RGIA, f. 821, op. 8, d. 743, l. 960b.
[58] RGIA, f. 821, op. 8, d. 594, ll. 40, 420b.
[59] RGIA, f. 383, op. 24, d. 37141, ll. 3–4, 21.

terrupted Muslim population" consisting of several tens of millions of people—a "continuous mass of people who confess a faith according to whose dogmas we, Christians, are considered the natural and irreconcilable foes of all true believers."[60] Likewise, in 1883 B. Iuzefovich, commissioned by Chief Procurator Konstantin Pobedonostsev to investigate the issue of Islam, wrote that if Kazan and Ufa provinces had at one time been "isolated from the rest of the Mohammedan world," they now threatened to merge with that world "thanks to our Central Asian territorial acquisitions."[61] To the extent that Central Asia was considered to be even more fanatical than the rest of Muslim Russia, these connections could only cause alarm.

As such perspectives became rooted in Russian consciousness, moreover, it became more and more difficult to resist the proposition that Muslim opposition was to some degree politically motivated. Already in the days of the Anti-Muslim Division, students had begun to highlight the antipathy of Muslims toward everything Christian.[62] As Il'minskii became increasingly hostile toward Islam, he used his influence with highly placed officials in St. Petersburg whenever possible to restrict the activities of Muslims.[63] Iuzefovich, who was apparently deeply influenced by Il'minskii, concluded in 1883 that while Muslim "fanaticism" and "propaganda" had so far remained largely within religious parameters, it could very easily "serve also as tool for political agitation among Muslims."[64] The commentator E. N. Voronets, who launched a kind of anti-Islamic crusade in print, was even more alarmist. Noting that within European Russia alone there were over five million Muslims, kept by their faith in "stubborn alienation from everything Russian," he contended that Islam represented "the principal link by means of which the non-Russian Muslim population in Russia constitutes within the state a religious state that is hostile to Russia and to which the whole life of those non-Russians, their activity and tendency, is subordinated."[65] To be sure, Voronets' position was extreme, and even missionary activists like Malov had difficulty accepting many of his arguments.[66] But the specter of an Islamic-inspired political challenge, especially after the

---

[60] RGIA, f. 821, op. 8, d. 594, l. 35.

[61] B. Iuzefovich, "Khristianstvo, magometanstvo i iazychestvo v vostochnykh guberniiakh Rossii," *Russkii vestnik* 164 (1883): 28.

[62] See, for example, Vasilii Petrov, "Prichiny upornoi priviazannosti tatar-mukhammedan k svoei vere," *Missionerskii protivomusul'manskii sbornik* 1 (1873): 90–139. Petrov was a student at the Academy in the years 1846–50, when this essay was written.

[63] See Geraci, "Window on the East," pp. 73–77, 171–75; Kreindler, "Educational Policies," pp. 120–21; and Il'minskii, *Pis'ma Nikolaia Ivanovicha Il'minskogo k Ober-prokuroru Sv. Sinoda K. P. Pobedonostsevu* (Kazan, 1898).

[64] Iuzefovich, "Khristianstvo, magometanstvo i iazychestvo," p. 28.

[65] E. N. Voronets, "Mirovozzrenie mukhammedanstva i otnoshenie ego k khristianstvu," *Missionerskii protivomusul'manskii sbornik*, no. 14 (1877): 20–21. See also Voronets's vitriolic essay, "K voprosu o svobode very i sovremennykh, vnutri Rossii, otpadeniiakh ot khristianstva v magometanstvo," *Pravoslavnyi sobesednik* 1 (1877): 226–58.

[66] See Ia. B. [Malov], "Russko-gosudarstvennyi vzgliad na otpadenie inorodtsev-khristian v mukhammedanstvo," *Tserkovnyi vestnik* 23 (1876): 7–10.

emergence of the Islamic reform (*jadid*) movement in the 1880s, had been raised and could not so easily be put to rest.[67]

It was in this context, and in the more conservative atmosphere of the reign of Alexander III (1881–94), that the Anti-Muslim Division was at least partially resurrected. In 1884 another new academy statute revived the division and raised the study of Tatar and Mongol missionary subjects to a more prominent place in the curriculum. Nonetheless, missionary studies continued to be plagued by small and inconsistent enrollments and by the absence of real missionary careers for the division's graduates. In 1889 the Academy attempted to broaden the appeal of missionary studies by establishing short, two-year missionary courses open to non-Academy students—that is, to priests in non-Russian parishes and to missionaries traveling through Kazan. In 1897 the Academy further revised these courses, making them more general and independent. The idea was to offer practical, general missionary education to rank-and-file clergy, as opposed to the more theoretical and advanced study in the Academy for a missionary elite.[68] In short, Islam represented far too formidable an opponent for the church not to prepare its servitors more effectively against it.

Containing Islam

Gradually, these new concerns about Islam led to calls for restrictions on Muslims and their religious activities or for the active application of laws that had remained on the books from earlier periods of repression. Initially, however, the measures adopted seemed tentative, as if religious and civil officials had begun to identify Islam as a major problem but were not sure what made Islam so tenacious and what could be done about it. Nor was it easy for many of them to reconcile (geo)political considerations, their own convictions about the inherent superiority of Christianity, and their commitment to a basic level of religious tolerance.

The earliest measure taken in response to Islam in the nineteenth century involved the publishing of religious books in Kazan. The missionary Vasilii

---

[67] On the emergence of jadidism, which can be seen in part, at least, as a Muslim response to these unsympathetic representations, see Edward J. Lazzerini, "Defining the Orient: A Nineteenth-Century Russo-Tatar Polemic over Identity and Cultural Representation," in *Muslim Communities*, pp. 33–45; idem, "Ismail Bey Gasprinski (Gasprali), the Discourse of Modernism, and the Russians," in *Tatars of the Crimea: Their Struggle for Survival*, ed. Edward Allworth (Durham, 1988), pp. 149–69; and several contributions in *L'Islam de Russie: Conscience communautaire et autonomie politique chez les Tatars de la Volga et d'Oural depuis le XVIIIe siècle*, ed. Stéphane A. Dudoignon, Dämir Is'haqov, and Räfyq Möhämmätshin (Paris, 1997).

[68] Ternovskii, *Istoricheskaia zapiska*, pp. 243–52; RGIA, f. 796, op. 170, d. 421; RGIA, f. 796, op. 179, d. 701; and "Missionerskie kursy pri Kazanskoi Dukhovnoi Akademii," RGIA Khranilishche pechatnykh zapisok, folder no. 3204.

Orlov, following his trips to Chistopol and Spassk districts in 1844, reported that the Koran and various textbooks were being printed "in an enormous quantity" and distributed in the countryside for free by wealthy Tatars. Considering these books to be a major source of apostasy, Orlov explained that "novokreshchenye Tatars view the printing of these books as an order by the government and on this basis conclude that 'it is clear that our faith is correct and that Russians have come to like it as well [*ruskim de ponravilas´*]'."[69] Data supplied by the governor of Kazan confirmed the impression that the printing of such books was increasing dramatically in the early 1840s.[70] Statistics on the output of one private press (run by the Rakemzanov brothers) were not even available, "for only Tatars work there, and they do not reveal their secrets to anyone."[71] Emperor Nicholas therefore called for a prohibition on the printing of the Koran and other Muslim religious books by private presses in Kazan.[72]

The ban was enforced for about four years (1845–49), but doubts soon began to arise concerning both the true relationship between books and apostasy and the consequences of the ban. By 1849 the Committee of Ministers had instructed the MVD to reinvestigate the effects of the books, and Il´minskii had submitted his report on baptized Tatars, in which books were not identified as a major source of apostasy. In fact, Il´minskii wrote that because baptized Tatars enjoyed few educational opportunities (as opposed to Muslims), "they are submerged in extreme ignorance. A literate person among them is a great rarity."[73] The new Archbishop Grigorii followed Il´minskii's lead. Noting that Muslim books had been found in the possession of only one apostate (and citing Il´minskii almost verbatim), he concluded: "All those books, in all likelihood, did not have currency among baptized Tatars. . . . [These Tatars] cannot use any books: they are submerged in such ignorance that among them a literate person is the greatest rarity." In fact, Grigorii argued, the ban simply made Muslim books more desirable by rendering them forbidden fruit, and in any event it was better to have copies of the Koran handy in order to point out its "obvious errors" and "to show the Tatars that Christianity fears no rivals and eliminates them

---

[69] RGIA, f. 796, op. 125, d. 1518, ll. 22–220b. (internal quotation marks added to clarify Tatar voice).

[70] A. G. Karimullin believes that the governor's figure of 220,000 Muslim religious books in 1841–44 was probably an exaggeration. But the volume of printing was nonetheless impressive and growing. See A. G. Karimullin, *U istokov tatarskoi knigi* (Kazan, 1992), pp. 159–65.

[71] RGIA, f. 796, op. 125, d. 1518, l. 41.

[72] The Chief Procurator's report to the Emperor along with the latter's decision is in RGIA, f. 797, op. 15, d. 35644, ll. 13–21. The DDDII justified the ban by claiming that out of respect for Allah and Mohammed, Muslims only allowed manuscript copies of the Koran. Thus the government was enacting the ban, paradoxically, on the basis of "religious tolerance," since "deviations from ancient rules and customs" could not be allowed, "especially for the benefit of private speculation" (NART, f. 1, op. 2, d. 483, ll. 1–2).

[73] Il´minskii, "Izvlechenie," p. 328.

all by its internal strength." In the end, Grigorii suggested merely that the printing of such books be better regulated.[74]

Moreover, it turned out that the majority of the printed books were sent to more distant markets—to the Caucuses, the Kazakh steppe, even to China. (Remarkably, the university press depended on the sale of these books for its economic survival and had been exempted from the ban, which applied only to *private* presses.)[75] Minister of Education Sergei Uvarov, meanwhile, noted the importance of these books for Russian orientalism and contended that such restrictions might violate provisions on religious tolerance.[76] But perhaps the most important considerations were geopolitical. If publication of these books were halted in Kazan, the governor argued, then "this trade will go into the hands of the English trading companies in the East and will be an object of significant contraband for Muslims within Russia. Besides that, the printing of Korans and other books in Eastern languages should spread trust in Russia's protection and religious tolerance among neighboring Muslim peoples, which is perhaps not without benefit."[77] A lenient policy on Islam could serve as the basis for further imperial expansion. The Committee of Ministers accepted these arguments, noting in conclusion that while the ban would have no effect on apostasy, it would have the harmful consequence of "having strengthened the influence of foreigners in the East."[78] The ban was accordingly repealed.

In the early 1850s attention also began to focus on Islamic institutions. While initially efforts involved gaining greater control over the election and approval of mullahs and regulating the size and spread of Muslim parishes, authorities subsequently began to consider more thorough transformations in the structure of Islam's administration, including even the elimination of the Muftii and the Spiritual Assembly altogether. The discussions on these reforms continued into the 1880s and produced a voluminous bureaucratic correspondence.[79] Most Russian administrators agreed that it was necessary to reduce the influence of the Islamic clergy in the Russian Empire and to break its ability to resist the government's reform initiatives, but their discussions did not introduce any major structural changes. Nonetheless, the MVD did remove the Kazakh steppe from the Assembly's jurisdiction and in 1865 appointed as Muftii Selim-Direi Tevkelev, a noble landowner who was

[74] RGIA, f. 796, op. 125, d. 1518, ll. 78–80.

[75] " 'Ex Oriente Lux,' " p. 50; NART, f. 10, op. 1, d. 1655, l. 19; and RGIA, f. 821, op. 8, d. 830, ll. 5–8.

[76] RGIA, f. 1263, op. 1, d. 2034, ll. 2900b.–91. On Uvarov's interest in orientalism, see Cynthia Whittaker, "The Impact of the Oriental Renaissance in Russia: The Case of Sergei Uvarov," *Jahrbücher für Geschichte Osteuropas* 26, 4 (1978): 503–24.

[77] NART, f. 1, op. 2, d. 483, l. 47.

[78] RGIA, f. 796, op. 125, d. 1518, l. 920b. The full decision of the Committee of Ministers (1849) is in RGIA, f. 1263, op. 1, d. 2033, ll. 92–95.

[79] For a survey of some of the issues involved in this correspondence, see Iuzefovich, "Khristianstvo, magometanstvo i iazychestvo," 38–51. Relevant archival files include RGIA, f. 821, op. 8, dd. 594, 607, 611, and 616, which cover the initial reform projects.

not a Muslim clergyman. Through Tevkelev, the government hoped to promote Russian language and secular values among the region's Muslims.[80]

Increasingly convinced of the scope of "Mohammedan propaganda," authorities also began to contend that mosques were proliferating beyond any effective control. Already in 1857 Il'minskii had targeted this as a potential area for government action.[81] The construction of all new mosques was regulated by two important provisions: first, each mosque was to have "not fewer than three hundred, or at the very least two hundred," male revision souls as parishioners; second, new mosques could be established "only if there is no possibility that the construction of the mosque will cause temptation [*soblazn*] for Christians and novokreshchenye Tatars living together with the Muslims."[82] Though these two provisions had their origins in eighteenth-century decrees and appeared in the 1857 edition of the Law Digest (*Svod Zakonov*), I have not been able to locate them in the 1832 and 1842 editions of the digest, which makes it unclear whether they were in force or local authorities knew about them.[83] Their reintroduction in the 1857 edition clearly suggests a heightened awareness of Islam, a growing concern for the unregulated construction of mosques, and a new acknowledgment that novokreshchenye's religious condition was threatened by the very presence of Muslim houses of worship.

As large-scale apostasy erupted in 1866, the calls for limitations on new mosques increased. Archbishop Antonii was especially active in requesting more decisive government intervention to combat "the excessive multiplication of mosques in Kazan diocese." Noting what he considered to have been a highly successful policy against the unauthorized construction of Catholic churches in the western provinces in the 1830s and 1840s, Antonii called for a similar campaign against mosques in Kazan diocese. He requested strict observance of the two-hundred-parishioner standard and an outright prohibition on mosques in areas with baptized non-Russian settlement or "where there can be unquestionable harm and temptation for the Orthodox population." Arguing that "partial measures" dependent on diocesan authorities were no longer sufficient, Antonii called for "a few general government directives, not to tear off the tops but rather to wrench out the very root of the evil and eliminate that which constitutes the strongest support of Islam and

---

[80] Steinwedel, "Invisible Threads of Empire," pp. 114–18; and Azamatov, *Orenburgskoe Magometanskoe Dukhovnoe Sobranie*, pp. 59–64. For a brief biography of Tevkelev that shows his distinguished record of service, see *V pamiat' stoletiia Orenburgskogo Magometanskogo Dukhovnogo Sobraniia, uchrezhdennogo v gorode Ufe* (St. Petersburg, 1892), pp. 34–35.

[81] NART, f. 10, op. 1, d. 1655, ll. 19–190b.

[82] *SZ* (1857), vol. 12, articles 260, 261, 262.

[83] The confusion surrounding these provisions is considerable. The two-hundred-soul minimum was established by a law in 1756 (*PSZ* I, vol. 14, no. 10597 [1756]) and was technically confirmed by an 1829 law that regulated building plans for mosques (*PSZ* II, vol. 4, no. 2902 [1829]). Nonetheless, as I noted above, the 1832 and 1842 editions of *SZ* do not contain references to these minimums, nor do they refer to the 1756 decree.

the barrier to appropriate action on it by Christianity."[84] Various requests were subsequently made in both Kazan and Simbirsk provinces with regard to specific mosques.

The policy on mosques demonstrates once again a significant shift in consciousness about Islam. In the first half of the nineteenth century Muslims had been left more or less to their own devices, and even Il'minskii, recognizing the tremendous institutional presence of Islam in the Volga region, had recognized that only "partial measures" against Islam were possible. Inspired by a historical record that they saw confirming the benefits of a hard line against Muslims, clerics like Malov and Antonii became less satisfied with "partial measures" and demanded more active government intervention. The Volga-Kama was now being construed as a space where two religious systems—Islam and Christianity—were to fight a battle for the hearts and minds of all the Finnic peoples, Chuvash, and baptized Tatars stuck between the two. Thus Il'minskii wrote in 1873, as he himself became more insistent on government action against Islam, "The arena for the struggle with Mohammedanism is extensive—almost the entire Volga region."[85]

As often as not, however, the requests of Antonii and other clerics were rejected by the secular authorities, who usually considered their arguments but did not feel obliged to accept them. Of the cases I have encountered, civil authorities upheld the requests of Muslim petitioners about as often as they gave the Orthodox clergy satisfaction. The MVD noted on different occasions that the bishop's opinion was only one of several factors, that rejection of a petition would only aggravate Muslims, or that a given petition addressed only the renovation of an old mosque and not the construction of a new one. In general, the MVD stuck closely to the law and even laid the burden of proof on the government, rather than on Muslim petitioners.[86] In response to Antonii's requests for "a few general government directives," the DDDII pointed to "the growing number of Muslim subjects on the Central Asian borders," which made any attack on Muslim institutions unwise from a geopolitical standpoint.[87] In 1875 the director of the DDDII, E. K. Sievers, reacted with irritation to Antonii's complaint that the government was displaying "indifference" toward the struggle with "Tataro-Muslim propaganda." The many punitive and administrative measures that the government had taken in response to the apostasy of 1866, Sievers wrote, "once again confirm the truth that they can neither create nor eradicate religious

---

[84] RGIA, f. 797, op. 37, otdel 2, stol 3, d. 216, l. 1; and RGIA, f. 821, op. 8, d. 743, ll. 23–30 (citation from l. 23).

[85] N. I. Il'minskii, ed., *Perepiska o trekh shkolakh Ufimskoi gubernii k kharakteristike inorodcheskikh missionerskikh shkol* (Kazan, 1885), p. 17.

[86] RGIA, f. 821, op. 8, d. 659; RGIA, f. 821, op. 8, d. 664; RGIA, f. 821, op. 8, d. 769; and RGIA, f. 821, op. 8, d. 775. The following two files contain whole series of cases concerning the construction and renovation of mosques: RGIA, f. 821, op. 8, d. 673; and RGIA, f. 821, op. 150, d. 404.

[87] RGIA, f. 821, op. 8, d. 743, ll. 33–48.

beliefs." Expressing faith in the eventual triumph of Christianity over Islam, Sievers concluded: "The government, in light of the size of the Muslim population, which lives both in the eastern edges of the Empire, as well as in contiguous countries, and due to other considerations must sometimes display a certain restraint concerning the use of punitive measures in matters of faith."[88] Charged with reviewing the problem of apostasy in the early 1880s, and confronted with new apostasies in Ufa province, the Committee of Ministers similarly decided in 1884 against taking any new and aggressive measures, opting instead for the less confrontational policy of supporting missionary schools.[89]

While apostasy had supposedly demonstrated the scope of "Mohammedan propaganda" underway among baptized Chuvash, Udmurts and others, there was also a growing fear that Islam might contaminate the remaining pagans (above all in Orenburg—later Ufa—province), thereby rendering impossible their eventual conversion to Christianity. Thus the authorities began also to grapple with the question: Should pagans be allowed to convert to Islam? This issue first arose in 1842, at which time the Synod registered its opinion that this act should be considered illegal: "The conversion of pagans by a Mohammedan to his faith is an action that violates the right of the ruling church, and it is all the more harmful since those subjected to a change of pagan beliefs for Muslim [belief] become infected with fanaticism and become even less accessible to the word of truth."[90] The MVD likewise denied pagans the intellectual capacities necessary to make a decision as complex as conversion, arguing that they "cannot achieve consciousness concerning the advantage of one or another non-Christian faith, and that they must naturally be brought to this by the suggestions of others; thus the conversion of pagans to Mohammedanism must render guilty not the ones who have converted but the ones who have converted them, or the ones who have assisted this in any way."[91] Intrinsic to pagan conversion was thus "Mohammedan propaganda." Since there was no law that explicitly prohibited conversion from one non-Christian faith to another, the proposition that Muslims had instigated pagans' acceptance of Islam—in violation of laws prohibiting non-Orthodox proselytism—was essential to the criminalization of this conversion.

More substantial reports of Muslim influence on pagans began to surface in the late 1840s, when Emperor Nicholas ordered that measures be taken to convert the large numbers of pagans under the jurisdiction of the Ministry of State Domains. In this context, the bishop of Orenburg reported that

---

[88] Ibid., ll. 61–640b.
[89] Ibid., ll. 180–89. On these developments, see also Elena Vorob′eva, "Khristianizatsiia musul′man Povolzh′ia v imperskoi politike samoderzhaviia," in *Imperskii stroi Rossii v regional′nom izmerenii (XIX–nachalo XX veka)* (Moscow, 1997), pp. 224–37.
[90] RGIA, f. 797, op. 12, d. 29894, l. 5.
[91] Ibid., ll. 7–8.

"temptation from Muslims" was significant in the region—that is, pagans were sending their children to Islamic schools and marrying Muslims, and mullahs were attracting pagans to their mosques.[92] Nicholas charged the Orenburg governor with taking the necessary measures "for the protection of these pagans from seduction [to Islam]."[93] While the government never issued a law specifically prohibiting the conversion of pagans to Islam, this directive served for several decades as the basis for rejecting pagans' requests for recognition as Muslims.

Yet there was considerable disagreement about how to interpret this directive. As petitions from pagans—mostly from Udmurts and Maris in Ufa and Perm province—requesting formal recognition as Muslims began to appear in greater numbers in the 1870s, the MVD argued that the directive was intended to be prophylactic rather than prohibitive. These pagans *already* confessed Islam, and the MVD added that "the transition to Mohammedanism for idolaters constitutes a progressive movement, a step toward the comprehension of Christian truths, since Mohammedans believe in a single God and they recognize Christ the Savior as one of the prophets."[94] War Minister D. Miliutin took a rather different line, arguing that "in a *political sense*" it was best to prevent such transfers, "since there remains hope to make a Christian out of an idolater, but a Mohammedan has already yielded irrevocably to the influence of Muslim fanaticism and will hardly go over to Christianity."[95] The Synod concurred, arguing that the recognition of pagans as Muslims "would serve for Mohammedans as a cause to strengthen their propaganda . . . and even to consider such propaganda permitted by the government."[96] This question was never resolved, although the reformist Minister of Internal Affairs M. T. Loris-Melikov was working on a project to allow such conversions and even approved a number of petitions before his dismissal in 1881.[97]

The policy on pagan conversion to Islam demonstrates the extent to which the church felt itself to be in a defensive position, having to call on civil authorities to preserve and create the conditions in which continued missionary activity could be effective. The need to cordon Islam off from pagans became much more pressing for religious figures as the focus of confrontation

[92] RGIA, f. 797, op. 18, d. 41173, ll. 27–28.

[93] Directive no. 647 (1854). RGIA, f. 821, op. 133, d. 432, l. 7; and RGIA, f. 821, op. 8, d. 1232, l. 13.

[94] RGIA, f. 821, op. 133, d. 432, l. 4.

[95] Ibid., l. 120b. (emphasis in the original). Even so, Miliutin acknolwedged that "It goes without saying that those who have actually become Muslims cannot be returned to paganism by government power" (l. 13).

[96] Ibid., l. 27.

[97] Ibid., ll. 37–85. On these developments, see my "Tsarist Categories, Orthodox Intervention, and Islamic Conversion in a Pagan Udmurt Village, 1870s–1890s," in *Muslim Culture in Russia and Central Asia from the Eighteenth to the Early Twentieth Centuries*, vol. 2: *Inter-Regional and Inter-Ethnic Relations*, ed. Anke von Kügelgen, Michael Kemper, and Allen J. Frank (Berlin, 1998), pp. 385–415.

between Islam and Christianity shifted into Ufa province, where there were many more pagans, many more Muslims, and a much smaller Orthodox institutional presence to combat "Mohammedan propaganda" than in the region's more western provinces. Indeed, as Il'minskii wrote in 1873, "In other provinces there are brotherhoods, [missionary] committees, and zemstvos, which in one way or another can forward the business of enlightenment; but Ufa province is deprived of all, decisively all, means."[98] The existence of pagans helped to raise the stakes of the struggle, since there was now a danger not only that "Russian civilization" would not be able to penetrate the seclusion of the Muslim world in Russia, but also that Islam would grow, increasing its numbers at the expense of people who might otherwise have been reasonably well disposed toward the government's initiatives and "Russian civilization."

While the "discovery" of Islam generated a range of new potential policies designed to limit Islam's influence, the civil government and religious figures tended to part ways on many of these issues. For clerics, Islam already enjoyed too many advantages over Christianity: its extensive institutional presence, the widespread literacy of Muslims and the availability of books, and the linguistic similarities between Tatar and the other non-Russian languages of the region. Containment of Islamic influence was thus construed by them above all as a leveling of the playing field, a matter—strange though it may sound—of fairness. For the civil government, the geopolitical situation—the conquest of Central Asia and, by the late 1870s, yet another Russo-Turkish war—combined with more general concerns for stability and commitments to religious tolerance to prevent any direct confrontation with Islam. While the government certainly did not abandon missionaries entirely—their central agreement about the fanaticism and potential danger of Islam was too great for that—it was clear that Orthodox "reinforcement" would require new methods for success. Fortunately for the missionary activists, there was some basis for hope.

[98] Il'minskii, ed., *Perepiska*, p. 17. Zemstvos were opened in Ufa province in 1875, and the Ufa Committee of the Orthodox Missionary Society opened in 1879. Il'minskii later considered the establishment of zemstvos in Ufa province to have been a big mistake, since, he claimed, Muslims eventually took control of them.

8 The Mari Religious Movement and Non-Russian Monasticism

If the dramatic rejection of Orthodox Christianity among baptized-Tatar communities in 1866 starkly revealed the limits of Russian and Orthodox hegemony in the Volga-Kama region, there were other, less dramatic indications that some non-Russians had begun to incorporate Orthodoxy into their lives. In particular, among the highland Maris in western Kazan province a "religious movement" began to appear by the 1840s and culminated in the consecration of an explicitly Mari monastery in 1871. Highland Maris began actively to spread Christianity among their neighbors, the authority of literacy and texts grew, and the keremet cult faced demise, thus giving Russian officials and clergy renewed hope that the Christianization of non-Russians was indeed possible. To the extent that these developments predated the missionary innovations of N. I. Il'minskii discussed in chapter 9, they offer valuable insights as to why Il'minskii's project met with considerable success among some non-Russian communities. An analysis of the Mari movement suggests that there were significant social changes underway in the region that helped precipitate religious change, making non-Russians more receptive to innovations in missionary practice once they appeared.

But while some Maris began to incorporate Orthodoxy into their lives, there was no a priori indication of what this would entail. Even when non-Russians embraced Christianity with enthusiasm, they had their own conceptions and hopes about what Christianity should mean in their lives. To develop a true Christian spirituality, was it necessary to repudiate indigenous habits and practices entirely and to become Russian in all respects? Did aspiration for an ascetic life require that one submit to an imposed monastic hierarchy? For Orthodox authorities, how much autonomy could indigenous religious movements tolerably entail, and was non-Russian monasticism an acceptable and desirable form of Christianization? The experience of the highland Maris demonstrates that conversion to Orthodoxy was not without its own perils for the religious authorities, at least until they could assert effective "supervision" over the movement and regulate its spiritual impulses. Even so, the monastery went on to serve as a model for a series of non-Russian monasteries and convents in the last decades of the tsarist regime, thus establishing monasticism as a significant element of indigenous spiritual life.

The Emergence of the Religious Movement

By the 1860s or so, there were many indications of a growing crisis in indigenous animist cosmologies. A number of sources show the emergence of more critical attitudes among non-Russians toward their traditional beliefs and practices, while indigenous conceptions themselves seem to have undergone important shifts. Most dramatically, the keremet began to appear to some non-Russians as a "dream," a "delusion of their ancestors," and even as "loathsome" and "intolerable."[1] One group of Maris remarked to their priest: "It seems, Father, that the time has come for our keremet to die and for the *muzhani* to go to God's church."[2] In response to missionary attempts to "diabolize" indigenous beliefs, keremet spirits were losing their positive significance in the native imagination as the kind souls of ancestors and instead became reconfigured as "evil spirits" or representatives of the devil.[3] Non-Russians now began to see the adoption of Christianity and a Russian lifestyle as a way to liberate themselves from these increasingly vilified keremets.[4] One observer noted how Maris claimed to have escaped an especially evil keremet: "Now, say the Cheremis, this keremet has become harmless, because we began to believe as Russians" (*verovat' po-russki*)."[5] In a similar fashion, eastern Maris in Ufa province saw conversion to Islam as a way to escape the power of the keremet spirits there: "It is sufficient to go

[1] Citations from Vasilii Sboev, *Issledovaniia ob inorodtsakh Kazanskoi gubernii* (Kazan, 1856), pp. 122–23; and P. N. Luppov, ed., *Materialy dlia istorii khristianstva u votiakov v pervoi polovine XIX veka* (Viatka, 1911), p. 204. See also P. Znamenskii, "Gornye cheremisy Kazanskogo kraia," *Vestnik Evropy* 4 (1867): 34; and Il'ia Sofiiskii, "O keremetiakh kreshchenykh tatar Kazanskogo kraia," *IKE* 4 (1877): 688.

[2] Mikhail Rozhdestvenskii, "Byt gornykh cheremis Kozmodem'ianskogo uezda v religiozno-nravstvennom otnoshenii (kakimi byli i kakimi sdelalis' gornye cheremisy?)," *IKE* 1 (1873): 19.

[3] See, for example, "Besedy k cheremisam kuznetskogo prikhoda kuznetskogo shkol'nogo uchitelia Ivana Iakovleva Moliarova," *IKE* 7 (1873): 221.

[4] N. I. Il'minskii, *K istorii inorodcheskikh perevodov* (Kazan, 1884), p. 34. See also A. Grekov, "Novye uspekhi v khristianskom obrazovanii mezhdu chuvashami, Cheboksarskogo uezda, Kazanskoi gubernii," *Tserkovnaia letopis'* 2 (1875): 28.

[5] L. Iznoskov, "Gorno-cheremiskie prikhody Kozmodem'ianskogo uezda," *Trudy Kazanskogo gubernskogo statisticheskogo komiteta*, no. 2 (1869): 20.

over to the Tatar faith, and the keremet will not touch you."[6] Thus even when belief in keremets was sustained, the significance of these spirits was in some cases dramatically reconfigured so as to render their further veneration undesirable.

Some of the non-Russians who were abandoning animism were also embracing Christianity, above all in the western end of Kazan province.[7] Most remarkable in this regard was the "religious movement" among the highland Maris in Kozmodem´iansk district. Based on the initiative of local Orthodox clergy in previous decades, by the early 1860s a cohort of young, literate Maris had begun a campaign to spread literacy and Christianity among their fellows. Every holiday before and after the liturgy, these activists gathered their fellow Maris and discussed important concepts in Holy Scripture, Christian teaching, and morality. They traveled from house to house teaching literacy, denouncing pagan beliefs, and restraining their "superstitious" neighbors from going to sacred groves. Their activism met with great success, as thousands of highland Maris became, by all accounts, the most fervent Christians. They began to go on pilgrimages to holy sites not only in Kazan but in a few instances as far away as Voronezh and Kiev. The most zealous among them began to espouse asceticism and petitioned the Synod for permission to establish their own monastery and school, for which they received permission in 1868. Female parishioners founded a women's commune and eventually a convent in Kozmodem´iansk in 1877. Literacy and the Russian language became widespread in the affected villages, and highland Maris even visited their meadow counterparts across the Volga as missionaries. This movement became famous as a major missionary achievement, bringing one missionary from as far away as Perm province to investigate the reasons for its success.[8] Thus as the apostasy movement signaled non-Russians' rejection of incorporation into the empire on religious terms, another movement simultaneously seemed to represent an enthusiastic acceptance of that vision.

The development of Orthodox religiosity among non-Russians has typically been associated with the pedagogical innovations of N. I. Il´minskii— in particular his promotion of native languages in education and missionary work. Central to the assertion of the efficacy of his "system" was the proposition that earlier missionary efforts had all been complete failures. The enthusiasm of Il´minskii's followers thus prevented them—and subsequent his-

[6] Petr Eruslanov, "Magometanskaia propaganda sredi cheremis Ufimskoi gubernii," *Pravoslavnyi blagovestnik* 16 (1895): 385.

[7] See, for example, A. G–v, "Religioznoe dvizhenie mezhdu inorodtsami Kazanskoi gubernii," *Tserkovnaia letopis´* 40 (1872): 216–24, 41 (1872): 232–38.

[8] Evgenii Popov, *Ob userdii k missionerskomu delu* (Perm, 1874), pp. 52–60. Accounts of the "religious movement" also include Znamenskii, "Gornye cheremisy," and especially idem, "Religioznoe sostoianie cheremis Kozmodem´ianskogo kraia," *Pravoslavnoe obozrenie* 10 (1866): 61–79, 12 (1866): 149–68.

torians—from seeing some of the successes that the church could claim even before Il´minskii's methods were implemented on a broad scale. In fact, the origins of the religious movement among highland Maris should be traced back to the 1840s or even earlier. The first indigenous activist, Afanasii Efremov, had appeared by the 1820s and received a copy of the catechism and biblical history from Archbishop Filaret personally in 1829.[9] By the early 1850s highland Maris had begun to distinguish themselves from other non-Russians more clearly. An 1853 article by a priest close to the emerging movement noted that highland Maris were largely abandoning their "superstitions" and more zealously fulfilled the rules of the Orthodox faith than their fellow Maris across the Volga. The Chuvash ethnographer Spiridon Mikhailov ventured in 1852 that highland Maris "are more religious even than Russians."[10]

By most accounts, highland Maris' religiosity was due in part to the efforts of local clergy, who made special efforts to teach their parishioners and to perform services and liturgy in the local language. Most notable, perhaps, was Andrei Al´binskii of Pertnury parish, who translated the liturgy into Mari, corresponded with the Russian Biblical Society in the 1810s and 1820s, and completed a Mari grammar that was published in 1837.[11] The priest Petr Urusov, meanwhile, cultivated Afanasii Efremov as the first indigenous proselytizer in the 1820s.[12] Mikhail Rozhdestvenskii helped convert the parish of Malyi Sundyr´ into a showplace of native Christian religiosity. Indeed, when he arrived in the parish in 1854, Maris celebrated Friday rather than Sunday as a day of rest and claimed that they had no time to attend church even on major Christian holidays. One Mari explained the relationship that perhaps many non-Russians had with their clergy: "Father, with previous priests I lived well. I always paid them *ruga,* and I didn't ever owe anything, no arrears. That's exactly how I want to live with you. Please don't give me trouble, don't sully me, and don't give me communion."[13] Admonishing his parishioners not to go to sacred groves and requiring that each of them learn at least one Christian prayer, Rozhdestvenskii also debated a *muzhan*, forcing the latter to admit that he had been deceiving his

---

[9] L. Iznoskov, "Selo Perniagashi i ego prikhozhane," *Kazanskie gubernskie vedomosti* 11 (1869): 56–57, 29 (1869): 173–74.

[10] "Gornye cheremisy v Kazanskoi gubernii," *Zhurnal MVD* 41, 2 (1853): 229. Other accounts from the early 1860s confirm this picture. See Sergei Nurminskii, "Ocherk religioznykh verovanii cheremis," *Pravoslavnyi sobesednik* 3 (1862): 287–92; M. Laptev, *Materialy dlia geografii i statistiki Rossii, sobrannye ofitserami General´nogo shtaba: Kazanskaia guberniia* (St. Petersburg, 1861), p. 251; S. M. Mikhailov, *Trudy po etnografii i istorii russkogo, chuvashkogo i mariiskogo narodov* (Cheboksary, 1972), pp. 29–30.

[11] Al´binskii's letter is in RGIA, f. 808, op. 1, d. 134, ll. 44–45. On his Mari grammar, see I. G. Ivanov, *Istoriia mariiskogo literaturnogo iazyka* (Ioshkar-Ola, 1975), pp. 22–23. On his promotion of the "religious movement," see Nurminskii, "Ocherk religioznykh verovanii cheremis," 286–87; and Znamenskii, "Religioznoe sostoianie," 63.

[12] Iznoskov, "Selo," 173–74.

[13] Rozhdestvenskii, "Byt gornykh cheremis," 10–11.

fellow Maris. Under Rozhdestvenskii's tutelage, many Maris were willing to have him remove from the ceilings of their homes and barns small bundles, each signifying an obligation to perform a sacrifice to one or another native spirit, and toss them into a nearby stream to be taken far away.[14]

If an activist clergy provided a crucial impetus to religious change, much of the initiative quickly passed to a group of young indigenous apostles, who promoted religious change in the villages through proselytism and the establishment of new schools, in which they served as teachers.[15] These Maris made religious instruction and a critique of animism central to their activities and eventually involved thousands of Chuvash and Maris in their quest for literacy and deeper religious knowledge. The core activists centered around a certain Mikhail Gerasimov, who was motivated by a dream calling on him to proselytize. Having settled in the forest along the Sura river, he and a number of his colleagues became ascetics. They cultivated a garden and bee-hives, took vows of celibacy (for fear that spouses might reintroduce pagan elements into their lives), and rejected the use of wine, beer, meat, and even butter. In 1861 Gerasimov suggested that the group establish its own monastery, which they hoped would become a center for Christianity and literacy for the entire Mari region. A significant number of men reacted positively to the call, and a group of women also began to request the establishment of a convent. A formal petition was sent to the Emperor in 1864, in which the ascetics expressed their desire "to abandon the superstitious blindness of the faith of [our] ancestors" and ventured that the monastery's establishment would lead to the conversion of "our neighbors who execute pagan rituals."[16]

Shortly thereafter, however, the activists suffered a series of setbacks that threatened to end the movement. Sergei Nurminskii, in his description of the movement in 1862, contended that the activists' emphasis on seclusion (*uedinenie*), based on Gerasimov's claim that married people could not attain the heavenly kingdom, had caused many activists to abandon their families entirely. The source of this view on marriage, according to Nurminskii, was almost surely local Skoptsy, religious sectarians whose deep commitment to sexual abstinence took the form of self-castration.[17] The accusation of schism was taken up by the newspaper *Sovremennyi listok*, which

---

[14] When Maris recognized the need to perform a sacrifice, they would hang such a bundle or a kettle in their barns or cellars as a sign of obligation until the sacrifice had actually been performed.

[15] The clergy themselves emphasized the role of Maris. NART, f. 10, op. 5, d. 515, ll. 18–18ob. On the schools, see N. I. Zolotnitskii, "Doklad sovetu Bratstva sv. Guriia," *IKE* 11 (1868): 287–95, 12 (1868): 322–29. Useful biographical information on this generation can be found in K. K. Vasin, "Mariiskie literatory-prosvetiteli vtoroi poloviny XIX veka," in *Mariiskaia literatura, iskusstvo i narodnoe tvorchestvo*, ed. K. K. Vasin and M. A. Georgina (Ioshkar-Ola, 1966), pp. 41–68.

[16] NART, f. 4, op. 1, d. 5851, l. 150b.

[17] Nurminskii, "Ocherk religioznykh verovanii cheremis," 291–92. On the Skoptsy, see Laura Engelstein, *Castration and the Heavenly Kingdom: A Russian Folktale* (Ithaca, 1999).

called the Maris' teaching "heresy" and accused them of promoting insubordination to the authorities.[18] These concerns apparently arose from a report of the Ministry of State Domains (MGI), which had jurisdiction over the land where the proposed monastery was to be erected. The MGI contended that a local priest had disingenuously convinced a group of Maris that seclusion was necessary for salvation in order to have someone look after beehives that he had set up in the forest. According to this account, an impressionable Mari (presumably Gerasimov) had become a "propagandist" for this enterprise and had managed to attract a number of "lazy, unmarried [Maris] who had fallen out with their families." These hermits settled in cells that they constructed out of trees cut down illegally in state forests, supported themselves for a time with items that they had stolen from their households, and then began pilfering more trees for sale across the Sura river in Nizhnii Novgorod province. Concluding that the Mari ascetics sought a monastery "to entrust their supervision to someone from among themselves," the MGI opposed the creation of the monastery, and the Synod agreed.[19] According to Petr Znamenskii, a clerical observer sympathetic to the movement, the two MGI officials charged with surveying the land that was to be provided for the monastery were a Catholic Pole and a sectarian, who were implicitly hostile toward the Maris' enthusiasm for Orthodoxy. Further investigations were conducted without the participation of a church deputy, who presumably would have tried to deflect guilt from the activists. Moreover, most local residents questioned on the matter were "half-pagans," who confirmed the activists' guilt and declared that they did not want the monastery in their midst. Gerasimov took all the blame for this accusation on himself and was sentenced to a prison term of five hundred days and a 470-ruble fine for the pilfered trees.[20]

At the same time, Maris with strong pagan inclinations—especially the older generation, who saw in the movement a direct threat to their authority—attempted to derail Gerasimov's initiative. They physically assaulted the activists—Gerasimov himself was severely beaten at one point, while another activist in neighboring Nizhnii Novgorod province was allegedly murdered by Mari pagans[21]—and spread rumors that those supporting the establishment of the monastery would be taken into the army or to workhouses. These rumors were so effective that many of the volunteers for the monastery withdrew their support.[22] In 1864 Father M. Krakovskii died, depriving the activists of one of their most ardent supporters. Most of Gerasimov's "hermits" (*pustynniki*) returned to their homes, leaving behind only a tiny brotherhood of the most dedicated Mari ascetics.

[18] As cited in Znamenskii, "Religioznoe sostoianie," 70–71.
[19] NART, f. 4, op. 1, d. 5851, ll. 17–22, 56–57.
[20] Znamenskii, "Religioznoe sostoianie," 74–75.
[21] Ibid., 158.
[22] Ibid., 74.

While the outlook certainly looked bleak, the tenacity of the few remaining activists eventually brought success. In particular, Ivan Zakharov, a Mari, made numerous trips to Kazan and even five trips to St. Petersburg to plead with the archbishop, the Synod, the Chief Procurator, the minister of state domains, and even the Emperor himself on behalf of the monastery project, thereby generating considerable sympathy for his cause.[23] Merchants from Kozmodem´iansk soon volunteered to fund the construction of the monastery, and local Mari craftsmen offered their services without compensation. By 1867 Zakharov had received promises from the region's inhabitants to contribute another 6,226 rubles. Meanwhile, in Kazan the passive Archbishop Afanasii was replaced by Antonii, an enthusiastic supporter of missionary work among non-Russians. Finally, the activists gained a patron of tremendous stature in the person of Chief Procurator of the Holy Synod Dmitrii Tolstoi, who concluded in 1866 that the growing apostasy of baptized Tatars "can have a most pernicious influence on Cheremis," and therefore requested the Archbishop to find a way to make the monastery possible.[24] Gerasimov's prison term soon ended, and in 1868 the Emperor gave his assent to the monastery's construction. In 1871 the monastery was blessed by the archbishop in a dramatic ceremony attended by five thousand people, mostly Maris.[25]

Archbishop Antonii obtained an icon directly from Mount Athos in Greece for the new monastery. The icon showed St. Panteleimon, whose life served as a metaphor for the religious experience of the highland Maris. Born and raised by a Christian mother, Panteleimon was instructed as a pagan by his father. Only through the efforts of a dedicated priest was Panteleimon made Christian again. Maris had followed a similar course: brought into the church through their baptism, they had subsequently deviated back to the keremet and were finally returned to the church by the efforts of their parish priests. The icon was transported ceremonially through various villages on its way to the monastery in 1873. Evgenii Popov, a missionary from Perm province visiting the region, witnessed this remarkable procession and left a striking account of Maris' reception of the icon: "Big groups of pilgrims walked behind the icon: some hurried to kiss the icon; others fell before the icon as it was being carried—they fell not individually,

[23] P. Rufimskii, *Cheremiskii Mikhailo-Arkhangel´skii muzhskoi obshchezhitel´nyi monastyr´ Kazanskoi gubernii Kozmodem´ianskogo uezda: Istoricheskoe opisanie i sovremennoe ego sostoianie* (Kazan, 1897), pp. 11–12. Zakharov described the encounter with the Emperor later by saying, "the Tsar treated us very graciously. . . . He took our request and, having learned what the matter entailed, told us to whom we should address ourselves." Cited in N. Ivanovich, "V 'cheremiskom' monastyre," *Nizhegorodskii birzhevoi listok* 250 (21 October 1888): 2.

[24] NART, f. 4, op. 1, d. 5851, ll. 58–61. See also Tolstoi's approving remarks about the movement in "Izvlechenie iz vsepoddanneishego otcheta Ober Prokurora Sv. Sinoda po vedomstvu Pravoslavnogo ispovedaniia za 1866," *Pravoslavnoe obozrenie* 25 (1868): 130–40.

[25] A. G., "Osviashchenie novogo muzhskogo monastyria, postroennogo cheremisami," *Tserkovnaia letopis´* 9 (1872): 185–92.

as is sometimes the case in our region, but by many scores, thus forming along the road one long row, which lay down on the ground beforehand; the people flocked even more when the procession stopped, for example, in the field for performance of a service."[26] Shortly thereafter Popov attended a liturgy in one village with two thousand parishioners, including Mari women who had traversed twenty-five versts to sing at the service. "After the liturgy and service I could not return to my quarters right away, although they were close to the church. During the break men, women, and children hurried to receive a blessing from me. I had to be careful of my feet, so as not to step on those in the crowd being blessed."[27]

The Mari women's religious commune in the village of Malyi Sundyr´ was no less remarkable than the monastery. Still lacking sufficient space and funding in the early 1870s, the commune was forced to turn away many who wished to join the group. Consisting of around thirty-five women, the commune's most remarkable achievement, by most accounts, was its singing, directed by a young deacon at the church.[28] One visitor declared in amazement, "You will hardly believe that you are listening to the singing of Cheremis girls."[29] The local priest provided religious instruction, while an elderly Mari woman taught them literacy, needlework, and arithmetic. The commune received the sanction of the Synod and the Emperor in 1877, when it established a convent in the city of Kozmodem´iansk based on contributions of a local merchant and funds collected by the Mari community. The women were to perfect their knowledge of Christianity, learn needlework and other handicrafts "intelligible to women," and spread this knowledge to Mari girls through a school.[30]

In the course of establishing the monastery, the Mari activists, and in particular Ivan Zakharov, exhibited great persistence and acumen. As well as seeking the support of highly placed officials they also strove to correct mistaken perceptions of them that had appeared in some of the earliest articles about the movement. Zakharov even went to the Kazan Ecclesiastical

[26] Popov, *Ob userdii*, pp. 52–53. See also the brief description in *Kratkoe opisanie Mikhailo-Arkhangel´skogo monastyria, Kazanskoi gubernii, Kozmodem´ianskogo uezda* (St. Petersburg, 1875), pp. 45–47. The monastery's earlier acquisition of two icons in 1869 had similarly been accompanied by a ceremonial transfer. See "Opisanie pereneseniia ikony sv. Arkhistratiga Mikhaila vmeste s chudotvornoi ikonoi Bozhiei materi, imenuemoi Vladimirskoi, v ustroennuiu na monastyrskom meste, bliz reki Sury, Kozmodem´ianskogo uezda, chasovniu," *IKE* 24 (1869): 633–42.

[27] Popov, *Ob userdii*, p. 55.

[28] This deacon, I. Kedrov, also published a manual for teaching Mari children reading in 1867: *Uproshchennyi sposob obucheniia chteniiu cheremiskikh detei gornogo naseleniia* (Kazan, 1867).

[29] A. G–v, "Religioznoe dvizhenie," 217.

[30] RGIA, f. 796, op. 158, d. 613; "Opredelenie Sv. Sinoda ob uchrezhdenii v g. Kozmodem´ianske obshchiny cheremiskikh devits s uchilishchem," *IKE* 21 (1877): 571–72; and "Ustav Kozmodem´ianskogo cheremiskoi troitskoi zhenskoi obshchiny," *IKE* 22 (1877): 606–11 (citation is from "Ustav," 608).

Academy in 1865 to speak with someone there about correcting Nurmin-skii's article, "because that article is not complete and is even untrue."[31] Recognizing the dangers of being (mis)represented by others, Zakharov and his comrades began to take a more active role in representing themselves, which suggests that non-Russians were perhaps not as powerless in the matter of representation as one might suppose. In his petitions, meanwhile, Zakharov marshaled published articles in support of his cause, noting that they endorsed the establishment of a monastery and school "for the spread of literacy and Christianity."[32] He also used the unsuccessful assassination attempt on the Emperor in 1866—"when Providence saved for us the precious life of the Sovereign Emperor from the hand of a murderer"—as a basis for soliciting contributions for the monastery among the region's inhabitants. By relating this fact very deliberately in his petitions, he demonstrated the loyalty of himself and local Maris to the monarchy.[33] Although Mari activists presumably turned for help to their clergy and to their peace mediator, L. Iznoskov, who served as a patron of the movement, they made use of these resources and gained valuable experience that Zakharov, at least, would later use for slightly different purposes.

Does the appearance of the movement allow us to speak finally of "conversion"—that is, of a substantial shift in self-identification and spiritual commitment? Conversion is a problematic concept, in that it tends to focus excessively on the discrete individual and thus makes questionable assumptions about reason, detached from cultural embeddedness, and about the rational, reflective self.[34] Yet some treatments of conversion have sought to account for religious change in terms of broader social, economic, and cultural processes. Robin Horton has argued that the incorporation of Africans, through modernization, into a larger social order served as a basic foundation for religious change. Rapid social change "obliterated many of the fields of experience with which the traditional cults concerned themselves," and in response the traditional African cosmology had already begun to undergo substantial change at the time that Islam and Christianity appeared on the scene. The beliefs and practices of the world religions were accepted, according to Horton, "only where they happened to coincide with responses of the traditional cosmology to other, non-missionary, factors of the modern

---

[31] Znamenskii, "Religioznoe sostoianie," 62. Nurminskii's article appeared in *Pravoslavnyi sobesednik*, which had been published at the Academy since 1855, and Zakharov went there presumably for this reason.

[32] Zakharov made explicit reference to the article by Nurminskii ("Ocherk religioznykh verovanii cheremis") and one in *Dukhovnaia beseda* 47 (1865).

[33] NART, f. 4, op. 1, f. 5851, ll. 59–60.

[34] Jean and John Comaroff, *Of Revelation and Revolution: Christianity, Colonialism, and Consciousness in South Africa* (Chicago, 1991), 1:248–51; and William L. Merrill, "Conversion and Colonialism in Northern Mexico: The Tarahumara Response to the Jesuit Mission Program, 1601–1767," in *Conversion to Christianity: Historical and Anthropological Perspectives on a Great Transformation*, ed. Robert W. Hefner (Berkeley, 1993), p. 153.

situation." Thus, Horton concludes, Islam and Christianity took on the role of catalysts—"i.e., stimulators and accelerators of changes which were 'in the air' anyway."[35] Critics have noted that by emphasizing these social determinants, Horton neglects the actual contributions that Islam and Christianity made in specific historical instances and construes local cultures and societies "as passive agents in a long historical process."[36] Still, Horton is probably right to suggest that religious change is more likely to occur in a context of larger social change. Our best approach is, as Robert Hefner has proposed, "to strike a balance between the two extremes of intellectualist voluntarism and structural determinism."[37]

While highland Maris undoubtedly interpreted Orthodox Christianity through frameworks of largely indigenous provenance,[38] there was clearly a substantial adjustment in their religious self-identification around the middle of the century. Certainly many Maris were themselves conscious that an important shift had occurred. The ascetics, in particular, referred to the old pagan beliefs, habits, ways of life, dress, ornamentation, songs, celebrations—in short, everything associated with the "old time"—as "secular" (*mirskii*).[39] Highland Maris in general exhibited a remarkable level of curiosity about Orthodox religious texts and strove to understand the precepts and practices of Christianity. A sympathizer of the movement, Petr Znamenskii, recounted on his own visit to the region that Maris "constantly besieged us with questions about the faith. . . . Most often of all, it was necessary to explain the teaching of the church on the characteristics of God, to explicate the Slavonic expressions of the psalms and prayers, that were unintelligible to the Cheremis, and to resolve moral questions. . . . In general, Cheremis curiosity revolves around the sphere of catechistic questions and confusion concerning the meaning of Russian words."[40] With their focus on catechism, these Maris sought not only to perform Orthodox rituals but also to understand their underlying principles. Evgenii Popov, describing his visit to highland Maris from Perm province, likewise underscored the profound interest parishioners displayed in Holy Scripture. Maris "are more

[35] Robin Horton, "African Conversion," *Africa* 41, 2 (1971): 85–108 (citations from pp. 92–93, 102–4).

[36] Aram A. Yengoyan, "Religion, Morality, and Prophetic Traditions: Conversion among the Pitjantjatjara of Central Australia," in *Conversion to Christianity*, p. 233. For other critiques of Horton, see Humphrey J. Fisher, "Conversion Reconsidered," *Africa* 43, 1 (1973): 27–40; E. Ikenga-Metuh, "The Shattered Microcosm: A Critical Survey of Explanations of Conversion in Africa," in K. Holst Petersen, ed., *Religion, Development, and African Identity* (Uppsala, 1987), pp. 11–27; Robert W. Hefner, "Introduction: World Building and the Rationality of Conversion," in *Conversion to Christianity*, pp. 20–25; and Terence Ranger, "The Local and the Global in Southern African Religious History," ibid., pp. 65–98.

[37] Hefner, "Introduction," p. 23.

[38] For an interesting discussion of this process in the Altai region of the empire, see Andrei Znamenski, *Shamanism and Christianity: Native Encounters with Russian Orthodox Missions in Siberia and Alaska, 1820–1917* (Westport, Conn., 1999), pp. 193–251.

[39] Znamenskii, "Religioznoe sostoianie," 157.

[40] Ibid., p. 156.

convinced of spiritual truth when it is brought to them through proof from Holy Scripture, and especially through the words of Christ the Savior."[41] All indications are that not only a change in religious self-identification but also a fundamental intellectual transformation was taking place.

To some degree, this religious change can, in accordance with Horton's contentions, be linked to a broader socioeconomic transformation. On the whole, one can discern a gradual process whereby Maris were increasingly integrated into a larger social order. In 1782 the state began to build a series of major roads, some of which went through Mari regions and facilitated contact with more distant places.[42] Kozmodem´iansk district, already closer to central Russia than the rest of the region, was located along major communication routes—above all the Volga river and the Moscow postal road, which linked that city with all of the eastern provinces.[43] The district itself was criss-crossed by roads connecting its capital with the cities of Vasil´sursk, Cheboksary, and Iadrin. To the south of this region, lines of communications were much sparser, and reports from the southern regions of Chuvash settlement showed the population in a much worse religious condition (from the church's perspective). To the north of the Volga, communications were extremely poor, and in 1890 the population density there was more than twenty times lower than to the south of that river.[44] This is not to posit a crude geographic determinism—that settlements closer to major roads and waterways automatically came to feel a deeper attachment to Christianity. At least one very distant settlement in northern Kozmodem´iansk district was among the most ardently Christian.[45] But these geographic factors are too significant to be ignored altogether.

In 1810–11, moreover, Maris received important privileges that had the potential, at least, to broaden their horizons. They were allowed to conduct trade; to be ascribed to cities; to conclude labor contracts; to join the merchant estate, clergy, or officialdom; and even to become nobility, if they could supply documentation proving their princely origins.[46] Some highland Maris took advantage of new opportunities, especially in the realm of trade. By most accounts, already in the 1850s highland Maris enjoyed a material existence superior (by Russian standards) to that of Chuvash and meadow Maris. In addition to farming, some hired themselves out as mail carriers and used their remuneration to invest in trade, buying grain, fish, and to-

---

[41] Popov, *Ob userdii*, p. 57.

[42] K. I. Kozlova, *Ocherki etnicheskoi istorii mariiskogo naroda* (Moscow, 1978), p. 227.

[43] Ibid., p. 239; D. E. Kazantsev, *Formirovanie dialektov mariiskogo iazyka* (Ioshkar-Ola, 1985), pp. 136–38.

[44] Kozlova, *Ocherki*, p. 232.

[45] Petr Dmitriev, "Missionerskaia deiatel´nost´ cheremisina Petra Dimitrieva sredi lugovykh cheremis Kazanskoi gubernii, Kozmodem´ianskago uezda v 1873," *IKE* 1 (1876): 13.

[46] F. Egorov, *Material po istorii Mari* (Kozmodem´iansk, 1929), pp. 105–6. I am not aware, however, that any Maris actually gained noble status.

bacco and reselling at the bazaars in Kozmodem'iansk district.[47] And it appears that migrant labor became more widespread in Kozmodem'iansk district than in other regions of Mari settlement.[48] There is certainly some truth, then, to Soviet claims that Maris were increasingly being drawn into broader trade patterns and markets. Although it is unclear whether emancipation was as detrimental to the peasant economy as Soviet historians have suggested, it seems fair to assert that the reform accelerated the breakdown of isolation in the countryside, as more peasants engaged in migrant labor and became integrated into broader economic and social systems.[49]

Perhaps still more detrimental to indigenous cosmology was the elimination of the large forests in Kozmodem'iansk district. Znamenskii reported that aside from the area along the Sura river, the entire district had been ploughed under by the 1860s or so. In historical terms this was a fairly recent development. "Even now old folks remember that this whole region was covered by thick deciduous forest." The forest had traditionally been central to Maris' way of life: they were raised in the forests, "and even now traits of their previous forest character are still visible. Even now a highland Mari retains in his soul love for the forest and always goes to the Sura river with great satisfaction." Highland Maris tried to offset the effects of the depletion by growing birch trees in their gardens, so that "a Cheremis village is completely hidden in the thick and lively verdure of birches [and] looks more like a group of summer cottages than a simple village."[50] Numerous accounts confirm this profound topographic transformation.[51] To the extent that Mari faith was closely connected to forest life, it is not surprising that these processes should have helped to precipitate a crisis in indigenous conceptions, or that religious change was decidedly less pronounced on the meadow side of the Volga, where deforestation was far less advanced.[52] While we need to acknowledge the particular role of parish clergy and Maris

---

[47] "Gornye cheremisy," 225, 235. E. Popov noted that highland Maris had fruit gardens and traded in grain, apples, and nuts (pp. 58–59).

[48] I. N. Smirnov, *Cheremisy: Istoriko-etnograficheskii ocherk* (Kazan, 1889), p. 90.

[49] See Ivanov, *Istoriia mariiskogo literaturnogo iazyka*, pp. 156–98; Kozlova, *Ocherki*, pp. 226–29; N. S. Popov, "K voprosu o religioznom dvizhenii v mariiskom krae vo vtoroi polovine XIX–nachale XX veka: Istoriografiia i istochniki," in *Istoriografiia i istochnikovedenie po arkheologii i etnografii Mariiskogo kraia*, Arkheologiia i etnografiia Mariiskogo kraia, no. 7 (Ioshkar-Ola, 1984), pp. 174–81; and M. I. Tereshkina, "Osvobozhdenie gosudarstvennykh krest'ian Mariiskogo kraia," in *Trudy Mariiskogo Nauchno-Issledovatel'skogo Instituta iazyka, literatury i istorii*, no. 9 (Ioshkar-Ola, 1956), pp. 3–35.

[50] Znamenskii, "Gornye cheremisy," 36–37.

[51] On the problem of deforestation in Russia more generally, see R. A. French, "Russians and the Forest," in *Studies in Russian Historical Geography*, ed. J. H. Bater and R. A. French (London, 1983), esp. 1:38–41. For an interesting consideration of the impact of deforestation among Cossacks in the North Caucasus, see Thomas M. Barrett, *At the Edge of Empire: The Terek Cossacks and the North Caucasus Frontier, 1700–1860* (Boulder, 1999), pp. 59–67.

[52] By 1889 Smirnov noted the depletion of forests throughout regions of Mari settlement and remarked that sacred groves had actually replaced the forest itself as the place of prayer because of this depletion. See Smirnov, *Cheremisy*, pp. 160–61.

themselves, the notions of exclusive religious allegiance that accompanied the adoption of Christianity, and the significance of literacy for consolidating and nourishing earlier changes in religious consciousness, the transformation of traditional structures of indigenous life should occupy a central place in any account of the movement.

Community and Conflict

Given the continued attachment of certain segments of indigenous society to pagan practice, it was perhaps inevitable that the religious movement would generate conflict in the villages, not least because religious affiliation had great communal significance for Orthodox Christians as well as for animists. As one priest explained the perspective of his Chuvash parishioners in 1866, "Chuvash always say that if they are to live in the Russian way, then it is necessary to force them all to do so. Otherwise, they are ashamed before one another, fear and avoid each other, because the old folks, especially women, in each unfortunate occurrence directly reprimand them, make speeches, and reproach them."[53] Non-Russians clearly viewed those in their midst who continued to practice animism not only as a potential source of "seduction" but as a concrete obstacle to their own practice of Christianity. In one Mari village, the five households that practiced Christianity complained that the others "do not fulfill anything Christian and in all that is holy they inhibit us in many various ways: when we go to God's temple to worship the Lord, they run into the field or the forest to revere their keremet."[54] In this formulation, the very fact that others performed animist rituals was construed as an obstacle to the Christian activities of the others.

Viewing religion as a communal enterprise and cognizant of their own frailties, some baptized non-Russians sought to institute mechanisms for collective control of religious practice. As early as the 1830s some parishioners suggested electing one person in each village "completely tested in good morality and in steadfastness in the Christian faith" to serve as "guardians" (*bliustiteli*) of the behavior of the others and to report to the priest in case of violations of Orthodox prescriptions.[55] By the early 1870s some Chuvash parishioners, having sent representatives to Archbishop Antonii to complain about the pagans in their midst, were willing to sign collective agreements (*mirskie prigovory*) promising to abandon pagan beliefs and to "live as Christians." The signatories promised to go to church regularly, take part in communion and confession, to observe Christian fasts, to abandon the keremet and *emzi* (a kind of native Chuvash sorcerer),

---

[53] NART, f. 4, op. 1, d. 5389, l. 12.
[54] Dmitriev, "Missionerskaia deiatel'nost'," 7.
[55] RGIA, f. 796, op. 118, d. 73, ll. 149–490b., 1520b.

and to cease observing *sin´ze* (a Chuvash agricultural festival) and Friday as holidays.[56] The agreements established significant fines for violations of these rules—in one case up to two rubles for a third offense—and in some cases established local "church councils" empowered "to look after anti-Christian actions of the parishioners."[57] Promoted by the church throughout Russia for the purposes of encouraging greater lay participation in parish affairs, such councils offered an institutional mechanism to ensure greater religious discipline, and there is evidence that some guardians were quite vigilant in reporting parishioners' deviations to their priests.[58]

Non-Russians themselves began to take greater initiative in enforcing religious discipline, for example, by informing the clergy about local pagan activities.[59] In 1862 several Mari "zealots of Orthodoxy" (Ivan Zakharov and four others) captured a group of Maris in the midst of animist prayer, confiscated their allegedly religious paraphernalia (bread and six barrels of beer), and brought them to the local priest, requesting that he report about the event to the civil authorities.[60] The arrest of the worshipers, according to Znamenskii, had a profound effect on those who continued to maintain animism and convinced them that public animist prayers were no longer possible.[61] Rozhdestvenskii reported a similar occurrence in the 1860s, when five zealots apprehended close to forty participants at an animist prayer. The apprehended Maris were so stunned by their capture that they marched back to the church without resistance, where Rozhdestvenskii had them kneel in church "and request from the Lord God forgiveness for their sins, which they did with the greatest of shame."[62] Some Maris even began to threaten others openly, as did one in Arda parish: "Look! If you go into the forest to pray to the keremet, then I'll catch you and lock you in a dark basement and beat you every day and starve you for a week or two without any food or drink!"[63] In

---

[56] For more on *emzi*, see N. Zolotnitskii, *Kornevoi chuvashko-russkii slovar´* (Kazan, 1875), pp. 162–72; Judith Szalontai-Dmitrieva, "The Etymology of the Chuvash Word *Yumsa*, 'Sorcerer,'" in *Chuvash Studies*, ed. Andras Rona-Tas (Budapest, 1982), pp. 171–77. *Sin´ze* began after the sowing fields and lasted for most of June. At this time Mother Earth was considered pregnant, and it was forbidden to disturb her with agricultural and certain kinds of domestic work.

[57] See Grekov, "Novye uspekhi," 22–29 (citation from p. 26). This article contains the original texts of three such agreements. Grekov identified ten parishes in which such agreements had been concluded, as well as another eight parishes where such agreements were being drawn up. See also Rozhdestvenskii, "Byt gornykh cheremis," 19.

[58] See for example K. Riabinskii, "Ardinskii prikhod Kozmodem´ianskogo uezda," *IOAIE* 16 (1900): 192, writing about the guardianship established in one parish in 1871. On the promotion of these councils, see Glennys Young, "'Into Church Matters': Lay Identity, Rural Parish Life, and Popular Politics in Late Imperial and Early Soviet Russia, 1864–1928," *Russian History* 23, 1–4 (1996): 367–84.

[59] The activist Efremov informed clergy of forthcoming pagan prayers, for example (Iznoskov, "Selo," 174).

[60] Znamenskii, "Gornye cheremisy," 59; and RGIA, f. 796, op. 143, d. 2117, ll. 1–10b.

[61] Znamenskii, "Religioznoe sostoianie," 165–66.

[62] Rozhdestvenskii, "Byt gornykh cheremis," 18–19.

[63] Dmitriev, "Missionerskaia deiatel´nost´," 16.

some cases it was the parish priest who had to argue for leniency for apprehended villagers in the face of less compromising demands from parishioners.[64] The ethnographer I. N. Smirnov faulted the activists for their "intolerance toward paganizers," which frequently led to fights in Mari villages: "unfortunately, individual Cheremis missionaries offer an example of proselytism by fist."[65] Highland Maris ran into particular hostility when they took their movement across the Volga into parishes on the meadow side. In 1873 Petr Dmitriev was confronted by three villagers in Kuz´ma parish, "who were prepared to give me a mortal beating," and was only barely able to escape this altercation unharmed, eventually subduing the "insurgents" with threats of incarceration.[66] But at least on the highland side of the Volga, these activists were able to make large public sacrifices a thing of the past, forcing those with animist inclinations to venerate keremets secretly.[67]

In general, information about the opposition of the "pagan party" is sparse, since the accounts we have were produced predominantly by the activists and their sympathizers. It seems that many Maris viewed adoption of "the Russian faith" as a kind of treason, calling the new Christians "traitors [*izmenniki*] to the Cheremis faith."[68] Others complained that they were being coerced "to bow down before empty boards [icons] and be servile to the priest, as if to some kind of devil." They also complained about the economic demands of the priest and the distractions that "Christian obligations" represented to their economic pursuits.[69] Otherwise, the "pagan party" appears to have agitated more generally for paganism, organized animist prayers, and interpreted unfortunate circumstances as retribution from animist spirits.[70]

While some Soviet historians have portrayed this conflict between the "pagan party" and the Christian activists in terms of the growing stratification within non-Russian villages, and the collective agreements as the products of a "triple alliance" among the clergy, police, and the "rural bourgeoisie,"[71] N. S. Popov seems closer to the mark in his assertion that the movement represented a challenge by youth to patriarchy.[72] The conflict in large measure involved an older generation, reluctant to change its ways,

---

[64] Ibid., 12.

[65] Smirnov, *Cheremisy*, pp. 173–74.

[66] Dmitriev, "Missionerskaia deiatel´nost´," 21–22.

[67] G. Iakovlev, *Religioznye obriady Cheremis* (Kazan, 1887), p. 84.

[68] Dmitriev, "Missionerskaia deiatel´nost´," 9–11. However, this proud pagan soon had a dream that his cellar was infested with demons, which caused him to reverse his position and accept Christianity.

[69] Ibid., 13–14.

[70] Znamenskii, "Religioznoe sostoianie," 164–67.

[71] See, for example, Petr Denisov, *Religioznye verovaniia chuvash: Istoriko-etnograficheskie ocherki* (Cheboksary, 1959), p. 347.

[72] N. S. Popov, "Iz istorii sotsioreligioznogo dvizheniia v mariiskom krae v 50–70-kh gg. XIX veka (po materialam Mikhailo-Arkhangel´skogo muzhskogo monastyria)," in *Polozhenie i klassovaia bor´ba krest´ian Mariiskogo kraia*, ed. Popov (Ioshkar-Ola, 1990), pp. 140–41, 151.

and a younger generation (25–35 years of age), who evidently saw in Christianity a way to challenge their elders' authority. Zakharov's petitions relate that it was "some young Cheremis" who had now "converted to Orthodoxy, as a result of which they are persecuted and hampered by their parents," who "with all their strength try to divert them from Orthodoxy."[73] Znamenskii concurred that there was "constant disagreement and heavy war" within individual families, "all the more since Christians are for the most part the younger members of the family." Family heads forbade the study of Orthodox scripture and attendance at church and forced subordinate family members to work on Sunday and rest on Friday. Because sexual abstinence had become a sign of Christian attachments, heads of household tried to marry off their children as soon as possible in order to force them into sexual relations.[74] The ethnographer Smirnov, writing in the late 1880s, contended that parental authority was weakening among Maris, as reflected in the frequent complaints of parents in the local courts that they were being insulted and even beaten by their children.[75] In this respect, non-Russians did not differ greatly from Russians, whose households were experiencing similar personal tensions within the extended family, accompanied by increasing household division.[76] Thus, while the activists contended that their seclusion in the most remote and heavily forested corner of Kozmodem′iansk district was necessary for the purposes of escaping pagan seductions and achieving salvation, there seems also to have been a desire for freedom, an aspiration to escape the supervision of elders and to live in accordance with their own dictates.[77]

In fact, teachers and clergy had by this time recognized that the authority of elders and ancestors constituted a fundamental barrier to Christianization and therefore had begun to call upon their parishioners and students to challenge this authority directly. The priest P. Vasil′evskii made this challenge an important part of his sermons in Chuvash. Arguing that elders were the ultimate source of strife in the villages, he called on Chuvash parishioners to assert their independence: "Your old folks frighten you with the idea that for

---

[73] NART, f. 4, op. 1, d. 5851, l. 150b.

[74] Znamenskii, "Religioznoe sostoianie," 159. See also Dmitriev, "Missionerskaia deiatel′nost′," 9–11, where one man allegedly kept his entire household in paganism, despite the wishes of the other family members to be Christians.

[75] Smirnov, *Cheremisy*, p. 111. Smirnov was trying to demonstrate the growth of individualism among Maris, part of his attempt to apply E. B. Tylor's evolutionist anthropology to the Finnic peoples. For details on this appropriation, see Robert Paul Geraci, "Window on the East: Ethnography, Orthodoxy, and Nationality in Kazan, 1870–1914" (Ph.D. diss., University of California, Berkeley, 1995), chap. 4.

[76] See Cathy Frierson, "*Razdel*: The Peasant Family Divided," in *Russian Peasant Women*, ed. Beatrice Farnsworth and Lynne Viola (New York, 1992), pp. 73–88. Smirnov contended, in the 1880s, that "Family division constitutes a most widespread phenomenon in the modern Cheremis way of life." Smirnov, *Cheremisy*, p. 111.

[77] N. S. Popov highlights this aspiration for freedom in his interpretation ("Iz istorii," p. 151).

violating *sin´ze* God will become angry and will pound your fields with hail. It is shameful for you, my friends, to be unthinking infants, who accept any lie as the truth and themselves do not know what frightens them."[78] The missionary Evgenii Popov made similar arguments in his discussions with non-Russians in Perm province, who often referred to their parents' commands prohibiting baptism. Arguing that parents were ignorant and uninformed, Popov demanded, "And why should you refer to your father and mother? Are you really children? Do you really lack your own mind, your own soul, your own life, so that even in [matters of] faith you must obey your parents?"[79] The Mari activists took up this campaign with particular vigor. They stressed that their ancestors had been ignorant of the meaning of their baptism, as symbolized by their habit of concealing a piece of horse meat under their tongues during baptism to signal their continued allegiance to the old faith. Ivan Moliarov, in particular, derided traditional Mari beliefs as "very ignorant understandings about faith" and concluded that "all our fathers' legends are unlawful."[80] While this rejection of the indigenous was by no means universal, nonetheless adopting Christianity for some meant adopting the Russian way of life wholesale and rejecting Mari ways of life altogether.

Subordinating the Religious Movement

Though the monastery represented the crowning edifice of the religious movement, tensions quickly developed between the Mari ascetics, who had expended tremendous efforts to establish a religious institution of their own, and Orthodox authorities, who felt compelled to ensure that the new monastery conformed to established standards. Recent research on "popular Orthodoxy" in Russia has shown that church authorities in general retained suspicions of more spontaneous and less conventional forms of spirituality and arrogated to themselves the privilege of legitimizing and co-opting those practices, even as common believers sought greater participation in religious affairs.[81] To the extent that the monastery's founders were Maris and the appointed monastic elite was Russian, the tension inherent in

---

[78] P. Vasil´evskii, "Poucheniia k chuvasham," *Tserkovnaia letopis´* 3 (1875): 47.

[79] Popov, *Ob userdii*, pp. 97–98.

[80] "Besedy k cheremisam," 212–16. Moliarov appears to have meant "unlawful" in a religious sense, that is, contrary to God's will as revealed through scripture.

[81] Works that address these tensions include: Chris J. Chulos, "Peasant Religion in Post-Emancipation Russia: Voronezh Province, 1880–1917" (Ph.D. diss., University of Chicago, 1994); Gregory L. Freeze, "Institutionalizing Piety: The Church and Popular Religion, 1750–1850," in *Imperial Russia: New Histories for the Empire*, ed. Jane Burbank and David L. Ransel (Bloomington, 1998), pp. 210–49; Vera Shevzov, "Miracle-Working Icons, Laity, and Authority in the Russian Orthodox Church, 1861–1917," *Russian Review* 58, 1 (1999):

the religious bureaucracy's efforts to dictate popular piety could hardly fail to acquire ethnic connotations.

The religious movement was admirable, to be sure, but imperial authorities could not permit it to continue developing "almost without supervision." Accordingly, as one observer contended, the movement "received correct orientation" only when the schools had been brought under the "protection" of the officially sanctioned Brotherhood of St. Gurii in Kazan and under the "supervision" of clergy.[82] Likewise, the Mari activists were clearly in no position, from the church's perspective, even to begin to administer the monastery themselves, since none of them was initially monastic or even ordained; therefore, Russian religious authorities appointed a father superior (Paisii) and brethren from among Russians.[83] Convinced that Russians had taken over their enterprise, several of the Mari activists complained that they were being pushed aside, and conflicts with the (Russian) brethren soon developed. According to one account, "An ordinary, so to speak, occurrence in the life of the fraternity was an open enmity among its members that sometimes went as far as the most savage fights and mutual brawls."[84] Within a short time, Mikhail Gerasimov, the founder of the "religious movement," had left the monastery, telling those on the outside, "This monastery is ours, and we should be the masters in it." He subsequently devoted his attention to establishing a convent, in which the mother superior would be a native Mari.[85] Shortly thereafter, another Mari, Andrei Kirillov, requested his release from the monastery as well, after the father superior alleged that he "conducts himself completely at variance with the monastery's rules."[86] Thus within a few years, some of the original founders had left the monastery in frustration.

Much of the trouble revolved around Father Superior Paisii, who was faced with the difficult task of bringing order to the monastery and rendering it financially solvent, which at times required him to resort to rather "extraordinary" methods. As the monastery's historian Porfirii Rufimskii relates, one strategy Paisii adopted was to spread rumors that the heir to the throne was soon to visit the monastery, and as this news made its way into the surrounding villages, the residents "hurry swiftly to the monastery to see

---

26–48; and Nadieszda Kizenko, *A Prodigal Saint: Father John of Kronstadt and the Russian People* (University Park, Penn., 2000).

[82] Such, at least, was Zolotnitskii's interpretation (Zolotnitskii, "Doklad sovetu Bratstva sv. Guriia," 331).

[83] NART, f. 4, op. 1, d. 5851, ll. 146–48. For a short biography of Paisii, see A. G., *Neskol'ko slov k biografii Nastoiatelia Mikhailo-Arkhangel'skogo Cheremiskogo Monastyria o. Igumena Paisiia* (St. Petersburg, 1883).

[84] NART, f. 10, op. 5, d. 515, l. 112. This archival file represents a draft of Rufimskii's book (based in part on the monastery's own archives), from which numerous passages were edited prior to publication.

[85] Citations from Rufimskii, *Cheremiskii Mikhailo-Arkhangel'skii monastyr'*, pp. 98–99.

[86] Cited ibid., p. 102.

the heir." This was done, Rufimskii related, "to teach the surrounding inorodtsy to visit the monastery," but also for the "enrichment" of the monastery through the contributions of pilgrims. Paisii sometimes left the monastery for several months at time in order to raise money, "and the multiethnic fraternity of the young cloister at this time lived in a way that could be prompted only by their natural habits and inclinations." To the extent that wealth for the monastery was acquired through his personal efforts, Paisii sometimes held part of the funds in his personal possession without proper accounting, which led some to question his propriety, and there are indications that he eventually developed a drinking problem. Rufimskii emphasized that Paisii's actions were necessary to get the monastery on its feet, and that Paisii's intimate relationship with the hierarchy in Kazan allowed him greater freedom of operation than he might otherwise have enjoyed.[87] But there was some foundation for suspicions about him, especially among the Mari brethren who were less appreciative of the financial needs of a "properly" constituted Orthodox monastery.

One of Paisii's most vocal opponents in the monastery was Zakharov, who, unlike Gerasimov and Kirillov, remained in the monastery and took monastic vows to become Iona in 1872. As Iona, Zakharov denounced Paisii's financial dealings directly to the Chief Procurator of the Synod and in fact filed two petitions in 1876 and 1877 relating that Paisii had closed the monastery's school for Mari boys and had prohibited Iona from using his violin to teach children polyphonic singing. Emphasizing that Maris in the region had made substantial contributions to the monastery with the understanding that there would be such a school, Iona argued that "without a school it will be very difficult and slow to attract Cheremis to prayer at the monastery in a big mass of people, for very many Cheremis sincerely regret that there is no school at the monastery." While calling for the appointment of either a Mari teacher or someone who had completed the seminary (and presumably knew Mari), Iona also suggested that he himself could teach, since he had taken singing lessons for two years and now had "sufficient understanding" to teach Mari boys literacy "not only in the Cheremis but also in the Russian language or dialect. I am even able to do church readings well in Cheremis during church liturgies, for Cheremis can sooner understand their natural dialect in the service than Slavonic, with which Cheremis are not at all acquainted." Iona considered singing to be central to the school's efforts and to attracting visitors to the monastery, for "each pilgrim can completely feel in his soul how wonderfully the monastery is elevated by the beauty of the singing." He had been using his violin to teach polyphonic singing since serving as a teacher in the early days of the movement and now complained that even outside the temple (Orthodoxy prohibited the use of

---

[87] NART, f. 10, op. 5, d. 515, ll. 84–87. See also A. G.'s praise of Paisii's efforts in *Neskol'ko slov*, p. 11.

instruments inside churches) Paisii had forbidden the use of the violin for divine verses, prayers, and choir singing.[88] While a sympathetic observer was inclined to see in Iona's actions "a few misunderstandings, or more accurately, misguided zeal," others saw in Iona an enemy of the existing order who sought to oust Paisii as father superior and take his place.[89] Iona's concerns about the school were apparently misplaced—the previous teacher had in fact passed away and the monastery was seeking a new one—but the affair evidently helped to spoil the atmosphere even more.

In fact, Iona's accusations seem to have emerged from a broader set of tensions involving the monastery's ethnic balance and growing "Russian influence." Rosters show that while a few Maris made their way into the monastic ranks, the numbers of Mari novices fell steadily over the course of the 1870s and 1880s, thus threatening the Mari character of the institution.[90] To be sure, Iona acknowledged that the monastery's school "in this region of Cheremis should serve as a local buttress of Orthodoxy, education, and unification of inorodtsy with the Russian people," and that the monastery as a whole should serve "to draw inorodtsy to the Christian religion." But he also stressed the need to teach children both Russian and Mari literacy. Maris better understood the liturgy in Mari, he argued, and neither Paisii nor the other servitors knew that language.[91] According to a religious superintendent sent to investigate the monastery's problems, Iona feared that Paisii viewed all Maris "as illiterate and inexperienced in church service [and] will push them into the background and will bring in from Sarov [his previous monastery] a whole set of servitors. . . and that in such a case the Cheremis monastery would remain only in name, and that all their previous labors will be completely spoiled."[92] In other words, a *Cheremis monastery*, for Iona, was one in which Maris constituted the defining element, and not one in which they were in a subordinate position.

It is difficult to ascertain the extent to which Iona represented the fears and aspirations of Mari participants in the monastery more generally,

[88] RGIA, f. 797, op. 46, otdel 2, stol 3, d. 231, ll. 1–30b.; and RGIA, f. 796, op. 158, d. 841, ll. 1–4. On Zakharov's earlier use of the violin, of which an observing priest had approved, see Zolotnitskii, "Doklad sovetu Bratstva sv. Guriia," 290.

[89] A. Grekov, "Stroitel' cheremiskogo monastyria ieromonakh Iona (nekrolog)," *Tserkovnyi vestnik* 33 (1885): 531; Ivanovich, "V 'cheremiskom' monastyre," 2; and Rufimskii, *Cheremiskii Mikhailo-Arkhangel'skii monastyr'*, pp. 102–12.

[90] NART, f. 10, op. 5, d. 515, l. 1010b. This trend seems to have continued into the early twentieth century (NART, f. 4, op. 135, d. 24). Ivanovich confirms that Russian influence became "predominant" and that the Mari servitors were not able to reconcile themselves to this immediately. Rufimskii at several points emphasized that Maris constituted less than half of the monks at the monastery.

[91] RGIA, f. 797, op. 46, otdel 2, stol 3, d. 231, ll. 2, 30b., 70b. Rufimskii reports that the whole church service in the monastery was conducted in Church Slavonic (*Cheremiskii Mikhailo-Arkhangel'skii monastyr'*, p. 134).

[92] Cited in Rufimskii, *Cheremiskii Mikhailo-Arkhangel'skii monastyr'*, p. 106. Rozhdestvenskii tried to convince Zakharov that the predominance of Russians was only temporary, until Maris were in a position to run the monastery themselves.

though it was certainly Rufimskii's impression that they were collectively guilty of "tribal enmity." "The Cheremis brothers treated all non-Cheremis monks with a kind of secret malice. Every novice from among the latter was met by the Cheremis as a kind of rival, a personal enemy who would take from them what they had acquired with such labor and what by right should belong to them exclusively."[93] More than this, the monastery initially attracted many Maris who arrived without passports or other authorization and who were even less willing than Iona to submit to the monastery's discipline. According to Rufimskii, Maris sought to establish "their own, so to speak, national cloister," and the resulting "quarrels" and "clashes" made it necessary "to attract to the monastery a non-Cheremis element, which would, so to speak, restrain and neutralize Cheremis national impulses."[94] Indeed, the situation stabilized, allegedly, only after the monastery instituted a more formal procedure for the selection of monks, in order to prevent the acceptance of "the kind of person who could constitute an undesirable element."[95] Rufimskii thus concluded that while the monastery succeeded in spreading Christianity more widely among the surrounding pagans, it was less successful in fulfilling another of its goals: "the weakening among Cheremis of the peculiarity of their alien character and their merging with the Russian population."[96]

Although Rufimskii's account is clearly tendentious in its treatment of the Mari brethren, it nonetheless seems reasonably clear that, much like Russian parishioners who also wanted more say in their religious affairs, some Maris considered the monastery to be their own creation and wanted it to reflect the efforts they had put into it.[97] With a Russian father superior and fraternity, there was very little space left for Maris to have a decisive say in its governance. If the Maris exhibited a certain dislike of other non-Russians, this may have been because they feared that the presence of the latter would increase the need for Russian as a lingua franca for the monastery and further dilute the specifically Mari character of the institution. In any event, we can assume that only a profound disappointment could have forced Gerasimov, who had spent close to a year-and-a-half in prison for the sake of the monastery, to abandon it so soon after its founding.

The subsequent history of the monastery is murky. Paisii died in 1883, and Iona two years later, and by 1888 an observer contended that the Mari brethren had by then reconciled themselves to the "fully legitimate order of things"—that is, the predominance of "Russian influence."[98] A report from

[93] Ibid., p. 124.
[94] NART, f. 10, op. 5, d. 515, ll. 1150b.–16.
[95] Rufimskii, *Cheremiskii Mikhailo-Arkhangel'skii monastyr'*, pp. 123–31 (citation from p. 131).
[96] Cited ibid., p. 160, from the original approval for the monastery's establishment.
[97] On the aspirations of Russian peasants, see Chulos, "Peasant Religion."
[98] Ivanovich, "V 'cheremiskom' monastyre," no. 252, 2.

1903 shows that there were 155 people at the monastery, only a minority of whom were Maris.[99] While Rufimskii contends that the monastery was famous and popular among non-Russians of the region, and that the pupils from the school played an important role in that population's "enlightenment," the ethnographer Smirnov asserted that the monastery was more popular among Russians, and that the money for its operation was collected in Moscow and Nizhnii Novgorod rather than locally.[100]

Whatever the direct impact of the Archangel Michael Monastery, it served as a model, implicitly or explicitly, for other non-Russian monasteries and convents in the Volga-Kama region. After the creation of the convent in Kozmodem'iansk in 1877, numerous petitions by local residents to establish another Mari convent in Kozmodem'iansk district finally bore fruit when an almshouse established in 1882 was raised to the status of a convent in 1898.[101] Other non-Russian monasteries, convents, and communes appeared in the late nineteenth and early twentieth centuries as well, although these continued to be concentrated in and around Kozmodem'iansk district.[102] A fair number of these new institutions were convents, which offered non-Russian women more opportunities to manifest their Orthodox spirituality and to contribute meaningfully to the religious and moral "development" of their co-ethnics.[103] Some people argued that women were especially well-suited to this task, since they "are more religious, more capable of preaching all the time and everywhere."[104] Thus, at least for some

---

[99] NART, f. 4, op. 135, d. 24, ll. 1–50. Ethnicity is not listed for all those at the monastery, but enough are listed as not being Mari to make it clear that Maris were only a minority, even if a substantial one.

[100] Smirnov, *Cheremisy*, p. 174.

[101] NART, f. 4, op. 125, d. 10; and NART, f. 4, op. 145, d. 299 (Vershino-Sumskii Vvedenskii cheremiskii zhenskii monastyr'). This transition from almshouse to convent was characteristic of the development of women's monastic communities more generally. See Brenda Meehan, "Popular Piety, Local Initiative, and the Founding of Women's Religious Communities in Russia, 1764–1907," in *Seeking God: The Recovery of Religious Identity in Orthodox Russia, Ukraine, and Georgia*, ed. Stephen K. Batalden (DeKalb, 1993), p. 96.

[102] "Inorodcheskaia zhenskaia obshchina v Permskoi gubernii," *Pravoslavnyi blagovestnik* 9 (1899): 34–39; "Iz zhizni chuvashskoi zhenskoi obshchiny," *Pravoslavnyi blagovestnik* 3 (1899): 130–34, 4 (1899): 166–73; "Kuzhenerskii Nikolaevskii cheremiskii zhenskii monastyr' v Urzhumskom uezde, Viatskoi Eparkhii," *VEV* 30, 31, 33, 35, 37, 44, 47 (1910); Roman Daulei, "O trekhsviatitel'skom kreshcheno-tatarskom monastyre, Kazanskoi eparkhii," *Ufimskie eparkhial'nye vedomosti* 4 (1915): 177–83; N. A. Arkhangel'skii, "Aleksandrinskii zhenskii chuvashskii monastyr' Iadrinskogo uezda," *IKE* 12–13 (1912): 393–407; and L. I. Denisov, *Pravoslavnye monastyri Rossiiskoi Imperii: Polnyi spisok vsekh 1,105 nyne sushchestvuiushchikh v 75 guberniiakh i oblastiakh (i 2 inostrannykh gosudarstvakh) muzhskikh i zhenskikh monastyrei, arkhiereiskikh domov i zhenskikh obshchin* (Moscow, 1908).

[103] The notable development of convents also situates non-Russian Orthodox religiosity in a broader Russian context, for in general by the second half of the nineteenth century, monasticism in Russia was being profoundly feminized. See William G. Wagner, "Paradoxes of Piety: The Nizhegorod Convent of the Exaltation of the Cross, 1807–1919" (paper delivered at the workshop, "Orthodoxy in the Russian Historical Experience," University of Michigan, March 1999).

[104] RGIA, f. 797, op. 77, otdel 2, stol 3, d. 57, l. 27.

non-Russians in the Volga-Kama region, monasticism had become an important aspect of non-Russian Orthodox life by the early twentieth century, and if anything seemed to be gaining momentum by 1917.

Significantly, not everyone enthusiastically supported the idea of non-Russian monasticism. Rufimskii's account, though sympathetic on some level, hardly constituted a resounding endorsement of the idea. He contended, rather, that the situation of non-Russians "amid the prevailing Russian population will be normal only when they concern themselves least of all with their tribal peculiarities and [when] they exert all efforts toward being true sons of their fatherland and loyal executors of its laws."[105] Kazan Archbishop Dmitrii was even more skeptical in 1907, contending that Maris were still "more children in terms of faith than mature people." Arguing disdainfully that "[it] is difficult even to imagine what would emerge in a religious and moral sense from a monastery consisting exclusively of Cheremis," he underscored that the "enlightenment" of Maris was closely connected to their Russification, and therefore "every Russian person should desire not the establishment of exclusively inorodtsy monasteries (Tatar, Chuvash, Cheremis, and others), *but a large influx of inorodtsy into Russian monasteries.*"[106] For many officials—even clerical ones—Christianization thus remained desirable principally to the extent that it also promoted Russification.

---

[105] Rufimskii, *Cheremiskii Mikhailo-Arkhangel'skii monastyr'*, p. 160.

[106] RGIA, f. 797, op. 77, otdel 2, stol 3, d. 57, ll. 21–21ob. (emphasis in the original). Note that Dmitrii's concern was with the desires of "every Russian person," but not with non-Russians.

9   From Missionary Reform to "Freedom of Conscience"

By the 1860s the itinerant model of missionizing that had prevailed from 1830 was losing ground to a model of missionary education.[1] Nikolai Il'minskii, whom we have already met in connection with the Anti-Muslim Division, was a pivotal figure in the elaboration of this missionary reform, which became known simply as "the Il'minskii system." These innovations, applied first and foremost to Kazan province beginning in the 1860s, facilitated a much deeper engagement with Orthodoxy on the part of many of the region's non-Russians. But this missionary success also raised new questions, precisely because it came to rest on the promotion of non-Russian ethnic identity as an antidote to Islamization. By creating small native intelligentsias, the rudiments of indigenous literatures, and the basis for emerging ethnic and national consciousness, the reform made inorodtsy more resistant to the larger project of Russification. And because Il'minskii's methods were not applied with equal enthusiasm throughout the region, the legacy of this missionary reform can only be considered mixed.

Moreover, the problem of apostasy remained unresolved. Although the new missionary practices did much to minimize the rejection of Orthodoxy among the remaining baptized Tatars, they enjoyed little success in bringing apostates back into the Orthodox fold. With time, the state found itself having to deal with apostates' children and grandchildren, who had never been baptized but continued to be denied official status as Muslims. Faced with similar religious "recalcitrants" (*uporstvuiushchie*) elsewhere in the empire, secular officials (and even a few ecclesiastical ones) felt more and more pressure to terminate this unwieldy situation and to recognize these

[1] A similar transition from itinerancy to missionary schools was underway in British India at about the same time. See Antony Copley, *Religions in Conflict: Ideology, Cultural Contact, and Conversion in Late-Colonial India* (Delhi, 1997), esp. chap. 1.

apostates-by-descent as Muslims. It was only in 1905, however, that the government finally permitted the exclusion from Orthodoxy as a general policy, even then adding significant caveats to maintain a privileged (if modified) position for the Orthodox church. The religious reform of 1905 thus represented a resolution of the problem of apostasy (at least for many of the region's inhabitants), but it stopped short of fully instituting the "freedom of conscience" promised by the October Manifesto of 1905.

Taken together, these developments constituted a significant revision in the nature of religious affiliation in the Russian empire. Il'minskii's system was geared toward bringing non-Russians' religious convictions into conformity with their formal confessional status. The reform of 1905 represented the opposite: a willingness to modify formal confessional status on the basis of apostates' religious convictions. Although not all non-Russians would be either touched by Il'minskii's project or satisfied by the reform of 1905, status and belief were nonethless brought into much closer alignment by the last decade of tsarist rule.

Il'minskii's Innovations and Their Implications

Il'minskii's methods replaced a missionary itinerancy that was already in decline. By 1859 the last of the active missionaries in Kazan diocese had retired for health reasons, and the Kazan mission of 1830 ceased to exist. At that time the Anti-Muslim Division was already in operation, and by all indications, church hierarchs put their faith in the division for the time being.[2] The Viatka mission retained its itinerant missionaries, although their activities in these years are not particularly well documented.[3] In Orenburg province the authorities were preoccupied with the transfer of Bashkirs and Teptiars to civilian status and opposed the introduction of any missionary measures until this process had been completed.[4] The idea of mission was now understood in somewhat different terms. As the archbishop of Kazan wrote in 1869, "The question of the mission in Kazan diocese is being transformed into the question of the education of non-Russians, or of non-Russian schools."[5] And indeed the education of non-Russians became a matter of extensive debate near the end of the decade, as the Ministry of Education contemplated how schooling could best effectuate the Russification of non-Russians.[6]

---

[2] RGIA, f. 796, op. 442, dd. 13, 27, and 52; and N. Razumov, *Vysokopreosviashchennyi Afanasii, Arkhiepiskop byvshii Kazanskii i Sviiazhskii* (Kazan, 1868), pp. 24–25.

[3] I have no information on what happened to the Simbirsk mission, although it would appear that it, like the Kazan mission, slipped into obscurity.

[4] TsGIARB, f. I-11, op. 1, d. 560. See also Charles Robert Steinwedel, "Invisible Threads of Empire: State, Religion, and Ethnicity in Tsarist Bashkiria, 1773–1917" (Ph.D. diss., Columbia University, 1999), pp. 93–100.

[5] RGIA, f. 796, op. 442, d. 270, l. 370b.

[6] These debates have by now been analyzed many times, and I therefore make no concerted effort to address them here. But see Steinwedel, "Invisible Threads of Empire," pp. 101–14;

The essence of Il'minskii's approach was to employ native languages and native instructors for the transmission of the Christian message to non-Russians. Translation, schooling in non-Russian languages, and the promotion of non-Russians to positions as teachers and clergy were thus at the core of his "system." The idea of using native languages was, of course, not entirely new. Some clerics had earlier comprehended the importance of native languages and translations for the "reinforcement" of non-Russians in Christianity, and the Synod had promoted the training of Mari boys at the Viatka Seminary for their eventual placement in clerical positions. But Il'minskii's efforts met with much greater success than earlier ones. He sought to translate texts in new ways, above all by using an idiomatic vernacular, verifying the texts with native non-Russians to ensure their coherence and intelligibility, and simplifying Christianity. As he wrote in one instance, "With inorodtsy it is necessary to begin from the very beginning, and to look on the mass of inorodtsy as children, who have gathered to learn and to whom the instructor must teach elementary knowledge."[7]

Il'minskii based these conclusions on his earlier participation in a project to translate the liturgy into Tatar using the literary language and Arabic script in the late 1840s and 1850s. Disappointed with the results of that endeavor, Il'minskii turned for help in his translation of a new Tatar-language primer to the Kräshen Vasilii Timofeev (1836–96), who had joined the Kazan Ecclesiastical Academy in 1862 as a tutor of Tatar.[8] Il'minskii soon concluded that a modified Cyrillic alphabet more accurately represented the phonetics of the Tatar language than did the Arabic and had the added advantage of restricting Kräshens' access to Islamic texts.[9] By 1869 the Orthodox liturgy had been translated into Tatar using this new approach, as the Kazan diocesan authorities encouraged the use of native languages in religious discussions and for the most oft-used prayers and songs. In 1883 the

---

Jean Saussay, "Il'minskij et la politique de russification des Tatars, 1865–1891," *Cahiers du monde russe et soviétique* 8, 3 (1967): 404–26; Isabelle Teitz Kreindler, "Educational Policies toward the Eastern Nationalities in Tsarist Russia: A Study of Il'minskii's System" (Ph.D. diss., Columbia University, 1969); Robert Paul Geraci, "Window on the East: Ethnography, Orthodoxy, and Russian Nationality in Kazan, 1870–1914" (Ph.D. diss, University of California, Berkeley, 1995), pp. 110–84; and Wayne Dowler, "The Politics of Language in Non-Russian Elementary Schools in the Eastern Empire, 1865–1914," *Russian Review* 54 (1995): 516–39.

[7] N. I. Il'minskii, "Prakticheskie zamechaniia o perevodakh i sochineniiakh na inorodcheskikh iazykakh," *Pravoslavnyi sobesednik* 1 (1871): 163–64.

[8] On Timofeev, see his "Moe vospitanie"; "Dnevnik starokreshchennogo tatarina," in N. I. Il'minskii, ed., *Kazanskaia tsentral'naia kreshcheno-tatarskaia shkola: Materialy dlia istorii prosveshcheniia kreshchenykh tatar* (Kazan, 1887), pp. 9–28, 34–76; P. Z., "O. Vasilii Timofeevich Timofeev (Nekrolog)," *Pravoslavnyi sobesednik* 1 (1896): 143–62; and David Grigor'ev, "Pervenets inorodcheskogo sviashchenstva," *Ufimskie eparkhial'nye vedomosti* 10 (1905): 753–62, 11 (1905): 822–31, 12 (1905): 887–96.

[9] NART, f. 10, op. 1, d. 3418; N. I. Il'minskii, "O primenenii russkogo alfavita k inorodcheskim iazykam," in *Nikolai Ivanovich Il'minskii: Sbornik statei* (Kazan, 1916), pp. 106–20; *Perepiska o chuvashskikh izdaniiakh perevodcheskoi komissii* (Kazan, 1890), pp. iii–xiv.

Synod authorized the conduct of liturgy in non-Russian languages wherever there was "a more or less substantial population" of non-Russians.[10]

Il'minskii not only promoted non-Russians into teaching and clerical positions far more energetically than had his predecessors but also established a set of special institutions for their training. In 1863, building on Timofeev's effort to teach young boys from his native village in his spare time, Il'minskii established the Kazan Central Baptized-Tatar School, which became the cornerstone of his "system."[11] The school offered Kräshens a basic education in Tatar with a strong Orthodox-Christian component, and many of its graduates went on to serve as teachers in branch schools that were established one by one in Kräshen villages. After the Ministry of Education's endorsement of Il'minskii's principle of native-language instruction for the eastern portions of the empire in 1870, the Ministry created a non-Russian teachers' seminary with Il'minskii as its director in 1872.[12] By 1867 Il'minskii had obtained from the Synod a directive that authorized the training and ordination of non-Russian clergy and exempted them from the normal seminary course.[13] Deeply convinced that each non-Russian ethnicity had its own worldview, Il'minskii contended that to render Christianity "the foundation for [non-Russians'] thinking and life," one needed "to adapt to their religious conceptions and moral convictions."[14] Non-Russians themselves were obviously in the best position to effectuate this cultural translation.

Il'minskii was able to secure for this emerging set of institutions a remarkable degree of autonomy, in part because of the Synod's desire, after the apostasy of 1866 and the perceived failure of the Anti-Muslim Division, to minimize its direct involvement in missionary matters. Thus, while the baptized-Tatar school began to receive a stipend from the Ministry of State Domains and the Synod, it was ultimately a private institution that relied on individual contributions and remained unsubordinated to official regulations.[15] Likewise, the Brotherhood of St. Gurii, which was founded by Il'minskii and others in 1867 and essentially replaced the older mission, was a voluntary society consisting of church hierarchs, merchants, government

---

[10] *IKE* 11(1869): 327–31; *IKE* 7 (1874): 191–93; "Ob otkrytii v g. Kazani bogosluzheniia na tatarskom iazyke," *IKE* 2 (1870): 48–55; and N. I. Il'minskii, "O tserkovnom bogosluzhenii na inorodcheskikh iazykakh," *Pravoslavnyi sobesednik* 1 (1883): 258–72.

[11] *Kazanskaia tsentral'naia* contains the most extensive materials on the history of the school.

[12] NART, f. 93, op. 1, d. 7; NART, f. 93, op. 1, d. 17; and "Uchrezhdenie Kazanskoi uchitel'skoi seminarii," in *Kazanskaia tsentral'naia*, pp. 424–45. On the 1870 regulations on education, see Kreindler, "Educational Policies," pp. 78–88; Geraci, "Window on the East," pp. 151–54; and Dowler, "Politics of Language," pp. 516–39. The Russian language was to be the central tool of Russification among Muslims.

[13] RGIA, f. 797, op. 26, otdel 2, razriad 3, d. 251; RGIA, f. 796, op. 162, d. 1417; and N. I. Il'minskii, ed., *Iz perepiski ob udostoenii inorodtsam sviashchenno-sluzhitel'skikh dolzhnostei* (Kazan, 1885).

[14] Il'minskii, *Iz perepiski*, p. 9.

[15] Kreindler, "Educational Policies," p. 71.

officials, and educational specialists.[16] Although the Brotherhood maintained ties with the government, as well as with the Orthodox Missionary Society in Moscow, it was in fact an independent organization that enjoyed the right of censorship over its own publications (mainly translations).[17] True, as director of the teachers' seminary Il'minskii was officially an employee of the Ministry of Education, and he also maintained a correspondence with important officials in St. Petersburg.[18] Nonetheless, the institutions under his direction retained an essentially "private" character and served as the foundation for a highly personalized regional bureaucracy.[19] This independence allowed these institutions to minimize the formalities and

A group of pupils at the Simbirsk Chuvash Teachers' School (1896). The seated pupil on the far right is a Russian. RGIA, f. 835, op. 3, d. 506, photograph #9.

[16] According to its original statute, the group was called the Brotherhood of Bishop Gurii—*Bratstvo sviatitelia Guriia* (*sviatitel´* = bishop). In most of its subsequent publications, however, the group was listed as *Bratstvo sv. Guriia*, so that most scholars refer to it as the Brotherhood of St. Gurii. Since Gurii, the first bishop of Kazan, was eventually canonized, I follow the latter convention.

[17] RGIA, f. 796, op. 149, d. 102; and M. A. Mashanov, *Obzor deiatel´nosti Bratstva sv. Guriia za 25 let ego sushchestvovaniia, 1867–1892* (Kazan, 1892).

[18] Kreindler, "Educational Policies," pp. 94–96. Il'minskii's letters to Pobedonostev have been published as *Pis´ma Nikolaia Ivanovicha Il'minskogo k Ober-prokuroru Sv. Sinoda Konstantinu Petrovichu Pobedonostsevu* (Kazan, 1895). The latter's responses are in RGIA, f. 1574, op. 1, d. 1146. Il'minskii's correspondence with Ministers of Education Dmitrii Tolstoi and I. D. Delianov are in NART, f. 968, op. 1, d. 8.

[19] P. Z., "O. Vasilii Timofeevich Timofeev," 154. As Kreindler remarks, Il'minskii "became in effect a quasi-minister for native affairs" ("Educational Policies," p. 98).

Students of the Shikhozamovskaia school, Tsivil´sk district, Kazan province. RGIA, f. 835, op. 3, d. 178, photograph #3.

Violin lesson for pupils at the Khornovar-Shiglainskaia Chuvash school in Simbirsk diocese. RGIA, f. 835, op. 3, d. 504, photograph #2.

the associations with the state that constituted a substantial liability for missionary efforts.[20] In general, this arrangement corresponded well with the spirit of the reform era, which valued initiative from society and active participation of the laity in religious affairs.[21] The Synod, for its part, was content to allot a few thousand rubles a year to the Missionary Society, the school, and the Brotherhood, leaving them to conduct missionary affairs.[22]

Il'minskii at times spoke of Russification, but his principal concern was the salvation of non-Russians and the development of their Christian spirituality.[23] Indeed, although he claimed that Russification would be the ultimate result of his approach, the purpose of his system was at least temporarily to *uphold* ethnic difference in order to fortify baptized non-Russians within Orthodoxy and to protect them from Islamization. As Il'minskii had written at one point, if Christianity could be made available in native forms, "Tatars will be convinced that upon accepting the faith of Christ they can maintain their nationality [*narodnost'*], which is so dear to them." Christianity, he later asserted, "does not encroach on ethnic particularities, does not smooth them out in a formal or external way, [and] does not deprive a person of individuality."[24] Il'minskii was in fact committed to the retention by non-Russian teachers and clergy of the spirit, appearance, and simplicity of their rural non-Russian compatriots, precisely to ensure the connection of his students with the village.[25] The practical essence of the project was to create a kind of intermediate class of people, who would maintain ties with both the Russian Orthodox world (i.e., with Il'minskii and his colleagues) and the ethnicities from which they came.[26] In short, whatever Il'minskii might have said about Russification, his principal and immediate goal was to convince non-Russians that they could confess Orthodoxy *without* becoming Russian.

[20] On Il'minskii's desire to avoid formalism, see "'*Ex Oriente Lux*': Odna iz neizdannykh zapisok Nikolaia Ivanovicha Il'minskogo ob ustroistve uchebnykh zavedenii," *Pravoslavnyi sobesednik* 1 (1901): 40–53 (originally written in 1862 or 1863).

[21] Gregory L. Freeze, *The Parish Clergy in Nineteenth-Century Russia: Crisis, Reform, Counter-Reform* (Princeton, 1983), pp. 248–97; A. Papkov, "Nachalo vozrozhdeniia tserkovno-prikhodskoi zhizni v Rossii," *Russkii vestnik* (February / March 1900): 605–28, 131–54; and Glennys Young, "'Into Church Matters': Lay Identity, Rural Parish Life, and Popular Politics in Late Imperial and Early Soviet Russia, 1864–1928," *Russian History* 23, 1–4 (1996): 367–84.

[22] Indeed, the Synod cited the Brotherhood, the baptized-Tatar school, and the provisions on the promotion of non-Russian clergy as rendering the Academy's Anti-Muslim Division "superfluous" (RGIA, f. 796, op. 152, d. 876, ll. 14–15).

[23] See Kreindler, "Educational Policies," pp. 6–9, 125–29, 144–47.

[24] NART, f. 10, op. 1, d. 5964, l. 200b.; and Timofeev, "Dnevnik," p. 445.

[25] One Kräshen told how he and a comrade, having finished the baptized-Tatar school, "now feeling ourselves to be teachers," had bought themselves pants and coats (i.e., non-peasant dress). Il'minskii was dismayed and made it clear to them that he wanted to be able to recognize a Kräshen by outward appearance. Recounted in S. Chicherina, *U privolzhskikh inorodtsev: Putevye zametki* (St. Petersburg, 1905), pp. 107–8. See also Kreindler, "Educational Policies," pp. 148–50.

[26] Geraci, "Window on the East," p. 184; P. Z., "O. Vasilii Timofeevich Timofeev," 151; and *Kazanskaia tsentral'naia*, pp. 271–73.

Many observers credited Il′minskii and his indigenous disciples with insti-
gating a spiritual revolution in the countryside. Non-Russians previously considered to have had virtually no sense of attachment to Orthodoxy now
"throng[ed] in crowds" into the schools, which in effect served as houses of
prayer. Enchanted by singing in native languages, adults learned about "truths
of the Orthodox faith" through their children and visited the schools and increasingly the parish churches where the liturgy was conducted in native languages.[27] Non-Russians were ever more willing to open schools in their villages, often themselves passing resolutions requesting teachers.[28] To be sure,
the Brotherhood's financial constraints limited its impact, and in part because
Il′minskii's system was largely informal, we lack the kinds of sources that permit a fuller assessment of the system's results. Undoubtedly, Il′minskii's supporters often succumbed to hyperbole, exaggerating the contrast between "before" and "after." Nonetheless it is difficult to gainsay that in the last few
decades of the nineteenth century some kind of profound spiritual transformation, involving both Orthodoxy and Il′minskii's methods, was occurring.

These methods had the greatest impact on Kräshens and Chuvash, and
Il′minskii's efforts were concentrated on these two peoples. Kräshens, the
group most linguistically and culturally akin to Muslim Tatars, were seen to
be in the greatest danger of apostasy, while Chuvash constituted the largest
single non-Russian Orthodox ethnic group aside from Mordvins.[29] Il′minskii's
Chuvash protégé, the equivalent of the Kräshen Vasilii Timofeev, was Ivan
Iakovlev, who went on to head a special Chuvash Teachers' Seminary in Simbirsk beginning in 1875.[30] As regards translations, schools, and clergy, by
Il′minskii's death the Brotherhood had done far more for these two groups
than it had for Maris and Udmurts, and their success was far greater in Kazan
and Simbirsk provinces than elsewhere.[31] Buoyed by native teachers and clergy
and an extensive network of schools, and equipped with an impressive range
of religious texts in their native vernacular, Kräshens increasingly developed
an indigenous Orthodoxy and even began to assert that they, as Kräshens,
constituted a people entirely distinct from Muslim Tatars.[32] And by 1905 a

---

[27] Mashanov, *Obzor*, pp. 234–39.

[28] Ibid., p. 237. Examples of such resolutions among Kräshens are in GAKO, f. 811, op. 1,
dd. 207 and 349.

[29] Mordvins, as we have seen, were generally considered to have been already substantially
Russified.

[30] Kreindler, "Educational Policies," pp. 157–59; and P. D. Denisov, *Religioznye verovaniia
chuvash: Istoriko-etnograficheskie ocherki* (Cheboksary, 1959), pp. 320–29.

[31] Mashanov, *Obzor*, pp. 72–75, 130–48, 179–83; and Kreindler, "Educational Policies,"
p. 159.

[32] On these trends, see the various contributions to *Kazanskaia tsentral′naia*; Ia. E.
Emel′ianov, *Stikhi na kreshcheno-tatarskom iazyke* (Kazan, 1879), especially the poem "Sat-
nashkanny uiatyu" (p. 22); Filipp Gavrilov, "Slovo inorodtsa-khristianina k inorodtsam-
magommedanam," *VEV* 6–8 (1889): 157–64, 177–86, 209–18; and A. N. Grigorief,
"Keräshen matur ädäbiaty," in *Shigrlär jiyntyghy (Kräshen-tatar shaghirläreneke)* (Kazan,
1931).

religious superintendent in Simbirsk diocese could remark, "The present condition of the Chuvash, with the exception of a small number of the older generation who have had their day, hardly differs in a religious-moral respect from the condition of a Russian Orthodox Christian."[33]

Il'minskii's approach was not without controversy. His most vocal critics feared that his project would give native languages literary status and thus foster conscious ethnicities resistant to Russification. Already in the late 1860s, some observers contended that the Russian language should be the principal tool for cultural assimilation and that a focus on Orthodoxy in indigenous form was not sufficient.[34] Il'minskii and his associates defended their position by stressing that the message—Christianity and associated values—was more important than the medium, and that their project was designed to serve a transitional function for non-Russians, preparing them for eventual instruction in Russian while protecting them from the pernicious influence of "Mohammedan propaganda." But the distinction between making Christianity accessible to non-Russians and promoting ethnic

Baptized Tatars of the village Iantsovary, Laishevo district, Kazan province, exiting their church. Date unknown. RGIA f. 835, op. 4, d. 72, photograph #2.

[33] RGIA, f. 796, op. 442, d. 2114, l. 11.
[34] See Kreindler, "Educational Policies," pp. 78–84. For other accounts critical of the idea of the promotion of non-Russian languages, see the discussion in *Sbornik dokumentov i statei po voprosu ob obrazovanii inorodtsev* (St. Petersburg, 1869), as well as *Perepiska o chuvashskikh izdaniiakh*, esp. pp. 1–18.

particularism was not so easy to draw. Il'minskii's methods came under ever greater fire, especially after his death in 1891. Already in the 1880s, the Brotherhood was forced to defend itself from growing attempts by the Kazan diocesan authorities to assert formal control over its staffing and activities. In 1898 the bishop managed to gain greater power of appointment over the Brotherhood's council and made membership mandatory for all diocesan clergy in 1900 in order to improve the Brotherhood's finances.[35] Several prominent figures, including Il'minskii's adopted son and successor at the Teachers' Academy, Nikolai Bobrovnikov, resigned from the Brotherhood in response to this interference.[36] At the same time, officials of the Ministry of Education began quietly to dismantle Il'minskii's system on the grounds that, though successful from a missionary standpoint, it had failed to achieve the linguistic "unification" of inorodtsy with the Russian population and was too narrowly "religious-moral" in its orientation. The curator of the Kazan Educational District removed Iakovlev from his position at the Chuvash Teachers' Seminary in 1903, while also planning to transform the Kazan Teachers' Seminary into an exclusively Russian institution. Even as these figures dismantled significant parts of Il'minskii's system, however, Il'minskii's stature prevented them from attacking him personally, leaving them instead to present their acts as modifications or "corrections" with which he would surely have agreed were he still alive.[37]

Nor was the idea of itinerant missionaries entirely dead. The Brotherhood sometimes dispatched Timofeev or Malov to villages where apostasy appeared, and students of the Ecclesiastical Academy might visit Kräshen villages during their summer vacation.[38] In 1884 Archbishop of Kazan Palladii (Pisarev) sought to resurrect missionary activity on the basis of the 1830 decree, which was still technically in effect, though he was transferred to a new diocese before anything came of this proposal.[39] The idea of reintroducing some kind of mission received new impetus toward the end of the 1890s, when a special commission in Kazan was formed to address (once again!) the problem of baptized-Tatar apostasy. By 1901 a new mission in Kazan diocese had been created more or less on the traditional model, with Iakov Koblov at its head and with twelve missionary assistants from among the

---

[35] Geraci, "Window on the East," pp. 335–37; Kreindler, "Educational Policies," pp. 189–90.

[36] Chicherina, *U privolzhskikh inorodtsev*, pp. 422–25.

[37] Geraci, "Window on the East," pp. 344–51; Kreindler, "Educational Policies," pp. 182–85; Denisov, *Religioznye verovaniia chuvash*, p. 327–30. On the educational issues, see also Wayne Dowler, "Pedagogy and Politics: Origins of the Special Conference of 1905 on Primary Education for Non-Russians in the East," *Nationalities Papers* 26, 4 (1998): 761–75.

[38] Such a visit was the basis, for example, of M. A. Mashanov's account, *Religiozno-nravstvennoe sostoianie kreshchenykh tatar Kazanskoi gubernii Mamadyshskogo uezda* (Kazan, 1875).

[39] RGIA, f. 799, op. 13, d. 803, ll. 1–5; and Mashanov, *Obzor*, pp. 185–88. Only one priest, Aleksandr Miropol'skii from the village of Apazovo, actually made any missionary trips at this time.

parish clergy. As before, these missionaries took trips to parishes in their jurisdictions, conducted discussions with inorodtsy, and tried to promote zeal among the local clergy. Although Koblov was in effect appointed as an "anti-Muslim missionary," he quickly came to the conclusion that conducting public missionary discussions with Muslims was "dangerous, indeed impossible."[40] His excursions accordingly focused on the few remaining pagan settlements in Kazan diocese, where he did succeed in baptizing forty-eight Maris in 1902.[41] Not everyone was supportive of this endeavor, however. Bobrovnikov argued that schools and liturgy in non-Russian languages were by far the most effective means of Christianization. Rather than engage in traditional missionary activity, which as a "state affair" (*kazennoe delo*) would never inspire non-Russians religiously, it made sense to promote more non-Russian clergy, whose numbers were still inadequate.[42]

Indeed, the issue of non-Russian clergy and teachers had by this time long been a source of particular acrimony.[43] Convinced that non-Russians were especially well-suited for the transmission of Orthodoxy to their fellow villagers, Il'minskii aggressively supported their candidacy for such positions, even when their formal qualifications were low. As he wrote in defense of one Kräshen candidate whose knowledge of the catechism had been deemed insufficient for priestly status, "It seems to me that in a religious matter, during a struggle of heterodoxy [*inoverie*] with Orthodoxy, much more vital and important than theological knowledge are the moral and pastoral qualities of priests."[44] Exempted from the normal course of seminary study, non-Russians were instead trained at the baptized-Tatar school, the Teachers' Seminary, and the Chuvash school in Simbirsk. As they went through these institutions and began to receive clerical appointments, opposition from Russian clergy grew. Il'minskii noted in 1881 that some members of the Brotherhood were inclined to see in his efforts to attract non-Russians

---

[40] Ia. Koblov, "O sostoianii missionerskogo dela v Kazanskoi eparkhii za 1903," *IKE* 43 (1904): 1461–62.

[41] Ia. Koblov, "Kreshchenie 48 chelovek iazychnikov cheremis v prikhode Bol'shikh Musheran', Tsarevokokshaiskogo uezda," *IKE* 9 (1902): 400–407. Another forty-two were baptized in the same locale later that year. See Aleksei (Bishop), "Kreshchenie cheremis-iazychnikov v sele Musherani, Kazanskoi eparkhii," *IKE* (1902): 726–33.

[42] N. Bobrovnikov, "Nuzhny li tak nazyvaemye protivomusul'manskie i protivoiazycheskie eparkhial'nye missionery v guberniiakh Evropeiskoi Rossii?" *Pravoslavnyi sobesednik* 1 (1905): 301–16; idem, "Inorodcheskoe dukhovenstvo i bogosluzhenie na inorodcheskikh iazykakh v Kazanskoi eparkhii," *Pravoslavnyi sobesednik* 2 (1905): 177–81. For Koblov's defense of the new mission, see his "O neobkhodimosti inorodcheskikh missionerov v dele prosveshcheniia inorodtsev," *Pravoslavnyi sobesednik* 1–2 (1905): 706–16, 108–18.

[43] A thorough treatment of this issue is provided by Robert Geraci (though principally as regards Kazan diocese) in "The Il'minskii System and the Controversy over Non-Russian Teachers and Priests in the Middle-Volga" in *Kazan, Moscow, St. Petersburg: Multiple Faces of the Russian Empire*, ed. Catherine Evtuhov, Boris Gasparov, Alexander Ospovat, and Mark von Hagen (Moscow, 1997), pp. 325–48.

[44] RGIA, f. 796, op. 205, d. 621, l. 260b.

"injury and censure for the Russian clerical estate." Most notably, he began to detect in his long-time colleague E. A. Malov a "strong disinclination" to allow non-Russians clerical status, which he understood to proceed from the latter's "jealous guarding of the rights and privileges of the Russian clergy."[45] Based in part on Malov's diary, Robert Geraci confirms this was indeed the case: Malov saw Il'minskii's convictions on the absolute irreplaceability of non-Russians as an "extreme view," and he became a key figure in the attempt to modify Il'minskii's method after the latter's death.[46]

Perhaps most damaging to Il'minskii's project, particularly in the increasingly nationalist reign of Alexander III, was the accusation of non-Russian "separatism." From this perspective, the promised Russification had failed to materialize, as non-Russians developed attitudes that appeared to some observers to be outright anti-Russian.[47] For the most part these concerns were probably somewhat overdrawn, since many non-Russians seem to have been eager to hide their non-Russian origins and to blend as quickly as possible with Russians. One Mari teacher (writing to Il'minskii, no less) related that, "desiring to Russify my descendants, [I] married a Russian girl of delicate upbringing in 1876," adding that he was experiencing tremendous "woe" due to the fact that "*I have left one shore behind but have not reached the other.*"[48] Non-Russians who went through Russian schools, where designations like "Cheremis" and "Votiak" were used as terms of abuse, were particularly likely to emerge shorn of attachment to their native milieu.[49] Writing in 1907, the Kräshen David Grigor'ev contended that many "Russified inorodtsy" "would gladly reject the designation of inorodets and consider themselves Russians." However, he complained, even the most Russified inorodets "remains for now an inorodets for the sole reason that he was born an inorodets, of inorodtsy parents." From this perspective, if there was any foundation at all to accusations of "separatism," this was because Russians "roughly push already Russified inorodtsy away from the gates of Russianism" (*russitsizm*).[50]

Despite the purported desire of inorodtsy to Russify, Il'minskii's critics clearly had grounds for concern. Although the promotion of non-Russian ethnicities made a great deal of sense in terms of the perceived threat from Islam, Malov was not far off the mark when he complained that inorodtsy

[45] Ibid., ll. 150b., 34.

[46] Geraci, "The Il'minskii System," pp. 332–34; idem, "Window on the East," pp. 333–37.

[47] Geraci, "The Il'minskii System," pp. 335–36.

[48] NART, f. 93, op. 1, d. 128b, l. 2320b. (emphasis in the original).

[49] A. I. Emel'ianov, "Zhelatel'nyi kharakter missionerskoi inorodcheskoi shkoly," *VEV* 10 (1904): 603; and "O missionerskikh inorodcheskikh kursakh v g. Viatke," *VEV* 11 (1905): 607–15. See also Seppo Lallukka, "Kazan' Teachers' Seminary and the Awakening of the Finnic Peoples of the Volga-Urals Region," *Studia Slavica Finlandensia* 4 (1987): 143–65.

[50] David Grigor'ev, "Polozhenie obruselykh inorodtsev," *VEV* 3 (1907): 63–64; idem, "Russifikatsiia inorodtsev," *VEV* 14 (1907): 361–62.

soon started to understand the project "in their own way."[51] Especially after 1905, inorodtsy became more self-conscious and assertive, more convinced of their own self-worth (vis-à-vis both Russians and Muslim Tatars), and more insistent on their own version of assimilation and integration into the broader imperial polity. In Viatka diocese, in particular, non-Russian clergy after 1905 quickly made up for all the time that Il'minskii's principles had not been in effect there. They became especially vocal in defending the collective interests of inorodtsy against "narrow" (principally linguistic) forms of Russification, arguing instead that obrusenie was above all a spiritual matter entirely compatible with non-Russian ethnic development. By 1907 these non-Russian clerics had their own mission, headed by a Mari from Ufa province, and enthusiastically promoted non-Russian forms of Orthodoxy in the diocese.[52] Il'minskii's project thus forged stronger bonds between many non-Russians and Orthodoxy, but also more conscious opposition to the project of Russification in its narrow, linguistic sense.

Animism and Its Reformation(s)

If Il'minskii's project had its greatest results in Kazan province, for several decades its impact was more limited elsewhere. In 1881 Il'minskii himself complained that in Ufa diocese "there are almost no people who are soundly acquainted with the matter of inorodtsy and mission," and in Viatka diocese "apparently incomprehension reigns."[53] Virtually no missionary work of any kind was undertaken in Ufa province until the founding of a local committee of the Orthodox Missionary Society in 1879, and it was really only when apostasy appeared there in the early 1880s that bishop Nikanor (Brovkovich) began to promote non-Russians into clerical positions—without official exams (which, as elsewhere, antagonized the Russian clergy).[54] The situation was similar in Viatka diocese. Only in the early 1880s did the first few native priests, principally Kräshens, make their debut in the diocese, and there was still only a handful of such priests by the early 1890s.[55] In 1900 a correspondent wrote that Il'minskii's precepts were not prevalent in Viatka province: there was no liturgy in Mari or Udmurt, and some missionaries did not know these languages. Russian was the language of

---

[51] Cited in Geraci, "The Il'minskii System," p. 335.

[52] I have considered these developments in "*Inorodtsy* on *Obrusenie*: Religious Conversion, Indigenous Clergy, and the Politics of Assimilation in Late-Imperial Russia," *Ab Imperio* 2 (2000): 105–34.

[53] RGIA, f. 796, op. 205, d. 621, l. 160b.

[54] S. M. Matveev, "Religiozno-nravstvennoe sostoianie kreshchenykh tatar Ufimskoi eparkhii do 70-kh godov," *Ufimskie eparkhial'nye vedomosti* 14 (1895): 477; and idem, *O kreshchenykh inorodtsakh Ufimskoi eparkhii* (Ufa, 1910), p. 44. For more on Nikanor, see Steinwedel, "Invisible Threads of Empire," pp. 146–56.

[55] Mashanov, *Obzor*, pp. 74–75, 183; and GAKO, f. 811, op. 1, d. 239, l. 1.

instruction in most schools, and some of the so called non-Russian schools were, ironically, located in predominantly Russian areas.[56] Only in 1904 were special "missionary inorodtsy courses" established in Viatka diocese with the goal of training "native-born inorodtsy" for clerical positions with special missionary functions.[57]

Perhaps in part because Il′minskii's precepts appeared so late, animism remained especially resilient in Viatka diocese.[58] To be sure, some observers contended that paganism was disappearing, and that merely its "remnants" (*ostatki*) were actually detectable.[59] One account from Iaransk district in 1902 reported that Maris were cutting down sacred groves (or were asking Russians to do this for them so as not to anger indigenous spirits), and that most remaining groves had become simply places for rest and relaxation.[60] But considerable evidence suggests that such conclusions were premature. Missionary reports from the 1860s show that many Udmurts and Maris remained committed to animism, even as some were also becoming better Christians.[61] Chapter 2 discusses how the village of Kuprian-Sola (Urzhum district) became the "Cheremis Jerusalem"—or as one missionary put it, "the center of the pagan-religious life of the Cheremis world"—and continued to draw Maris from Viatka, Kazan, and Ufa provinces even in the twentieth century.[62] One grove there was known as *Tünia-küs-oto* (worldwide prayer grove), which underscored its broad significance, and there remained numerous "parish" groves (*mer-küs-oty*) that served a number of villages more locally.[63] Convinced of the legality of these prayers, Maris sent petitions and even telegrams to the governor in defense of their animist practices and made explicit references to the laws of the Russian empire on religious tolerance and freedom of conscience. The author of one account concluded, citing choice phrases from missionary reports: "Thus before us is the

---

[56] D. Z., "Iazychestvo v Viatskoi gubernii (pis′mo iz provintsii)," *Zhizn′* 12 (1900): 399–400. The traveler Sofia Chicherina confirmed most of these observations during her visit to the region in 1904 (Chicherina, *U privolzhskikh inorodtsev*, pp. 188–89, 214, 228–29, 235).

[57] L. S–kii, "Missionerskie inorodcheskie kursy v gorode Viatke (o missii voobshche a v Viatskoi eparkhii v chastnosti)," *VEV* 22 (1904): 1254–68.

[58] Animism also remained strong in Ufa province, where most of the Maris and Udmurts were still officially pagans.

[59] See, for example, Sergei Nurminskii, "Ocherki religioznykh verovanii cheremis," *Pravoslavnyi sobesednik* 3 (1862): 278–79; and S. K. Kuznetsov, "Ostatki iazychestva u cheremis," *Izvestiia Imperatorskogo Russkogo Geograficheskogo Obshchestva* 21, 6 (1885): 453–79. One doctor even claimed that meadow Maris themselves were on the verge of extinction as a result of disease (especially goiter), chronic poverty, unproductive land plots, and limited intermarriage with other peoples. See M. Kandaratskii, *Priznaki vymiraniia lugovykh cheremis Kazanskoi gubernii (endemiia zoba i kretinizma)* (Kazan, 1889).

[60] N. Kibardin, "Iz nabliudenii inorodcheskogo missionera nad cheremisami," *VEV* 15 (1902): 809–10.

[61] The reports are in GAKO, f. 237, op. 170, d. 76.

[62] A. Odoev, "Po povodu iazycheskikh zhertvoprinoshenii u cheremis-khristian," *VEV* 24 (1897): 1200. Odoev was quoting the local missionary Timofei Semenov.

[63] "Selo Sernur, Urzhumskii uezd," *Viatskie gubernskie vedomosti* 84 (20 October 1882): 3. The village of Sernur was the same as the village of Makarovo discussed in chapter 2.

fact that whole villages, consisting '*exclusively* of Orthodox Christian Cheremis,' even whole cantons with thousands of people, 'in the *complete* absence of Cheremis pagans,' '*annually*' conduct pagan prayers with blood sacrifice, and this is 'a *usual occurrence*.'"[64]

Nor was this all simply a matter of Maris blindly following tradition. On the contrary, they were quite able to adapt animism to changing times. Maris (and Chuvash as well) were presenting their animism as the faith of Adam or of Abraham, hoping thereby to invest it with greater weight and authority. Perhaps most remarkably, in the 1870s a group of baptized Maris initiated a reformation of animism, involving a systemization of indigenous conceptions, the rejection of blood sacrifice, and the abandonment of polytheism in favor of a more abstract monotheism. Adept in the matter of public relations, these reformers, who later became known as the *Kugu-Sorta* (or "Big Candle") sect, even brought artifacts from their religious rituals to Kazan and presented their faith to the public at the Kazan Scientific and Industrial Exhibition in 1890.[65] Similarly, in a petition of 1891 to the Emperor requesting exclusion from Orthodoxy, they very explicitly described their prayers to show that there was nothing harmful in them.[66] They also made use of the modified Cyrillic orthography that the Brotherhood had created for its translations of Orthodox scripture into Mari—an ironic appropriation, to say the least! These were all substantial innovations designed to enhance the stature and relevance of indigenous animism. As one insightful observer remarked, the sectarians "wish to place their religion, despite the absence of books, on the same level as organized Mohammedanism and the true Christianity." Warning against the proposition that these reformers were naive or simple, this author concluded, "People who have undertaken the task of reforming paganism can in no way be called simpletons." Their endeavor indeed required that they evaluate their faith consciously and critically.[67] The leaders of the group were exiled to Siberia in 1893, but they were allowed to return to the Volga-Kama region in 1896, and they continued to promote Kugu Sorta even into the Soviet period.[68] Far from dying out, animism was being reformed and defended in new and sophisticated ways.

[64] Odoev, "Po povodu," 1206. For a similar complaint, see also Uchastnik-nabliudatel' (pseud.), "Episkop na iazycheskom mol'bishche u cheremis," *VEV* 19 (1901): 976.

[65] I. N. Smirnov, *Etnografiia na Kazanskoi nauchno-promyshlennoi vystavke* (Kazan, 1890), pp. 30–31.

[66] RGIA, f. 796, op. 172, d. 2686, ll. 3–5. The description itself is in Mari (ll. 6–11).

[67] *Sekta "Kugu Sorta" sredi cheremis Iaranskogo uezda* (Viatka, 1893), pp. 7, 16. I have considered this movement in greater detail in "Big Candles and 'Internal Conversion': The Mari Animist Reformation and Its Russian Appropriations," in *Of Religion and Empire: Missions, Conversion, and Tolerance in Tsarist Russia*, ed. Robert Geraci and Michael Khodarkovsky (Ithaca, 2001), pp. 144–72.

[68] Soviet authorities eventually condemned Kugu Sorta as a "reactionary" peasant group. See N. A. Martynov, "Perezhitki religioznoi sekty 'Kugu Sorta' i ee reaktsionnaia rol' v sotsialisticheskom stroitel'stve," *Trudy Mariiskogo Nauchnogo Issledovatel'skogo Instituta*, fasc. 1 (1940): 82–92.

Apostasy: Steps toward 1905

Nor was the church making much headway in bringing apostates back into the Orthodox fold. To be sure, the establishment of schools and the appointment of native clergy to Kräshen parishes were probably crucial to the prevention of further apostasy. But the years after 1870 also saw a factual (though gradual) capitulation by the state to those who had already renounced Orthodoxy, especially novokreshchenye Tatars. The government was unable to execute many of the court's verdicts, and in 1876 the Kazan Ecclesiastical Consistory formally requested to be relieved of the duty of keeping track of all those who had apostatized in 1811–63.[69] This led to a stalemate. Though the state was unable to compel the apostates' submission, it could still withhold the one thing they truly wanted: formal recognition as Muslims.

In a sense, apostates were the unfortunate victims of the fact that religious reform failed to take place in the 1860s–70s. As Aleksandr Polunov has suggested, the Great Reforms should logically have been accompanied by a liberalization of religious policy—the equalization of confessions and indeed even a certain separation of church and state.[70] No doubt, a few concessions to religious minorities were made in the reform period. Many of the administrative measures against Old Believers were terminated in the early 1860s, and from 1874 Old-Believer marriages were recognized as legal. As regards the many Estonian and Latvian converts to Orthodoxy in the 1840s, the government unofficially lifted the requirement that children of mixed marriages be raised in Orthodoxy in 1865, and it ended its persecution of Lutheran pastors who administered rites to these formally Orthodox subjects in 1874. This amounted, for all intents and purposes, to the factual recognition of those subjects once again as Lutherans, although they remained Orthodox in a purely technical sense.[71] As late as 1883, Alexander III (1881–94) approved a law repealing certain restrictions on the religious life of Old Believers and sectarians, who could now occupy public positions and obtain passports, conduct public religious services and build and repair houses of worship within certain parameters.[72]

Even under Alexander II, however, the state was also moving in the opposite direction. In response to the Polish insurrection of 1863, the state imposed repressive measures on the Catholic church and clergy. In 1875 the last remaining Uniates in the empire, in the Kholm region of the King-

---

[69] See especially RGIA, f. 796, op. 163, d. 1231; f. 796, op. 172, d. 2667, ll. 40b., 390b.; and RGIA, f. 821, op. 8, d. 788. Though not actually approved by the Synod, this proposal was essentially adopted.

[70] A. Iu. Polunov, *Pod vlast´iu Ober-Prokurora: Gosudarstvo i tserkov´ v epokhu Aleksandra III* (Moscow, 1996), pp. 96–97.

[71] Ibid., pp. 19–20; Toivo Raun, "Russification in Education and Religion," in *Russification in the Baltic Provinces and Finland, 1855–1914*, ed. Edward Thaden (Princeton, 1981), p. 324.

[72] Polunov, *Pod vlast´iu*, p. 103; Peter Waldron, "Religious Reform after 1905: Old Believers and the Orthodox Church," *Oxford Slavonic Papers* 20 (1987): 114; and idem, "Religious

dom of Poland, were bureaucratically "reunited" with Orthodoxy, much like their counterparts in the western provinces in 1839. This "reunification" was effectuated in a remarkably brutal fashion, so that even the Chief Procurator of the Synod admitted, "The population was forced to endure a great deal. Deprivation of freedom, exile, corporal punishment, and the disruption of economic life produced in them such bitterness that the people were prepared to accept any faith whatsoever, so long as their suffering would end."[73] Such trends only intensified under Alexander III. Though he approved the law of 1883, several groups were immediately or subsequently excluded from its provisions. Skoptsy were considered too "harmful" from the very beginning, and so-called "shtundists" (essentially Russian Evangelical Christians), who were rapidly establishing an alternative to Orthodoxy in the 1880s, were also classified as a "most harmful sect" in 1894, which placed them beyond the protections of the 1883 law.[74] In the mid-1890s Dukhobors, who had already been resettled to Transcaucasia under Nicholas I, also found themselves subject to increasing persecution, in conjunction with their resistance to military service.[75] In 1885 the state's earlier concessions to the converts from Lutheranism in the Baltic provinces were withdrawn: the state's ascription of religious confession once again trumped the declaration of the believers themselves. All but four of the Lutheran pastors in Livland province soon found themselves being prosecuted in the courts.[76] The situation for Jews in the empire also deteriorated substantially after 1881, as they became scapegoats for many of the regime's problems.[77]

Compromise with "foreign" faiths became more difficult in these years in part because the regime under Alexander III invoked Orthodoxy much more

Toleration in Late Imperial Russia," in *Civil Rights in Imperial Russia*, ed. Olga Crisp and Linda Edmondson (Oxford, 1989), p. 110.

[73] Quoted in A. Iu. Polunov, "Dukhovnoe vedomostvo i uniatskii vopros: 1881–1894," in P. A. *Zaionchkovskii, 1904–1983 gg.: Stat'i, publikatsii, i vospominaniia o nem*, ed. L. G. Zakharova (Moscow, 1998), p. 257. On the "reunification," see also Theodore R. Weeks, "The 'End' of the Uniate Church in Russia: The *Vozsoedinenie* of 1875," *Jahrbücher für Geschichte Osteuropas* 44, 1 (1996): 28–39.

[74] Laura Engelstein, *Castration and the Heavenly Kingdom: A Russian Folktale* (Ithaca, 1999), pp. 52–53; and Heather Jean Coleman, "The Most Dangerous Sect: Baptists in Tsarist and Soviet Russia, 1905–1929" (Ph.D. diss., University of Illinois, 1998), pp. 42–43.

[75] Polunov, *Pod vlast'iu*, p. 109; Nicholas Breyfogle, "Heretics and Colonizers: Religious Dissent and Russian Colonization of Transcaucasia, 1830–1890" (Ph.D. diss., University of Pennsylvania, 1998), pp. 190–92. The sectarians in Transcausia worried tsarist authorities also because they had been among the first Russians to become Baptists (Breyfogle, "Heretics and Colonizers," pp. 177–78).

[76] Raun, "Russification in Education and Religion," p. 325; Polunov, *Pod vlast'iu*, p. 113; M. E. Iachevskii, "Zapiska ob otpavshkikh iz pravoslaviia v inoverie" (1905), RGIA, Khranilishche pechatnykh zapisok, folder 2349, p. 57.

[77] Andreas Kappeler, *Russland als Vielvölkerreich: Entstehung, Geschichte, Zerfall* (Munich, 1992), pp. 222–24; Hans Rogger, *Jewish Policies and Right-Wing Politics in Imperial Russia* (Berkeley, 1986); and John D. Klier, "The Concept of 'Jewish Emancipation' in a Russian Context," in *Civil Rights*, pp. 136–39.

energetically as a legitimizing principle than it did under Alexander II. Richard Wortman has shown that these years saw a crucial shift in the monarchy's self-presentation from a motif of conquest by foreign rulers, transformed into Westernized Russian monarchs, toward an explicit identification with the Russian nation and people. A revitalized Orthodoxy became absolutely central to the elaboration of this new scenario of power. Alexander III looked back to early modern Muscovy for his model of an ethnically and religiously united people, ruled by an Orthodox Tsar. The government increasingly sought to project itself as a Russian master subjecting lesser peoples of the empire, and policies of Russification found new targets—most significantly, the Baltic region and eventually Finland.[78] Chief Procurator of the Holy Synod Konstantin Pobedonostsev (1880–1905), who had served as Alexander III's tutor, embraced a similar vision of Orthodoxy providing the indispensable unity of the Russian state, and thus broke decisively with the secular, bureaucratic orientation of his predecessor, Dmitrii Tolstoi. As a kind of conservative populist, Pobedonostsev sought to instill a deeper connection to Orthodoxy among the Russian people, particularly through the energetic promotion of parish schools and the extensive publication of religious literature.[79]

This Orthodox revival was not merely a government enterprise, however, for recent scholarship has demonstrated a range of ways in which Orthodox believers became more deeply engaged in spiritual matters, whether through monasticism, social work, or veneration of the charismatic Ioann of Kronstadt.[80] The attraction of a growing number of Orthodox Christians to Old Belief and "rationalistic" sects like the Baptists in this period can be understood as a reflection of a spiritual searching that some people, at least, could not satisfy within the official Orthodox fold.[81] In this context, it was even less likely that the state would make any compromise with the baptized-Tatar apostates of the Volga-Kama region.

The problem of apostasy, however, was itself changing and becoming more complex by the 1880s or so. Those who had renounced Orthodoxy now occupied a strange and nebulous legal space somewhere between Christianity and Islam. They could not hold any local office, since they were

---

[78] Richard S. Wortman, *Scenarios of Power: Myth and Ceremony in Russian Monarchy*, vol. 2: *From Alexander II to the Abdication of Nicholas II* (Princeton, 2000), pp. 196–97, 219, 235–56.

[79] Thomas C. Sorensen, "Pobedonostsev's Parish Schools: A Bastion against Secularism," in *Religious and Secular Forces in Late Tsarist Russia*, ed. Charles E. Timberlake (Seattle, 1992), pp. 168–84.

[80] Simon Dixon, "The Church's Social Role in St. Petersburg, 1880–1914," in *Church, Nation, and State in Russia and Ukraine*, ed. Geoffrey A. Hosking (New York, 1991), pp. 167–92; and Nadieszda Kizenko, *A Prodigal Saint: Father John of Kronstadt and the Russian People* (University Park, Penn., 2000).

[81] Polunov, *Pod vlast'iu*, p. 103; Coleman, "The Most Dangerous Sect," chap. 2.

unwilling to take the Christian oath that their religious status required. Children of apostates were not allowed to marry Muslims. Mullahs were not permitted to perform marriages and keep registers for apostates, since this would constitute their recognition as Muslims. Petitioners increasingly complained that they could not conclude a legal marriage and that their children were therefore illegitimate. They were excluded from inheritance and could not prove their age and social status, which was especially problematic with respect to the military draft.[82] This strange state of affairs rendered administration difficult and confusing. The Kazan governor explained that "in light of the confusion of record keeping regarding Tatar apostates from Orthodoxy to Mohammedanism . . . the collection of information on cases involving them is extremely difficult and gives rise to extended correspondence."[83] Local authorities were confused about whether they should make special lists for apostates and which names they should enter in the list: apostates had no Russian names (since the young among them had not been baptized), while the use of Tatar names would create the impression that they had been recognized as Muslims. Moreover, any attempt to collect information about apostates aroused their hope that their aspirations were finally about to be fulfilled.[84] Thus authorities had to perform a tortuous balancing act in creating some kind of administrative order for apostates that would not produce the impression that they were now formally Muslims. Such a situation was hardly consonant with efficient governance.

Even more problematic was the fact that the supplicants in petitions were increasingly the children and grandchildren of apostates—that is, people who had never been baptized and who therefore "belonged" to the Orthodox church only because the state regarded Orthodox status as hereditary and unalterable.[85] In their petitions they accordingly emphasized that they themselves were not apostates and should not be treated as such. They recounted that "these so-called apostates are nothing other than the children and in general the descendants of Muslim Tatars, and despite all the strenuous efforts of the Christian clergy [they] remained adamant and in the majority of cases converted again to Islam, after which their children were not baptized by Christian ritual."[86] Noting that several generations had passed since the apostasy, another group wrote: "Judging by this, what are we guilty of? If indeed our ancestors apostatized from the Orthodox faith to the Mohammedan, we were not yet even on the face of the earth, and no one

---

[82] RGIA, f. 821, op. 8, d. 788. At draft selection, apostates' ages were determined by appearance.

[83] RGIA, f. 821, op. 8. d. 790, l. 84. Religious figures registered similar complaints (RGIA, f. 796, op. 172, d. 2667, l. 125).

[84] RGIA, f. 821, op. 8, d. 788, l. 1150b.

[85] RGIA, f. 796, op. 172, d. 2667, ll. 20–23, 129–32.

[86] RGIA, f. 821, op. 8, d. 774, ll. 56–560b.

Apostates of the village Kibiak-Kozi who have gathered for prayer near their "secret mosque," ca. 1904. RGIA, f. 835, op. 4, d. 72, photograph #12.

taught us the Orthodox faith."[87] In short, a generational shift had occurred, whereby most of those still considered apostates in a legal sense had virtually no connection whatsoever with Orthodoxy. In most cases, however, the government rejected or simply ignored their petitions, remarking that they did not merit consideration. As a result, many of these Tatars filed multiple petitions to various government agencies, almost always to no avail.

Yet the persistence of these second- and third-generation apostates was not entirely without effect. Some officials cautiously began to consider the possibility of granting apostates Muslim status out of concern for administrative efficiency. In 1882 the governor of Kazan province, less out of a principled sense of religious tolerance than a desire "to be rid of" apostasy as a chronically recurring problem, held out the idea of recognizing those who had apostatized before a certain date as Muslims ("although not openly"), which would allow the police more effectively to keep the remaining baptized Tatars from visiting mosques and sending their children to Islamic schools.[88] In

[87] RGIA, f. 796, op. 172, d. 2667, l. 20b.

[88] See "Zapiska N. I. Il'minskogo po voprosu ob otpadeniiakh kreshchenykh tatar Kazanskoi gubernii v 1881 g.," *Pravoslavnyi sobesednik* 2 (1895): 262.

1895 a special Editorial Committee for a new criminal code, contending that the law's deprivation of apostates' rights created too much confusion to be included in the newest edition of the code, proposed the deletion of article 185 (punishment for apostasy), leaving the matter entirely to religious authorities.[89] Also in 1895 the governor of Samara province signaled his willingness to recognize one set of petitioners as Muslims, since they were not listed in parish registers and did not have even grandparents who had officially been considered Christian.[90] These arguments centered on the practical hardships engendered by an intransigent stance on the issue of apostasy, but they also implicitly recognized that there was a compelling social reality that resisted efforts to subordinate it to official dictates. Yet another batch of petitions in 1896, apparently filed on the occasion of the coronation of Nicholas II (1894–1917), created new pressures to reconsider this issue.[91]

Most ecclesiastical figures continued to maintain that even the grandchildren of apostates should not be separated from the church, adding that the recognition of some as Muslims would produce a massive exodus of non-Russians from Orthodoxy. As Chief Procurator K. P. Pobedonostsev wrote in 1898 on the basis of reports from local bishops, "Granting to all apostates the right to confess Mohammedanism will constitute a victory for the bitterest opponents of Christianity—Muslims—will strengthen their fanaticism and propaganda, and will serve as a seduction for all those who are weak and unsteady in the faith, and in any case threatens great harm for the Holy Church."[92] Though forced to admit that a given set of petitioners were "Mohammedans in the full sense of the word," Archbishop of Kazan Vladimir (Briantsev) argued in 1895 that granting Muslim status would constitute "a great loss for the Orthodox Church."[93] Likewise, prominent missionaries such as Il'minskii and E. A. Malov remained adamantly opposed to sanctioning apostates' return to Islam. Yet even among clerics there were doubts about the appropriateness of continued intransigence. In 1895 the bishop of Samara diocese acknowledged with respect to two families that because they had Muslim names and were not entered into Orthodox parish registers, their apostasy could be considered "completed" (*sovershivshimsia*), and their children should be released from Christianity.[94] Most remarkably, having received such opinions from local bishops, even Pobedonostsev was

---

[89] RGIA, f. 796, op. 172, d. 2667, ll. 130–31. The Committee's conclusion was based partly on the idea that it was inappropriate for secular criminal courts to sentence people to "church repentance."

[90] RGIA, f. 821, op. 8, d. 790, l. 1640b.

[91] RGIA,, f. 796, op. 172, d. 2667, l. 112. The Synod noted thirty-four petitions in the first three months of 1896, evidently filed with the knowledge of the upcoming coronation of Nicholas II (May 1896).

[92] RGIA, f. 821, op. 8, d. 788, ll. 1130b–14. Pobedonostsev was citing almost verbatim from a report by the archbishop of Kazan (RGIA, f. 796, op. 172, d. 2667, l. 1340b.).

[93] RGIA, f. 821, op. 8, d. 790, l. 570b.

[94] Ibid., ll. 330b–34. The DDDII nonetheless rejected the petition.

prepared to have the petitioners' requests satisfied, thereby signaling his willingness to compromise in certain particular cases, even as he remained resolutely opposed to more general reform on the apostasy issue.[95]

As a result of this growing willingness to compromise, petitioners from three villages actually received satisfaction in 1894–95 because of the extremely tenuous nature of their connections to the Orthodox Church.[96] Other petitions, in contrast, were rejected with the simple justification that "the petitioners are among the descendants of baptized Tatars who have apostatized from Orthodoxy."[97] As a commission established in Kazan considered ways to prevent further apostasy, all incoming petitions were shelved, and nothing changed until the Committee of Ministers took up the question of religious tolerance early in 1905.

In these years the state found itself slowly capitulating to other religious "recalcitrants" as well: the former Uniates and the Estonian and Latvian converts to Orthodoxy. Although official policy on the former Uniates had been quite harsh in the 1880s, secular authorities for the most part remained unenthusiastic about creating further disturbances through the application of repressive measures, and by the late 1880s even Pobedonostsev acknowledged that earlier policy had painted the church into an extremely uncomfortable corner. Unable to retreat by reinstating the Uniate church, he also sensed the futility of continuing repressive policies. But even as Pobedonostsev fretted about the fact that any concession would be construed as a major victory for Orthodoxy's opponents, the civil administration became more inclined to seek some kind of compromise. As in the Volga-Kama region, a whole mass of petitions from former Uniates appeared in 1894–95, apparently in conjunction with Nicholas II's upcoming coronation. These petitions made claims similar to those of baptized-Tatar apostates, and they, too, were rejected with the explanation that the petitioners or their parents had been baptized into Orthodoxy.[98] Even so, the state did make a compromise in 1898, when the second generation of those raised in Catholicism were allowed to transfer to that confession officially.[99] Representing a constant source of irritation for state authorities and a clear

---

[95] Ibid., ll. 59, 94, 168.

[96] RGIA, f. 821, op. 8, d. 788, l. 1130b.; RGIA, f. 821, op. 8, d. 790, ll. 37–59, 85–94, 163–68. The villages were Novaia Kadeeva (Chistopol district), Risovaia Poliana (Spassk district), and Novaia Mansurkina (Buguruslan district, Samara province). Some other petitions also found satisfaction in 1896 and 1898, but only in the complete absence of evidence of connections to the Orthodox church. In the three villages mentioned above, the petitioners were identified explicitly as descendants of apostates and were thus not legally entitled to satisfaction.

[97] RGIA, f. 821, op. 8, d. 794; and RGIA, f. 821, op. 8, d. 795. Eighty-three new petitions were filed in 1895–98 alone.

[98] Polunov, "Dukhovnoe vedomstvo," pp. 261–63.

[99] Iachevskii, "Zapiska," p. 41.

indication of the limits of bureaucratic confessional ascription, these three groups of "recalcitrants" and "apostates"—baptized Tatars, Baltic peasants, and former Uniates—gave the authorities a strong incentive to revise the prevailing policy on Orthodox status.

1905 and "Freedom of Conscience"

Impetus for religious reform grew substantially the few years prior to the revolution of 1905. To a degree, the regime was compelled to adopt a reformist policy in response to liberal and revolutionary opposition, especially after the assassination of Minister of Internal Affairs V. K. Pleve in 1904. But Rafael Ganelin has argued that there was in the government a substantial "reformist idea" whose development over the course of the revolution did not depend entirely on revolutionary pressure.[100] As early as February 1903 the Emperor promised "to strengthen the steadfast observance by the authorities concerned with religious affairs of the guarantees of religious toleration contained in the fundamental laws of the Russian Empire." A decree of December 1904, raising a number of issues that were to be considered for reform, called on the government to review statutes on the rights of religious minorities and "to take now in the administrative order appropriate measures for the elimination of all constraints on religious life not directly established by law."[101] The government found itself considering these issues in the early months of 1905, just as the revolution was beginning to unfold.

With its jurisdiction over "foreign faiths," the DDDII took up the problem of the "recalcitrants"—the former Uniates, Baltic converts, and baptized Tatars. The Department's acting director, M. E. Iachevskii, assembled a detailed historical survey in which he documented the inability of state and church to break the resistance of the three groups. Apparently none of the conversions had been based on spiritual convictions, Iachevskii asserted, and therefore "the phenomenon of apostasy from the supreme church . . . depends directly on those abnormal circumstances in which Orthodoxy has been accepted by non-Orthodox people in Russia." Moreover, it was intolerable that many of these subjects were unable to visit temples and consult with their clergy and that the Baltic converts "little by

---

[100] R. Sh. Ganelin, *Rossiiskoe samoderzhavie v 1905 godu: Reformy i revoliutsiia* (St. Petersburg, 1991); and idem, "Krizis samoderzhavnogo stroia i poiski vykhoda iz nego v 1905–1907 gg.," in *1905 god: Nachalo revoliutsionnykh potriasnenii v Rossii XX veka*, ed. P. V. Volobuev (Moscow, 1996), pp. 142–55.

[101] *PSZ* III, vol. 23, no. 22581 (26 February 1903); and ibid., vol. 24, no. 25495 (12 December 1904). It should be emphasized that the question of religious toleration was only one of the issues raised by the decree of 1904, and far from the most significant.

little are losing their religious feeling and becoming atheists." Iachevskii countered the arguments that his reform would represent a loss for the church, arguing that the church gained "no advantages whatsoever from the artificial ascription to itself of these zealots of other confessions." Nor would the reform constitute a blow to "national pride," since the Uniates had long inclined toward the Poles, and there was no real hope of making "Great Russians" out of Tatars. Finally, the reform would not set a bad example for others, as many feared, since "recalcitrants" (approximately 200,000 people) represented only about 1 / 400 of the empire's population. On the contrary, Iachevskii declared that the reform would represent a great statement of religious toleration, "each deviation from which so greatly agitates the conscience of Russian society." Regarding baptized Tatars specifically, Iachevskii concluded, the numerous petitions that were still being processed, "in conjunction with the complete alienation of the petitioners from contact with the Orthodox church and with everything Russian, can only be recognized as clear proof of the hopelessness of all attempts to return these people to the bosom of the Orthodox church." In general, Iachevskii saw the "recalcitrants" and the state as divided by an impenetrable wall: "on one side stands the government in all its previous impotence, and on the other [stand] the apostates, in all their desperation." The only real solution to this "chronic ailment" was to offer each person the right to choose his or her own faith.[102]

The apostates' cause was aided by the lobbying of Muslims, who articulated a series of demands to the Committee of Ministers, which was then considering the issues raised by the decree of December 1904. "Among the members of our beloved fatherland," the Muslims wrote, were the "unfortunate" baptized Tatars: "These people, Muslims in spirit, but Christians by registration, appear as something pitiful in the extreme, something that calls forth sorrow. As they are our kinsmen by ethnicity [*po plemeni nashi sorodochi*], we naturally cannot look upon them with indifference." The Muslims therefore requested that these "Christians by registration" be allowed "to confess Islam openly and without fear, with the right of their registration with the Muslim community."[103] The Committee was inclined to regard the empire's Muslims favorably. It concluded, contrary to the arguments of many missionaries and some officials about Muslims' "fanaticism" and hostility to Russian civilization, that the empire's Muslims had always fulfilled their duty to the state, had never presented any political challenges, and had never proselytized among Russians. "Moreover, despite some remaining differences in external and internal way of life, this population has become intimate with Russia [*srodnilos´ s Rossieiu*] and has become com-

---

[102] Iachevskii, "Zapiska," citations from pp. 8, 10–11, 13–15, 60.

[103] "Dokladnaia zapiska upolnomochennyh ot Kazanskogo musul´manskogo obshchestva, Predsedateliu Komiteta Ministrov," RGIA, Khranilishche pechatnykh zapisok, folder 2349, p. 7.

pletely friendly with her. These historically constituted relations should be valued, and one should avoid ruining them."[104]

The leading figure in the Committee at this time was Sergei Witte, who sought to speed the erosion of social and religious distinctions in Russian society for the purposes of establishing more direct contact between the state and its citizens.[105] Under his tutelage, the Committee was clearly receptive to the idea of significant religious reform. Its members found particularly disturbing the fact, underscored by petitioners themselves, that "these recalcitrants and apostates remain entirely without religion." Unable to attend mosques legally or to receive religious rites from Islamic clergy, and thoroughly alienated from Orthodox religious institutions, apostates had no opportunity to develop their religious lives or to sanctify (or even legalize) their marriages and the births of their children.[106] The Committee lamented "the moral sufferings experienced by people who remain without any spiritual consolation in the difficult moments of life," and it acknowledged that particular attention should be directed toward baptized Tatars, since "those unfortunate people lead a very miserable life, located between two confessions."[107] Apostates' lack of access to religion, particularly in a time of revolutionary turmoil, was intolerable, as well as dangerous for simply political reasons: "There can scarcely be a less desirable element in a state than subjects without religion, that principal foundation of morality; such people can all the more easily become fertile soil for the birth of sedition and lawlessness of every kind." The Committee's deliberations were simplified by the fact that the church's representative at the relevant sessions, Metropolitan Antonii of St. Petersburg and Ladoga concluded that the church itself, "always ailing on account of the apostates," did not desire their forcible restraint. Noting that "any force is alien to the very nature of the Church of Christ," Antonii concluded that "from the standpoint of the Orthodox church, there can be no obstacles to the abolition of the law that prohibits apostasy from Orthodoxy, as long as that abolition is dictated by concerns of the state's benefit and fairness." Even so, the Committee made clear that its actions were by no means intended to compromise the predominant position of the Orthodox faith in the Russian Empire. The Sovereign would still have to be an Orthodox Christian, and the church retained

[104] "Osobyi zhurnal Komiteta Ministrov 22 fevralia i 1 marta 1905 o poriadke vypolneniia punkta 6 Imennogo Vysochaishego ukaza 12 dekabria 1904 po voprosam, kasaiushchimsia inoslavnykh i inovernykh ispovedanii," RGIA, Khranilishche pechatnykh zapisok, folder 2349, p. 22.

[105] This is a major theme for Steinwedel, "Invisible Threads of Empire" (see esp. pp. 267–72).

[106] The deliberations of the Committee of Ministers on these questions in the winter of 1905 are reproduced in N. P. Solov'ev, *Polnyi krug dukhovnykh zakonov* (Moscow, 1907) (citation is from p. 12).

[107] "Postupivshee k Ministru Zemledeliia i Gosudarstvennykh Imushchestv zaiavlenie magometan," RGIA, Khranilishche pechatnykh zapisok, folder 2349, p. 4.

its monopoly on proselytism and would continue to receive state funds.[108] The issue was not *whether* the Orthodox church would remain privileged in the new order, but to what extent.

The result of these discussions was a decree of 17 April 1905 that significantly altered the place of Orthodoxy in state and society. Transfer from one Christian faith to another was now fully legalized, sects like the Russian Baptists received at least implicit recognition, and the Old Belief even gained something close to the status of a recognized non-Orthodox Christian faith.[109] Furthermore, in June 1905 many people who had been convicted and punished for "religious crimes" had their sentences reduced or eliminated entirely, thereby providing even the adherents of criminalized sects with some relief.[110] True, the law of 1905 continued to criminalize adherence to certain "barbarous dogmas," and it did not reconstitute the Uniate Church, thus leaving former Uniates with a choice merely between Orthodoxy and Catholicism.[111] Moreover, the state upheld the prohibition on non-Orthodox proselytism and therefore continued to criminalize "seduction" (*sovrashchenie*).[112] Still, the law established the fundamental principle that those born or baptized into Orthodoxy could leave that faith for another Christian confession.

The situation was considerably more complex as regards non-Christian confessions. In its deliberations the Committee of Ministers had insisted that a law explicitly permitting Orthodox Christians to accept non-Christian faiths "would not conform with the deep recognition of the truth [*istinnost´*] of the high principles at the base of the faith of Christ and is hardly necessary in light of the undoubtedly exceptional nature of such cases." Even while acknowledging that a convert to Islam or Judaism should not endure "repressive" measures, the Committee insisted that unfavorable civil disabilities remain in place, in order to reflect "the nonrecognition by the state that such a transfer has occurred." At the same time, the Committee felt compelled to make an explicit exception for baptized-Tatar apostates and a

---

[108] Solov´ev, *Polnyi krug dukhovnykh zakonov*, pp. 11–13.

[109] *PSZ* III, no. 26126 (17 April 1905); Coleman, "The Most Dangerous Sect," p. 16; M. A. Reisner, *Gosudarstvo i veruiushchaia lichnost´* (St. Petersburg, 1905), p. 420; and V. N. Shiriaev, *Religioznye prestupleniia: Istoriko-dogmaticheskie ocherki* (Yaroslavl, 1909), p. 333.

[110] *PSZ* III, no. 26480 (25 June 1905). Skoptsy could thus petition to leave Siberian exile, provided they had served nine years of their terms and could demonstrate a record of good behavior. See Engelstein, *Castration and the Heavenly Kingdom*, p. 128.

[111] The criminal code that went into effect in 1906 upheld this criminalization. See S. V. Poznyshev, *Religioznye prestupleniia s tochki zreniia religioznoi svobody: K reforme nashego zakonodatel´stva o religioznykh prestupleniiakh* (Moscow, 1906), p. 286. On Uniates, see Theodore R. Weeks, *Nation and State in Late Imperial Russia: Nationalism and Russification on the Western Frontier, 1863–1914* (DeKalb, 1996), pp. 175–76.

[112] Diliara Usmanova, *Musul´manskaia fraktsiia i problemy "svoboda sovesti" v Gosudarstvennoi Dume Rossii, 1906–1917* (Kazan, 1999), pp. 88–89, 93; Poznyshev, *Religioznye prestupleniia*, pp. 258–59, 265–66; and Shiriaev, *Religioznye prestupleniia*, p. 374.

few other groups who "in reality" confessed non-Christian faiths.[113] Taking these important distinctions into account, the law of 17 April 1905 granted the right of exclusion from Orthodoxy to "those people who are registered as Orthodox, but who in reality confess that non-Christian faith to which they themselves or their ancestors belonged before their adherence to Orthodoxy."[114]

Thus the law retained the notion of religious confession as a hereditary trait, since it allowed one to return only to one's ancestral religion. The MVD subsequently directed local governors to ascertain in each case "that the petitioner or his ancestors truly did belong to that non-Christian faith" that he or she now wished to join.[115] Even more problematic, however, was the fact that the law gave no indication as to how those wishing to leave the Orthodox fold were to prove that they "in reality" confessed a non-Christian faith. When the MVD attempted to clarify the procedure, it introduced an important temporal element that was absent in the original law: to receive satisfaction, one had to have clearly confessed the non-Christian religion *prior to the appearance of the law*. As the MVD circular stated, if there was any confusion in establishing the religious affiliation of the petitioner (or his ancestors) before conversion to Orthodoxy, then "administrative authorities limit themselves to confirming that the petitioner truly did deviate from fulfilling the rituals of the Orthodox church (did not go to confession, take communion, etc.) *prior to the appearance of the Decree of 17 April 1905*."[116] At a minimum, then, clear evidence of "deviation"—the refusal to fulfill "Christian obligations"—was an essential precondition for the legalization of the transfer. There was, of course, a certain irony in all this: those who had *violated* the law before 1905 by ignoring their "Christian obligations" were now rewarded, whereas those who had fulfilled those obligations, even when it went against their convictions, could expect difficulty in obtaining release. In effect, the MVD clarified what was perhaps only implicit in the wording of the actual law: the state was willing to recognize those cases of apostasy that had *already* occurred, but by no means to recognize *new* cases.

Although fairly straightforward on the issue of conversions *within* Christianity, the new law erected a clear barrier between Christianity and non-Christianity. In principle, the October Manifesto, issued later in 1905, should have erased this barrier, since Nicholas II now instructed his

---

[113] Solov'ev, *Polnyi krug dukhovnykh zakonov*, pp. 11–14.

[114] *PSZ* III, no. 26126 (17 April 1905), section I, article 3. A later circular interpreted this provision to include cases of proposed conversion from non-Orthodox Christian faiths to non-Christian religions, provided that analogous circumstances pertained (DDDII circular no. 3192 [25 June 1906] in TsGIARB, f. I-9, op. 1, d. 714, ll. 3–30b.).

[115] RGIA, f. 821, op. 8, d. 795, l. 1020b.

[116] DDDII circular (no. 4628, 18 August 1905), in RGIA, f. 821, op. 8, d. 795, ll. 102–103 (emphasis added).

Table 4
Numbers Rejecting Orthodoxy for Other Faiths (17 April 1905 to 1 January 1909)

Faith	No.
Buddism	3,468
Christianity	
Armeno-Gregorian	407
Evangelical and Lutheran	14,527
Orthodox Old Believers	4,240
Orthodox sectarians	3,093
Roman Catholic	232,705
Islam	49,759
Judaism	409
Paganism	150
Total	308,758

Source: "Svedeniia o chisle lits, otpavshikh za vremia s 17 aprelia 1905 g. po 1 ianvaria 1909 g. ot gospodstvuiushchei very," RGIA, Khranilishche pechatnykh zapisok, folder 2349. Numbers include both sexes.

government "to grant to the population the firm foundations of civil freedoms on the bases of the true inviolability of person, freedom of conscience, word, association, and union."[117] Despite this reference to "freedom of conscience," in deciding subsequent cases of religious affiliation, local officials continued to refer to the provisions outlined in the April law and its supplement.

The DDDII had correctly predicted that former Uniates, Baltic peasants, and baptized Tatars were the groups most likely to transfer to other faiths in the new order (see Table 4).[118] Muslims in Kazan paid for the distribution of copies of relevant sections of the new law and preprinted petitions in which apostates needed only to fill in their names and villages.[119] It appears that most baptized Tatars who wished to be registered as Muslims had little difficulty receiving satisfaction. Although there were some reports of local Orthodox authorities attempting to hinder this transfer, baptized Tatars had been identified explicitly as one of the "exceptions" to which the law was meant to apply. To my knowledge, their petitions were rejected very

[117] *PSZ* III, no. 26803 (17 October 1905).
[118] Iachevskii, "Zapiska," p. 14.
[119] S. Bagin, *O propagande Islama putem pechati* (Kazan, 1909), p. 9. Numerous copies of these petitions are in several files in NART, f. 2, op. 2, dd. 12720, 12721, 12722, 12723, 12724, 12732, 12733, and 12736. Even handwritten petitions were virtually identical in content and form to the printed ones.

rarely.[120] Local Orthodox bishops, though of course dismayed to witness such a mass rejection of Orthodoxy, for the most part accepted the change with relative equanimity. In his survey report for 1906, for example, the bishop of Ufa noted that the petitioning "does not represent anything remarkable. Almost all the received petitions concerning transfer to Mohammedanism received satisfaction," since each individual inquiry revealed that "all the petitioners were merely de jure included in the lists of Orthodox parishioners; factually they had all long been true adherents of Mohammedanism." Indeed, the bishop went so far as to claim that there had so far been no transfers among those baptized Tatars "who prior to the publication of the manifesto of 17 April remained in the bosom of the Orthodox church" (i.e., those who had been willing adherents of Orthodoxy).[121] The archbishop of Kazan likewise noted in 1906 that the majority of the "numerous petitions" were receiving satisfaction "in accordance with the new statutes."[122] In the first few years after 1905, most of those who sought to transfer did so, leaving behind those who were more committed to Orthodoxy or who were at least less certain about their desire to abandon it.

The new order appears also to have simplified conversion from paganism to Islam, which, though never actually prohibited, had often been hindered by the government. Noting that the law itself made no mention of the issue, but that the October Manifesto had granted "freedom of religious confession and conscience," the DDDII concluded in 1907 that "the silence of the law alone on the right of pagans to transfer from paganism to Mohamedanism cannot serve as a basis for the negation of that right." Such transfer was therefore to be permitted, as was conversion in the opposite direction.[123]

---

[120] On accusations of the clergy's alleged hindrance to conversion, which the governor of Ufa concluded were unfounded, see TsGIARB, f. I-9, op. 1, d. 831, ll. 21–220b. Orthodox authorities could postpone the approval of petitions by insisting on a period of admonition, but their opinion on whether a given petitioner should receive satisfaction had no legal significance. In a few cases, communities claiming that their ancestors had been baptized in the aftermath of the conquest of Kazan (1552) were denied permission to become Muslims, but this was principally because their "belonging" (*prinadlezhnost'*) to Islam was so far in the past (RGIA, f. 821, op. 8, d. 796, ll. 88, 95–97).

[121] RGIA, f. 796 op. 442, d. 2124, l. 20. For more on the implementation of the new order in Ufa province, see Steinwedel, "Invisible Threads of Empire," pp. 281–98.

[122] RGIA, f. 796, op. 442, d. 2148, l. 17. The numbers of apostates in the years 1905–9 were by far the highest in Kazan province (38,958) and notably lower in other provinces: Simbirsk (4,355), Ufa (4,247), Penza (866), Orenburg (513), and Viatka (427). See "Svedeniia o chisle lits." The conflict was somewhat more acrimonious and even violent in the west. See Robert Blobaum, "Toleration and Ethno-Religious Strife: The Struggle between Catholics and Orthodox Christians in the Chelm Region of Russian Poland, 1904–1906," *The Polish Review* 35 (1990): 111–24.

[123] TsGIARB f. I-9, op. 1, d. 714, l. 13 (DDDII circular no. 6068, 12 November 1907). The MVD had argued this position to the Holy Synod as early as June 1906 (RGIA, f. 821, op. 10, d. 510, ll. 2–3).

Less fortunate were baptized non-Russians, principally Maris, who sought official recognition as pagans. In almost all cases, their requests were summarily rejected, usually with the claim that the petitioners had fulfilled their "Christian obligations" until 1905 and therefore could not be construed as having confessed paganism "in reality" before then. The prevailing assumption among most officials was that the new laws simply did not apply to paganism. Thus religious authorities in one case argued for the rejection of a petition by noting that "those desiring to transfer from Orthodoxy to paganism have no legal right to such a transfer," to which the investigating police official added, "because the law on religious toleration does not give the right of return to pagan beliefs."[124] In fact, the law in no way singled out paganism in this way, but a return to "idolatry" was apparently more than many officials could tolerate. I have encountered only one concrete case in which permission to return to paganism was granted, in this case to two households, because almost all of their relatives were formally pagan.[125]

The failure of would-be pagans was not for lack of trying. Many of them quite compellingly invoked the October Manifesto in their requests. One baptized Mari woman pointed to the Manifesto and interpreted it to mean that "whichever faith one wishes to confess, no one can hinder him. And thus I make the open, unforced declaration to abandon new-convert status and to confess 'paganism,' which I consider to be correct."[126] Another group of petitioners, requesting the right to perform sacrifices in accordance with their "Old-Testament faith of Abraham" (*po vetkhozavetnoi Avraamskoi vere*), also referred to the Manifesto with the claim that it gave freedom of conscience to "all the people of the Russian empire," so that "each person can have the faith that he desires."[127] Another group indicated that upon learning of the Manifesto's granting of "freedom of conscience and religion, we gave the priest our holy icons and refused in the presence of the clergy and authorities to fulfill Christian rituals, to baptize our children and to bury our dead, since our ancient religion of Abraham is very dear to us."[128] These petitions reflect the profound resonance that the Manifesto had in the countryside, but their rejection demonstrates that in the minds of most officials, the October Manifesto by no means superceded the more specific pronouncements of the April law and follow-up rulings.

Similarly unsuccessful were nominally Orthodox Chuvash, Maris, and Udmurts who sought to transfer to Islam. Whereas Muslim "ancestry" was

---

[124] TsGIARB, f. I-9, op. 1, d. 967, ll. 6–7.

[125] GAKO, f. 582, op. 148, d. 91., ll. 16–160b. See also N. S. Popov, "K voprosu o religioznom dvizhenii v Mariiskom krae vo vtoroi polovine XIX–nachale XX veka," *Istoriografiia i istochnikovedenie po arkheologii i etnografii Mariskogo kraia*, Arkheologiia i etnografiia Mariiskogo kraia, fasc. 7 (1984), p. 190.

[126] GAKO, f. 582, op. 150, d. 60, l. 4. Her request was nonetheless rejected.

[127] GAKO, f. 582, op. 148, d. 187, l. 4.

[128] GAKO, f. 582, op. 150, d. 73, l. 30.

assumed in the case of baptized Tatars, other baptized peoples usually found it impossible to demonstrate that either they or their ancestors had ever been Muslims, the basic condition for transfer. The protests of some of these unsuccessful petitioners are quite compelling and demonstrate once again the broad appeal of ideas of "freedom of conscience." In 1906, for example, a baptized Chuvash from Ufa province, Nikolai Tikhonov,[129] complained that his earlier petition to the Ufa governor requesting Muslim status had been rejected and that, instead of consulting him, investigators had interviewed "only my mother and brothers, who wish to remain in the Orthodox faith." They had testified that Tikhonov had never been a Muslim, "which is quite understandable, for in the earlier order all Orthodox Christians, even a sham Orthodox Christian like me, were prohibited from confessing the Mohammedan religion." Underscoring his "spiritual inclination" toward Islam and the imperial acts granting freedom of faith and conscience, Tikhonov remarked, "If I assert that I am not an Orthodox Christian, can witnesses' testimony really alter the essence of the matter or force me to change my conviction? This is a matter that depends exclusively on a person's freedom of conscience, that is on that freedom that was proclaimed from the heights of the Throne, and not on the results of a police inquiry."[130] The Ufa governor asserted, however, that Tikhonov was the son of religious Orthodox parents, that there were neither Muslims nor even pagans among his father's kin, and that his ancestors had resettled to the region from Kazan province more than a century earlier as Orthodox Christians. Since neither Tikhonov nor his parents had ever belonged to Islam, his petition was rejected.[131] Another group of Chuvash petitioners in Ufa province expressed similar disappointment at the failure of their request:

> Such a rejection of our genuine desire [to be Muslims] will of course not change the situation and in essence represents coercion of us to accept the Orthodox faith and therefore contradicts the law on freedom of conscience and toleration in religious affairs. Under the previous order, when a sense of faith and devotion were instilled in the disobedient with the lash, prison, exile, and so on, we could not request recognition as Muslims, as long as other people considered us to be Orthodox.[132]

But whatever the strength of their arguments and the ostensible power in the words of the October Manifesto, the experience of these supplicants demonstrates that there were distinct limits to "freedom of conscience" even after 1905.

---

[129] Nikolai Tikhonov was his name "in Russian." He referred to himself otherwise as Mukhamet´din (his Muslim first name is not listed).

[130] RGIA, f. 821, op. 8, d. 796, ll. 86–86ob.

[131] Ibid., ll. 93–93ob.

[132] Ibid., l. 181ob.

Whatever the fate of these unfortunate petitioners, on the whole 1905 represented a crucial break in the religious life of the Russian empire. Orthodoxy retained certain advantages over other faiths but was now forced to compete much more openly with other confessions. For the first time, Muslims in the Volga-Ural region gained the opportunity to develop a native-language periodical press, and they began to organize politically in a series of Muslim congresses to express their support for a Muslim bloc in the State Duma. Many sectarians, too, organized congresses, new parishes, and religious publications, through which they were able to attract a growing number of adherents from among the Orthodox. Meanwhile, baptized non-Russians became more insistent about having priests from their own ethnicity.[133] Missionaries were forced to regroup and to reconsider their methods, which became the principal focus of missionary congresses, including one in Kazan in 1910. Those who attended the Kazan congress became much more introspective, focusing on the need to restructure Orthodox parish life and to increase Russians' own religiosity as much as on specifically missionary tasks. Some even looked to Muslims as a model for Orthodoxy's own spiritual improvement.[134] But even as the church faced a setback in 1905, the new situation was not without its positive side. If the "recalcitrants" had finally been liberated from the Orthodox church, then the converse was also true. And as Orthodox authorities in several diocese became more willing to support the ordination of non-Russian priests, the level of religiosity in many communities grew, especially among Kräshens.[135] There was therefore both a challenge and an opportunity for the people and government of the Russian empire—Russians and non-Russians, Orthodox Christians and others—to construct a new religious order after 1905.

[133] On these developments, see Usmanova, *Musul'manskaia fraktsiia*, pp. 31–80; Coleman, "The Most Dangerous Sect," pp. 118–62; Werth, "*Inorodtsy* on *Obrusenie*," pp. 119–34; and Roy Robson, *Old Believers in Modern Russia* (DeKalb, 1995).

[134] On the Kazan congress, see Geraci, "Window on the East," pp. 421–28; *Missionerskii s˝ezd v gorode Kazani, 13–26 iiunia 1910 g.* (Kazan, 1910); and Frank McCarthy, "The Kazan´ Missionary Congress," *Cahiers du monde russe et soviétique* 14, 1 (1973): 308–32.

[135] For more on these developments, see my article, "From 'Pagan' Muslims to 'Baptized' Communists: Religious Conversion and Ethnic Particularity in Russia's Eastern Provinces," *Comparative Studies in Society and History* 42, 3 (2000): 497–523.

Conclusion

The confessional politics addressed in this book grew out of state attempts to regulate religious affiliation and to promote religious change in the culturally diverse Volga-Kama region. Beginning under Catherine II, but principally under Alexander I, the imperial state constructed a system of administration for "foreign faiths" that rendered them inferior to Orthodoxy, accessible to state authority and intervention, but still relatively autonomous within their own communities. In the case of the Volga-Kama region, this system was supplemented with attempts to promote baptism (with varying degrees of force) and to enforce religious discipline among novokreshchenye after conversion. The state thus combined recognition of confessional diversity with a conscious attempt to transform religious identities in certain cases. As a result, it was compelled to find a balance between promoting Orthodoxy and enforcing religious discipline, on one hand, and respecting its own provisions on religious toleration, on the other.

Balancing these different imperatives proved difficult in light of non-Russians' reluctance to embrace Orthodoxy and to abandon animist practices and their aspirations for Muslim status. Unwilling to acknowledge baptism as the exclusive foundation of their religious affiliation, many novokreshchenye sought to maintain connections with their non-Christian faiths. Often they submitted petitions of protest, in almost all cases appealing over the heads of local officials to more highly placed figures. They also challenged the authority of missionaries and local officials in more subtle ways. In almost all cases, these challenges were rooted in circumstances that cast doubt on what missionaries and their allies had to say. Detached from their original contexts and given out to novokreshchenye (usually for a fee), various documents from within the tsarist bureaucracy served as excellent grounds for rumors that undercut official policy. Nicholas I's own directive not to persecute novokreshchenye for their "ignorance" could easily be turned against all attempts to induce them to abandon animist practices. The state's general, if limited, toleration of those remaining in Islam or paganism also divested the missions of legitimacy, for attempts to promote Orthodoxy and discipline novokreshchenye appeared to contradict this more tolerant practice. Even explicit efforts by central officials to invest local missions with greater authority—such as Nicholas's provision of two elaborate caftans to the missionary Pokrovskii in Viatka diocese—could later be reinterpreted as signs of the Emperor's patronage of animism. In some cases, circumstances made it easy for novokreshchenye to conclude that their religious aspirations were truly compatible with the law and the Sovereign's wishes. Non-Russians' actions appear to have been motivated not by a desire to oppose tsarist and church authority as such but rather by the recognition that this authority was fragmented in opportune ways.[1] What is striking is the way in which local inhabitants were able to reinterpret virtually *any* document, event, or circumstance in accord with their desire to maintain connections with the "old faith."

Still, the fact that non-Russian protest often took forms similar to those adopted by Russians suggests that the Volga-Kama peoples had imbibed the political culture of Russia to a substantial degree.[2] Similarly, the fact that many baptized Tatars found it insufficient to confess Islam secretly and therefore sought official Muslim status suggests that they had largely accepted the state-controlled system of confessional classification. Here the distinction between Islam and paganism is notable. Whereas the state fully recognized Islam by providing it with its own spiritual administration and creating a "clergy" out of the *ulema*, paganism was recognized only in the sense that the unbaptized were permitted to practice their faith openly. It was partly for this reason that those seeking to return (or even to convert) to Islam made use of petitions much more frequently than those whose allegiances were to animism: the more official and institutionalized nature of Islam in the empire required a more formal and officially sanctioned transfer of religious identity. Part of being Muslim was having one's vital statistics kept by Islamic clerics, and this would occur only if one enjoyed official Muslim status. Because paganism had no such institutional or clerical recognition, it was enough for most baptized Maris, Chuvash, and Udmurts merely to practice animism to the extent that circumstances allowed. With a few exceptions, it was really only in the unique context created by the religious reform of 1905 that some baptized non-Russians (primarily Maris)

---

[1] This distinction is made in another context by Lauren Benton, "Colonial Law and Cultural Difference: Jurisdictional Politics and the Formation of the Colonial State," *Comparative Studies in Society and History* 41, 3 (1999): 576.

[2] For example, the work of David Moon suggests that much of what we have encountered—rumors, often inspired by local scribes or other literate "brokers"; petitions; "misunderstanding" of legislation and decrees—was characteristic of Russian serfs' interactions with officialdom as well. See David Moon, *Russian Peasants and Tsarist Legislation on the Eve of Reform: Interaction between Peasants and Officialdom, 1825–1855* (London, 1992).

actually petitioned for official recognition as pagans. The terms and forms of non-Russians' resistance had thus been to a significant degree prefigured by state-imposed categories, administrative structures, and practices, thus lending credence to the proposition that "episodes of resistance themselves rarely mark pure forms of escape from domination; struggle is constantly being conditioned by the structures of social and political power."[3]

The spiritual disposition of different non-Russian groups in the nineteenth century depended also on the state's thoroughness in its earlier attempts at conversion. The very existence of officially non-Christian communities of a given ethnicity constituted a serious source of "seduction," as many missionaries themselves realized. The problem was most acute with regard to novokreshchenye Tatars, since they represented such a small portion of the larger Tatar-speaking community. But even in the case of Maris, of whom a majority had been formally baptized, a similar dynamic appeared. A fairly large segment of the Mari population (numbering over 100,000 by the beginning of the twentieth century) had managed to remain officially pagan by migrating eastward into Bashkiria in the eighteenth century. As we have seen, Maris in Viatka province, most of whom were baptized, maintained contact with these migrants and invited them to participate in important animist prayers. Settled in dense forests in Orenburg and Perm provinces, and largely free to practice animism as they wished, these eastern Maris remained more isolated from external influences and proved quite resistant to assimilation. They remained beacons of Mari particularity—that is, cultural resources for their baptized counterparts in Viatka and Kazan provinces, who were under much greater Orthodox influence.

Because eastern Maris had migrated almost exclusively from the so-called meadow side (the left bank) of the Volga, highland Maris by all accounts felt little or no sense of association with this eastern population. Given the almost complete absence of pagans (in the official sense) along the Volga's right bank and the deeper and earlier implication of the population there in processes of social and economic change, it is not surprising that highland Maris became among the most fervently Orthodox of the region's non-Russians by the second half of the nineteenth century. Similarly, there were few Chuvash, Udmurts, and especially Mordvins who had escaped baptism in the eighteenth century, which meant that there was only a handful of communities among these peoples that could sustain animism without hindrance. The historical record accordingly reveals less resistance on the part of Chuvash and Udmurts—and almost none on the part of Mordvins—to Orthodoxy in the nineteenth century. As in many respects, Kräshens constitute a special case. Some, clearly, saw Muslims as kinsmen who were

---

[3] Douglas Haynes and Gyan Prakash, "Introduction: The Entanglement of Power and Resistance," in *Contesting Power: Resistance and Everyday Social Relations in South Asia*, ed. Haynes and Prakash (Berkeley, 1991), p. 3.

upholding the true faith. Others apparently did not regard themselves as baptized Tatars but instead saw themselves as a distinct group. As such, they had no unbaptized counterparts who could maintain an "old faith" without Orthodox interference. Kräshens were therefore a more malleable group, and the promotion of Kräshen clergy and teachers helped to create among many of them a strong sense of attachment to Orthodoxy—so strong that communist authorities in the 1920s complained about Kräshens' deeply "clerical" and even "fanatical" Orthodox disposition.[4] It would appear that the comprehensiveness of the original conversions within a particular ethnic or linguistic community was a crucial factor in determining that group's subsequent trajectory.

Non-Russians' actions and behavior also helped shape the nature of tsarist rule, although in ways that are more difficult to specify. In the vast majority of cases petitioners received little or no satisfaction, but the tenacity of baptized Tatars in seeking Muslim status over many decades not only led finally to the satisfaction of these requests in 1905 but also contributed to a crucial revision of religious policy more generally in the same year. Together with equally tenacious former Uniates and Baltic converts to Orthodoxy, baptized Tatars demonstrated that there were distinct limits to religious ascription—that is, to the state's ability to assign religious status without regard to the wishes of the people in question. These protestors thus exposed the contradictions in policy between religious toleration and Orthodoxy's privileged status. In doing so, they also contributed to the elaboration of new notions of faith, which involved conviction and belief as much as external practice and bureaucratic ascription.

The confessional politics considered in this book demonstrate that religious affiliation was significant for governance and local life in different ways. Confessional categories represented important tools for the imperial state in its attempt to impose structure on a culturally diverse society whose internal social demarcations were relatively amorphous. The ability of many baptized animists to continue practicing animism, at least in a modified form, long after their baptism suggests that the boundaries of confessional categories were sufficiently flexible to accommodate informal or even illicit relationships and self-definitions, as Elise Kimerling Wirtschafter has suggested was the case for social identities in imperial Russia more generally.[5] The decades-long struggle of baptized Tatars, in contrast, reveals that the boundaries of these categories were malleable only to a point. It may be that the boundaries of these confessional categories were, if anything, more rigid than those of other social distinctions.

---

[4] Paul W. Werth, "From 'Pagan' Muslims to 'Baptized' Communists: Religious Conversion and Ethnic Particularity in Russia's Eastern Provinces," *Comparative Studies in Society and History* 42, 3 (2000): 497–523.

[5] Elise Kimerling Wirtschafter, *Social Identity in Imperial Russia* (DeKalb, 1997).

The state's manipulation of religious affiliation through the promotion of Orthodoxy also provided a way to subordinate non-Russians to administrative structures prevalent in the empire's central provinces (above all the Orthodox church itself). This was perhaps the principal achievement of the mass baptisms of the eighteenth century: combined with the creation of the Muslim Spiritual Assembly, these baptisms brought almost all the region's non-Russians under the control of state-sanctioned religious institutions. (Only those who were officially pagans remained outside this system.) The state's promotion of Orthodoxy also represented a potential means to assimilate non-Russians to the dominant culture of the empire's central Russian provinces. Yet here the picture becomes more complicated, for one may legitimately question whether the state's commitment to assimilation was actually clear and consistent. Categorized as inovertsy (non-Christians) before their conversion, baptized non-Russians remained novokreshchenye—that is, less than full-fledged Orthodox Christians—generations after their ancestors' baptism. The state's retention of this particularistic designation was to some extent consistent with converts' weak sense of attachment to Orthodoxy, but the retention of this term also segregated non-Russian converts from other Orthodox Christians and reified their position at the margins of Orthodoxy. And just as some non-Russians, particularly the highland Maris, began to confess Orthodoxy more consciously and enthusiastically in the mid-nineteenth century, non-Russians of all confessions in the region rhetorically became inorodtsy, whose Orthodox status might mitigate their difference from Russians but could never eliminate it entirely.[6] Despite significant transformations in their religious consciousness, therefore, baptized non-Russians remained only tenuously affixed to the Orthodox community.

Still, many missionaries and officials believed that Orthodox affiliation was crucial to non-Russians' effective and meaningful participation in the postemancipation order. The establishment of new forms of local self-government and the elimination of the authority of the nobility and the Ministry of State Domains over local peasant communities presupposed that rural inhabitants had imbibed (or would imbibe) a set of civic attitudes and norms often referred to as *grazhdanstvennost'* (civic-mindedness). Missionaries contended that Orthodoxy represented by far the most effective means for promoting these norms among the non-Russians of the Volga-Kama region. Along the same lines, N. I. Il'minskii argued effectively that the promotion of religious ties between non-Russians and Russian civilization, with significant concessions to native-language liturgy and indigenous personnel, would prove far more effective in the long run than efforts designed to promote linguistic Russification. Thus, even as state officials and publicists were adopting more secular standards for marking difference and defining community, religious distinctions did not lose their significance.

---

[6] It bears emphasizing, however, that these non-Russians never became inorodtsy in a strictly legal sense.

For non-Russians, religious confession offered primarily a way of constituting and maintaining community. Conversion (especially when imposed from without) accordingly raised serious dilemmas. For many, especially in the first part of the nineteenth century, to abandon non-Christian practices entirely would be to renounce their previous community—to cease being Mari, Chuvash, or Muslim—and "to become Russian" (which itself seems to have been understood largely in a religious sense). Given the strength of filial piety among most non-Russians, the misfortunes that they could expect from native spirits, and the scorn and derision that they would face from neighbors and friends, few were willing to take this step. Many baptized Tatars were particularly reluctant to accept their exclusion from a regional Islamic identity that was then being constructed by the *ulema*, and they therefore petitioned the government for official Muslim status. With time, however, some non-Russians came to see in Orthodoxy not just a threat to existing forms of community but a basis for creating new ones. The participants in the highland-Mari religious movement stand out in this regard, although with the development and spread of Il′minskii's methods, it became possible for many communities to embrace Orthodoxy—and to enjoy the benefits that it offered, such as literacy—without fear of losing their distinctiveness. On the whole, it would seem that Orthodoxy offered a realistic basis for forging a conscious and effective bond between baptized non-Russian communities and the imperial state, as long as both church and state were willing to make *some* concessions to local particularity.

In all these processes, however, non-Russians were by no means entirely unified. On the contrary, the redefinition of community along new confessional lines involved a good deal of conflict and confusion. Although we may offer broad sociological and anthropological explanations for both the processes and the outcomes of these developments, undoubtedly much had to do with the psychology of individuals, which remains too complex and poorly documented to permit more than speculation.

The experience of the peoples of the Volga-Kama region over the course of the nineteenth century was both similar to and different from that of other peoples in the empire. Conquered in the sixteenth century, substantially colonized by Russian peasants, incorporated into the administrative institutions and social structure of the central provinces, the region could hardly be considered a borderland or colony akin to the Kazakh steppe, Transcaucasia, or Central Asia. If the Volga-Kama peoples were ruled by an "imperial center," then the same was true for the Russians in the region (and elsewhere). Yet the eventual designation of the peoples there as inorodtsy (if only unofficially) and the application to them of at least some colonial outlooks and practices clearly differentiated the region from purely Russian provinces.

In many respects, the Volga-Kama region is perhaps best compared to the western region—the nine provinces immediately to the east of the Kingdom of Poland and Austrian Galicia. Much like Islam and the Tatar language, Catholicism and Polish culture represented a rival to Russian civilization that—according to worried tsarist officials—threatened to expand into neighboring territories and render hostile to Russia subjects who would otherwise have been amenable to the government's projects. In both cases, the Russian state had sought to extend or reinforce the control of Orthodoxy over the populations "in between" (Ukrainians, Belorussians, the Finnic peoples, and Chuvash) through mass conversion or bureaucratic confessional "reunification." Many baptized Tatars and "reunified" Uniates behaved in a similar fashion, petitioning for return to their previous faith and leaving Orthodoxy when the opportunity finally arose in 1905.

Of course, the comparison can only be taken so far. Poles and Catholicism surely represented a greater threat to the Russian empire, given that Polish aspirations for full political independence were quite strong. Muslims seem not to have aspired to more than cultural autonomy within the Russian empire, at least before the twentieth century. The western region was also larger and much more populous and had greater strategic significance for the empire's security. Finally, to the imperial state Ukrainians and Belorussians obviously represented something quite different from the Volga-Kama peoples: they were, many Russians believed, branches of a single Russian people, connected to "Great Russians" of the central provinces by Orthodoxy and their historical descent from Kievan Rus´. Maris, Chuvash, Udmurts, and Kräshens, in contrast, were related to Russians only in the sense that many officials presumed, especially by the 1860s, that these peoples would naturally be assimilated by Russians as long as no one interfered in this process. They were clearly held to be more backward than Ukrainians and Belorussians and could even fit into larger ideologies of colonialism in ways that the latter peoples could not.

Still, officials regarded a portion of the population in both regions as being slated for eventual fusion with the Great Russian people. And in both cases, some among the local population felt a strong attraction toward the alternative to Orthodoxy (Catholicism or Islam) or, toward the end of the nineteenth century, began the process of constructing their own alternative *within* Orthodoxy.[7] Finally, the Volga-Kama peoples *did* have a historical connection with Russians, if not through Kievan Rus´, then by their relatively early incorporation into the Muscovite state. While recognizing the specificity of all regions within the empire, we may nonetheless consider the Volga-Kama region similar to the western provinces in important respects. Cases need not be identical, after all, to be comparable.

[7] On the western provinces, see Theodore R. Weeks, *Nation and State in Late Imperial Russia: Nationalism and Russification on the Western Frontier, 1863–1914* (DeKalb, 1996); and A. I. Miller, *"Ukrainskii vopros" v politike vlastei i russkom obshchestvennom mnenii (vtoraia polovina XIX v.)* (St. Petersburg, 2000).

As for many people in the empire, the years after 1905 offered new opportunities and presented new challenges to Orthodox non-Russians. Although some returned to Islam or tried to return to paganism, as we have seen, others embraced their identity as Orthodox inorodtsy and construed their interests as extending across divisions separating different ethnicities.[8] After the February revolution in 1917, representatives of the region's baptized non-Russians established a Society of the Small Peoples of the Volga Region to promote their cause.[9] Its first congress met in May and made a series of unanimously accepted resolutions on religious questions. Delegates insisted on native-language liturgies and the creation of "pastoral inorodtsy courses" for the preparation of church servitors and declared that any non-Russian teacher or sexton who had served at least ten years and had demonstrated a high degree of religious activism could be ordained and assigned to a parish without examination. Moreover, they declared, "We inorodtsy, the original [korennye] inhabitants of the Great Russian land, must have our own national bishops [narodnye episkopy], able to teach the word of truth in the native language of their flocks." They also called for a new metropolitan of the Kazan region, who would act "as the manager of the activities of the national inorodtsy bishops not as a boss, but as a first among equals."[10] Thus in the dynamic context of 1917, Orthodoxy and a supraethnic sense of non-Russianness informed the project of the most active segments of these communities.

By the fall of 1917, however, centripetal forces were dividing this supraethnic community into its constituent ethnic groups. Like the "nationalization" of politics observable among Muslims,[11] the tendency over the

[8] On developments in the region after 1905, see Robert Paul Geraci, "Window on the East: Ethnography, Orthodoxy, and Russian Nationality in Kazan, 1870–1914" (Ph.D. diss., University of California, Berkeley, 1995); Charles Robert Steinwedel, "Invisible Threads of Empire: State, Religion, and Ethnicity in Tsarist Bashkiria, 1773–1917" (Ph.D. diss., Columbia University, 1999); Christian Noack, Muslimischer Nationalismus im Russischen Reich: Nationsbildung und Nationalbewegung bei Tataren und Baschkiren, 1861–1917 (Stuttgart, 2000); and Paul W. Werth, "Inorodtsy on Obrusenie: Religious Conversion, Indigenous Clergy, and the Politics of Assimilation in Late-Imperial Russia," Ab Imperio 2 (2000): 105–34.

[9] Ustav Obshchestva melkikh narodnostei Povolzh'ia (Kazan, 1917). The Society included Chuvash, Maris, Udmurts, Mordvins, Komi, Komi-Permiaks, Kräshens, Mishars, Nagaibeks, and Kalmyks. The designation "small peoples" (melkie narodnosti) was clearly designed to replace the term "inorodtsy," though many of the participants continued to use the latter term.

[10] Protokol pervogo obshchego sobraniia predstavitelei melkikh narodnostei Povolzh'ia (Kazan, 1917), pp. 1–4, 23–27. See also the overview provided by M. Korbut, "Natsional'noe dvizhenie v Volzhsko-Kamskom krae," Revoliutsionnyi vostok 7 (1929): 180–87.

[11] Whereas the all-Muslim congress in May 1917 had included representatives of almost all the empire's Muslims, by August the Muslims of Azerbaijan, Kazakhstan, and Turkestan were boycotting the second congress in Kazan in the hopes of attaining territorial autonomy (and preventing Tatar domination of their affairs), and by the fall even the Muslims of the Volga-Ural region were separating into their Tatar and Bashkir components. See Daniel Evan Schafer, "Building Nations and Building States: The Tatar-Bashkir Question in Revolutionary Russia, 1917–1920" (Ph.D. diss., University of Michigan, 1995), pp. 72–76, 106–7, 115–48; and Adeeb Khalid, The Politics of Muslim Cultural Reform: Jadidism in Central Asia (Berkeley, 1998), pp. 265–67.

course of 1917 was toward the narrowing of the functions of the Society, as national organizations—that is, societies and congresses consisting exclusively of Chuvash, Maris, or even Kräshens—took on more aspects of organized political life. Collective affiliations were increasingly construed in ethnic terms, and the October Revolution only accelerated this process, since the Bolsheviks' acceptance of the principle of federalism (national self-determination on a territorial basis) induced non-Russian populations to articulate their interests in a national, as opposed to regional, religious, or supraethnic idiom. Eventually, each of the peoples considered in this study—Tatars, Bashkirs, Maris, Chuvash, Udmurts, and Mordvins—was outfitted with its own autonomous republic within the larger Russian Federated Republic of the USSR.[12] Even Kräshens, though denied their own territorial unit, for a time in the 1920s received their own publishing house, newspaper, and section within the Communist party of the Tatar republic.[13] But there was little room for religion in the new order. And although Islam, Orthodoxy, and even animism have all seen a revival in the post-Soviet period, only time will tell how—and if—the state will regulate their interrelationship in the twenty-first century.

[12] Schafer, "Building Nations and Building States," pp. 345–446; Yuri Slezkine, "The USSR as a Communal Apartment, or How a Socialist State Promoted Ethnic Particularism," *Slavic Review* 53, 2 (1994): 414–52; and K. I. Kulikov, *Natsional'no-gosudarstvennoe stroitel'stvo vostochno-finskikh narodov v 1917–1937 gg.* (Izhevsk, 1993).

[13] On this section—the so-called *Kriashsektsiia*—and other developments among Kräshens in the 1920s, see Werth, "From 'Pagan' Muslims," 515–21.

Selected Bibliography

Bibliographic Essay

My purpose is to highlight the most important works, both primary and secondary, concerning the issues raised in this book. This essay makes no effort to provide a comprehensive bibliography. My goal instead has been to provide a manageable list of the most relevant sources, on the assumption that readers interested in particular issues will refer to footnotes in the individual chapters, where the first reference to each source is given in full.

In a unique category as source material are the imperial law codes, which provide much background on the reasons for implementing specific laws: *Polnoe Sobranie Zakonov Rossiiskoi Imperii,* first series, 45 vols. (St. Petersburg, 1830), second series, 55 vols. (St. Petersburg, 1830–84), third series, 28 vols. (St. Petersburg, 1911). *Svod Zakonov Rossiiskoi Imperii* (with editions in 1832, 1842, 1857, and subsequent supplements) represents a compilation of active legislation. In some cases, legislation on one or another particular question has been usefully gathered in one publication. See, for example, Ia. A. Kantorovich, ed., *Zakony o vere i veroterpimosti* (St. Petersburg, 1899); and F. Kh. Gumerov, ed., *Zakony Rossiiskoi Imperii o bashkirakh, mishariakh, teptiariakh, i bobyliakh* (Ufa, 1999). On religious crimes, see the criminal code *Ulozhenie o nakazaniiakh ugolovnykh i ispravitel'nykh* (editions in 1845 and 1866). Directives of the Orthodox church are gathered in *Polnoe Sobranie postanovlenii i rasporiazhenii po vedomstvu Pravoslavnogo ispovedaniia Rossiisskoi Imperii,* five series, 19 vols. (St. Petersburg / Petrograd, 1869–1915).

In terms of periodicals, the most illuminating source material may be found in the *eparkhial'nye vedomosti* (including *Izvestiia po Kazanskoi eparkhii*), the *gubernskie vedomosti* of various provinces, and religious journals such as *Pravoslavnoe obozrenie, Pravoslavnyi sobesednik, Pravoslavnyi blagovestnik,* and *Missioner.* Official ministerial journals, such as *Zhurnal Ministerstva Narodnogo Prosveshcheniia* and *Zhurnal Ministerstva Vnutrennikh Del,* also contain many useful articles, as do ethnographic journals, such as *Etnograficheskoe obozrenie, Izvestiia Obshchestva*

Arkheologii, Istorii, i Etnografii pri Kazanskom universitete, and *Vestnik Russkogo Geograficheskogo Obshchestva*.

On the early history of the Volga-Kama region after its conquest in the mid-sixteenth century, see Nikolai Firsov, *Inorodcheskoe naselenie prezhnego Kazan-skogo tsarstva v novoi Rossii do 1762 goda i kolonizatsiia zakamskikh zemel' v eto vremia* (Kazan, 1869); G. Peretiatkovich, *Povolzh'e v XVII i nachale XVIII veka: Ocherki iz istorii kolonizatsii kraia* (Odessa, 1882); N. V. Nikol'skii, *Sbornik is-toricheskikh materialov o narodnostiakh Povolzh'ia* (Kazan, 1920); and Andreas Kappeler, *Rußlands erste Nationalitäten: Das Zarenreich und die Völker der Mit-tleren Wolga vom 16. bis 19. Jahrhundert* (Cologne, 1982).

On the history of specific ethnic and ethno-confessional groups, see K. I. Kozlova, *Ocherki etnicheskoi istorii Mariiskogo naroda* (Moscow, 1978); N. E. Egorov, *Ocherki istorii kul'tury dorevoliutsionnoi Chuvashii* (Cheboksary, 1985); G. N. Aiplatov and A. G. Ivanov, eds., *Istoriia Mariiskogo kraia v dokumentakh i materi-alakh*, fasc. 1 (Ioshkar-Ola, 1992); A. G Ivanov, *Ocherki po istorii Mariiskogo kraia XVIII veka* (Ioshkar-Ola, 1995); V. V. Pimenov, ed., *Udmurty: Istoriko-etnografich-eskie ocherki* (Izhevsk, 1993); D. M. Iskhakov, *Istoricheskaia demografiia tatarskogo naroda: XVIII–nachalo XX vv.* (Kazan, 1993); idem, *Etnograficheskie gruppy tatar volgo-ural'skogo regiona* (Kazan, 1993); idem, *Ot srednevekovykh tatar k tataram novogo vremeni* (Kazan, 1998); I. G. Mukhametshin, *Tatary-kriasheny: Istoriko-etnograficheskoe issledovanie material'noi kul'tury, seredina XIX–nachalo XX vv.* (Moscow, 1977); F. S. Baiazitova, *Govory tatar-kriashen v sravnitel'nom osveshchenii* (Moscow, 1986); idem, *Keräshennär: Tel Üzenchälekläre häm iola ijaty* (Kazan, 1997); Maksim Glukhov-Nogaibek, *Sud'ba gvardeitsev Seiumbeki* (Kazan, 1993); and Paul W. Werth, "From 'Pagan' Muslims to 'Baptized' Communists: Religious Conversion and Ethnic Particularity in Russia's Eastern Provinces," *Comparative Studies in Society and History* 42, 3 (2000): 497–523.

On missionary activity in the region prior to the nineteenth century, see *PSZ* (cited above) and the published *opisi* (registries) of the Holy Synod, which cite extensively from archival files: *Opisanie dokumentov i del, khraniashchikhsia v arkhive Sv. Pravit. Sinoda*, 31 vols. (St. Petersburg / Petrograd, 1869–1916). The following sources offer detailed accounts, in some cases with extensive citation from original source material: E. A. Malov, *O Novokreshchenskoi kontore* (Kazan, 1878); A. Mozharovskii, *Izlozhenie khoda missionerskogo dela po prosveshcheniiu kazan-skikh inorodtsev s 1552 po 1867 goda* (Moscow, 1880); P. N. Luppov, *Khristianstvo u votiakov so vremeni pervykh istoricheskikh izvestii o nikh do XIX v.* (Viatka, 1901); N. V. Nikol'skii, *Khristianstvo sredi chuvash Srednego Povolzh'ia v XVII–XVIII vekakh: Istoricheskii ocherk* (Kazan, 1912); S. L. Ursynovich, "No-vokreshchenskaia kontora: K voprosu o roli pravoslavnogo missionerstva v kolo-nizatsionnoi i natsional'noi politike samoderzhaviia," *Ateist* 54 (1930); A. N. Grigor'ev, "Khristianizatsiia nerusskikh narodnostei, kak odin iz metodov nat-sional'no-kolonial'noi politiki tsarizma v Tatarii," *Materialy po istorii Tatarii*, fasc. 1 (Kazan, 1948): 226–85; Joseph Glazik, *Die Russische-Orthodoxe Heidenmission seit Peter dem Grossen* (Münster, 1954); idem, *Die Islammission der Russisch-Orthodoxen Kirche* (Münster, 1959); Petr D. Denisov, *Religioznye verovaniia chuvash: Istoriko-etnograficheskie ocherki* (Cheboksary, 1959); Chantal Lemercier-Quelquejay, "Les Missions Orthodoxes en pays Musulmans de Moyenne-et Basse-Volga, 1552–1865," *Cahiers du monde russe et soviétique* 8 (1967): 369–403;

Michael Khodarkovsky, "'Not by Word Alone': Missionary Policies and Religious Conversion in Early Modern Russia," *Comparative Studies in Society and History* 38, 2 (1996): 267–93; I. K. Zagidullin, "Khristianizatsiia tatar Srednego Povolzh'ia vo vtoroi polovine XVI–XVII vv.," *Uchenye zapiski Tatarskogo Gosudarstvennogo Gumanitarnogo Instituta* 1 (1997): 111–65; Paul W. Werth, "Armed Defiance and Biblical Appropriation: Assimilation and the Transformation of Mordvin Resistance, 1740–1810," *Nationalities Papers* 27, 2 (1999): 245–70; and F. G. Islaev, *Pravoslavnye missionery v Povolzh'e* (Kazan, 1999).

On missionary activity in the nineteenth century prior to the innovations associated with N. I. Il'minskii, see, aside from the sources listed above, N. I. Il'minskii, ed., *Opyty perelozheniia khristianskikh verouchitel'nykh knig na tatarskii i drugie inorodcheskie iazyki v nachale tekushchego stoletiia* (Kazan, 1885); A. Odoev, "Stranichka proshlogo (Istoricheskie nabroski)" *VEV* 7 (1901): 363–94; P. N. Luppov, *Khristianstvo u votiakov v pervoi polovine XIX veka* (Viatka, 1911); idem, ed., *Materialy dlia istorii khristianstva u votiakov v pervoi polovine XIX veka* (Viatka, 1911); N. V. Nikol'skii, ed., *K istorii khristianskogo prosveshcheniia cheremis v XIX v.* (Kazan, 1915); L. A. Taimasov, *Khristianizatsiia chuvashskogo naroda v pervoi polovine XIX veka* (Cheboksary, 1992); and Paul W. Werth, "Baptism, Authority, and the Problem of *Zakonnost'* in Orenburg Diocese: The Induction of Over 800 'Pagans' into the Christian Faith," *Slavic Review* 56, 3 (1997): 456–80.

On the innovations of Il'minskii and the Brotherhood of St. Gurii, see N. I. Il'minskii, ed. *Kazanskaia tsentral'naia kreshcheno-tatarskaia shkola: Materialy dlia istorii khristianskogo prosveshcheniia kreshchenykh tatar* (Kazan, 1887); Petr Znamenskii, *Na pamiat' o Nikolae Ivanoviche Il'minskom: K 25-letiiu Bratstva sv. Guriia* (Kazan, 1892); idem, *Istoriia Kazanskoi Dukhovnoi Akademii za pervoi (doreformennyi) period ee sushchestvovaniia, 1842–1870*, 2 vols. (Kazan, 1891–92); M. A. Mashanov, *Obzor deiatel'nosti Bratstva Sv. Guriia za 25 let ego sushchestvovaniia, 1867–92* (Kazan, 1892); *Pis'ma Nikolaia Ivanovicha Il'minskogo k Ober-prokuroru Sv. Sinoda K. P. Pobedonostsevu* (Kazan, 1898); S. V. Chicherina, *U privolzhskikh inorodtsev: Putevye zametki* (St. Petersburg, 1905); Jean Saussay, "Il'minskij et la politique de russification des Tatars, 1865–1891," *Cahiers du monde russe et soviétique* 8, 3 (1967): 404–26; Isabelle Teitz Kreindler, "Educational Policies toward the Eastern Nationalities in Tsarist Russia: A Study of Il'minskii's System" (Ph.D. diss., Columbia University, 1969); and Robert Paul Geraci, "Window on the East: Ethnography, Orthodoxy, and Russian Nationality in Kazan, 1870–1914" (Ph.D. diss., University of California, Berkeley, 1995).

On the Mari religious movement and the Archangel Michael Cheremis Monastery, see P. Znamenskii, "Gornye cheremisy Kazanskogo kraia," *Vestnik Evropy* 4 (1867): 30–71; idem, "Religioznoe sostoianie cheremis Kozmodem'ianskogo uezda," *Pravoslavnoe obozrenie* 10, 12 (1866): 61–79, 149–68; *Kratkoe opisanie Mikhailo-Arkhangel'skogo monastyria, Kazanskoi gubernii, Kozmodem'ianskogo uezda* (St. Petersburg, 1875); P. Rufimskii, *Cheremiskii Mikhailo-Arkhangel'skii muzhskoi obshchezhitel'nyi monastyr' Kazanskoi gubernii Kozmodem'ianskogo uezda: Istoricheskoe opisanie i sovremennoe ego sostoianie* (Kazan, 1897); and N. S. Popov, "Iz istorii sotsioreligioznogo dvizheniia v mariiskom krae v 50–70-kh gg. XIX veka (po materialam Mikhailo-Arkhangel'skogo muzhskogo monastyria)," *Polozhenie i klassovaia bor'ba krest'ian Mariiskogo kraia* (Ioshkar-Ola, 1990): 132–57.

On the problem of baptized-Tatar apostasy in the ninteenth century, see Il'minskii, ed., *Opyty*; idem, ed., *Kazanskaia tsentral'naia*; E. A. Malov, "Prikhody starokreshchenykh i novokreshchenykh tatar v Kazanskoi eparkhii," *Pravoslavnoe obozrenie* 17 (1865): 449–94, 18 (1865): 283–308, 499–513; idem, *Pravoslavnaia protivomusul'manskaia missiia v Kazanskom krae v sviazi s istoriei musul'manstva v pervoi polovine XIX veka* (Kazan, 1868); idem, "Ocherk religioznogo sostoianiia kreshchenykh tatar, podvergshikhsia vliianiiu magometanstva," *Pravoslavyi sobesednik* 3 (1871): 234–55, 397–418; 1 (1872): 62–78, 124–39, 237–50, 377–405; 2 (1872): 38–78; idem, *Missionerstvo sredi mukhammedan i kreshchenykh tatar* (Kazan, 1892); *Materialy po istorii Tatarii vtoroi poloviny XIX veka: Agrarnyi vopros i krest'ianskoe dvizhenie v Tatarii XIX veka* (Moscow, 1936); Jean Saussay, "L'Apostasie des Tatars christianisés en 1866," *Cahiers du monde russe et soviétique* 9, 1 (1968): 20–40; Pol Uert [Paul Werth], "Otpadenie kreshchenykh tatar," *Tatarstan* 1, 2 (1995): 106–11; Agnès Kefeli, "Constructing an Islamic Identity: The Case of Elyshevo Village in the Nineteenth Century," in *Russia's Orient: Imperial Borderlands and Peoples, 1700–1917*, ed. Daniel R. Brower and Edward J. Lazzerini (Bloomington, 1997), pp. 271–91; idem, "L'Islam populaire chez les Tatars Chrétiens Orthodoxes au XIXe siècle," *Cahiers du monde russe* 37, 4 (1996): 409–28; and Paul W. Werth, "The Limits of Religious Ascription: Baptized Tatars and the Revision of 'Apostasy,' 1840s–1905," *Russian Review* 59, 4 (2000): 493–511.

On the question of Muslims and Islam in the Volga-Kama region, see B. Iuzefovich, "Khristianstvo, magometanstvo i iazychestvo v vostochnykh guberniiakh Rossii," *Russkii Vestnik* 164 (1883): 5–64; Serge Zenkovsky, *Pan-Turkism and Islam in Russia* (Cambridge, Mass., 1960); Azade-Ayşe Rorlich, *The Volga Tatars: A Profile in National Resilience* (Stanford, 1986); Michael Kemper, Anke von Kügelgen, and Dmitriy Yermakov, eds., *Muslim Culture in Russia and Central Asia from the Eighteenth to the Early Twentieth Centuries*, vol. 1 (Berlin, 1996), vol. 2: *Inter-Regional and Inter-Ethnic Relations* (Berlin, 1998); Stéphane A. Dudoignon, Dämir Is'haqov, and Räfyq Möhämmätshin, eds., *L'Islam de Russie: Conscience communautaire et autonomie politique chez les Tatars de la Volga et d'Oural depuis le XVIIe siècle* (Paris, 1997), also available in a slightly different Russian version: *Islam v tatarskom mire: istoriia i sovremennost'* (Kazan, 1997); Allen J. Frank, *Islamic Historiography and "Bulghar" Identity among the Tatars and Bashkirs of Russia* (Leiden, 1998); Elena Vorob'eva, "Musul'manskii vopros v imperskoi politike Rossiiskogo samoderzhaviia: Vtoraia polovina XIX veka–1917 g" (cand. diss., Institute of Russian History, St. Petersburg, 1999); Charles Robert Steinwedel, "Invisible Threads of Empire: State, Religion, and Ethnicity in Tsarist Bashkiriia, 1773–1917" (Ph.D. diss., Columbia University, 1999); Robert D. Crews, "Allies in God's Command: Muslim Communities and the State in Imperial Russia" (Ph.D. diss., Princeton University, 1999); D. D. Azamatov, *Orenburgskoe Magometanskoe Dukhovnoe Sobranie v kontse XVIII–XIX vv.* (Ufa, 1999); and Christian Noack, *Muslimischer Nationalismus im Russischen Reich: Nationsbildung und Nationalbewegung bei Tataren und Baschkiren, 1861–1917* (Stuttgart, 2000).

On the practice of "paganism" and official efforts against it, see (in addition to works already cited) V. A. Sboev, *Issledovaniia ob inorodtsakh Kazanskoi gubernii* (Kazan, 1856); A. Filimonov, "O religii nekreshchenykh cheremis i votiakov Viatskoi gubernii," *Viatskie gubernskie vedomosti* 12–14, 22, 23, 28, 29, 48, 49

(1868); 2–4, 25, 26 (1869); A. Andrievskii, "Dela o sovershenii iazycheskikh zhertvoprinoshenii kreshchenymi inorodtsami Viatskoi gubernii," in *Stoletie Viatskoi gubernii, 1780–1880: Sbornik materialov k istorii Viatskogo kraia* (Viatka, 1881), 2:535–80; V. K. Magnitskii, *Materialy k ob˝iasneniiu staroi chuvashskoi very* (Kazan, 1881); A. G. Ivanov, "Vsemariiskoe iazycheskoe molenie 1827 i deistviia vlastei," *Mariiskii arkheograficheskii vestnik* 8 (1998): 48–74; and Paul W. Werth, "Big Candles and 'Internal Conversion': The Mari Animist Reformation and Its Russian Appropriations," in *Of Religion and Empire: Missions, Conversion, and Tolerance in Tsarist Russia*, ed. Robert Geraci and Michael Khodarkovsky (Ithaca, 2001). pp. 144–72.

For general treatments of religious minorities in Russia, see M. A. Reisner, *Gosudarstvo i veruiushchaia lichnost´* (St. Petersburg, 1905); K. K. Arsen´ev, *Svoboda sovesti i veroterpimost´* (St. Petersburg, 1905); Peter Waldron, "Religious Toleration in Late Imperial Russia," *Civil Rights in Imperial Russia*, ed. Olga Crisp and Linda Edmondson (Oxford, 1989), 103–19; A. Iu. Polunov, *Pod vlast´iu Ober-Prokurora: Gosudarstvo i tserkov´ v epohku Aleksandra III* (Moscow, 1996); E. A. Vishlenkova, *Religioznaia politika: ofitsial´nyi kurs i "obshchee mnenie" Rossii aleksandrovskoi epokhi* (Kazan, 1997); and Robert Geraci and Michael Khodarkovsky, eds., *Of Religion and Empire: Missions, Conversion, and Tolerance in Tsarist Russia* (Ithaca, 2001).

Archival Sources

1. Rossiiskii Gosudarstvennyi Istoricheskii Arkhiv (RGIA), St. Petersburg

Fond 381	Kantseliariia Ministra Zemledeliia
Fond 383	Pervyi Departament Ministerstva Gosudarstvennykh Imushchestv
Fond 515	Departament Udelov
Fond 796	Kantseliariia Sviateishego Sinoda
Fond 797	Kantseliariia Ober-Prokurora Sviateishego Sinoda
Fond 799	Khoziaistvennoe Upravlenie Sviateishego Sinoda
Fond 802	Uchebnyi Komitet Sviateishego Sinoda
Fond 808	Rossiiskoe Bibleiskoe Obshchestvo
Fond 821	Departament Dukhovnykh Del Inostrannykh Ispovedanii
Fond 1263	Komitet Ministrov
Fond 1405	Ministerstva Iustitsii
Fond 1473	Sekretnyi Komitet po delam raskola
Fond 1574	K. P. Pobedonostsev
	Khranilishche pechatnykh zapisok

2. Natsional´nyi Arkhiv Respubliki Tatarstan (NART), Kazan

Fond 1	Kantseliariia Kazanskogo Gubernatora
Fond 2	Kazanskoe Gubernskoe Pravlenie
Fond 4	Kazanskaia Dukhovnaia Konsistoriia
Fond 7	Chistopol´skoe Dukhovnoe Pravlenie
Fond 10	Kazanskaia Dukhovnaia Akademiia

Fond 13   Kazanskaia Palata Ugolovnogo Suda
Fond 92   Popechitel′ Kazanskogo Uchebnogo Okruga
Fond 93   Kazanskaia Uchitel′skaia Seminariia
Fond 319   Tsentral′naia Kreshcheno-tatarskaia Shkola
Fond 968   Nikolai Ivanovich Il′minskii

3. Otdel Rukopisei Kazanskoi Nauchnoi Biblioteki im. Lobachevskogo, Kazan

Fond 7   Evfimii Aleksandrovich Malov

4. Gosudarstvennyi Arkhiv Kirovskoi Oblasti (GAKO), Kirov

Fond 582   Kantseliariia Viatskogo Gubernatora
Fond 237   Viatskaia Dukhovnaia Konsistoriia
Fond 811   Viatskii Komitet Pravoslavnogo Missionerskogo Obshchestva

5. Tsentral′nyi Gosudarstvennyi Istoricheskii Arkhiv Respubliki Bashkortostan (Ts-GIARB), Ufa

Fond I-2   Orenburgskii General-Gubernator
Fond I-6   Orenburgskii Grazhdanskii Gubernator
Fond I-9   Ufimskoe Gubernskoe Pravlenie
Fond I-11   Kantseliariia Ufimskogo Gubernatora
Fond I-294   Ufimskaia Dukhovnaia Konsistoriia
Fond I-295   Orenburgskoe Magometanskoe Dukhovnoe Sobranie

6. Gosudarstvennyi Arkhiv Respubliki Marii El (GARME), Ioshkar-Ola

Fond 165   Tsarevokokshaiskoe Dukhovnoe Pravlenie

7. Nauchno-Rukopisnyi Fond Mariiskogo Nauchno-Issledovatel′skogo Instituta (NRF MarNII), Ioshkar-Ola

Various files and documents

Index